# Internet-Enabled Business Intelligence

## William A. Giovinazzo

*Prentice Hall PTR*
*Upper Saddle River, NJ 07458*
*www.phptr.com*

ISBN 0-13-040951-0

9 780130 409515

90000

**Library of Congress Cataloging-in-Publication Data**

A CIP catalog record for this book can be obtained from the Library of Congress.

Editorial/production supervision: *Laura Burgess*
Composition: *Sean Donahue*
Cover design director: *Jerry Votta*
Cover design: *Nina Scuderi*
Art director: *Gail Cocker-Bogusz*
Interior design: *Meg Van Arsdale*
Manufacturing manager: *Alexis R. Heydt-Long*
Acquisitions editor: *Victoria Jones*
Editorial assistant: *Michelle Vincente*
Marketing manager: *Debby van Dijk*

© 2003 Pearson Education, Inc.
Publishing as Prentice Hall PTR
Upper Saddle River, New Jersey 07458

Prentice Hall books are widely used by corporations and government agencies for training, marketing, and resale.

For more information regarding corporate and government bulk discounts please contact:
Corporate and Government Sales (800) 382-3419 or corpsales@persontechgroup.com

Printed in the United States of America
10   9   8   7   6   5   4   3   2   1

ISBN 0-13-040951-0

Pearson Education LTD.
Pearson Education Australia Pty. Limited
Pearson Education Singapore, Pte. Ltd.
Pearson Education North Asia Ltd.
Pearson Education Canada, Ltd.
Pearson Educatión de Mexico, S.A. de C.V.
Pearson Education—Japan
Pearson Education Malaysia, Pte. Ltd.

To My Bride Carol with all my heart,
The sound of your laughter is as the tinkling of bells.
It is to my soul as a snow-fed spring in a parched and arid land.

# Contents

# ACKNOWLEDGMENTS

Whenever they give out the Academy awards, the recipients always say "there are so many people I need to thank." Invariably, they ramble on and on until the band starts to play and someone turns off their mike. This is what's nice about a book. There is no band to silence me. In bringing this book together, I had a great deal of help from many intelligent, kind, and professional individuals. I am continually grateful for their support in this effort. The challenge is to sufficiently thank them all.

First and foremost is Eric Hanson. Our daughters are in the same Indian Princess tribes. One late night over the campfire I had expressed concern that the book was drifting and I was very interested in ensuring that I was providing substantive content. As is his nature, he volunteered to help. Even then I didn't believe he understood what was involved. I took him up on his offer regardless. I owe him a debt of gratitude. He kept me focused and provided an excellent sounding board for ideas, as well as providing excellent ideas of his own. When I was carried away with my own rhetoric he attempted to bring me back down to earth. There are times, however, when he did not always succeed.

I also want to thank the people at Prentice Hall. This book has been two years in the making, and they have demonstrated enormous patience. In this time, I went through my share of editors, all of whom were very helpful. Starting with Tim Moore, an all-around terrific guy and ending with Victoria Jones, my current editor, they have all been both patient and helpful. I am not sure why Victoria still speaks to me. Every month for the past six months I have been telling her the book will be done the end of next month. Don't say anything to her, but I think I might really be done writing this soon.

I would also like to thank the reviewers, Jeff Kirk and Jody Giles. They suffered through my poor grammar, mixed metaphors, and indecipherable spelling. Their corrections and suggestions are of great value to me.

Another group of people I wish to thank are the many fine folks at Oracle. They were supportive of this effort and provided much needed advice. Of that group, there are several people I wish to thank specifically. Marty Gubar assisted with Oracle Business Intelligence JavaBeans. Mark Hornick provided input on the Java Data Mining API. Lisa Alms was kind enough to provide feedback on Oracle 9i Application Server. In addition, Gregory Dorman provided help with the Java Multidimensional Database API. I wish to thank each of them for taking time out of their busy schedules to assist me in this effort, receiving in return only this note of gratitude.

There are some people I need to thank on the personal level. My wife and children have been very patient. This work at times affected them more than it affected anyone else and yet they were always supportive. Thanks to my good friend Bill Hayes; if it weren't for his assistance in other areas, I would never have had the time to write this book. I must also thank my dearest and oldest friend and supporter, Tonoose Dimeo. In all the things I have done he has been there with his friendship, advice, humor, and, when necessary, correction. This book would never have come into existence if it were not for him.

Finally, I must thank the one to whom I owe the greatest of all debts, my Lord Jesus Christ. I am thankful that I have been blessed with so many things, not the least of which is the gift to be living at this time, in this place. I am grateful for being able to work in this industry, doing the thing that I love, with a truly terrific organization. More than this, as you can tell by reading this long list of acknowledgments, God has blessed my life with so many wonderful people, with so much kindness, and so much love. To say that I am not worthy of such blessings is obvious to anyone who knows me, which makes me all the more grateful.

As I approached the daily task of writing this book, I prayed that it would be something of quality, something that would be of real benefit to the reader. Where the book accomplishes that objective, I give all the credit to Jesus and I thank him for his blessing. If there are places where this book falls short of achieving this goal, I can only say that it is, to steal a line from my altar boy days, "through my fault, through my fault, through my most grievous fault."

# INTRODUCTION

So, what's the problem? In this book, we present Internet Enabled Business Intelligence (IEBI) as a solution. Unfortunately, the word *solution* has been so abused by marketers that it has lost meaning. We begin, therefore, by looking at the characteristics of a solution. One of the responses I received to this approach from an early reviewer caught me a bit off guard. "Great, Internet Enabled Business Intelligence is a solution," he said. "So, what's the *problem*?" At first I sputtered out some inarticulate platitude, aggravated that he was giving me a hard time. Then, after some reflection, I realized that often, as system engineers, we forget the real issue when we build systems. Whether they are Business Intelligence (BI) systems, supply chain management, or even email, they all have a problem for which we are trying to find a solution.

So, let's ask the question one more time. What's the problem?

The easy access to information provided by the Internet has intensified the competitive environment. Today we live in what has become known as the *information age*. Information has taken on more value today than at any other time in human history. People are more informed, more connected, than ever before. Politicians struggle with a 24-hour news cycle. Governments wrestle with the conflict between freedom of information and national security concerns. During the Persian Gulf war, CNN was a major source of strategic information for Iraq. The same is true of consumer information. Product reviews, consumer advocacy groups, and individual customer opinions are all there for anyone to read. That's the good news. There is a lot of information out there.

The bad news is that there is a lot of information out there. We all know by now that our organizations are awash in data. In the summer of 2001, the White House received warnings of a terrorist attack. FBI field agents sent in warnings concerning possible terrorists attending flight schools. The problem was that all these separate pieces of information were couched in a cacophony, other nonrelated pieces of information. Imagine yourself for a moment at your local consumer electronics store, standing in front of a wall of televisions. Then imagine each television on a different channel with the volume turned up as loud as possible. Think of the challenge in trying to understand all those different information feeds and develop some consolidated view of the world. That is what the average organization faces today. We are drowning in data. Do we sleep, perchance to dream? Or, do we take up arms against a sea of data? If we sleep, if we continue to try to do business as usual, then we will most certainly die. Our organizations will lose out in the marketplace to those competitors who have adapted to this changing environment, to those who have learned how to harness the power of this sea of information.

In short, our problem is twofold. On one hand, we are competing in an environment where consumers and competitors are better informed. On the other hand, there is so much information flowing through the organization that it is almost impossible to make any sense of it. This is the problem; IEBI is the solution.

This text is divided into four sections. The first section, chapters 1 through 3, describes the IEBI solution. We begin this section by differentiating a solution from a mixture. The text then describes the ingredients of the IEBI solution. In Chapter 2, we discuss the evolution of the Internet from both a technical and economic perspective. Chapter 3 discusses the anatomy of BI, exploring the BI loop and its components in detail.

In the second section, chapters 4 through 6, we study the Internet itself. In Chapter 5, we discuss servers, the heart of the Internet, distinguishing between the different architectural alternatives available to systems designers. We discuss how communication occurs over the Internet in Chapter 6. How does a thing called a *URL* connect a client to a server on the other side of the planet? While this may seem basic to some, understanding the nuances of this architecture will have an impact on our implementations.

The third section, chapters 7 through 10, studies the software of the Internet. We discuss application development on a multi-tier architecture in Chapter 8. In Chapter 9, we discuss how XML provides a structure for sharing data over the Net. We then discuss in Chapter 10 how the Common Warehouse Metadata Interchange (CWMI) uses this structure for the communication of metadata between systems.

In the final section, we examine the ultimate objective, using IEBI to be more competitive in the information age. The key to being more competitive is to create a customer-driven culture in our organizations. We discuss what this means in

Chapter 12. In Chapter 13, we see how we can use the Internet to capture the information necessary to understand our customers, and in Chapter 14, we see how to use it.

You will note that I have provided a recommended reading list as an Appendix to the book. I am not so foolish to believe that any one book can be *the* one book a person will ever need to read on this subject. I don't know of any topic so narrow that any one book can be the exclusive work on that subject, much less so broad a subject as IEBI. Even if such an accomplishment were possible, I am not so vain as to believe that I could write it. Rather, I see this book as one step in a very long journey. For some, it may be the first step, for others it may be much farther down the road. In either case, the books I've listed provide additional resources for you to continue your study beyond what we have done here.

Now that we understand what it is we are discussing, let me tell you about my sister's kitchen. Having inherited the old homestead, she has become the matriarch of the family. When any of my siblings or I go back home, we are going back to our actual home. As we sit in her kitchen, my mother's kitchen, the phantoms of those who have gone linger in the shadows. The thousand raucous family gatherings with all the laughter, debates, shouting, and roughhousing, still reverberate in the very structure of that old house. In the increasingly rare quiet moments, you can hear them. I can see my father sitting at the head of the table telling stories of his own childhood, my uncle leaning over telling me his own version of the story. In my mind's eye my Mother is at her post, cooking. "Get out of here with your long hair," she tells my sisters. She lived in fear of their hair getting in the food. They are all still there, faint echoes you can only hear with your heart.

While most of my father's generation has gone on, new memories are being created. If you sit at my sister's kitchen table long enough, you will eventually meet everyone in my home town. Everyone passes through. It is the stereotypical Italian kitchen, lots of food and lots of conversation, lots and lots and lots of *very* loud conversation. In all that talk, there is no tangent too wild, no reference too obscure, no metaphor stretched too thin to be leveraged for forensic advantage. The only rule of engagement seems to be, the more wild the claim or ludicrous the statement, the louder it must be stated. Most participants in family discussions leave one very hoarse and a little deaf.

This is how I have learned to discuss topics. Wild tangents and clever anecdotes only deepen the discussion. Many topics we will discuss in our exploration of IEBI have their traditional explanations. Rather than opt for the same worn, trite examples, I have attempted to take a different route, a more scenic excursion. We will go down paths that seem tangential, or make references that are somewhat wild, but in the end, they will only add to our understanding of the subject. I hope through this unorthodox style to provide you with a richer, more rewarding experience than typically found in technical books.

Everything is connected. We cannot be myopic in our view of any one subject. We must endeavor to see the whole as well as the individual parts. It is my objective that through such an experience, I can share with you the same thrill, the same excitement that I feel for this subject. It is my desire that after reading this book, you will feel the same eager anticipation I feel for what we—you and I—can accomplish with Internet Enabled Business Intelligence.

*William A. Giovinazzo*

*2002*

# Part 1

# The Solution

# Chapter 1

# THE SOLUTION

*"... A first rate soup is more creative than a second rate painting, and ...*
*generally cooking or parenthood or making a home could be creative while poetry need*
*not be...."*

*Abraham Maslow*

The subject of this book is Internet-Enabled Business Intelligence (IEBI). Then
again, you know that—it's on the cover of the book. What we need to discover is
what is meant by this phrase. Let's start by establishing that it is really one thing,
not two or even three. IEBI is something different than just Business Intelligence
(BI); it is *bigger*. It isn't a data warehouse accessed via the Internet, although that is
part of it. It isn't just click-stream analysis either, although that is part of it as well.
What is it? Well, it is really a *solution*.

Don't you just hate that word? Solution! What the heck is a solution? It wasn't
more than a couple of years ago that I sat in a marketing meeting where a consulting manager was trying to convince me that a disk array was a solution. We
worked for a disk array vendor and we were planning our attack on the data warehousing space. He had maintained that in some cases a disk array was a solution.
*Wrong!* A disk array is a disk array. A solution is something much more than a
piece of hardware.

When I was a boy in upstate New York, my dear sainted mother was to the
culinary arts what Michelangelo was to sculpture. As does every good son, I loved
my mother's cooking. It was, however, more than filial devotion. She was truly an
artist in the kitchen. Her lasagna, for example, was heaven on a plate.

My mother would start her sauce for Sunday dinner on Saturday morning. She began by browning beef in garlic and olive oil. Imagine being a 13-year-old boy with a bottomless stomach, waking with that delightful aroma wafting through the house. My endless hunger was only sharpened by the scents that came from her kitchen on those distant mornings. When my mother left for her job at the local textile mill, she left the sauce to simmer all day long over a barely perceptible flame. The deep red marbled with the sinewy black lines of spices that rose to the top. As my father and I set about our weekly home repair projects, it coddled. Large molten bubbles surfaced from the depths of that tub-sized white sauce pot, only to lazily plop and sink back down. Intermittently, my father or I would stir the sauce. Roughly translated, this meant that we would run a spoon through it two or three times and ladle a bit into a nearby bowl for tasting purposes. For lunch, my father and I would sit behind bowls of the steaming red sauce. We would break off hunks of freshly baked Italian bread, scattering the light brown flakes across the Formica top of the kitchen table. I would then pluck out the soft white interior, hungrily eating it as I smeared a heavy coat of butter on the inside of the hard crust. I would then dip the bread into the sauce, repeating the process until the bowl was wiped clean.

The next day Mother would serve the sauce over perfect squares of lasagna, lightly dusted with Parmesan cheese. She would set our plates down in front of us, a link of homemade sausage resting comfortably at four o'clock on the plate and two meatballs at eleven. My mother had a special twist to her lasagna. Just beneath the top layer, she would add a few lengthwise slices of hard-boiled egg. On the side was an antipasto salad topped with its familiar cross of anchovies. Years later, when I was married, my ex-wife would discretely remove the anchovies from the salad before eating. She would also pick out the egg from the lasagna as we ate. *(This probably explains why she is my ex-wife; she didn't like my mother's lasagna.)*

Right about now you are wondering what any of this has to do with IEBI. Well, it demonstrates the difference between a solution and a mixture. In a mixture, the entities comprising that mixture remain distinct. When they are added to the mixture, they continue to maintain their own identity. In a solution, the entities comprising the solution go through a transformation. They are no longer unique, separate entities, but are transformed; the characteristics of each element within the solution are affected by the other elements of the solution. In my little story, the sauce undergoes a process that transforms the individual ingredients. The meat browning with the garlic changes the flavor of the meat. The tomato paste, tomatoes, red wine, and spices that are added to the sauce all react with one another, changing the characteristics of each. In a solution, the whole is greater than the sum of the parts. If, once it was fully cooked, you removed the meat from the sauce, the flavor of the meat was still there.

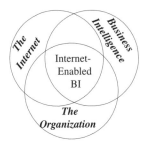

**FIGURE 1.1** Internet-enabled business intelligence.

The salad topped with the cross of anchovies or the hard-boiled egg in the lasagna were mixtures. While they were in close proximity to one another, they did not exchange characteristics. Once the anchovies were removed from the salad, the salad tasted as if the anchovies had never been there. Once the egg was removed from the lasagna, you would never have known it had been there. These are mixtures.

IEBI is a solution, not a mixture. Figure 1.1 is a simple diagram of the ingredients that comprise this solution: the Internet, BI, and the organization. Let's take a brief look at each.

We begin with perhaps the most important ingredient in the solution, the base of the sauce if you will. This is the organization itself. The reason for the very existence of IEBI is for the health and well-being of the organization. In Chapter 3, we discuss how an organization is like an organism, a common metaphor. An organism is a body that is composed of organs that work together towards a common goal. Organizations are pretty much the same types of entities. The different departments work together for the common good of the organization. Every organism has a nervous system. Not all nervous systems are the same; there are different levels of development. As we shall see, in a very real sense the information infrastructure of an organization is its nervous system. Just as there are different levels of nervous system development in the world of biological systems, there are different levels of development in the realm of organizational systems.

This is brings us to the second ingredient in our solution, business intelligence (BI). BI is not YAA (Yet-Another-Application). Figure 1.2 presents BI as an iterative process. Although we will revisit this figure in Chapter 3, I present it here to describe the loop. It begins with the operational environment. Data is extracted from this environment and stored in the data warehouse. As the data is stored, it is cleansed and transformed so that it can be integrated with the other data in the warehouse. The warehouse is some central repository of data, which is separated from the operational data. The decision maker uses Decision Support Systems (DSS) to retrieve data from the data warehouse. Based on this information, he or she is able to formulate some plan of action. This change in course, or lack thereof, is reflected in the operational environment, which is recorded in the operational systems. This change in operational information starts the next iteration of the BI loop.

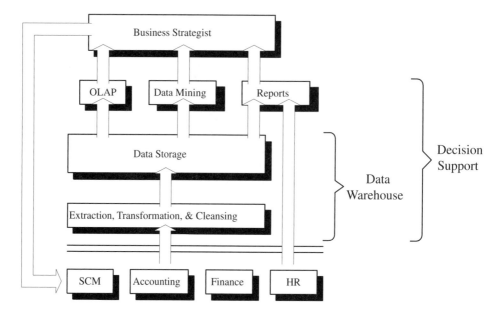

**FIGURE 1.2**   The business intelligence loop.

There are some basic truisms to BI. One is that the impetus for any BI system must come from outside the Information Technology (IT) department. When we sell BI, we sell to the C-level executive, the CFO or CEO, for example. Consider why this is the case. Earlier we said that with BI the decision maker bases his or her decisions on the information extracted from the DSS. For BI to be effective, it must change the way the organization does business. BI must be integrated into the daily operations and procedures of the organization. It is the C-level executive who has the organizational authority and political clout to enforce the integration of BI into the business process. In short, the C-level executive can create the heat that will cause our ingredients to simmer.

In this discussion, we can see how the first two ingredients of our solution are transformed. BI changes the decision-making process of the organization. Decision makers now have a tool to collect data concerning the organization's environment. They can then base their decisions on this data. BI permeates the entire organization. Activity Based Management (ABM) systems provide management with costing information to design and refine business processes. Customer Relationship Management (CRM) systems assist organizations in developing more profitable, stronger relationships with their customers. Balanced Scorecard systems provide a concise way to measure how well the organization is meeting its strategic objectives.

As we said earlier, *all* the ingredients in a solution are transformed by one another. So how is BI changed? A BI system is not some monolithic system that sits in the bowels of the IT department. It is a dynamic system that changes to meet the needs of an organization that is evolving to meet a changing business environment. One such change is in fact the third ingredient in our solution, the Internet.

The organization and BI are just two elements of the solution, two ingredients of our sauce. The third, the Internet, is the spice that provides the zing. The entire world has been caught up in this net. Years ago, as part of my masters work, I studied management science. Back then the organization was at times viewed as a black box. Very real walls divided the organization from its suppliers and buyers. This was all well and good for that timeframe. Tight integration along a supply chain was difficult and therefore expensive. The benefits simply did not justify the costs. As we shall see in Chapter 2, the Internet came along and crashed through those walls. The lines that divide an organization from its partners and customers are no longer drawn as boldly. We now discuss tighter integration of supply chains and the sharing of strategic information. We start to think in terms of a virtual organization that spans the entire value chain.

We can see the ripple effect. The Internet changes the organization. The walls are torn down between the business and its suppliers, customers, and partners. We can see a mingling between the businesses, tentacles of one reaching into the other. Where appropriate, information is shared with partners and suppliers. This change in the organization also mandates a change in BI. As we said above, BI permeates the organization. As the business expands its view of the world, as the business seeks tighter forward and backward integration, so does the BI system. An IEBI system is something that no longer sits in the black box of our organization, but reaches outside of that organization as it grows and expands. We are tempted to say that BI reaches outside of the box, but there isn't even a box.

IEBI truly is a solution, a solution in which its three main ingredients—the organization, BI, and the Internet—all change each other in a very real and dramatic way. In Chapter 2 we review the rise of the Internet and how it has transformed business. In Chapter 3 we define BI and examine the anatomy of an intelligent organization's information infrastructure.

# EVOLUTION TO E-ENTERPRISE

*It is change, continuing change, inevitable change, that is the dominant factor in society today. No sensible decision can be made any longer without taking into account not only the world as it is, but the world as it will be. . . . This, in turn, means that our statesmen, our businessmen, our everyman must take on a science fictional way of thinking.*

*Issac Asimov*

Asimov on Science Fiction[1]

Isaac Asimov was correct in saying that we must not only consider the world as it is, but the world as it will be. This is especially applicable to the Internet age. The Internet bubble has popped. Dotcom stock has become the proverbial swampland in Florida, as in "If you believe that, I've got some dotcom stock to sell you." As we take our fist step in the exploration of Internet-Enabled Business Intelligence (IEBI), we must take heed of Dr. Asimov's advice. We must not only consider the world as it is, but the world as it will be. What will be the fate of the Internet in the world to come? Where have we been, and where are we going? As we understand this, we can understand how to position our organization's IEBI solution for the future.

We begin by asking about the nature of the Internet itself. Is it merely a lot of hype? Is it "a tale told by an idiot, full of sound and fury, signifying nothing"? Or is the hype really wisdom, wisdom that "is better than the merchandise of silver, and the gain thereof than fine gold." We will explore the grandiose claims made by its proponents and the derision espoused by its detractors. We will attempt to decide if the Internet is really all that some say it is.

---

[1]Asimov, Isaac, *Asimov on Science Fiction*, Random House, 1981. Used by permission.

Asimov talked of thinking in a *science fictional* way. As we go on to discuss the history of the Internet, we will meet such visionaries as J. C. R. Licklider, Ivan Sutherland, Bob Metcalfe, and Tim Berners-Lee, influential people who thought in the future. We will come to see how the Internet was the culmination of many advanced ideas, developed independently and in parallel. We will come to see how truly revolutionary was the dream of an *Intergalactic Network*, how truly extraordinary that it could become a reality.

We then ask, What does all this mean to business? After all, the subject of this book is not just the Internet, but Internet Enabled *Business* Intelligence. How does the Internet affect business? After reviewing the Internet's history, this chapter discusses how businesses developed over the Internet and the possible future for those businesses. We will travel from the era of *brochureware*, billboards along the information superhighway, to the integration of supply chains across the Net.

Finally, we will discuss the different types of businesses we will encounter on the Internet. Not all businesses have developed their Internet capabilities to the same level. Some have just scratched the surface. These e-commerce organizations are just now developing ways to reach their customers over the Internet. Others have advanced to a stage in which they are integrating their entire supply chain. As these organizations move to the Internet, they all have one thing in common: the need for IEBI. In this chapter, we will survey the landscape in which this intelligence is to reside.

## 2.1   The Internet: Hype or Hope?

The Internet is the catalyst for a tectonic shift in industrialized societies throughout the world. The metaphor, while appropriate for the magnitude of the shift, breaks down when it comes to the speed in which these changes have taken place. Tectonic shifts are rather slow in human terms. The Internet, however, has revolutionized the worlds of entertainment, communications, and business at an astonishing pace. The Internet has transformed the exchange of information. The entire world has been caught within this net, taking it to…*yada, yada, yada*. Are you as sick of the same old Internet hype as I am?

It seems that everything you read lately about the Internet fluctuates between two camps. The first camp, the "it serves those start-up rich kids right" camp, portrays the dotcom mania as all a hoax and the burst of the Internet bubble as well deserved. Now that it is thankfully over and we have all wised up, we can get back to real work. The second camp is the "ever faithful." As soon as we pull out of this slump, things will get back to normal and we can all be rich again.

Let's try to attack this from a different angle and possibly avoid both the derision and the hype. In the 2000 presidential election, Vice President Al Gore suffered a fair amount of ridicule after he *supposedly* claimed to have invented the

Internet. While the media may have exaggerated his remarks, we cannot deny that the man is a visionary who did have more than a little part to play in bringing about the Internet age. In his book, *The Digital Economy*, Don Tapscott quotes Al Gore as saying "Guttenberg's invention, which so empowered Jefferson and his colleagues in their fight for democracy, seems to pale before the rise of electronic communications and innovations, from the telegraph, to the television, to the microprocessor and the emergence of a new computerized world—an information age."[2] Guttenberg pales before the Internet? What causes so much hoopla about a network of computers? Do you really think the ability to email Aunt Lorraine pictures of your trip to Hawaii can compare with the Guttenberg press, the most important invention of this past millennium?

Perhaps comparing the Internet to Guttenberg's press is not all that great a stretch. In Victor Hugo's *Notre Dame de Paris* there is a scene in which Jacques Coictier visits Dom Claude Frollo. There is a discussion between the men, during which Dom Claude opens the window of his cell and points to the massive Notre Dame. "The archdeacon contemplated the gigantic cathedral for a time in silence, then he sighed and stretched out his right hand towards the printed book lying open on his table and his left hand towards Notre Dame, and looked sadly from the book to the church: 'Alas,' he said, 'this will kill that.'" He continues "Alas and alack, small things overcome great ones! A tooth triumphs over a body. The Nile rat kills the crocodile, the swordfish kills the whale, the book will kill the building."

The same thing is happening with the Internet today. Rather than attempt to explain Dom Claude's thoughts, allow me to provide Hugo's own explanation:

> As we see it, this thought has two facets. Firstly it was the thought of a priest. It was the alarm felt by the priesthood before a new agent: the printing press. It was the terror and bewilderment felt by a man of the sanctuary before the luminous press of Guttenberg. It was the pulpit and the manuscript, the spoken and the written word, taking fright at the printed word; something like the stupor felt by a sparrow were it to see the angel legion unfold its six million wings. It was the cry of the prophet who already hears the restless surge of an emancipated mankind, who can see that future time when intelligence will undermine faith, opinion dethrone belief and the world shake off Rome. The prognosis of a philosopher who sees the human mind, volatilized by the press, evaporate from the theocratic receptacle. The terror of a soldier examining the bronze battering-ram and saying: "The tower will give way." It meant that one power was going to succeed another power. It meant: the press will kill the church.[3]

Hugo was partially correct. Although the press did not destroy the church, it certainly had a role in transforming it. Prior to Guttenberg, the church was the center of society. The center of many a town was the cathedral. The clergy were not just men of God but men who were the keepers of knowledge. The western world was orthodox because the church controlled what was said and what was written.

---

[2]Tapscott, Don, *The Digital Economy*, McGraw Hill, 1996.

[3] Hugo, Victor, *Notre Dame de Paris*.

Then came Guttenberg and messed everything up. The press allowed the free expression of ideas, bypassing church censors. While the powers that existed tried to suppress this form of speech, it survived and transformed the world. Direct access to the Bible allowed the populace to define Christianity for themselves, giving rise to Protestant reforms. Even democracy owes a debt to Guttenberg in that the printed word gave rise to the age of enlightenment, empowering men like Jefferson.

Let's jump ahead in history to Edison. Reportedly, he once said that movies would eliminate the need for books. After all, why invest all that time reading when you can catch the same thing in a movie? The answer is simple: You can't. Despite his brilliance, Edison was wrong. Books and movies are distinctly different. Books communicate ideas that cannot be expressed on film. The same is also true of films; they present things that cannot be expressed in books. A culturally rich society requires both.

So what does this have to do with the Internet? Just as movies did not eliminate books, the Internet will not eliminate the structures of the industrial age. Each delivers something that the other cannot. As we said earlier, Hugo was *partially* correct. The press did not destroy or bring down the church; it transformed it. Similarly, the Internet will not destroy, but transform, the structures of the past. This should sound familiar. We are simply restating what we discussed in Chapter 1: The Internet is part of a solution. In a solution, each of the ingredients is transformed by the other.

Like the Guttenberg press, the Internet transforms the structures of the past by providing a conduit for the free and open exchange of ideas. Just as Guttenberg could not be suppressed, neither can the Internet. It is global; no single power can suppress the thoughts expressed on it. The Internet also provides a voice. Freedom of speech means nothing if you have no voice, if you cannot be heard. The Internet provides this voice. Anyone can set up a Web site anywhere and be instantly heard anywhere in the world. As you can see, it is an extraordinarily powerful tool for the communication of ideas. Freedom of speech and voice were tremendous tools in the emancipation of humanity. While it is obvious that we can easily fill the remaining chapters with the sociological implications of the Internet, that is not what we are here to discuss.

Just as these changes have affected the social and political worlds, they have also affected the business world. The ability to easily communicate globally has had enormous impact on the marketplace. When a competitor's offering is only a mouse-click away, customers can easily price shop or change suppliers when dissatisfied with a service. Manufacturers of new, innovative products now have immediate access to global markets. For these and other reasons, the information age has changed the business world.

At the dawn of the American industrial revolution, Eli Whitney transformed the manufacturing process. The story is actually quite fascinating. Whitney received contracts from the government for the manufacture of rifles in a time of war, but did not actually deliver on that contract until well after the war was over. It wasn't that he was slacking in his obligation. He was perfecting a process, a process that created products with interchangeable parts. The trigger mechanism of one rifle fit the stock of another. This enabled production to move from artisans to mass production. It gave birth to the American industrial revolution. During the ensuing industrial age, companies succeeded by capturing economies of scale and scope.

The industrial age view of technology was to employ it in the automation of an existing manual process. The vestiges of this thinking are with us to this day. How often do systems designers simply automate a manual process rather than explore the use of these systems in new and more efficient ways? In moving from the industrial age to the information age, businesses no longer derive sustainable competitive advantage by injecting new technology into physical assets. Doing things the same old way with new technology just doesn't cut it. Today organizations need to do more than manage their assets and liabilities well. Organizations must find new ways to differentiate themselves. They must look to some of the following areas:

❑ Introduce products and services that fulfill the desires of targeted customers;

❑ Deliver products and services with short lead times and at low cost;

❑ Develop long-term relationships with customers that retain customer loyalty; and

❑ Develop employee skills to improve the ability of the organization to achieve the previous objectives.

Well, I guess I wasn't able to avoid the hype, and I am guilty of being one of the *ever faithful*. The world is caught up in the Internet, and it is changing everything. Perhaps, just perhaps, Gore was correct. Maybe future historians will one day look back and see the dawning of the Internet and the information age as having a greater significance than Guttenberg's press. I don't know. I still have a hard time swallowing that one.

## 2.2 Building the Internet

The emergence of the Internet was the result of several technologies developing in parallel. The Internet's story begins at the height of the cold war, back in 1962. John F. Kennedy was in the White House and Camelot was in full bloom. The gauntlet had been thrown down, and we were facing the Russian challenge to reach the moon. (When they make this book into a movie, the screen will go all wavy at this point.) The good sisters of Saint Agnes School would gather my classmates and me in front of a small black and white television screen to watch the latest space shot.

While we pondered how the space race would change our future world, another development was occurring with much less fanfare. This other development, however, would have as great, if not greater, an impact on all our lives. This was the year that the visionary J. C. R. Licklider was appointed the first head of the Information Processing Techniques Office (IPTO), a department of the then 4-year-old Advanced Research Projects Agency (ARPA) of the U.S. Department of Defense. Even at this early stage, Licklider envisioned a network spanning the globe. He dubbed this network the *Intergalactic Network,* where anyone in the world can access any system's applications and data from anywhere. We must emphasize that, for this time, such a vision was remarkable. We are talking about an age before even the simplest of computer networks, much less one that spanned the globe! Even if such a network were in place, data was not standardized. How were systems, all of which were proprietary, to communicate? Still, Licklider had a vision.

The Internet, as stated previously, is the result of many technologies developing in parallel. Two other developments occurred in 1962 that would affect the development of the Internet. First, Ivan Sutherland created Sketchpad, which laid the foundation for today's graphical user interfaces. Also, the Semi Automatic Ground Environment (SAGE), an early warning system, was fully deployed. SAGE was significant in that it used a light-gun to identify moving objects on radar screens. The following year, 1963, Licklider hired Sutherland to work at ARPA. In this same year the American Standard Code for Information Interchange (ASCII) was developed. ASCII was the first standard for computers that allowed systems to exchange information regardless of manufacturer.

Although Licklider left ARPA in 1964, his successor, Ivan Sutherland, continued to work on making a network that spanned the globe a reality. Shortly thereafter, Larry Roberts and Thomas Marill connected a system at MIT with one in Santa Monica using a dedicated telephone line and acoustic couplers. With ARPA funding, they created the first wide-area network. They were still, however, a good way off from the dream that would become the Internet.

Sutherland's stay at IPTO was short, and in 1965 Bob Taylor took over as director. He, like other researchers within ARPA, was faced with the same problem of computer systems that do not easily communicate with one another. Taylor presented these issues to the head of ARPA, Charles Herzfeld. To remedy this situation, a million-dollar networking project was launched to connect all the IPTO contractors. Taylor hired Larry Roberts of MIT to head up this project. Roberts began by convening a conference of ARPA researchers that concluded with Wesley Clark proposing *Interface Message Processors*. These IMPs, as they were called, were the precursors of modern-day routers.

Again, we see the parallel development of technologies that ultimately led to the Internet. While Roberts and Marill may have succeeded in having systems communicate, their method of using telephone lines wasted bandwidth and was expensive. In 1964, MIT, RAND, and the National Physical Laboratory in Britain developed packet-switching networks. In this scheme, data was put together into fixed-length packets. Network nodes routed the packets by passing them on to the other nodes in the network. Replacing Roberts' and Marill's telephone lines with packet-switching technology for the ARPANET increased line speeds from 2.4 Kbps to 50 Kbps.

In 1968 things began to happen at a quickened pace. ARPA refined the specifications for ARPANET. They also requested quotes for the development of the IMPs. Bolt, Beranek, & Newman (BBN) won the bid and began 1969 with the formation of a team to develop IMP software. Teams were formed at the University of California Los Angeles (UCLA), Stanford Research Institute (SRI), and University of California Santa Barbara (UCSB) to write the software that enables computers to communicate with the IMP. Each team delivered an important piece of the developing Internet. The UCLA team evolved into the Network Working Group and developed the Network Control Protocol (NCP). SRI used it as an opportunity to develop wide-area distributed collaboration while the UCSB team experimented with the display of mathematical functions, using a storage display.

The chaotic decade of the 1960s ended with two momentous events. First, man walked on the moon. Second, October 25, 1969, the Internet was born. Just like any other newborn, the Internet entered the world crying. The first logon attempt crashed the IMP. The second attempt succeeded, and a host-to-host connection was established between UCLA and SRI. While the 1960s gave birth to the Internet, it was in the 1970s that this infant that came crying into the world started to mature. ARPANET began the decade as an experiment, but concluded it as an uncontested success. Throughout this decade developments occurred, sometimes independently of one another, that led to the ultimate success of the Internet.

The first development of the 1970s was the completion of the UNIX operating system by Dennis Ritchie and Ken Thompson. While it may seem by today's standards that a universal operating system such as UNIX was inevitable, this was not always the case. Back in that era there was a great deal of cynicism concerning the possibility of a single operating system that would be supported by all platforms. In the days of proprietary hardware and operating systems, the very concept of having a single operating system was so alien that it was chided by many. Today, UNIX support is table stakes for any Independent Software Vendor (ISV) that wants to develop an enterprise class solution.

The other groups that were involved in the development of ARPANET weren't sitting idle either. In 1971 the Network Working Group delivered the Telnet protocol. The protocol provided a way to establish sessions on remote systems over a network. Within this same timeframe, the Networking Working Group also defined the File Transfer Protocol (FTP) and the Transmission Control Protocol

(TCP). FTP allowed the exchange of files between differing systems. Both TCP/IP and UUCP (UNIX-to-UNIX Copy) were incorporated into Berkeley UNIX, a version of UNIX enhanced at UC Berkeley. We will discuss the structure of TCP/IP when we take a closer look at some of the technologies upon which the Internet is based.

Additional developments included the introduction by Bell Labs of a new programming language called C. Ray Tomlinson of BBN introduced the @ sign for email headers. Unfortunately, this conflicted with other networks that used this symbol as a control character, and the controversy over email headers began. Also at this time, Bob Metcalfe of Xerox PARC developed a protocol for Local Area Networks (LANs) that eventually became Ethernet. By the mid-1970s over 3 million packets were traveling across ARPANET among 61 nodes. The network was a success. With IPTO's assignment complete, Licklider (who had temporarily returned to IPTO) turned over the operational responsibilities of ARPANET to the Defense Communications Agency. The first chapter of the Internet story drew to a close.

The next step in the history of the Internet began in 1977. Larry Landweber built THEORYNET, a network that connected part of the University of Wisconsin and provided email to over 100 researchers. Recognizing the importance of what he had created, Landweber started to discuss with other universities the construction of a computer science research network, CSNET. Robert Kahn, representing the U.S. Defense Advanced Research Projects Agency (DARPA), and Kent Curtis of the National Science Foundation (NSF) participated in these discussions. The idea caught on and was refined into a three-tier architecture that included ARPA-NET, TELENET, and an email-only service. CSNET was built using TCP/IP.

The inclusion of TCP/IP is significant. Many protocols were contending to become the standard, and there was no one clear leader at this time. Even the International Organization for Standards proposed its own Open Systems Interconnection (OSI). In addition to being used for CSNET, however, TCP/IP received greater and greater acceptance in the industry. Berkeley incorporated it into its version of UNIX, which shipped with the newly developed SUN workstations. Finally, in January 1983, ARPANET standardized on TCP/IP. TCP/IP continued to gain popularity, becoming available on most workstations and personal computers.

The NSF took the concept of CSNET a major step forward in 1984. Rather than just supplying an email service between researchers, the NSF sought to establish a way to provide researchers throughout the entire United States with access to supercomputers. In 1985, five supercomputer centers were selected: Cornell Theory Center, the John Von Neumann Center at Princeton, the National Center for Supercomputer Applications (NCSA), the Pittsburgh Supercomputing Center (PSC), and the San Diego Supercomputer Center (SDSC). A 56Kbps backbone was established between these centers around which grew regional networks. By the close of 1987, there were approximately 30,000 interconnected networks.

Despite its success, the very nature of ARPANET created limitations. UUNET was established to resolve these issues. This network provided commercial access to UUSCP and USENET newsgroups. At about this same time, 1988, the NSF backbone connection between supercomputers was upgraded to T1. The network also took on more of an international scope with connections to other parts of North America and then to Europe and Japan.

At about this time, Tim Berners-Lee of CERN in Switzerland wrote a proposal for a hypertext markup language. This in and of itself was nothing new. There were at the time various hypertext projects, such as those at Brown University and at Stanford Research Institute. The proposal from CERN, however, described a markup language that was able to execute in a heterogeneous distributed environment. Two years later, students at the NCSA at the University of Illinois at Urbana-Champaign created MOSAIC based on Berners-Lee's proposal. The World Wide Web took flight.

In the past 40 years we have seen private industry work together to develop what Licklider called an *"Intergalactic Network."* Even legislation played an important role in the development of the Internet: The Gore Bill, for example, was passed in 1991 by Congress to create the National Research and Education Network. All of these things played together to create this vast network in which we have all become entangled. What we have described up to this point is the network itself. Business and the development of the e-enterprise was still a few years in the future.

## 2.3 The Evolution to e-Commerce

In the 1800s, when telegraphic communication was first established between Texas and Maine, Thoreau pondered the possibility that it perhaps was an improved means to an unimproved end. He observed that "our inventions are wont to be pretty toys, which distract our attention from serious things. They are but improved means to an unimproved end." The essence of Thoreau's point is that we may have improved the mechanics of communication, but we may not really have improved what we are communicating. In this information age, have we really anything meaningful to say to one another? Simply establishing the infrastructure, the hardware and the software that enables the Internet, is one thing; having something meaningful to say is quite another.

Consider the role played by the telegraph in America's westward expansion. Without it, the railroads would not have been able to span the western frontier. How many times have we seen in movies about the Old West telegraph lines strung alongside railroad tracks? This is actually one of the few cases where Hollywood got it right. The telegraph provided railroad management with a means to coordinate the resources of the organization over a wide geographic area. During the Civil War, the telegraph was used to coordinate the movement of units and deliver intelligence information. Grant, recognizing the telegraph's use in command and control, would often cut his own telegraph lines to free himself of centralized command. In answer to Thoreau's question concerning the telegraph, yes, we did have something meaningful to say. The first attempts at e-commerce, however, were an entirely different matter.

### 2.3.1 BILLBOARDS ALONG THE INFORMATION SUPERHIGHWAY

In 1994 I was involved in a large data warehouse project. The system, when all was said and done, required a budget of approximately $1.5 million. In order to receive funding, I had to justify this cost in front of the board during the semiannual budget review. On the schedule, just prior to my presentation, was the manager in charge of researching new technologies. No one really knew what he did, and he didn't really have anyone working for him. Yet, he always seemed to be doing something. In the couple of months prior to our meeting with the board, he had been fooling around with the Internet. He was trying to create a *presence* for our company on the Web. When he demonstrated a corporate Web site to the board, they were impressed. The site gave a rundown on our company, our office locations, and even a picture of the CEO. The concept he presented was simple, a new slick way to promote the organization. The Internet, as far as the board was concerned, was just another communication medium, not much different from a newspaper or television. The data warehousing stuff was something radical, something requiring change, something entailing risk. The data warehouse was a solution: Being a solution it was going to change the way the company did business. Unfortunately, it was a solution to a problem they didn't realize they had. Hence, they did not see the ROI. In the end, the new technologies manager received funding, and I did not.

What my colleague had demonstrated was something safe, something to which the CEO could relate. It was what has become known in the industry as *brochureware*. At first, companies didn't know how to take advantage of the World Wide Web. People began with simply creating Web sites that provided information about a company or product. These early Web sites were mere billboards along the information superhighway. They were little more than electronic copies of company brochures. Business processes such as purchasing and sales were still carried out in the traditional manner. Some sites went as far as providing a way to contact the company over the Web, but no real transactions were carried out.

Contrast these early attempts at e-commerce with the telegraph. The telegraph was used to do things differently. It enabled a nation to expand. It allowed industry to coordinate resources across great distances. The telegraph was part of a solution. Brochureware did nothing new. It used the Internet as just another venue for publication, little more than an electronic newspaper. Brochureware lacked the imagination and innovation to take advantage of the capabilities of the Web.

### 2.3.2 THE CHALLENGES OF EARLY E-COMMERCE

Before we start to vilify these early Web designers, we should remember that most organizations *couldn't* do much more than brochureware. To achieve true e-commerce, three main issues needed to be resolved. As we shall see, two of them weren't even technological. The first was how to actually sell something over the Internet. We needed to develop a means by which we could carry out secure transactions. If I were giving you all the information necessary to purchase something, I needed to feel secure that you were the only one to receive this information. Then, assuming you received the information, I had to feel secure that you would use it only for the purposes for which it was sent.

Creating a secure transaction was only part of the problem of carrying out a sale over the Internet. The second issue was order fulfillment. Sure, the Internet was a great way to exchange information, but we still had to get the product in the hands of the customer. Even with a T1 line, this was a problem. The challenge of order fulfillment varies with the characteristics of the product. With some products, an order must be delivered immediately, while other products lend themselves to delivery times of a week or more. Order fulfillment is dependent on the nature of the products and the way in which people otherwise purchase the item.

When purchasing a book, for example, I might find a week to 10 days an acceptable period to wait. My alternative to buying a book over the Web is to go down to my local bookstore. If they don't have the book, which is usually the case for me, I have to order it, wait, and then make another trip back to store when the book arrives. Purchasing over the Web eliminates most of this process. I just order the book and wait approximately a week. Purchasing groceries over the Web has a different set of characteristics. Order fulfillment must be immediate. When I normally buy groceries, I simply go to the store, buy what I want, and go home. When I purchase groceries over the Web, I order what I want, and when I get home, the order is there. The process is simpler than the normal method, and fulfillment is easier. Each product has its own set of fulfillment requirements. When moving to e-commerce, a company needs to understand the normal purchasing patterns of the consumer and the demands it must meet to compete.

The third issue was perhaps the most important. No one knew what kind of market we were facing. Why should I, Billy Boy Bowling Balls, supplier to King Pins across the world, be interested in resolving these issues? Why should I make that investment in technology? Who the heck wants to buy bowling balls over the Internet anyway? Remember that most people in the mid-1990s *didn't* have an Internet connection in their home. True, some people were getting online, but mostly it was through some service that charged on an hourly basis. While the person with an email address is the norm and not the exception today, it was just the opposite back then. If you weren't connected to a business that used the Internet, you probably didn't have Internet access. The Internet was still the domain of geeky programmers who wore thick glasses and pocket protectors. (As a spokesperson for this group, I must say that pocket protectors have been greatly maligned. When one invests good money in a nice shirt, it is only natural to not want to mess it up with ink and pencil marks!)

### 2.3.3  THE NAKED TRUTH ABOUT EARLY E-ENTERPRISES

This brings us to a part of the Internet story that most people don't like to discuss. There was one industry that was extraordinarily well suited to e-commerce. The characteristics of the Internet made it the perfect medium for this industry to conduct business. It is one that has consistently blazed new cybertrails across the Internet. What developed between this industry and the Internet was a type of symbiotic relationship in which each thrived off the other. In spite of its contribution to the health of the Internet, most professionals seldom give it credit for its contributions. In fact, many work at suppressing the first true e-commerce industry. Which industry has done so much for the Internet? The adult entertainment industry—in short, pornography. The benefits of *cyberporn* we are discussing here are technological. It is not my intention to suggest that pornography is beneficial either socially or morally. As the old expression says, however, one must give the devil his due. Sociologists and ministers can best deal with whether this expression is either figurative or literal when applied to cyberporn. Here, we are simply discussing the technological benefits this industry has brought to the Internet.

Cyberporn did three things for the Internet, two of which resolved the initial challenges to e-commerce. First, it helped spur the market. People became interested in the Internet. Let's face it: Sex sells. In the early 1990s, the traditional media spent more time discussing the evils of cyberporn than reporting the educational benefits of Internet communication. The evening news did stories on chat rooms and online sex. Talk shows discussed pornography on the Internet. News magazine programs did stories on sexual addiction and the Internet. A technology users' group in the Santa Monica area held a symposium on cybersex. In addition to discussing the current state of sex over the Internet, there were designs for peripheral devices that would allow people to do more than just *talk* about sex on the Internet.

It was all about sex. Radio and television broadcasters along with publishers had their own motivations: Titillate the viewer and drive up ratings. These shows did something else though. They also sold people on the Internet. Just as the sex stories drove people to tune in, they also drove people to get connected. The image of the Internet went from some network frequented by techno-nerds to a place where something exciting was happening. People were meeting other people over the Internet. Heck, people were even having affairs over the Internet! It wasn't necessarily that people were getting connected to be sexually stimulated, although some obviously were. It was really that the basic image of the Internet had changed. It was where things were happening. If all this sex stuff was going on, what else was happening?

Second, cyberporn demonstrated that money can be made over the Internet. The right product with the right profile could create a profitable market on the Internet. The pornography industry is perhaps the most successful because it is so well suited to the Internet. The entire transaction is carried out over the Internet, from the purchase to the delivery of the product. There is no need for the supplier to develop relationships with third parties for product delivery. The transaction completes immediately. Product purchase and delivery is virtually simultaneous. This is different than with books or groceries that involve product shipment. Most importantly, the Internet offered anonymity. Normal purchasing methods are embarrassing for the consumer. Think of the embarrassment one would feel if his or her minister or neighbor were to see him or her with a copy of *Hot, Nasty Monkey Love.* The Internet is private; no one other than the individuals involved know about the transaction. As we can see, cyberporn has advantages over traditional pornography.

Finally, cyberporn developed some of the basic technology necessary for e-commerce. Since this industry was the first, it was the one that had to figure out how to carry out secure transactions over the Web. It was among the first to deliver large volumes of images, sound, and video over the Web. It pushed the technology.

Cyberporn in fact serves as an excellent case study for companies attempting to go to the Web. It was able to find ways to leverage the technology to compete with traditional distribution channels. It was also able to offer products and services that were not readily available in other venues. What is the equivalent of a chat room? Where could one go to receive the benefits of a chat room and still maintain his or her anonymity? As companies explore e-commerce, they must offer more than the standard distribution channels. To do this, some companies may have to do away with the old way of doing things. Again, we return to the concept of a solution. Applying the new technology means doing things differently.

### 2.3.4  THINKING DIFFERENTLY

It is all well and good for us to sit here and extol the virtues of thinking differently, of doing things in bold new ways, but what does it mean to think differently? As we have seen in the first section of this chapter, the Internet has been the catalyst for enormous change in our culture. How we do business is part of this culture and has not been impervious to these changes. This should be obvious to anyone who has been not been trapped on a deserted island for the last 10 years. Yet, many do not understand how business has been transformed. To many, the Internet is just another way of doing the same old thing. To others, it is all encompassing, completely transforming the purchasing process. We are back to the two camps, derision and hype.

In their book *Convergence Marketing*,[4] Yoram Wind and Vijay Mahajan discuss a third and more accurate alternative: convergence. Convergence is where the two markets—the traditional and the Internet-enabled—come together. No longer do we have consumers who are completely in one camp or the other. Modern consumers are a hybrid of the two, combining the two different methods of purchas-

---

[4] Wind, Yoram, and Mahajan, Vijay, *Convergence Marketing: Strategies for Reaching the New Hybrid Consumer,* Prentice Hall, 2001.

ing into one. Wind and Mahajan describe this hybrid consumer as the centaur. They discuss in their book strategies for reaching this new mixed breed. The first step in their strategy is to understand the centaur. They then explain how to use this understanding to *run with the centaurs*.

A realization that the focus for the e-business is on a new breed of consumer is critical to success. The first Business-to-Consumer (B2C) sites moved the actual process of sales and support to the Internet. The emergence of B2C gave rise to an entirely new set of Internet organizations. Companies such as Amazon.com gave customers the ability to search catalogs, choose an item, purchase the item, and select the method of delivery, all from the comfort of their own homes. We now know that not all B2C sites were successful; most weren't. The successful ones recognized that the automation of a manual process was not enough. They had to do more. They had to take what was the normal process and improve it.

This improvement came in the form of *personalization*. The Internet provides capabilities that cannot be met in the brick-and-mortar world. On the one hand, the Internet gives the e-business a global reach, a market in which there are tremendous economies of scale. On the other hand, through personalization, the organization can give each customer individualized attention. No longer are customers dealing with a cold, impersonal corporation. They are dealing with a trusted advisor, someone with whom they have a relationship. In Chapter 12, we will discuss how to personalize the customer's experience and develop a relationship.

What we are saying is that we use the Internet as a tool in our Customer Relationship Management (CRM) strategy. Let's be clear: Establishing a relationship with the customer is not just some warm fuzzy way of doing business. It is something of actual and real value to both the customer and the business. The objective of CRM is to establish a *mutually* beneficial relationship with the customer. As we shall see, it is impossible to manage your customer relationships without customer knowledge. It is impossible to have this knowledge without intelligence, business intelligence. In the Internet age, this intelligence needs to be Internet-enabled. It needs to be IEBI.

### 2.3.5 INTEGRATING THE SUPPLY CHAIN

For the most part, when people discuss e-commerce, they have focused their attention on the B2C market. The burst of the dotcom bubble has caused those with such myopic views of the Internet to become disenchanted. The B2C market is, however, only a part of the Internet revolution. The real money to be made over the Internet in the future is not in the B2C market, but in the Business to Business (B2B) market.

The repercussions of B2B markets will be far greater on the economy than anything we have seen in B2C. It is a new infrastructure, a new way of doing business. To understand these implications, look at B2B from a historical perspective. One of the reasons for the success of the American industrial revolution was that we started with a clean slate. There was no infrastructure. Industry was able to carry out business in unique ways. For the Europeans to develop a new way of doing business, they would have to replace a preexisting infrastructure. This European resistance crushed innovation. One such modification that was actually developed in France and implemented in America is the concept of manufacturing a product all in one factory. Raw materials go in one end of the factory and finished goods come out the other. Europeans visiting the early states were amazed by American industry. This was drastically different than in Europe, where each step of the supply chain was carried out by different suppliers. Wool was converted to yarn in one location, dyed in another, and made into garments in yet another. Germany and Japan in World War II had their infrastructures destroyed. During reconstruction, they found new and more efficient means of production that spurred tremendous economic growth. Keep in mind that the Internet is a new phenomenon. We are just beginning to understand how to take advantage of its capabilities.

One example of how the Internet can improve how businesses work together is in the procurement process. For most organizations, the procurement process has remained relatively unchanged for years. Figure 2.1 shows the typical flow for purchasing a product. First, some employee identifies a need. Perhaps his or her laptop is no longer functioning properly, or he or she is running low on direct materials. The employee manually completes a requisition, which is manually forwarded to a manager for approval. The approval process, especially for items that are out of the ordinary, may require the signature of several managers. If there is some question, the requisition is bounced back to the original employee, who must justify the purchase and start the process over again. When the appropriate approvals are finally received, the requisition is sent to purchasing. Purchasing may in turn question the requisition, and the employee or the manager must then justify the expense. In many cases, purchasing sends requests to suppliers for quotes. Once a supplier has been chosen, a purchase order is manually generated and the product is ordered. After the product is received, purchasing pays the supplier. As we can see, this is primarily a manual process and remains so in most companies today.

Organizations that move from a manual process to e-procurement will experience significant savings and operational efficiencies. It has been projected that a significant percentage of purchasing costs are attributed to the manual effort involved in processing and managing the purchase request. It is common for the administrative cost of a purchase to be greater than the purchase itself. The electronic processing of these requests removes the manual intervention and reduces overall cost. We have emphasized throughout this text that systems need to do more than automate a manual process. This holds true for e-procurement as well. When implementing an e-procurement system, we need to look beyond the manual process and understand how we can truly leverage the power of the Internet.

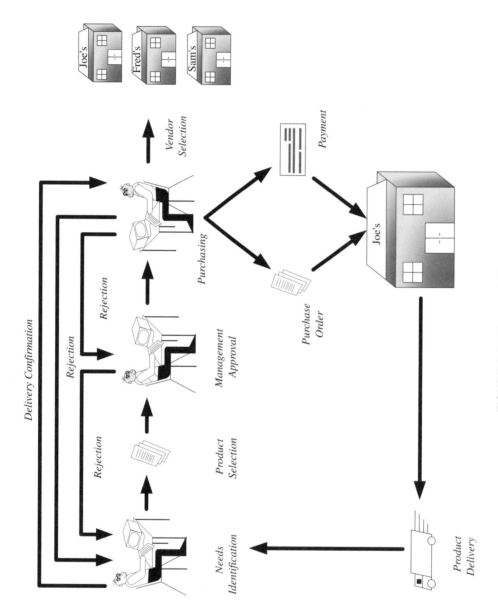

**FIGURE 2.1** The requisition process.

We should begin with putting as much of the process as possible in the hands of the employee making the request. Employees with a need for direct or indirect materials should be able to *easily* select from catalogs of preapproved vendors. They should be able to compare similar products of multiple vendors to get not only the best price, but also the best product for that price. Once an employee has selected a product, the system should provide online forms that can be processed electronically. Management approval should be electronic as well, automatically routing the request to the appropriate managers. If the manager does not approve it within a specific period, the request should be sent either back to the original requestor or to the manager's superior. When the request receives all the required approvals, it should be passed to purchasing to be consolidated with other requests prior to being electronically sent to the supplier.

One of the most important features of the e-procurement system is improved purchasing intelligence. The integration of IEBI into this environment provides purchasing with the information it needs to improve the purchasing process. With purchasing consolidated into a single electronic system, detailed reports can be easily generated. Purchasing can see which suppliers are providing what products to whom. We will be able to detect individuals and departments that purchase products outside of our accepted purchasing practices. Online Analytical Processing (OLAP) provides analysis of purchasing by individuals, departments, and divisions within the organization. Data-mining applications can detect patterns in the organization's purchasing habits. Armed with this information, purchasing can forecast needs more accurately, plan more efficiently, and negotiate with suppliers more effectively.

As we become more intelligent in our purchasing, competition among our suppliers increases and markets become tighter. A true free market is very much a Darwinian environment; only the fittest survive. As markets tighten and competition intensifies, the battle for survival becomes much more fierce. It is the ability of the organization to adapt to this changing environment that will mean the difference between survival and extinction. As we learned in the pervious section, we need to learn to do things differently to meet the challenges of an evolving market. The answer to competing in a more demanding B2C market is to establish a relationship with our customers. The answer for suppliers competing in a more demanding B2B market is to establish a relationship with their customers and other trading partners.

When we discussed CRM in the B2C market, we talked about personalization. We could see how personalization changes the customer's view of our organization from a faceless corporation to a trusted advisor. In the B2B space, businesses seek to do the same with one another. Both the supplier and the supplier's customer recognize the value of establishing a long-term mutually beneficial relationship. Both organizations recognize that just as the Internet has created a market in which a relationship is necessary, it has also provided the means to establish it. We can envision this relationship as establishing a virtual company, a single, uninterrupted supply chain that extends from the consumer through the distributors and manufacturers to the actual suppliers of raw material. For a more complete under-standing of such a virtual organization, refer to *e-Procurement from Strategy to Implementation*[5] by Dale Neef.

Consider for a moment what such a virtual organization can do for our man-ufacturing processes. As our organizations work in conjunction with one another, we are able to meet one another's needs in a more timely and efficient manner. Organizations can begin to implement Just-In-Time (JIT) manufacturing, where we reduce safety stock and excess inventories. For example, let's say that I am the map king of Southern California. I make every kind of street, city, and state map for which you could ever possibly hope. One of my hottest products is a map to the homes of both the famous and infamous. My suppliers are the printers. My dis-tributors are the folks who sell the maps on the street corners of Hollywood and Los Angeles. When one of my distributors goes to my Web site and orders another shipment of maps, the system immediately checks the inventory levels. If we are unable to fulfill the order, the system communicates with our printer and we receive a shipment date. The system responds to the distributor with a promised delivery date based on the printer's commitment to deliver the maps to our offices.

In Chapter 1 we discussed how business intelligence permeates the organiza-tion. We discussed how the information infrastructure is to the organization what the nervous system is to the organism. If we are to extend our organization to form a virtual organization with partners and supplier, must we also extend this infor-mation infrastructure. In the past there were significant barriers to establishing such tight integration between information systems. Remember that it was little more than 10 years ago that the passage of the Gore Bill made it possible to do busi-ness over the Internet. The power of this integration is more than just the ability to pass information between companies. The real benefit, the real power, the real strategic competitive advantage is in the organizations' ability to work as one. It is the power to act intelligently with one another. In order to work and cooperate with one another in this manner, we need intelligence, business intelligence. The Internet is the medium through which we communicate, the link between our information systems. This, of course, means that we will need to employ IEBI.

## 2.4  The Internet Marketplace

So far in this chapter, we have followed the growth of the Internet from a concept in the minds of some forward thinkers to an actual reality that has had profound effects on our society and business. The Internet has evolved from an environment where researchers share ideas to a ubiquitous medium of commerce. We have seen how business has gone from merely posting information on billboards along the

---

[5] Neef, Dale, *e-Procurement: From Strategy to Implementation*, Prentice Hall, 2001.

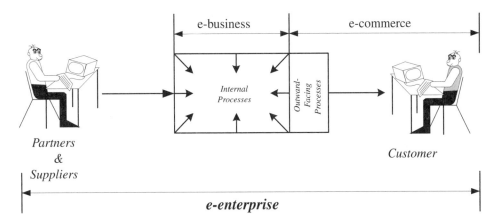

**FIGURE 2.2**  Types of e-organizations.

information super highway to leveraging the technology to integrate their information infrastructures. We have also seen how the Internet has given businesses the ability to form a single virtual organization that spans the entire supply chain.

Before proceeding, let's stop and look at the different types of organizations that we now encounter in the Internet age and their interaction with the market. There are four basic categories: traditional brick and mortar; e-commerce; e-business; and e-enterprise. With the exception of the traditional brick-and-mortar company, these organizations have embraced the Internet as a way to exchange information. What distinguishes them from one another is what information they exchange and with whom they exchange it. Figure 2.2 demonstrates the distinctions between each of these groups. In the following subsections, we will discuss each of these categories in a bit more detail.

### 2.4.1   BRICK AND MORTAR

We begin with the traditional brick-and-mortar company. These organizations are really outside the scope of our discussion. They have chosen, for one reason or another, not to participate in the Internet revolution. The point of mentioning them at all, however, is to note that the market in which the company competes mandates the extent to which an organization participates in the Internet revolution. Some companies may have nothing to do with the Internet. While this may be blasphemy in some circles, how a company applies Internet technology to its business processes must be driven by the conditions of its individual market.

One company that comes to mind is a map-making company with which I am familiar. The company receives orders over the phone; the vast majority of its customers are not set up for ordering over the Internet. It makes its own maps and deals with one or two local printers. Only two or three maps are produced a year, so it is not cost effective to set up some way of transmitting the maps other than carrying a tape to the printer. In fact, the printer isn't even set up to receive the information electronically. There is no ROI for this small company to become Internet-enabled. Organizations should leverage the Internet where the solution requires this level of communication. One should not look on the brick-and-mortar company with disdain when the market conditions for that organization do not require an Internet-enabled solution.

### 2.4.2 E-COMMERCE

Certainly, e-commerce has captured the imaginations of many in the media. When people think of an Internet-enabled organization, they typically envision e-commerce. An e-commerce company is one whose forward-facing functions are Internet-enabled. Forward-facing functions include such activities as marketing, sales, and support. These companies compete in B2C markets. Of course, there are degrees of e-commerce. Some companies may still use traditional outlets for the sale of their products while providing post-sales support over the Internet. Others have integrated the Internet into their brick-and-mortar enterprises: the brick-and-click enterprise.

The brick-and-click company integrates the Internet into its brick-and-mortar infrastructure. While such integration poses its own set of challenges, significant benefits can be derived from this approach. Organizations attempting to transform themselves to brick-and-click need to understand how the Internet can complement current business processes. Keep in mind the *centaur* described in Yoram and Mahajan's *Convergence Marketing*. The purchasing process is not Internet-enabled or done by physically visiting retail stores. It is not exclusively one or the other; it is a matter of both. The brick-and-click company can market directly to this hybrid consumer.

There are also variations on the B2C theme. One variation is the customer-to-customer (C2C) site, where one customer sells directly to the other. In such markets the e-commerce organization becomes a facilitator of the exchange between the two customers. Customer-to-Business (C2B) sites are another variation, where the consumer actually determines the conditions of the transactions to be carried out. These are sites where businesses compete with one another for the consumer's business.

In all of the cases cited above, IEBI plays a key role in driving business. We noted earlier in the chapter how the objective of CRM is to establish with the customer a mutually beneficial relationship. The organization does this by striving to understand the needs and desires of the consumer and fulfilling them. It is through this fulfillment that we are able to drive business in B2C, C2C, and C2B markets.

There is a difference between a need and a desire. We need to eat. We desire a porterhouse steak smothered in onions with a baked potato and asparagus in Hollandaise sauce on the side. We need to drink liquids. We desire a nice California Merlot vintage 1998. A need is something without which we cannot achieve necessary objectives. A desire is something that we want but can live without. Through personalization, companies can understand the customer's needs and create desires. The creation of these desires will generate new business. We can do this in each of these environments.

In a Web-based environment we can record and store the customer's interactions with our site. We can then analyze these activities, comparing them to other customers who demonstrated similar behavior with the same general demographics. Based on this analysis, we can then tailor the customer's shopping experience to address his or her specific needs and desires. In a B2C environment, we can offer products that complement products purchased by the customer. We can also recommend products that were rated favorably by other customers who had similar tastes as the current customer. We can use a similar method in the C2C space. In an online auction, for example, we can notify a customer when a particular product that may be of interest is up for bid. Not only does this benefit the buyer, but the seller has a larger market for the sale of his or her product. In C2B markets, companies can negotiate more effectively with customers. Perhaps companies can offer additional functionality or service to secure a purchase at a desired price.

In all of the markets described above, companies use the Internet to reach their customers in some way. The organizations that will be successful in these markets, however, are those that are able to use the Internet to do more than simply reach their customers. They are able to use it to forge a more enduring relationship with those customers.

### 2.4.3  E-BUSINESS

The e-business organization is the company that has taken its information infrastructure and moved it to the Internet. As shown in Figure 2.2, e-business is internally focused. This is not by any means as glamorous an undertaking as e-commerce, but its reward can be substantial. An example of such a system and the associated benefits is the e-procurement system we discussed earlier. Through Internet-enablement of just this one application, the organization was able to be more effective in purchasing and realized significant cost savings.

We need to emphasize that the information infrastructure is to the organization what the nervous system is to the organism. Think of the devastating effects of diseases that attack the nervous system—leprosy, for example. Victims can't feel pain in parts of their body; they don't know when they injure themselves. Consequently, infections set in. Is a sick information infrastructure any different? Inordinate levels of safety stock, the production of unwanted goods, and excess inventories are all symptoms of a sick information infrastructure. These are signs that parts of our organization are not communicating with one another.

Think of the power of a tightly integrated information infrastructure. Imagine an environment where the finance, budgeting and planning, forecasting, supply chain management, and manufacturing systems all work together as one, not for just a department or a division but for the entire enterprise. For this to be truly effective, every part of the organization must have access to the same set of applications. Geographically dispersed departments, remote offices, foreign divisions, all must be able to tie into this one system. The vehicle for this integration is, of course, the Internet.

We return to our theme of a solution. The e-business uses the Internet to change the business processes of the organization. They transform one another. As the organization becomes Internet-enabled, so too must business intelligence. As the organization moves its internal processes to the Internet, it must also transform its business intelligence systems to provide IEBI.

### 2.4.4 E-ENTERPRISE

Returning to Figure 2.2 we see that the e-enterprise is the organization that has fully Internet-enabled its value chain. The e-enterprise has succeeded in creating the virtual company we discussed earlier. In this environment, the information infrastructures of the organizations within the value chain have become fully integrated with one another. We are reminded of our analogy between information systems and the nervous system. Two organisms can form a symbiotic relationship in which each thrives off the other yet maintains its distinct identities. When two organisms start to share the same systems, nervous systems or cardiovascular systems, for example, they cease to be two organisms and become one. When organizations integrate information systems, their nervous systems, they form one virtual organization. The two have evolved through adaptation into a new more powerful organism—an organism fighting for survival in a market of lesser, weaker competitors.

You may have noticed a difference in terminology from what we used earlier in this chapter. Here we use the term *value chain* as opposed to supply chain. You can envision the supply chain as the process that is carried out *within* an organization that entails the procurement of materials, the processing of those materials to create finished goods, and the distribution of those finished goods to customers. For the purposes of our discussion, the value chain is a chain of supply chains. The value chain extends from the customer all the way back through retailers, distributors, manufacturers, and suppliers. The entire length of the value chain reaches from the customer to the actual supplier of raw materials.

As we stated earlier, while the B2C aspects of the Internet have certainly captured the imagination of most industry watchers, the real action is occurring in the B2B space. In their book *B2B Exchanges*,[6] Sculley and Woods project that the B2B market will reach $1.5 trillion in the United States by the year 2004, while more than $600 billion of that market will pass through B2B exchanges. Compare this to a B2C market of $108 billion.

---

[6] Sculley, Arthur, and Woods, William, *B2B Exchanges: The Killer Application in the Business-to-Business Internet Revolution*, Harper Business, 2001. Copyright © 1999 Arthur B. Sculley and W. William A. Woods. All rights reserved. Reprinted by permission of the authors and ISI Publications.

As the expression says, there is nothing new under the sun. The concept of supply chain integration has been with us for some time. Electronic Data Interchange (EDI) has been with us since the late 1960s. Since then organizations have attempted to share information using a number of different technologies. Some organizations attempted direct connections between systems. Others attempted to create Value Added Networks (VANs) or clearing centers. In these environments, a company will post a message with a destination address in a post box. The VAN takes the messages from the various boxes, sorts them, and distributes them to the recipients. The exchange of files between systems, however, was just one piece in the EDI puzzle. Receiving a message is one thing, understanding it is quite another. Of course, it was always possible to share flat ASCII files. To do this, however, both the sender and the receiver needed to understand the structure of the file in advance; deviation from the agreed upon structure caused errors and possibly the failure of the entire transmission.

As one can see, these systems, in addition to their exclusivity, were complex, which made them difficult to implement. This in turn made them expensive. These drawbacks made EDI the domain of large organizations that could afford such costs. Smaller companies that could not afford this investment in technology were excluded from the party. Internet technology solved some of these problems, opening the world of EDI and the ensuing integration of information systems to even the smallest of organizations.

The first issue resolved by the Internet is the communication between systems. In the Internet age, anything from a PDA to a supercomputer can communicate. Organizations with the smallest of budgets can easily establish communications with suppliers, sharing data in a variety of ways. Such methods as email, HTTP, and FTP are all simple, inexpensive, and easy ways of sending files over the Internet. The eXtensible Markup Language (XML) was soon seen as a solution to the second part of the problem, which was understanding what was being sent. Being a cousin of HTML (Hypertext Markup Language), XML was viewed as a better way of transmitting data over the Internet. XML is not necessarily the panacea some would claim. There are still issues with XML, such as the extraction and integration of XML data. Yet, it is far simpler than maintaining communication between systems using flat ASCII files. Organizations can now develop communications systems that interact with not only one supplier, but many.

Who hosts the system is another important advantage over EDI in the Internet age. In the past, a ball bearing company, interested in EDI, suddenly found itself in the business of setting up a communications network. This was an expensive undertaking. Beyond the initial development costs were network maintenance and support costs. In the Internet age, companies focus on what they do best. Organizations wishing to participate in B2B markets can enter via Application Service Providers (ASPs). The entire system can be outsourced. As we shall see, organizations can become part of exchanges with virtually no additional hardware or software.

The Internet has provided the foundation upon which we build our virtual organization. It provides the vehicle for the communication of data along the value chain in addition to a common language, XML. We have Internet-enabled our information infrastructure, expanding it across the entire value chain. As we enhance the power of our information infrastructure with the power of the Internet, we must also enhance the power of our intelligence systems. We transform our business intelligence to IEBI.

### 2.4.5  THE EXCHANGE

When EDI was first attempted, many of the connections between companies were peer to peer. The Internet improves on this. Using the Internet, organizations can maintain many simultaneous connections. It is interesting that Bob Metcalfe described the value of a network as the number of people on that network squared. Networks with 10 people on it would have a value of 100, while a network with 100 people would have a relative value of 10,000. This observation was made in the context of a point-to-point network. Kevin Kelly noted in *New Rules for the New Economy*[7] that in the Internet age multiple simultaneous connections can be maintained. In such environments the value of the network increases not by squaring the number of people on the network but by raising the number of people on the network to power of that number. Using Metcalfe's example, the value of a network of 10 people is 10 to the 10th power, or 10 billion. The network of 100 people has the relative value of 100 to the 100th power, or 1.e + 200.

As we can see, the wider the audience, the more effective and ultimately the more profitable our efforts. For this reason, we see that B2B exchanges have enormous power. Consider the nature of an exchange. In the traditional brick-and-mortar exchange we have a place where a number of people come together to do business. We see this in stock exchanges. Stockbrokers come together to buy and sell stock. We see similar activities in B2B markets. Buyers and sellers come together in one virtual space. The business of the exchange itself is to facilitate business between the participants within the exchange. To this end, the exchange acts as a neutral and independent third party in transactions. If we continue the analogy between B2B exchanges and the stock exchange, the organization operating the B2B exchange would be the equivalent of the Securities and Exchange Commission.

There are four basic types of exchanges. The first, *aggregate exchanges,* collect the products offered by multiple suppliers into one place. The buyer can then compare similar products from multiple vendors. Vendors whose products are included in this aggregation may not necessarily have a Web presence of their own. This is another way for companies that may not otherwise be able to participate in EDI to find entry into B2B markets. In our discussion on e-procurement we proposed that organizations have a catalog of approved vendors. We can easily implement

---

[7] Kelly, Kevin, *New Rules for the New Economy*, Penguin Books, 1999.

this through an aggregate exchange. The exchange provides for the management of the catalogs, such as maintaining content, approving vendors, and monitoring quality. As new vendors enter the marketplace, the exchange can determine their acceptability. Companies participating in the exchange can accept all or a subset of the vendors as suppliers.

The second type of exchange is an *auction exchange.* In these exchanges, bids are submitted for products and services. These bids can originate from either the buyer or the seller. Auction exchanges can operate in a variety of ways. In the basic auction exchange, blind bids are submitted and evaluated. The auction process can also be fully automated, where the system matches bids between buyers and sellers. Obviously, such markets are highly competitive and offer advantages to both buyers and sellers. While buyers are able to drive prices down, sellers have a distribution channel where they can offload excess inventory.

The third type of exchange is a *trading hub.* A trading hub is a virtual marketplace in which vendors can advertise and sell their products. Trading hubs have a distinct benefit to the buyer in that they typically set up communities comprised of both buyers and sellers. These communities provide the buyer with information concerning their businesses. They can learn the latest on industry trends. Buyers can share information on where certain products fail and helpful tips on the use of other products. Again, we see similarities between B2B and B2C markets. Earlier, we discussed personalization. Part of personalization is the ability to create communities of users. These communities can be centered on basically any aspect of the B2B exchange, whether it is related to product sets, product utilization, or industries that use a particular type of product. All are valid types of communities that can be established within a trading hub.

The fourth type of exchange is the *video dating exchange.* I refer to these types of exchanges as video dating because they provide introductions between potential buyers and sellers. The exchange is involved only in the initial introduction of the two parties. Subsequent activities occur outside of the exchange. A buyer or seller posts a description of the product or service in which he or she is interested. The second party responds, and from there they go on to carry out the transaction as they normally would.

## 2.5 Conclusion

We have reached the end of our exploration of the Internet world. What have we learned? What conclusions can we draw?

To begin, we see that the Internet is truly more than hype. It is also more than mere technology. The Internet is a new medium by which we can communicate. As Guttenberg's press transformed the old world, the Internet is transforming the current world. It is transforming society, business, governments, all aspects of our daily lives. Such a transformation has created a much more competitive business environment. Just as the Internet has posed a problem, it has also provided a solution. It has equipped businesses with the tools necessary to succeed in this more competitive world.

What is staggering, perhaps, is that the Internet began as the dream of J. C. R. Licklider. His dream was to establish an *intergalactic network*. Certainly the Internet started simply enough—two computers in two different universities communicating with one another. From little acorns, mighty oaks grow, and that little acorn grew into the mightiest of oaks. From this modest beginning the network grew, adapted, and incorporated other networks until it formed a massive oak in whose branches many organizations have come to nest.

At first, how to do business over the Internet was not so obvious. Many began simply by creating a Web *presence*. As companies became more sophisticated in their use of the Internet, more of the business processes began to be carried out over the Internet. Forays onto the Internet ranged from e-commerce sites, where the forward-facing part of the company were Internet-enabled, to e-enterprises. An e-enterprise has achieved the long sought after goal of integration of the entire value chain.

As we look into the future, we cannot help but conclude that the Internet will continue to expand and that it will continue to strengthen its influence on business. There will come a day in the not too distant future when we will no longer discuss Internet-enabled this or Internet-enabled that. The Internet will so permeate society, business included, that we will simply discuss business. It will be understood that the Internet forms the backbone of communication. Of course, this is a pretty safe statement to make—the conclusion is all but confirmed.

# INTERNET-ENABLED
# BUSINESS INTELLIGENCE

*If you're good at finding the one right answer to life's multiple-choice questions, you're smart. But there's more to being intelligent—a creative aspect, whereby you invent something new "on the fly." Indeed, various answers occur to your brain, some better than others.*

> *Every time we contemplate the leftovers in the refrigerator, trying to figure out what else needs to be fetched from the grocery store before fixing dinner, we're exercising an aspect of intelligence not seen in even the smartest ape. The best chefs surprise us with interesting combinations of ingredients, things that we would never think "went together."*

—*William H. Calvin*
How Brains Think[1]

In Chapter 1, we learned that Internet Enabled Business Intelligence (IEBI) is a solution. We also noted that each of the elements within a solution is changed by the other. In Chapter 2, we discussed the rise of the Internet and the environment it has created. As part of this examination, we saw how the organization has evolved to compete in this changed world. This is only part of the story, two ingredients in our solution. The third is Business Intelligence (BI).

---

[1]Calvin, William H., *How Brains Think*, Perseus Books, 1997. Used by permission.

My youngest daughter and I are part of a father and daughter program that entails monthly weekend campouts. In addition to providing some one-on-one time with my daughter, the program gives me the opportunity to spend time with other fathers of young daughters. Typically, once we get all the girls tucked away, the dads sit by the fire and solve the world's most pressing problems. In one of these discussions, one of the dads noted that *intelligent* people, in his experience, are not always the most successful. He described how intelligent people at his company often lacked common sense. Although they had book learning, they lacked creativity. My friend had never read William Calvin.

Many misunderstand the true nature of intelligence. It would be pointless for me to drone on about intelligence unless we first understand the nature of intelligence. We begin this chapter, therefore, by exploring intelligence and examining how intelligence relates to business.

Far too often when people hear "BI," they think "data warehouse." The data warehouse is just one part of the information systems that support BI. As the chapter progresses, we will find that the data warehouse and associated information systems really are implementation *details* of BI. They are not BI in and of themselves.

This chapter describes BI as an iterative loop composed of Extraction, Transformation, and Loading (ETL) processes, the data warehouse, decision support systems, BI applications, and decision makers. We will examine each component of this loop in detail. Some of you may recognize the discussion on data warehousing from my previous book, *Object-Oriented Data Warehouse Design*.

## 3.1   Intelligence

Let's start by talking about thinking. That's what BI is all about: *thinking*. In their book *The Ape at the Brink of the Human Mind*, Sue Savage-Rumbaugh and Roger Lewin discuss how oranisms with a complex nervous system are all faced with a common question. They describe how in each moment of life they must decide what to do in order to survive. From the lowliest earthworm to man, we are all faced with one common question: What shall I do next? We find intelligence in how an organism finds an answer to this question.

Organisms and organizations are very similar. An organism is a body that is composed of organs that work together towards a common goal: staying alive. An organization is made of people or groups of people who work together towards a common goal: staying in business. This is a common metaphor. The apostle Paul described the church as a body in which each member has its own particular function. We can conclude, therefore, that in the same way we find intelligence in how an organism decides what to do next, we find intelligence in an organization by how it defines what to do next.

In 1575 the Spanish physician Jaun Huarte defined intelligence as the ability to learn, to exercise judgment, and to be imaginative. We can extend this definition of intelligence as the ability to think abstractly, to be able to organize volumes of information, and then to reason. When we discuss BI, therefore, we are talking about thinking abstractly about the organization, reasoning about the business, and organizing large quantities of information about the business environment. The development of a strategy requires that the decision maker take a set of facts and create something new. This is the very essence of BI. The sheer size of most organizations, however, requires that there be an information infrastructure present to facilitate this level of intelligent thought.

The central nervous system of the organism facilitates intelligence. The central nervous system of an organization is the information infrastructure. Consider the similarities between the two. The central nervous system receives information from the outside world and transmits that information to the rest of the organism. The brain processes that information and directs the behavior to the rest of the organism. In the organization, the information infrastructure receives data from the outside world as transactions. Some server receives the transactions and takes appropriate action. If the transaction is a purchase, orders are filled and customers are billed. The presence of a central nervous system, however, does not create intelligence.

The human brain is composed of three distinct concentric layers. The innermost layer is the oldest; it controls the automatic biological functions. These are the things that we do not think about, such as digesting, breathing, and sleeping. Often, this innermost layer is referred to as the reptilian brain. The second layer controls the emotions; this is the limbic system. The third layer, the new brain, is where thinking is done. This is the cerebral cortex. The cerebral cortex carries out such functions as observing, organizing, and responding.

In scanning the business world, we see organizational intelligence has evolved to varying levels. Organizations that have only operational systems are at the lowest rung of the evolutionary ladder; they function with only a reptilian brain. The operational system receives a stimulus and passes that stimulus on to other parts of the organization. It signals when there is pain or pleasure. For example, when stock levels fall too low, it registers hunger, and the organization reacts by ordering more stock. When sales exceed expectations, it registers pleasure, and the payroll department issues bonus checks. Organizations with purely operational systems are unable to make meaningful information out of the volumes of data locked within the operational systems.

Some companies have evolved to the level of the limbic system. These companies are often worse off than those at the reptilian level. Limbic companies are continually buffeted by market forces, reacting and overreacting to events in the marketplace. Earnings drop a cent per share and a thousand people lose their jobs. Six months later, a new promising market opens and a hiring frenzy commences. Organizations in this mode are emotional companies. Strategy cannot exist in this environment. Rather than shaping their market, the market shapes them. They optimize the stock price often at the expense of the long-term health of the company. The information systems of these organizations provide some analytical capabilities, but it is only a snapshot of the current environment. It is not within the context of what has occurred in the past or projections of the future.

The new brain, the cerebral cortex, is the thinking brain. This is where the capacity to think abstractly exists. It is in the cerebral cortex that reasoning occurs and the vast quantities of information are organized into meaningful systems. The data warehouse is the part of the information infrastructure that transforms the volumes of information into something meaningful. Within the warehouse is a detailed history of past experiences. Decision Support System (DSS) tools allow the strategist to find patterns in these experiences for comparison to the current situation. In this way, the strategist can better predict the future.

So, why does an organization need BI? In order to survive, the organization must develop a winning strategy. In order to develop a winning strategy, one must be able to anticipate future conditions. Understanding the past is the best way to be able to predict the future. For this reason, information is the meat upon which a strategy feeds. It is only through the eyeglass of the DSS that the decision maker can look out on the organization's environment and see behaviors amidst the havoc.

## 3.2 Anatomy of Business Intelligence

Examining your environment, *understanding* what is going on around you—this is what BI is all about. As we discussed in Chapter 2, the very fabric of our environment has undergone a massive transformation. The threads of this fabric have gone from person-to-person interactions to person-to-system interactions and in many cases to system-to-system interactions. The catalyst for this transformation is the Internet. The Internet has changed the way organizations interact with one another as well as with their customers. An organization's BI must evolve to meet the challenges of this new environment.

Figure 3.1 presents the BI loop described in Chapter 1. As we look at this figure, we see the components of BI. Each component has the potential to be changed in significant ways by the Internet. Data from outside the data warehouse flows into the BI loop through the operational environment. This data contains information about customers, suppliers, competitors, products, and the organization itself. The Internet expands the information sources of the warehouse. It reaches beyond what is contained within the organization's internal systems, across the Internet, to include partner, supplier, and customer systems. It spans the entire breadth of the value chain.

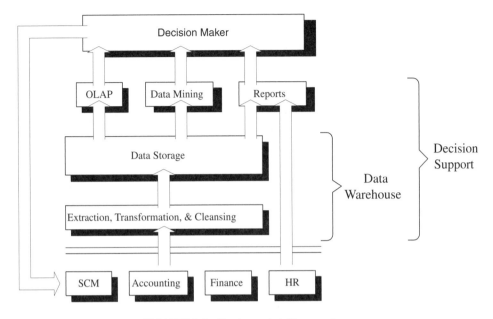

**FIGURE 3.1**  Business Intelligence loop.

As we extract the data from the operational environment, we cleanse and transform it to make it more consistent with the data in our warehouse. It is then stored in some central repository. This central repository can be either a multi-dimensional or relational database. The extraction, cleansing, transformation, and storage of data is the data warehouse/data mart portion of the BI loop. We will discuss the data warehouse in more detail in section 3.2.1.

DSS is the next step in the loop. DSS retrieves data and presents it to the decision maker. We often think of DSS as a multidimensional tool that is a complex, advanced system. At times, it is. At other times, we can consider simple reporting as DSS. In fact, DSS is a full spectrum of systems, ranging from reporting through OnLine Analytical Processing (OLAP) to data mining. As we discuss IEBI, the tremendous impact the Internet has had on DSS will become clear. We will see that Java provides support for developing Web-enabled DSS and XML, a common way to share data to devices with drastically different capabilities; Common Warehouse Metadata Interchange (CWMI) provides a means to share metadata between systems. In later chapters, we discuss how DSS can use the capabilities of the Internet to deliver support to decision makers throughout the entire organization. We will examine DSS in more detail in section 3.2.4.

Data warehousing and DSS are just a means to an end; they might even be considered implementation details. BI is the process and systems used by the organization to define its strategic direction. As such, BI also includes applications that are often overlooked by the novice. Two such applications are the Balanced Scorecard and Activity Based Costing (ABC). What is most interesting about these applications is that they did not originate within IT departments but within the business community. We will examine each of these applications in section 3.2.5.

Integral to this loop is the decision maker. He or she takes information extracted from the data warehouse and delivered by the DSS to define some plan of action. This plan is not necessarily a change in course; the data may support maintaining the present direction. Rather than considering the decision maker as the end user of BI, we should consider him or her as part of the process. The operational environment reflects the result of his or her decisions. These results are then fed back into the data warehouse and another iteration of the loop begins again. Decision makers are just as much a part of the BI loop as any other component. We will examine the role of the decision maker as well as the different types of decision makers in section 3.2.6.

As we discussed in Chapter 1, the loop is composed of three basic steps: acquire the data, analyze the data, and take action based on the data. We can describe this data as the three A's: acquire, analyze, and act.

### 3.2.1 THE DATA WAREHOUSE[2]

The previous section discussed the unique purpose of BI. This section describes how the data warehouse, the heart of the BI loop, meets these special needs. In this section we define a data warehouse and identify each of its components. We already know that the warehouse sits outside the operational environment and receives its data from it. We also know that the purpose of the warehouse is to provide a central repository for strategic information that will be used as a basis for business strategy.

Given this understanding of the data warehouse, we see it is a system sitting apart from the operational environment that feeds off of it. What is it, though? The very term *data warehouse* evokes images of large buildings of corrugated metal where dingy yellow forklifts loaded down with crates of information scurry between bare steel girders. To the computer literate, there is some nebulous vision of big computers with petabytes of disk drive space, seasoned with a dash of some sort of online archive of operational data. In this idealized world, users magically fly through volume upon volume of information, routing out that one piece of information that is going to make all the difference.

The situation is similar to the old story of the blind men and the elephant. One blind man felt the legs and thought the elephant was like a tree, while another felt the trunk and thought it was like a snake. Finally, a third felt the tail and thought it was like a rope. Each view grasps some element of the truth while missing the overall picture. It is true that data moves data from the operational environment to the warehouse, but the warehouse is more than an archive. It is also true that the warehouse contains large volumes of data, but the central repository where the

---

[2] Giovinazzo, William, *Object-Oriented Data Warehouse Design*, Prentice Hall, 2000.

data is stored is only part of the overall warehouse. The key to understanding the data warehouse is how the parts interact with one another, a Gestalt, if you will, of the data warehouse. The data warehouse is clearly a case where the whole is greater than the sum of the parts. Figure 3.2 presents each of these parts and their place in the warehouse.

Let's follow the path data takes from the operational environment to the decision maker:

1. **Operational Environment**—The operational environment runs the day-to-day activities of the organization. Such systems as order entry, accounts payable, and accounts receivable reside within the operational environment. These systems collectively contain the raw data that describes the *current* state of the organization.

2. **Independent Data Mart**—A common misconception is that a data mart is a small data warehouse. The difference between the data mart and the data warehouse is scope. The data mart focuses on an individual subject area

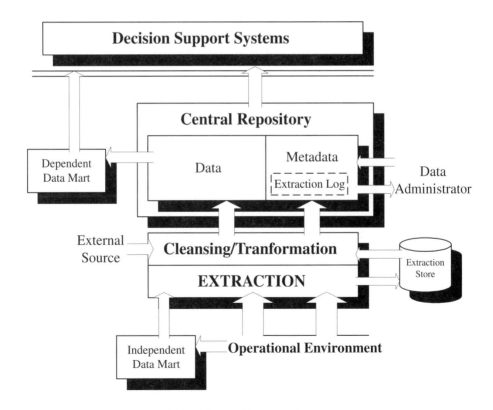

**FIGURE 3.2**  Data warehouse.

within the organization, where the scope of the data warehouse is the entire organization. An independent data mart receives data from external sources and the operational environment independent of any data warehouse.

3. **Extraction**—The extraction engine receives data from the operational environment. The extraction process can occur in a variety of ways. The warehouse can be the passive recipient of data, where the operational environment passes the data to the warehouse, or it may actively retrieve data from the operational environment. Transportable tables and data replication are examples of alternative techniques for moving data into the warehouse.

4. **Extraction Store**—Data received from the operational environment must be *scrubbed* before it is incorporated into the data warehouse. The extraction store holds the extracted data while it is awaiting transformation and cleansing. It is like the Ellis Island of data warehousing.

5. **Transformation and Cleansing**—Scrubbing consists of data transformation and cleansing. Data transformation is the process of converting data from different systems and different formats into one consistent format. Cleansing is the process of removing errors from the data.

6. **Extraction Log**—As the operational data is integrated into the data warehouse, an extraction log is maintained to record the status of the extraction process. This log is actually part of the data warehouse's metadata and is critical in maintaining data quality. This log will serve as input to the data administrator to verify the quality of the data integrated into the warehouse.

7. **External Source**—Data originating from outside the organization is also included in the data warehouse. This external data could include such information as stock market reports, interest rates, and other economic information. An external source could also provide metadata such as Standard Industrial Classification (SIC) codes.

8. **Data Administrator**—The role of the data administrator is to ensure the quality of the data in the warehouse. This role should not be confused with the data*base* administrator. The database administrator is responsible for the operation of the system that supports the data warehouse. The data administrator is the team member responsible for the quality of the data within the warehouse. One of the responsibilities of the data administrator is to review the extraction log for changes in metadata, inaccurate data from the operational environment, or even data errors generated by the operational system. The data administrator will take the necessary corrective actions, such as making changes to the metadata repository, correcting erroneous data, or notifying operations of programming errors.

9. **Central Repository**—The central repository is the cornerstone of the data warehouse architecture. This central location stores all the data and metadata for the data warehouse.

10. **Metadata**—This is *data about data*. One way to describe metadata is that it provides the context of the data. It describes what kind of information is stored, where it is stored, how it is encoded, how it relates to other information, where it comes from, and how it is related to the business. Metadata also contains the business rules of the data—the use of the data within the organization.

11. **Data**—The data store contains the raw data of the data warehouse. The central data store can be either a multidimensional database or a relational database system. The structure of this data and how this structure is designed is the focus of this book.

12. **Dependent Data Mart**—A common misconception is that a data mart is a small data warehouse. The difference between the data mart and the data warehouse is scope. The data mart focuses on a specific subject area within the organization; the scope of the data warehouse is the entire organization. A dependent data mart relies on the data warehouse for the source of its data.

This description of the warehouse, however, examines only the parts. It does not provide us with a complete picture of the warehouse. Let's take a moment to look at the data warehouse as a complete entity. Almost everything written on data warehousing begins with the obligatory and often verbose comparison between the data warehouse and the transaction-oriented operational world. Despite what Emerson may have said concerning consistency, that it is the hobgoblin of little minds, a study contrasting these two environments clarifies some of the most important characteristics of the data warehouse.

W. H. Inmon defines the data warehouse as "a subject-oriented, integrated, nonvolatile, time-variant collection of data in support of management's decisions."[3] I find this definition of data warehousing to be most clear in that it highlights the most vital features of the warehouse. In the next few subsections we will discuss each of these characteristics and how they differ from the operational sources.

### 3.2.1.1  Subject-Oriented

The first characteristic of a data warehouse, as described by Inmon, is *subject orientation*. The operational environment focuses its attention on the day to day transactions that are part of the normal operation of the business. The data warehouse is concerned with the *things* in the business environment that are driving those transactions. Figure 3.3 shows the difference in data orientation. This difference has far-reaching effects on the entire system.

The transaction-oriented system structures data in a way that optimizes the processing of transactions. These systems typically deal with many users accessing a few records at a time. For reasons too numerous to discuss here, minimizing

[3] Inmon, William H., *Building the Data Warehouse*, Wiley-QED, 1992, 1993.

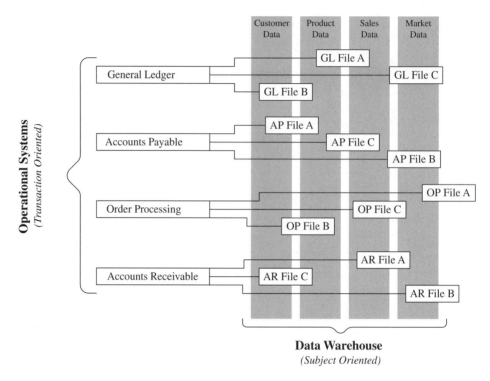

**FIGURE 3.3**  Data orientation.

record and table size improves overall system performance. System architects *normalize* transaction databases to structure the database in an optimal way. Although a complete discussion of normalization is outside the scope of this book, it is sufficient to note that data pertaining to a specific subject is distributed across multiple tables within the database. For example, an employee works in a department that is part of a division. The employee, department, and division information is all related to the subject employee. Yet, that data will be stored in separate tables.

Operational data is distributed across multiple applications as well as tables within an application. A particular subject may be involved in different types of transactions. A customer appearing in the accounts receivable system may also be a supplier appearing in the accounts payable system. Each system has only part of the customer data. We are back to the blind men and the elephant. Nowhere is there a single consolidated view of the one organization.

Considering the way in which the decision maker uses the data, this structure is very cumbersome. First, the decision maker is interested in the behavior of business subjects. To get a complete picture of any one subject, the strategist would have to access many tables within many applications. The problem is even more complex. The strategist is not interested in one occurrence of a subject or an individual customer, but in all occurrences of a subject and all customers. As one can easily see, retrieving this data in real time from many disparate systems would be impractical.

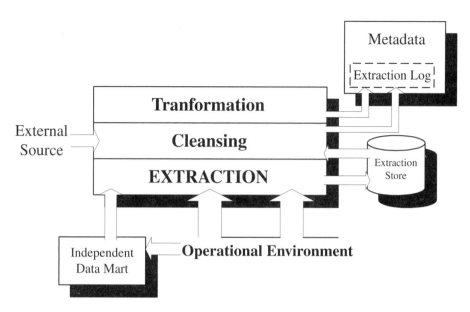

**FIGURE 3.4** Data integration.

The warehouse, therefore, gathers all of this data into one place. The structure of the data is such that all the data for a particular subject is contained within one table. In this way, the strategist can retrieve all the data pertaining to a particular subject from one location within the data warehouse. This greatly facilitates the analysis process, as we shall see later. The task of associating subjects with actions to determine behaviors is much simpler.

### 3.2.1.2 Integration

The difference in the orientation of the data drives the need to gather the data into one place. The warehouse, however, does more than gather the data. In a sense, it derives its data from the operational environment. The operational data is the basis of the warehouse. The integration process (see Figure 3.4) forms it into a single cohesive environment. The origin of the data is invisible to the decision maker in this environment. The integration process consists of two tasks: data cleansing and data transformation.

### Data Cleansing

Data cleansing is the process of removing errors from the input stream and is part of the integration process. It is perhaps one of the most critical steps in the data warehouse. If the cleansing process is faulty, the best thing that could happen is that the decision maker will not trust the data and the warehouse will fail. If that's the best thing, what could be worse? The worst thing is that the warehouse could provide bad information and the strategist could trust it. This could mean the development of a corporate strategy that fails. The stakes are indeed high.

A good cleansing process, however, can improve the quality of not only the data within the warehouse, but the operational environment as well. The extraction log records errors detected in the data cleansing process. The data administrator in turn examines this log to determine the source of the errors. At times, the data administrator will detect errors that originated in the operational environment. Some of these errors could be due to a problem with the application or something as simple as incorrect data entry. In either case, the data administrator should report these errors to those responsible for operational data quality. Some errors will be due to problems with the metadata. Perhaps the cleansing process did not receive a change to the metadata. Perhaps the metadata for the cleansing process was incorrect or incomplete. The data administrator must determine the source of this error and take corrective action. In this way, the data warehouse can be seen as improving the quality of the data throughout the entire organization.

There is some debate as to the appropriate action for the cleansing process to take when errors are detected in the input data stream. Some purists feel the warehouse should not incorporate records with errors. The errors in this case should be reported to the operational environment, where they will be corrected and then resubmitted to the warehouse. Others feel that the records should be corrected whenever possible and incorporated into the warehouse. Errors are still reported to the operational environment, but it is the responsibility of those maintaining the operational systems to take corrective action. The concern is making sure that the data in the warehouse reflects what is seen in the operational environment. A disagreement between the two environments could lead to a lack of confidence in the warehouse.

The cleansing process cannot detect all errors. Some errors are simple and honest typographical mistakes. There are errors in the data that are more nefarious and will challenge the data administrator. For example, one system required the entry of the client's SIC code for every transaction. The sales representatives did not really care and found two or three codes that would be acceptable to the system. They entered these standby codes into the transaction system whenever the correct code was not readily available. These codes were then loaded into the data warehouse during the extraction. While there are many tools available on the market to assist in cleansing the data as it comes into the warehouse, errors such as these make it clear that no software product can get them all.

Data cleansing is the child of the data administrator. This is an essential position on the data warehouse team. The data administrator must take a proactive role in routing out errors in the data. While there is no one component that will guarantee the success of a data warehouse, there are some that will ensure its failure. A poor cleansing process or a torpid data administrator is definitely a key to failure.

### Data Transformation

Rarely does one encounter operational environments where data is consistent between applications. In a world of turnkey systems and best-of-breed heterogeneous environments, it would be more surprising to see data consistency than not. Data transformation addresses this issue. The data transformation process receives the input streams from the different operational systems and transforms them into one consistent format.

The sheer task of defining the inconsistencies between operational systems can be enormous. Table 3.1 demonstrates the different types of integration challenges facing the data warehouse architect. The table shows that as each new source of data is identified, the complexity of the integration process increases. An analysis of each system contributing to the data warehouse must be performed to understand both the data elements that are of interest and the format of these elements. Once these elements have been selected and defined, an integration process must be defined that will provide consistent data.

**TABLE 3.1**   Integration Issues

|             | Sales Voucher | Purchase Order | Inventory |
|-------------|---------------|----------------|-----------|
| Description | Customer Name<br>IBM | Customer Name<br>IBM | Customer Name<br>International<br>Business Machines |
| Encoding    | Sex<br>1 = Male<br>2 = Female | Sex<br>1 = Male<br>2 = Female | Sex<br>1 = Male<br>2 = Female |
| Units       | Cable Length<br>Centimeters | Cable Length<br>Yards | Cable Length<br>Inches |
| Coding      | Key<br>Character (10) | Key<br>Integer | Key<br>pic '999999999' |

Table 3.1 presents some of the basic issues concerning data integration. Let's look at them in detail:

1. **Description**—This can be the most heinous of all integration issues. How does one determine that the three names presented in the table represent the same client? The transformation process must take each different description and map it to a specific customer name.

2. **Encoding**—There are four types of scales:[4] nominal, ordinal, interval, and ratio. When discussing encoding, we are concerned with a nominal scale. This scale is the simplest of all four scales. A number or letter is assigned as a label for identification or classification of that object. When integrating this data, map the input scales to the data warehouse scale.

3. **Units of Measure**—Integration of units of measure can be deceptive. While it may seem at first that it would be a simple mathematical calculation, issues such as precision must be considered when making these conversions.

4. **Format**—The originating operational systems may store data in a variety of formats. The same data element may be stored as character in one system and numeric in the next. As with the integration of all data elements, consider the ultimate use of the data within the warehouse.

One final note on the transformation process: Do not underestimate the task of defining an enterprise data format. It is necessary to get consensus on any format. The unfortunate truth is that when more than one person is involved in a decision, there are politics involved. Surprisingly, data elements can become highly controversial and political topics. Forewarned is forearmed. When defining data elements, expect political battles.

### 3.2.1.3  Nonvolatile

A major difference between the data warehouse and a transaction-oriented operational system is volatility. In the operational environment, data is volatile—it changes. In the data warehouse, however, once the data is written, it remains unchanged as long as it is in the warehouse. Figure 3.5 demonstrates the difference between the two system types as it relates to volatility. We begin on Monday. The quantity on hand for product *AXY* is 400 units. This is recorded in the inventory system in record XXX. During the Monday extraction, we store the data in the warehouse in record ZZZ. Tuesday's transactions reduce the quantity on hand to 200. These updates are carried out against the same record XXX in the inventory system. Tuesday night, during the extraction process, the new quantity is extracted and recorded in a completely separate data warehouse record YYY. The previous ZZZ record is not modified.

In essence, the nonvolatility of the data warehouse creates a *virtual* read-only database system. No database can literally be a read-only. Somehow, at some time, data must be stored in the database. The data warehouse does this in bulk. An extraction adds new records to the database; detail records already in the database are not modified. One of the challenges of a transaction processing system is that multiple users attempt to read and write to the same records, causing the database to lock records. This is not a concern in the data warehouse, since users only read the data.

---

[4] A scale is defined as any series of items that are progressively arranged according to value or magnitude and into which an item can be placed according to its quantification.

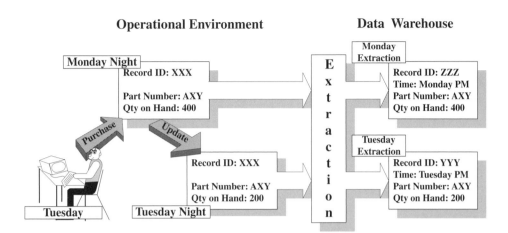

**FIGURE 3.5** Data volatility.

The database engine itself benefits from the nonvolatile nature of the data warehouse. While it is still critical that appropriate backup procedures be in place for the central repository, the database can eliminate many background processes used for recovery. For example, databases generally keep a *redo log*. These logs allow database administrators to return the database to its proper state after instance failure. Since updates are not being made against the data warehouse, there is no need to run this process.

### 3.2.1.4 Time-Variant Collection of Data

The nonvolatility of the data within the warehouse adds another *dimension* to the data warehouse, the dimension of time. If one were able to extract all the data from the operational systems in one specific moment in time, it would create a snapshot of the state of the organization. The warehouse, in essence, does this. At specified intervals, the warehouse takes a snapshot of the operational environment. The snapshots stored in the warehouse become frames on a roll of film, and this renders a movie. Time is not a variable for a snapshot; it is static. In a movie, however, time becomes a variable. The film can be run at whatever direction or speed the viewer may wish.

The data warehouse is like a movie. The decision maker can view the data across the field of time at whichever level of detail he or she may wish. This allows the business analyst to view patterns and trends over time. Time has become one variable that the analysis can manipulate. In short, the data warehouse is time-variant.

### 3.2.1.5 Supporting Management's Decision

The first section of this chapter discussed the strategic mission of the data warehouse. With this understanding, we see yet another difference between the data warehouse and the operational environment. The typical operational system is some automation of a manual process. The user community, therefore, is typically involved in the lines of production. As we said earlier, the data warehouse user is the decision maker. The strategist is any individual within an organization responsible for the strategy of any part of the organization. This includes product managers, marketing managers, department managers, and even CEOs.

It is very important that the actual decision maker interacts with the data. Management can no longer be satisfied acting as the passive recipient of static reports generated by the IT department. The average IT professional will not have the business acumen of the decision maker. When the strategist examines data, he or she will see things in the data that will lead to further inquiries. Some of these keys will be more overt than others; some may even be the result of a sixth sense on the part of the strategist. Static reports will not answer these inquiries, nor can the IT professional be expected to anticipate what questions may be asked. Regardless of the cause, the decision maker must be the main user.

The data warehouse architect must keep this difference in user communities in mind when building the system. It is critical that the system renders the appropriate performance to allow the decision maker to interact with the data in a timely and efficient manner. The user interface must also be so designed to allow the decision maker to explore the data within the warehouse. The challenge for the decision maker should be understanding the data, not retrieving the data from the system.

### 3.2.2  DISTRIBUTED VERSUS CENTRALIZED WAREHOUSE

One of the implications of the Internet is the ability to distribute the data warehouse. A distributed data warehouse is an integrated set of data stores that are physically distributed across a company's information infrastructure. Figure 3.6 presents the overall architecture of a distributed data warehouse. In this environment, we see independent data marts dispersed throughout the organization. These distributed data warehouses can be composed of homogenous environments in which the same database management system (DBMS) and operating system support the data marts, or they can be heterogeneous environments composed of multiple types of systems. As users query the data from the *distributed* data warehouse, the data is collated from these systems by either the client-tier or middle-tier application.

Proponents of the distributed data warehouse contend that distribution of the data solves several problems encountered by one large system. One of the key factors in the success of a data warehouse is timeliness. It is important to get the system up and running quickly, delivering the C-level executive who sponsored the system some proof that his or her support was well founded. To sift through the metadata of the many systems of even a moderately sized enterprise is a huge task that can take many months. In addition, the politics involved in finding consensus among the various departments within a single organization is enough to beach the launching of any data warehouse. This is, of course, a major impediment to delivering a system as quickly as possible.

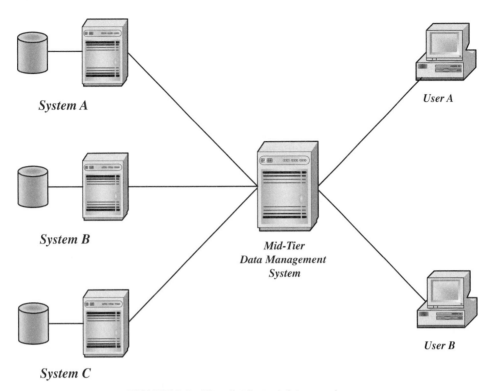

**FIGURE 3.6**   The distributed data warehouse.

Putting aside the "people" issues, one can see tremendous technical challenges to the single enterprisewide data warehouse. Even if we achieve consensus among the user community and we succeed in understanding all the metadata within our organization, we are still faced with the challenge of extracting that data and putting it into a single data repository. Once that is completed, imagine the size of such a system! Data warehouses running 20 to 30 terabytes are becoming more common, creating administration and maintenance challenges.

One would think that the decision whether to distribute or centralize the data warehouse is a no-brainer. Isn't it obvious that we should distribute? Well, on paper, even communism works if you are willing to ignore a few painful realities. Distributing the data warehouse is a patently BAD idea. At one time, the statements made above may have been true and the decision to distribute in some environments might not have been all that devastating. In today's world, it is not only possible to create a single enterprisewide data warehouse, it is preferable.

Let's start by thinking back to our metaphor. The information infrastructure is to the organization what the central nervous system is to the organism. The point of a central nervous system is that the intelligence is *centralized*. There are no organisms currently in existence that have more than one brain. In all organisms, one brain does the thinking and coordinates the activities of the entire organism. All parts of the organism work together for the common good. They do this through the coordination provided by the *central* nervous system. The organization must do the same—if all parts of the system are to work together in unison, then the intelligence of the organism must be centralized.

An important issue in BI is to define the true state of the organization. How certain values are calculated will vary between groups. In a distributed environment, there is no guarantee that all systems will calculate the data in the same way. Even when there is agreement on the calculations, the source data may vary. The reasons for these differences may be as simple as differing refresh rates. Regardless of the cause, multiple systems may disagree with one another and yet be correct within their own context. C-level executives often meet to discuss the state of the organization, and half the meeting is spent finding agreement in the numbers. In a distributed data warehouse, where two systems may not agree, there is no single version of the truth. In a centralized system, there is a single arbitrator of the truth: the data warehouse. By definition, it contains the authoritative version of the data. We are all drinking Kool-Aid from the same canteen.

By distributing the data warehouse, we were also hoping to avoid the political battles in defining the metadata. By moving the process to the client or middle tier, all we have done is postpone the debate; we haven't eliminated it. We have also removed many of the advantages we would have gained by going to a large centralized data warehouse. In the centralized system, we can pre-aggregate the data for faster retrieval. In a distributed environment, every time we wish to sum the data across systems, we have to extract the data then perform our calculations. The distributed alternative is to pre-aggregate the data in an independent system within the middle tier. When we do this, we are creating the centralized data warehouse. The only difference is in the granularity of the data. All we have done is further complicate a complex problem.

Hardware and software advances have eliminated many of forces that have driven people to attempt the implementation of a distributed data warehouse. For example, data warehouses up to 50 or 60 terabytes are no longer a problem. Advances in parallel database systems and storage arrays resolve the size issue easily. Pre-aggregated data reduces the need for full table scans, and bitmapped indexing enhances performance when such scans are necessary. For a more thorough discussion on how to structure your enterprise data warehouse to support very large databases, refer to my previous book, *Object-Oriented Data Warehouse Design*.

I am reminded of a scene in a movie where King Arthur is talking to Merlin. Merlin says to Arthur, "My days are drawing to a close. The old gods, the gods of stone, fire, and water will be no more. They will be replaced by the one God." This is what is happening in the data warehousing world. Market forces are such that the days of the custom-built data warehouse are drawing to a close. As more vendors develop BI extensions to their applications, fewer organizations will opt for a custom system. A BI system built into an already existing application will probably not meet 100 percent of a company's BI needs. It will, however, meet roughly half those needs, and in many cases, somewhat more than half. As long as the BI environment is *extensible*, a prebuilt solution is only logical. After all, why should a C-level executive commit funds to a risky million-dollar data warehousing project when there is a prebuilt solution that is sure to work?

We will discuss this in more detail later in this chapter. In the interim, consider the repercussions of such a change in the industry. Fewer companies build custom data warehouses. Vendors that specialize in databases and tools specifically for the data warehouse market find their market share shrinking. This results in smaller research and development budgets. The vendors who are gaining market share are the vendors who integrate BI. The R&D budgets expand, giving them greater functionality. Eventually, the specialized tools and databases fall behind the technology curve. They either fold or get purchased by the larger vendor. In the end, the only data warehouses that will be developed are enterprise-based systems that are integrated into the applications.

### 3.2.3 THE OPERATIONAL DATA STORE

The Operational Data Store (ODS) is a little discussed and often misunderstood system. Although it is mistakenly seen by some as a substitute for a data warehouse, it is actually a complement to it. Whereas the data warehouse is strategic in nature, the ODS is tactical. The data warehouse provides a historical context in which to understand the organization's current environment. With a data warehouse, we attempt to detect past trends in order to predict possible future outcomes of strategic decisions. Not all analyses, however, require a historical perspective. Tactical decisions deal with immediate needs; they are focused on what is happening in the organization *now*. This is not to totally discount the importance of the past, but in many situations, we need to deal with short-term operational issues. This is the point of the ODS: to provide information for tactical situations in the same way that the data warehouse provides information for long-term strategic decisions.

Since tactical decisions deal with the immediate present, the data supporting these decisions must reflect as nearly as possible the current state of the organization. Due to the large volumes of data involved as well as the processing requirements of integrating data into the data warehouse, it is difficult to refresh a data warehouse on real-time or even near real-time basis. Instead, we use an ODS. The ODS acts as the repository for the real-time information required to support tactical decision making.

How we integrate the ODS with the data warehouse is dependent upon the demands of the individual environment. Figure 3.7 presents the four classes of ODS, each with a varying level of complexity, depending on how closely integrated it is with the data warehouse. A Class 1 ODS is the simplest to construct. It is separate and independent of the data warehouse and contains a straightforward replication of the transactions carried out in the operational environment. The benefit here, of course, is that the data is integrated into a central repository much more easily than with a data warehouse. At the same time, we have all of our information located in one central system.

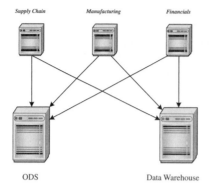

*Class 1 Operational Data Store*

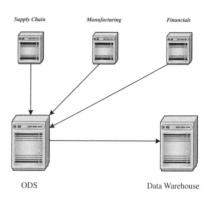

*Class 2 Operational Data Store*

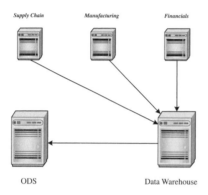

*Class 3 Operational Data Store*

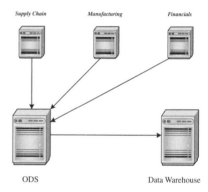

*Class 4 Operational Data Store*

**FIGURE 3.7**  ODS classification.

Consider the implications of a Class 1 ODS. We have discussed how difficult it is to get a complete view of a customer or other objects in our organization's environment when the data for that object is distributed across many systems. As we can see in Figure 3.7, a Class 1 ODS, when properly implemented, eliminates this problem. All the data from the various systems is brought together in one place for analysis. The difficulty with this class of ODS is its lack of integration with the data warehouse. One of the benefits of a central data warehouse is that we now have one source for truth. As you may recall from our discussion of distributed data warehouses, multiple asynchronous systems will often return conflicting results.

Although it is a bit more complex to develop, a Class 2 ODS resolves the data synchronization issue. The Class 2 ODS acts as a staging area for data that is to be integrated into the data warehouse. Just as in the Class 1 ODS, transactions are replicated from the operational environment. The data warehouse in a Class 2 ODS, however, extracts its data from the ODS and not from the operational environment, as does a Class 1. This is a rather nice solution. Its replaces the data warehouse ETL process in the operational environment with a simple transaction replication. The load of the ETL process is shifted to the ODS. A Class 2 ODS can be seen as straddling the operational transaction-oriented environment and the strategic BI environment. What is especially appealing about this solution is that it provides a tighter integration between the data warehouse and the ODS. The two systems work together, each sharing data, each supporting different types of decisions.

The Class 3 ODS reverses the integration of two systems. Rather than integrating the data from the ODS to the warehouse, the warehouse data is used to update the ODS. As we can see in the figure, it is very similar in where it sits within the information infrastructure to a dependent data mart. Note that the Class 3 ODS data is not as current as the data in the Class 2 ODS, since it undergoes the additional processing of passing through the data warehouse. The Class 3 ODS is useful in environments in which we wish to distribute subsets of the data within the warehouse to specific communities. Finally, the Class 4 ODS establishes a two-way dialog with the data warehouse. Just as with the Class 2 ODS, the transactions in the Class 4 ODS are integrated into the data warehouse. The data warehouse in turn provides the ODS with aggregated data and analysis data.

Personally, I am cynical of the long-term benefits of the ODS as a separate and distinct structure. Advances in technology are continually improving ETL performance. Depending on the data refresh rates and the resource requirements of the ETL process, in many instances all decision support questions may be handled by the data warehouse itself. In addition, an enterprise class database is able to pre-aggregate data and provide tactical analyses directly on the operational systems. More and more analyses that cannot be supported by the data warehouse may be addressed by these types of solutions. It seems, in light of these technological advancements, to be increasingly more difficult to justify the construction of an ODS. I wonder if there is really a necessity to add yet another system in the pantheon of systems that comprise that average information infrastructure.

### 3.2.4  DECISION SUPPORT SYSTEMS (DSS)

One could loosely define DSS as the presentation layer of the data warehouse. It is important, however, to emphasize the world *loosely*. When we discuss DSS, we are looking at more than just the presentation of the data within the warehouse. As shown in Figure 3.1, DSS extends from the extraction of the data through the warehouse to the presentation of that data to the decision maker. To classify these tools as mere presentation vehicles would greatly underestimate their value. These systems come in a variety of flavors, each meeting different needs within the organization.

In defining the role of the decision maker, we noted that he or she exists at all levels of the organization, from the department manager all the way up to the CEO. Each has his or her unique information requirements. The higher one moves

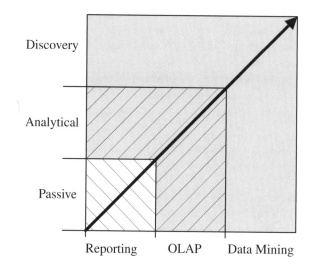

**FIGURE 3.8** DSS spectrum.

up in the organizational structure, the higher the level of detail he or she uses on a daily basis. There are different categories of DSS tools to meet the requirements of these different levels. We have presented the spectrum of DSS tools in Figure 3.8.

At the most rudimentary level, one could consider reporting a certain level of DSS. In comparison to the other levels of DSS, reporting is a passive consumption of data. This of course does not relegate it to the mere production of static green-bar reports. Today reporting systems are much more than that, as we shall discuss in the following subsection.

The next level of DSS is analytical; this is filled by OLAP tools. Where reporting simply presents the data, analytical tools take the user further. OLAP tools allow the decision maker to interact with the data. Data mining extends this interaction with the data to a level of discovery. This is where new behaviors within the data are unearthed and explored. We will discuss each category of tools in the subsections to follow.

### 3.2.4.1 Reporting

When discussing BI, reporting is often not recognized as a DSS. Reporting, however, fills an important role. As we said earlier, the higher the level of the decision maker in the organization, the higher the level of summarization required. Today most higher levels of management are not interested in *interacting* with data. At the highest levels within organizations, most strategists are interested in simple *dashboards:* systems that will display leading key indicators of an organization's health. While it is true that as younger, more technically astute management rises to the level of corporate leadership, this trend will change; most corporate leaders are more than happy to receive simple reports. While they may see them as simple reports, today there is nothing *simple* about reporting.

If an organization's initial foray into DSS is reports-based, the data warehouse architect must think beyond simple static green-bar reports to the overall enterprise. Enterprise class reporting in today's world should simplify the creation, maintenance, and distribution of reports. The enterprise reporting tool should make it as easy as possible to get the data to whomever may require it. For this reason, an enterprise reporting tool should have the following capabilities:

❑ **Rapid Development**—The tool should provide a wizard to walk the developer through the creation of the report. It should also allow the developer to view the report exactly as it will be seen.

❑ **Easy Maintenance**—The tool should allow the user to modify reports through a wizard.

❑ **Easy Distribution**—The report engine should be able to direct the same report or portion of a report to different media. For example, a portion of a report could be posted to a Web site, while another section is sent to management via email, and a third is sent via standard mail to stockholders.

❑ **Internet-Enabled**—The reports server should be able to receive requests from both Web-based and non-Web-based clients.

### 3.2.4.2 Online Analytical Processing

OLAP takes the decision maker to new levels in data analysis. With OLAP, the decision maker's analysis interacts with the data contained within the system. It leverages the time-variant characteristics of the data warehouse to allow the strategist to look back in time as well as into the future. In looking back, the strategist can identify trends that may be hidden in the data. In looking forward, these trends can be used to forecast future conditions. In addition, the characteristics of these trends can also be examined. The strategist can anticipate how possible changes in these trends will affect the organization's environment.

A variety of OLAP tools have been developed to achieve the objectives described above. Some of these tools are based on a *multidimensional* database, specially constructed and tuned for analytical processing. These tools are sometimes referred to as MOLAP, multidimensional On-Line Analytical Processing (OLAP). There are, however, shortcomings to multidimensional systems. To overcome these obstacles, many OLAP tools have taken a ROLAP approach. ROLAP is Relational On-Line Analytical Processing in which the multidimensional view of the data is implemented on top of some relational engine. There are also hybrid OLAP engines that are a combination of the two. These are frequently referred to as—you guessed it—HOLAP.

A complete discussion of OLAP could fill a book by itself, and that is not our objective here, but there are some points that will provide us with a general understanding of OLAP. Figure 3.9 presents a typical OLAP interface. Although it might appear to be a standard spreadsheet with rows and columns, an OLAP tool is much more powerful. OLAP allows the user to present the data in multiple dimen-

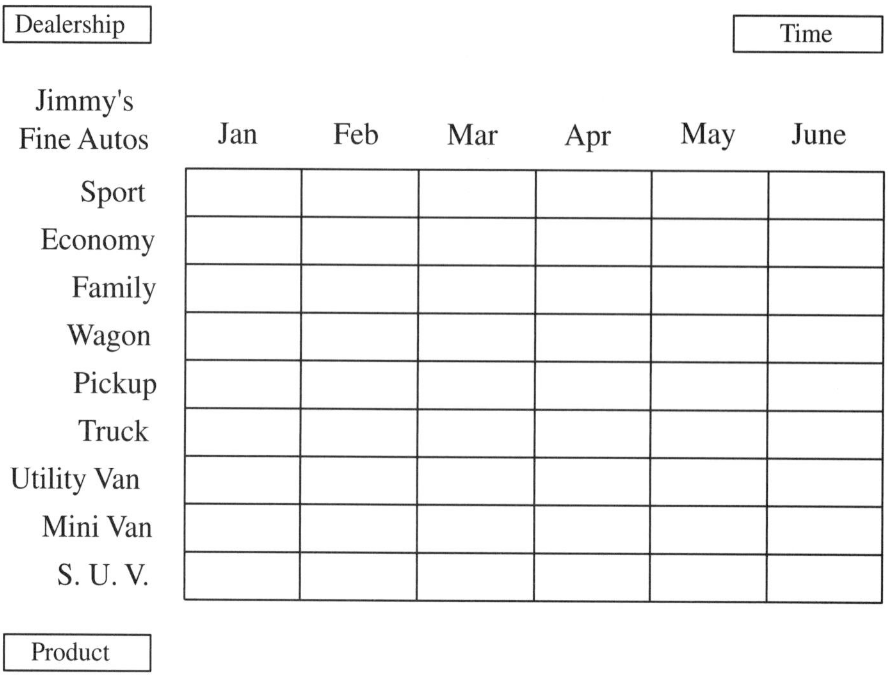

| Dealership | | | | | | Time |

| Jimmy's Fine Autos | Jan | Feb | Mar | Apr | May | June |
|---|---|---|---|---|---|---|
| Sport | | | | | | |
| Economy | | | | | | |
| Family | | | | | | |
| Wagon | | | | | | |
| Pickup | | | | | | |
| Truck | | | | | | |
| Utility Van | | | | | | |
| Mini Van | | | | | | |
| S. U. V. | | | | | | |

| Product |

**FIGURE 3.9**  OLAP interface.

sions. In our figure, we are presenting the sales data for automobile dealerships; the dimensions are time, product, and dealership. As we can see, time is spread across the columns, and the rows represent each product. Each *page* represents a different dealership. At an absolute minimum, OLAP must be able to present data in multiple dimensions at one time. Although our simple example shows three dimensions, the OLAP tool should be able to be extend the presentation of the data to many more dimensions.

The OLAP tool should also allow for the *rotation* of data. A rotation changes the orientation of the display. The dimension that runs across the columns is exchanged with the row data, for example. In Figure 3.9, a rotation would distribute the products across the columns, and each row would represent a month. The key is that with OLAP this can be done easily through an intuitive interface.

Another important feature of OLAP is the ability to *drill down* and *roll up* data. This allows the user to look at summaries of data. In our example, we have shown data at the dealership level. Each cell in the matrix is the sales of that particular product for that particular dealership. Rollup allows the strategist to sum the data of the different dealerships into a single regional sales number for each product. Drill-down is the same operation in reverse. The drill-down operation allows the strategist to look at the detail records of a summary. If we were to present regional sales numbers, a drill-down would allow the user to look at the sales numbers of the individual dealerships in those regions.

The point of OLAP is to give the decision maker the tools necessary to detect trends and analyze the characteristics of those trends. This includes the ability to perform *what-if* analysis. The OLAP tool must allow the strategist to build models based on the data and manipulate the variables in the model so that the strategist can examine both the effects of particular trends and how the changes in those trends will influence the business environment.

### 3.2.4.3 Data Mining

Not that long ago, hidden pictures were the latest rage. These were pictures of seemingly random patterns and colors that, when looked just right, revealed a hidden picture. The trick was to look at the entire picture at once, and after several hours (and a headache), you were able to see this hidden picture. I never could see the hidden pictures. You see, I am color blind. Really. No kidding. So I could stare at those patterns all day and never see anything but a bunch of squiggles. Data mining, in a way, is similar to those pictures. The data as a whole seems to be nothing but a collection of random events. Data mining allows us to see the picture hidden within those events—color blind or not.

There are two basic types of data mining: classification and estimation. With classification, objects are segmented into different classes. In a marketing data warehouse, for example, we could look at our customers and prospects and categorize them into desirable and undesirable customers based on certain demographic parameters. The second type of data mining, estimation, attempts to predict or estimate some numerical value based on a subject's characteristics. Perhaps the decision maker is interested in more than just desirable and undesirable customers. The strategist may be interested in predicting the potential revenue stream from prospects based on the customer demographics. Such a prediction might be that certain types of prospects and customers can be expected to spend $x$ percentage of their income on a particular product. It is common to use both classification and estimation in conjunction with one another. Perhaps the strategist would perform some classification of customers and then perform estimations for each of the different categories.

Whether performing a classification or an estimation, the process of data mining is basically the same. We begin with the data, or more appropriately, a subset of the data. This is our test data. The size of the data set is dependent on the deviation of characteristics of the data. In other words, if there are relatively few variables whose values do not greatly deviate from one another, then we can test on a small number of records. If the data has many variables with many possible values, then the test data is much larger. As with the data warehouse, the data is cleansed and merged into one database. If we are working directly from a data warehouse, we would expect this process to have already been carried out. This does not mean that we assume the data is cleansed and transformed. The data quality must still be verified to ensure accurate results.

We then define the questions that are to be posed of the data. Despite the common misconception of data mining, the strategist must be able to define some goal for the mining process. Perhaps we would like to segment our market by customer demographics or we would like to know the market potential of certain economic groups. In either case, we need to specify what we want to discover.

Using the test data, we construct a model that defines the associations in which we are interested. We have known results in the test data set. We know that certain records in the data set represent desirable or undesirable customers, or we know the market potential of a set of clients. The model will look for similarities in the data for those objects with similar results. Once we have built the model, we train it against subsequent test data sets. When we are confident in the model, we train it against the actual data we wish to mine. At times the model will not include some records that should be included, or it will include records that it should not. In either case, there will be some level of inaccuracy in the data model. No model can predict with perfect accuracy, so we should expect some margin of error. The models come in a variety of types.

### Decision Trees

Decision trees are a common modeling technique that has been used since before data mining was developed. In Figure 3.10, we see a typical decision tree. The decision is boxed, and each alternative is circled. The branches extending from each circle are labeled and assigned a probability. The company must decide whether to carry out a marketing campaign or invest the money where there would be a 10 percent return on the investment.

Between the two alternatives in the tree, there are three possible outcomes. In executing the campaign, there is a 50 percent chance that sales will increase by $1,000,000. There is also a 40 percent chance that sales will be constant, and a 10 percent chance that sales will decrease by $100,000. We multiply the probability of each outcome by the value of that outcome. We then deduct from the sum of these outcomes the cost of the campaign. We do the same with the decision to invest the money. In calculating the value of the decision to invest, we add the benefit derived from the investment to the sum of the possible outcomes. We see from the tree that the decision to increase the campaign has the value of $390,000, while the decision to invest the money has a value of $15,000. While the example shows two alternatives with three possible outcomes, decision trees can have many alternatives, outcomes, and subsequent decisions.

### Neural Networks

A neural network is an interesting approach to data mining. The structure of the model mimics the structure of the human brain. The brain is composed of neurons, each of which could be thought of as a separate processor. The inputs to the neuron are scattered over its dendritic tree. Axons are the white matter in the brain that insulate the neurons. The axon is, in a sense, an output device for the neuron; the dendrite is the input. The axon passes the output of one neuron to the dendrite of the next. Each neuron processes the information it receives and passes its results on down the line. How this results in human thought is the subject of another book.

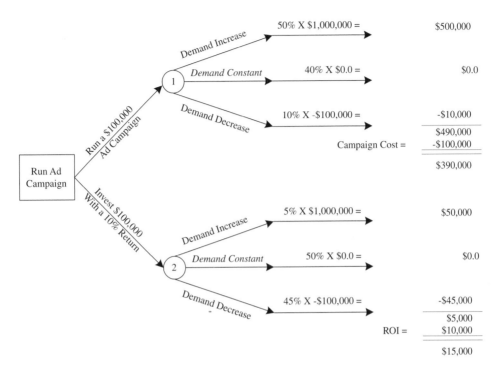

**FIGURE 3.10** Decision tree.

The neural network model attempts to perform this same kind of process. In the neural model, there are a number of nodes; these could be processors in a massively parallel processing system or simply processes in a multiprocessing system, as demonstrated in Figure 3.11. The network receives as input the location, age, gender, and income of the prospect. These are taken in by the neurons and, based on some algorithm, generate an output. These outputs are then added in a weighted sum to determine some final result, such as likely to buy or not to buy a particular product.

### Genetic Modeling

Genetic modeling is well suited for categorizing. It comes from the concept of survival of the fittest—in this case, survival of the fittest model. We begin by randomly placing the data into the desired categories. The model then evaluates each member of each category based on some function that determines the fitness of the member. Members that are not well suited to the class are moved to other categories. The class will continue to alter itself. Even as the class receives new data, it continues to alter itself to arrive at the best fit.

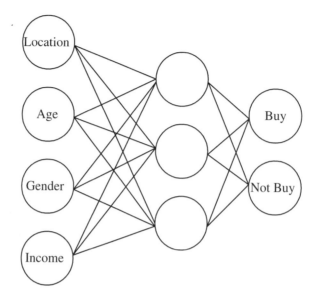

**FIGURE 3.11** Neural network.

### 3.2.5 BI APPLICATIONS

So far, we have discussed BI *tools*. There is a variety of tools in the software industry: compilers, code developers, documentation generators, and even testing environments. What they have in common is that they are used to build something in software. They are to the programmer what a hammer or saw is to the carpenter. They are not the product, what is actually turned over to the end user. Reporting, OLAP, and data mining are tools. Some software engineer uses them to build something. For many years, these were the height of BI. As the BI industry matures, it is inevitable that we should proceed to the next level, to BI applications.

It is interesting to watch applications as they come to maturity. Whether it be procurement, payroll, human resources, or BI, each has followed the same basic path. This path consists of four distinct stages. Figure 3.12 presents these stages and their relationships to market penetration. In the first stage, the "custom" stage, of development, every engagement is *homegrown*, built for that particular environment. At one time, you couldn't go out and buy a database system. Many of my early programming jobs involved building a database so that a custom application could sit on top of it. This is how BI began. When we first started developing BI applications, all we had was an operating system, a compiler, and a heck of a lot of courage. If we were really lucky, we had a database, but this wasn't always the case.

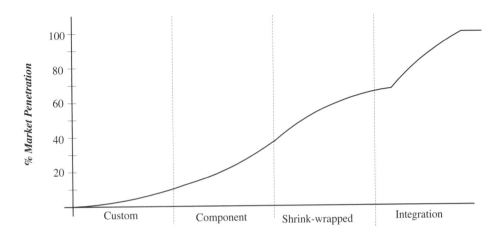

FIGURE 3.12 The stages of software maturity.

The second stage of maturity is the component stage. At this point, we don't quite have an application. Primarily what we saw in this era were packages of specialized tools that bolted together to form an application. In the BI world, these were the days when a number of independent vendors offered ETL tools, OLAP-engines, and data mining suites. People took a best-of-breed approach to solutions. They would cobble together the fender of one auto with the hood and tail fins of another. After they threw in an engine they picked up somewhere, they called it a car. Thankfully, BI has just completed this stage of maturity.

The next stage is the shrink-wrapped application. This stage brought us from offering tools to offering actual applications. The BI market is now in this stage of development. Many Enterprise Resource Planning (ERP) vendors offer prebuilt data warehouses, complete with ETL processes and warehouse data structures. Sitting on top of these warehouses are the reports, OLAP data cubes, and data mining applications. These shrink-wrapped solutions offer enormous benefits to the end user. While there may be some tuning of the BI application required to meet specific needs, the bulk of the development costs are eliminated.

We should also clarify the use of the term *tuning*. There is a huge difference between tuning an application and customization. Customization is the changing of the software itself, replacing one procedure with another procedure more tailored to a specific environment. Tuning is the process of taking what is already there and extending its use. By tuning we mean creating additional reports, adding elements to the data warehouse from external sources, or integrating the output into an executive dashboard. It is the equivalent to setting up a chart of accounts to a financial system.

When we think BI applications, we should not limit our horizons to a new way of applying OLAP or the integration of data mining into existing applications. Although these methods are valuable, there are new areas of analysis to explore. In the following subsections, we will examine two such applications: the balanced scorecard and activity-based costing. These are applications that fulfill our definition of BI, yet have their origins in the business community.

These stages of software maturity correlate well to the technology adoption life cycle described by Geoffrey Moore in *Crossing the Chasm*.[5] This life cycle consists of five stages: innovators, early adopters, early majority, late majority, and laggards. The innovators are the same people who bought the first cell phones back when they were still attached to a dictionary size battery. Any new technology turns them on. This group bought into BI in the custom stage of the application maturity cycle. The second group, the early adopters, are the folks who are willing to take a calculated risk if they see the payoff. This group bought into BI during the component stage.

The third group in Moore's life cycle is the early majority. To succeed in the software industry, a technology must succeed with the early majority. To succeed with any group of customers, you must understand the needs and desires that drive them. The early majority group is risk-averse. They want to see a proven record of accomplishment before they make a commitment. The risk involved in building a data warehouse in the component days was too great to attract this group to BI. In the component stage, most data warehouse implementations failed. The shrink-wrapped stage, however, is exactly what they want to see. A BI vendor can say to these users, "Here is the application. Touch it, feel it, understand how it will fit within your specific environment." The users get those all important warm and fuzzies. They aren't buying some nebulous concept. They are buying something that can actually be demonstrated. A smart vendor will tell them, "You can get this specific return on your investment. I know this is a fact because here is a list of your top competitors who are getting that return. This solution has been proven in your own industry."

In light of such a compelling case, more and more of the BI tools vendors, still in the component stage, will be forced from the market. They cannot meet the needs of the early majority. The early majority begins to look on BI as just another part of the application as more ERP vendors integrate it into their applications. In addition to a significant cost reduction, integration eliminates the biggest obstacle to penetrating the early majority: risk. This leads us to our fourth stage, integration. As integration tightens, specialty tools exit the market and the applications simply incorporate the new capabilities. BI is well on its way to this level of integration. Just as the Internet will become just another way of doing business, BI will become just another aspect of the application. Eventually, BI will be, as they say, *table stakes*. You can't play if you don't have it.

---

[5] Moore, Geoffrey, and McKenna, Regis, *Crossing the Chasm: Marketing and Selling High-Tech Products to Mainstream Customers*, Harper Business, 1999.

We will examine the next stage of the BI loop by reviewing two BI applications: balanced scorecard and activity-based costing. It is interesting that in the minds of many, these are not typically thought of as BI. Their inception actually lies outside the IT community, which perhaps is one of the reasons that they are so powerful. These concepts started with business people, people who had business problems to solve. They do fit nicely within the BI loop presented earlier. The applications extract data from the operational environment. The data is then cleansed and transformed to be presented to the decision maker for analysis. Based on this analysis, the decision maker then forms some course of action. Again we see the three A's: Acquire, Analyze, Act.

### 3.2.5.1  The Balanced Scorecard

Recent surveys have shown that most organizations do not have a written, well-defined strategy. Of those that do, a large percentage have no way of communicating that strategy to those who execute it or a means to measure how well the organization is performing towards achieving those objectives. All too often, organizations rely on financial reporting to be the vehicle by which organizations evaluate their performance. Unfortunately, financial reporting makes a poor tool for strategic analysis. Typically, financial measures are lagging indicators. They tell us how we did, but not necessarily how we are doing. By the time our financials reflect a problem, it may already be too late to take corrective action.

Balanced scorecard is an application first described by Kaplan and Norton in their book *The Balanced Scorecard*.[6] The scorecard views the health and well-being of the organization by more than its financial data. It views the organization according to the strategy established by the C-level executives and translates the vision established by the C-level executives to quantifiable measures. Figure 3.13 presents the structure of this translation process.

We begin at the top of the pyramid with the company vision: Where do the C-level executives see the organization in the next five years? What vision do they have for the organization? Where will they lead us? We are defining our journey's destination. Perhaps the vision is to be the recognized leader in our industry. In the automotive industry, we might see our company designing the next Rolls Royce, or in the writing instrument industry, crafting the next Mont Blanc. An alternate strategy would be to develop greater market penetration: We might envision our company producing a car that outsells Toyota or a pen that outsells BIC.

The next step is to define the strategy to achieve this vision. How are we going to realize the vision we have articulated? If we plan to be the industry leader, we would decide on a low-volume, high-quality strategy. In this case, we aren't as concerned with market penetration as we are with leading the market in product quality. We would focus on developing high-quality products and charging a premium for them. If our strategy is to penetrate the market, we would focus on high-volume, high-value. We would sell products that would deliver value at a low cost.

---

[6] Kaplan, Robert, and Norton, David, *The Balanced Scorecard*, Harvard Business School Press, 1996.

**FIGURE 3.13**   The Balanced Scorecard pyramid.

Quite often, the completion of these two steps alone will justify the balanced scorecard project. It is common for C-level executives to have some vague idea of where they want to the organization to be in several years, yet to lack a clear vision—as some would call it, "that vision thing." Others may have a vision, but no clear set of strategic objectives to achieve that vision. In creating a balanced scorecard, management is challenged to articulate both the vision and the strategy.

As we look at the strategy we will see certain themes emerge. These are the "doable" pieces of the strategy, the functions to be performed in order to enact the strategy. The market leader's low-volume, high-quality strategy would translate into producing high-quality products and developing high levels of customer satisfaction. We can see two themes here: production quality and customer satisfaction. We then take the next step and map these themes into the different perspectives by which we view the organization.

From these perspectives, we view how we are going to act on the strategy described in our strategic themes. A traditional Kaplan and Norton balanced scorecard views the organization's health from four different perspectives:

❑ **Learning and Growth**—This perspective focuses on how well members of the organizations are *tooled* to deliver on the strategy. Do they have adequate training and appropriate skills? Are they empowered to perform the assigned tasks?

❑ **Internal/Business Processes**—This perspective focuses on how well the internal processes of the organization can meet expectations. It evaluates the processes critical to attracting and retaining customers.

❑ **Customer**—This perspective focuses on how well we are satisfying our customers. It identifies our target markets and evaluates how successful we are in each.

❑ **Financial**—Finally, we evaluate how well the strategy of the organization is contributing to the overall financial well-being of the company.

The next step in the process is to define a set of Key Performance Indicators (KPIs). A KPI is a measure of the overall performance of the organization within a particular perspective. The novice scorecard designer is tempted to include a large number of measures. This actually defeats the purpose of the scorecard. A balanced scorecard is meant to provide a clear, concise view of the strategic position of the organization. Including measures that are not necessary or not indicative of the performance within a particular area will only cloud the issue. As a general rule of thumb, we should use three to four KPIs for each perspective.

If we plan to be the market leader, we would measure how well we are manufacturing high-quality items and satisfying our customers. In the internal processing perspective, we might define KPIs around our production process: In random quality testing, how many items were rejected? How many products required after-sale servicing? We might look at the customer perspective KPIs that indicate customer dissatisfaction. How many customer complaints were received in a given time period? How many products were returned by customers?

By examining each indicator, we can define where our performance is and isn't advancing our strategy. We might note that the number of rejects has risen sharply in the past month. This of course leads us to believe there is something wrong with our production process. After examining this process to determine the reason for the high rate of rejection, we discovered that the raw materials are of a lower quality. Perhaps we have switched suppliers in an attempt to reduce production costs. Perhaps we installed new machines without supplying adequate operator training.

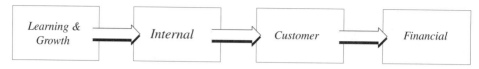

**FIGURE 3.14**   Relationships between scorecard perspectives.

As we look at the different perspectives, we can see that they are linked in a cause and effect relationship. We show this relationship in Figure 3.14. In order to achieve our financial objectives, we must satisfy our customers. In order to satisfy those customers, we must have the internal processes that will fulfill their needs and desires. In order to develop those processes, we must develop the skills of our internal staff to support those processes.

In developing a balanced scorecard, we define the relationship between each KPI in each perspective. This is often referred to as a *strategy-map* view of the scorecard. Figure 3.15 presents a typical strategy map. We start with a simple enough objective: increase profitability. To do this, we must increase sales and reduce expenses. All of these objectives are within the financial perspective. Let's follow the path of increasing sales. We determine that the best way to increase sales is to increase the customer's lifetime value; this is an objective within the customer perspective. We then ask ourselves, What is the best way to achieve this objective? First, we must improve service so that current customers, even when they have a problem, will want to deal with our company. Second, we must become a market-driven company, allowing the needs of the market to drive product design. Third, we must develop a better understanding of our customers so that we know their needs and desires.

To fulfill the objectives in the customer perspective, we must achieve objectives in the internal processes perspective. We must develop a CRM system so that we can better understand our customers and a BI system so that we can understand the market in which we compete. As we move back through the strategy map, we see how one objective is a cause of another. The results of one objective affect the results of the next objective.

The strategy map clearly shows that financial measures are lagging indicators; they occur at the end of process. If there is a problem, the cause happened months ago and the effect is just now being felt. The strategy map becomes the decision maker's early warning system. Our strategy map tells us that we need to increase customer lifetime value, but we see that the IT department is failing to implement the CRM system. We can see this before the delay has a detrimental effect on achieving our strategic objective, and we can correct the situation.

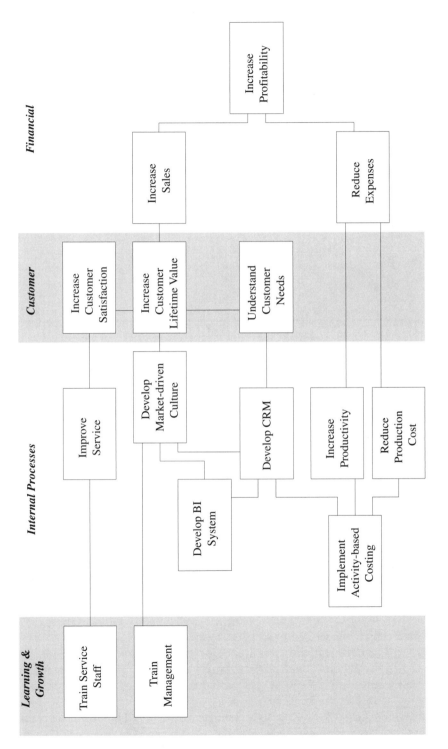

**FIGURE 3.15** A balanced scorecard strategy map.

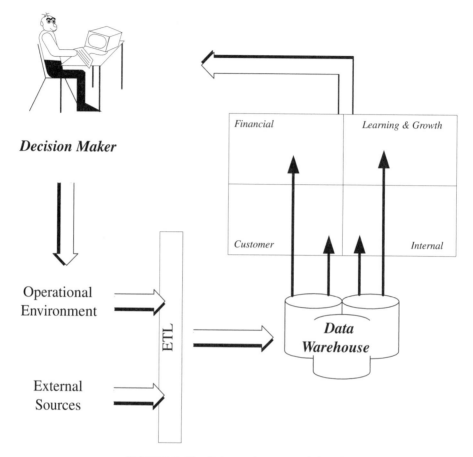

**FIGURE 3.16**  Balanced scorecard data flow.

Figure 3.16 presents the balanced scorecard data flow. Data is extracted from the operational environment, where it is used to calculate KPIs. These indicators are then grouped into the different perspectives. The decision maker reviews these perspectives to determine the state of the organization, taking corrective action when necessary. Compare this data flow to the one presented in Figure 3.1; they are essentially the same. The balanced scorecard is the embodiment of BI.

This section introduced the concept of balanced scorecards. There are a variety of methodologies for scorecard development as well as a number of different scorecard structures. For example, the perspectives presented in this section are the traditional perspectives seen in many scorecard implementations. This should by no means imply that these are the only perspectives that are permissible. The beauty of the scorecard is that it is a very flexible, commonsense approach to understanding corporate strategy. To truly understand balanced scorecards, read Kaplan and Norton's *The Balanced Scorecard*.

### 3.2.5.2 Activity-Based Costing

Activity-based costing is another BI application that addresses the deficiencies of traditional financial reporting. There are two audiences for financial data. The first group includes financial analysts, creditors, investors, and other company stakeholders. They use these traditional financial reports to understand the value of an organization. They depend on this data to determine if the company is worth an investment or solid enough to be extended credit. For this reason, the ways in which this data is reported is tightly regulated by a number of different agencies.

The second group interested in financial data is those managers and employees involved in the production and sale of products. As do any stakeholders in the organization, they of course want to understand the overall value of the company. This group has an additional need, however, a need for detailed cost information. This cost data is necessary for the efficient operation of the organization, to understand the cost of products and services. With this data, management has a way to understand how well the processes they use to create products and services are contributing to the financial well-being of the organization.

Let's think about what this means to an organization. Suppose we are a company, Billy Boy Bowling Balls. We've been making bowling balls for years. When we first began making bowling balls, we were fabulously profitable, but over the years, things have changed. Bowling ball styles have changed. The way we manufacture and distribute the balls has changed. One of our nephews just graduated from college with a BS in computer science and is trying to figure out how to distribute the balls over the Internet directly to the consumer. With everything that has changed, we don't really know which brands of bowling balls are profitable and which aren't.

One of the reasons we are unsure is based in the traditional accounting procedures. Direct costing systems ignore overhead costs. The rationale is that this cost data is fixed and is a small fraction of the overall costs of production. This assumption, however, is incorrect. There isn't any such thing as a fixed cost—just costs that may change over a longer period. Often, this isn't even the case. We sometimes see fixed costs increasing at an even faster rate than variable costs. Also, fixed costs can actually be many times greater than direct variable costs.

When our company first started, bowling balls were all pretty much one color, black. While there were a variety of sizes, the processing was the same. As time went on, we discovered that our competition was doing different things with balls. Some were making balls in a variety of colors and designs. One competitor even introduced a line of clear balls with objects embedded inside, such as a man positioned to look as though he were turning somersaults as the ball rolled down the lane. In an effort to compete, we did market research on some of the brands. The manufacturing of these balls differed as well; some were very inexpensive to make, and others entailed a complex and expensive manufacturing process.

In a traditional accounting system, these additional costs would be lost. Some brands underwent extensive market research before production; others did not. If both brands sold for the same price, the brand that was researched is obviously less profitable. After research, we decided to sell our own line of clear balls. Due to the special characteristics of the ball, shipping costs for these balls were much higher than for a standard ball. In traditional accounting, these differences would also be lost.

Figure 3.17 demonstrates the problem graphically. Traditional accounting methods aggregate cost according to the structure of the organization. Traditional accounting sees the company as an organization chart. Cost is divided into neat little silos, each cost representing the cost behind each little box in the organization chart. The problem is that products aren't manufactured vertically, in neat little organizational silos. Production occurs across the structure, horizontally. Traditional accounting doesn't see a process; it sees an organizational structure.

Activity-based costing looks at the cost horizontally. Imagine a factory in which raw materials go in one end and finished goods come out the other. If we were able to peel back the roof of this factory, we would be able to examine the steps in the transformation of the raw materials to finished goods. We can imagine the transformation process as a series of discrete steps. In our bowling ball example, the raw materials are prepared, then the balls are formed. The balls are then polished and passed on to the shipping department. Shipping packages the balls and ships them to our distributors. Each step in our manufacturing process is an activity. Every time we do something as part of our manufacturing process, we consume resources. Some of these resources include direct materials, such as the cost of the material to make the balls or the cleaning solution used to polish the balls. Other resources include labor and machines to form the balls and drill the holes.

We now have two sets of data. One set defines the steps in the manufacturing process. We call each step an *activity*. We also know the materials consumed by each activity. We can therefore calculate the cost of resources consumed by an activity each time that activity is performed. The sum of all the activity costs in the manufacturing of an individual product is the cost of making one unit of that product. The cost object is the product or service that we produce. The cost of making one unit of that cost object is the cost object unit cost.

To understand how we calculate the cost object unit cost, refer to Figure 3.18. We begin with two departments, production and packaging. The accounts associated with these departments are standard general ledger accounts. Both departments have an account to which labor is charged. The production department also has a machine account used to charge the cost of the machine that forms the bowling balls. The packaging department has a materials account used to charge the cost of shipping materials. The production department performs two tasks: forming and polishing the bowling balls. The packaging department is responsible for packing the bowling balls. Every month, the production department spends $100,000 on labor. The machine costs are $37,000. The packaging department spends $50,000 on labor and $26,000 on materials.

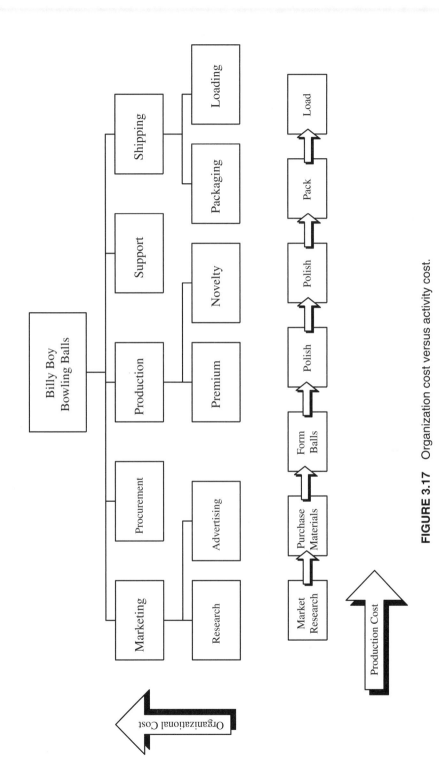

**FIGURE 3.17** Organization cost versus activity cost.

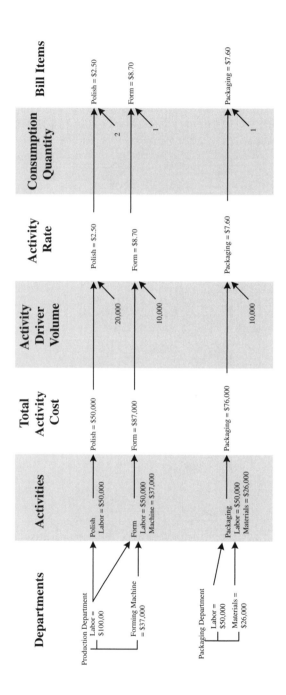

**FIGURE 3.18**  Calculating cost object unit cost.

Half of the labor in the production department goes into making the balls, and the other half goes into polishing them after production. The one function of the forming machine is the production of balls. The only activity carried out by the packaging department is the packing of bowling balls. We would distribute, therefore, the costs recorded in each account proportionally to the activities carried out by each department. As shown in the figure, 50 percent of production labor goes to the forming activity and 50 percent of the labor goes to the polishing activity. In a similar fashion, the entire cost of the forming machine is assigned to the forming process. Since the packaging department only packs the bowling balls, 100 percent of that department's labor and materials are assigned to the packing activity. In a given month, we can see that it costs us $87,000 to form the bowling balls. This is known as the total activity cost—the total an activity costs our department in a given period. We can see that polishing has a total activity cost of $76,000, and packaging has a total activity cost of $50,000.

Next, we determine how frequently we carry out each activity. This is the activity driver volume. In this example, the production department polishes bowling balls 20,000 times in a month, the same time period used for calculating our total activity costs. The activity driver volume for the activity driver is 20,000. The activity driver volumes for the packaging and forming activities are the same, 10,000. If we divide the total activity cost by the activity driver volume, we will know how much it costs us to carry out that activity just once. This is known as the activity rate. In the example, the total activity cost to form a bowling ball is $87,000, and we do this 10,000 times. It is safe to conclude that the activity rate is $8.70. It costs our company $8.70 to form one bowling ball. Similarly, polishing has an activity rate of $2.50, and packaging has an activity rate of $7.60.

We now understand what it costs us to do what we do every time we do it. The next question is, How often do we have to do it? This is known as our consumption quantity—how often we perform a specific activity to produce one unit of product, one cost object. In this case, we want to know how often we form, polish, and package during the production of one bowling ball. The consumption quantity for forming and packaging is one; we do this once for every bowling ball we produce. Due to the nature of the high-quality materials used in our bowling balls and the desire to have the prettiest bowling balls around, we polish our bowling balls twice. The consumption quantity for polishing is two. We then multiply the consumption quantity by the activity rate. This is a bill item, a charge that is added to the cost of the cost object.

The final step in the process is to sum the cost of the bill items, the cost of direct materials, and the cost of other cost objects to get the total cost object unit cost. Notice that we have added the unit cost of another cost object into the unit cost of our bowling balls. In this example, we may decide to include in every ball that we ship a premium, top-of-the-line bowling glove. In addition to including the glove with our ball, we also sell it as a separate item. Since it is sold independently, we have decided to make it a totally independent cost object whose cost is included in the cost of our bowling ball.

Keep in mind that what we have shown here is a simple example. There are many issues we did not discuss, such as yield and material cost calculations. In addition, we did this for only one product line. When we first described our bowling ball example, we said that we come out with different lines of bowling balls, each of which are processed differently. We would run these calculations for each unique production process. We also noted that prior to going into production, we spent time researching the market. These costs would also be included in the calculations. For a more detailed discussion of Activity Based Costing, refer to the masters, Kaplan and Cooper, and their book *Cost and Effect*.[7]

We should be aware of the enormous power granted to us by understanding the relationship between the activities to produce a product and the unit cost of that product. There are two outgrowths of Activity Based Costing. The first is Activity Based Budgeting (ABB). All companies go through a budgeting process. With ABB, we follow the path described earlier, but in reverse. The sales department has forecasted a demand for 20,000 bowling balls next month. Since our value chain is fully integrated over the Internet, we practice just-in-time manufacturing, which means we have no bowling balls in inventory. We then budget our production department's labor cost to be $100,000. Packaging will need to budget $52,000 for materials and $100,000 for labor. There is always the issue of capacity, but in this example, we will assume that we have the appropriate capacity to meet the demands.

We can also use activity-based costing to better manage our organization through Activity-Based Management (ABM). ABM is both operational and strategic. It is strategic in that it helps us do the right things. It is operational in the sense that it helps us determine how to do those things in the correct way. With this understanding of the production process, we can evaluate each stage and redesign it to reduce costs. Perhaps we discover that it is unnecessary to polish our bowling balls twice and that the incremental cost is not worth the demand.

Typically, companies determine price backwards. They first determine the cost of a product and then determine a price based on the return they desire on that investment. To determine the price of a successful product, we have to determine the customer's acceptable price range, not the company's. We then decide what margin we want. This leaves us with a maximum cost for producing the product. We can then analyze the proposed production process to determine if we can produce it for that cost. Since we are using activity-based costing, our numbers are more accurate and we can do a better job of predicting cost. Also, if the cost constraints can't be met, we can redesign the process.

---

[7] Kaplan, Robert, and Cooper, Robin, *Cost and Effect: Using Integrated Cost Systems to Drive Profitability and Performance*, Harvard Business School Press, 1997.

As we can see, activity-based costing fits squarely within the definition of BI. Our source data comes from the operational environment, typically from our financial system's general ledger. We take the data, store it, perform operations upon it, and deliver it to the decision maker. He or she then uses this information to define some course of action.

### 3.2.6 DECISION MAKERS

The decision maker is key to the BI loop. The decision maker takes information from the DSS and defines some course of action. Typically, we think of the decision maker as a member of our own organization, an individual who is working within the company, planning some strategy for the organization itself. At one time, this might have been true. In the Internet age, however, this broad definition of a decision maker actually includes individuals outside the organization as well.

The first group of decision makers we should consider is our partners. We have gone into great detail discussing how important it is for organizations to use the Internet to integrate the entire value chain. We have also noted that this integration means an expansion of the BI system's scope. As we expand the scope of the BI system, we also expand the user community. We begin to see how sharing strategic information with our partners benefits our own organization. Perhaps we can integrate our CRM system with our partners' systems. As our suppliers have better insights into our customer base, they can team with our organization more effectively. We can also share KPIs out of our balanced scorecard. Suppliers can see how the materials they supply our company affect production. They can use that information to improve the quality of their materials, thus improving the quality of our products. This leads to greater market share and greater profitability for both companies.

The second group of decision makers is the customers themselves. This may seem strange at first, but consider the role played by the decision maker in the BI loop and it will become clear. The decision maker receives information from the DSS and makes some decision based on the information provided. Isn't this the case every time a user logs onto a Web site and is given purchasing recommendations? Isn't the recommendation engine part of the DSS, and doesn't the customer receive its output? Based on this output, isn't he or she making some decision that is being reflected in the operational environment? In the end, we should consider the customer not only a decision maker, but perhaps the most important decision maker in the entire process.

The third group of decision makers is the organization's employees—the individuals employed by our company and responsible for defining some course of action. This can extend from the group leader all the way up to the C-level executive. As we can see with the balanced scorecard, there is a need to share strategic information at every level within the organization.

## 3.3  Conclusion

An organism is a body whose components, or organs, work together for the continued life of the whole, the *organism*. An organism has a central nervous system in which the intelligence of the organism resides. There are different levels of intelligence systems. The most advanced think abstractly, reasoning and organizing large quantities of information about environment. The same is true of the organization. It is composed of parts: departments and divisions that work together for the betterment of the organization. The organization's central nervous system is its information infrastructure. Organizations that have implemented a BI system, as described by the BI loop, have achieved the highest level of intelligence.

The Internet has changed BI as well as the organization. As the organization's information infrastructure expands across the Internet to encompass the entire value chain, so does BI. In the end, the organization, BI, and the Internet all undergo a transformation by being combined in a solution we have described as IEBI. Figure 3.1 presents the BI loop. Compare this loop to Figure 3.19.

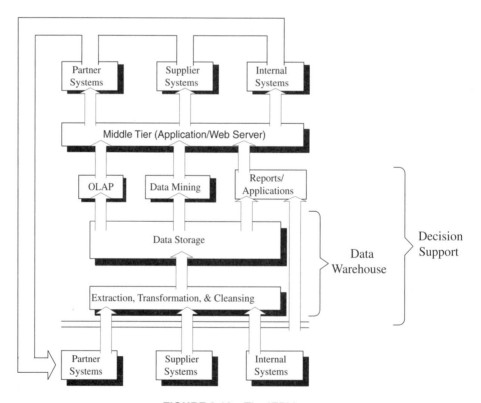

**FIGURE 3.19**  The IEBI loop.

The primary source systems for BI are the internal operational systems, while IEBI integrates data from partner and supplier information systems. The recipients of BI, the decision makers, are also more than just internal users. What truly differentiates IEBI from BI is the ability to collect and aggregate data across the value chain. Data is then analyzed and the results distributed to all parties along that chain, regardless of location.

There is enormous value to a centralized, Internet-enabled data warehouse. In Chapter 2, we explained that in a peer-to-peer network, the value of the network is the number of nodes on that network squared. In a network of many simultaneous connections, this value is the number of nodes raised to the power of the number of nodes. Apply this to IEBI. As the IEBI system spans more of the value chain, the value increases sharply. We are also expanding the most critical element of the IEBI loop, the decision maker. This also increases the value of IEBI. If multiple simultaneous connections of a network increase the value of the network exponentially, what does the expansion of IEBI do to the value of BI? Is it hyperbole to describe this increase as logarithmic? Is it an understatement? In either case, it is extraordinarily important to centralize the intelligence system.

The Internet has changed the organization, turning an entity bound by four walls into a single virtual organization that spans the value chain. This new organization has transformed BI to IEBI. Finally, IEBI has changed the organization to be a smarter, more competitive animal in the marketplace. It has also changed the Internet to be a much more competitive environment—a place where only the most intelligent survive.

# Part 2

# Making the Internet Work

# Chapter 4

# THE WEB-ENABLED INFORMATION INFRASTRUCTURE

*Every economy needs a national information infrastructure. This is the utility of the twenty-first century—a broadband highway for a broadband, high-capacity economy. And every organization needs to plug into this utility with an enterprise information infrastructure. The new infrastructure will change economic activity as significantly as did electrification. Just as business and wealth creation would be unthinkable today without electrification, so the new economy would be impossible without the power of information.*

—*Don Tapscott*
The Digital Economy[1]

Let us consider the nervous system of an organism again. If we look at the entire nervous system, we see that it permeates the entire organism. Our nervous system reaches every part of our body, both internally and externally. The tips of our fingers, our toes, our internal organs all integrate into this single internal information system. The input it receives passes through the network to the central nervous

---

[1] Tapscott, Don, *The Digital Economy: Promise and Peril in the Age of Network Intelligence*, McGraw-Hill Education, 1997. Used by permission.

system, where the brain takes this information and interprets its environment. In the same way, the information infrastructure permeates the organization—its nervous system. No part of a healthy organization is isolated from the rest. In an intelligent enterprise, data received in one department is passed on to the data warehouse, the central intelligence of the organization. There it is integrated with data from the rest of the organization.

If we were to close our eyes and try to envision the nervous system, what would we see? Imagine thinner than hair-like fibers running through the body, a mesh of microscopic threads in which we are all encased. We can see the sensations, little pinpoints of light, traveling along this thread until it reaches the spinal cord. Up the spinal cord it travels until it reaches the brain, where it joins the other points of light that make up our intellect. As we contemplate this vision, can we see how similar it is to our organization's information infrastructure? Each laptop, printer, server, and desktop system is linked together by the cabling of our network. We can see the data flow from one system to the next as it makes its way through our network. We can see a similar point of light flow from desktop to server to data warehouse. The challenge to many organizations is to have an infrastructure that is healthy enough for these connections to be made.

Figure 4.1 presents the information infrastructure of the company we discussed in Chapter 3, Billy Boy Bowling Balls. What is presented in this figure is typical of many organizations. As we look around Billy Boy's information systems, we see variations on a theme. We have a variety of clients connected to different types of servers over a number of network topologies. Each department manager, faced with the same set of problems, provides a different solution. The manufacturing area is an example of this problem. The machines that we use to form and polish our bowling balls are numerically controlled devices. These systems are connected to the shop floor's Local Area Network (LAN) with a departmental server. This LAN sits in isolation from the other parts of the network. This is Billy Boy's nervous system.

At the very ends of this infrastructure, the metaphorical tips of our organization's fingers and toes are the data entry and exit points. We are tempted to refer to these points as clients, but this is not the case. The administration department uses dumb terminals to access legacy applications that reside on a mainframe. We also see in administration a number of desktop systems that access the mainframe through some terminal emulator. These users are primarily concerned with the desktop applications on their system, occasionally accessing the mainframe. Most of the departments have a traditional environment, either a laptop or a desktop connected to some background server. In addition to the exception we have already discussed, we also see the C-level executives have their own environment. The CEO as well as the vice president of sales and marketing have no need of desktop systems; they have secretaries that do all the "stuff" for them. A simple thin client with an information portal is all they need. The CFO, however, won't give up her spreadsheets, which means that she still uses a desktop system. In addition to the clients on the network, the CIO and COO are set up for wireless communications. When there is a situation that requires immediate attention, they receive an electronic notification.

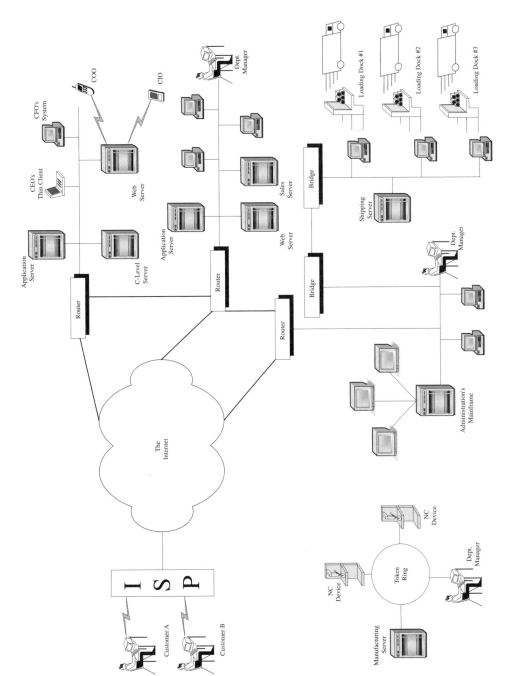

**FIGURE 4.1** Billy Boy's information infrastructure.

We also see in this structure several types of servers. Administration, shipping, and manufacturing each has its own network server. These systems provide the basic network services such as file sharing and network administration. In sales and marketing, however, we see that we have two additional server types, a Web server and an application server. As it turns out, Billy Boy's niece Francesca just graduated from Malibu State University with a degree in computer science and surfboard waxing. She convinced her uncle that Billy Boy needed to get into this dotcom stuff, so he put her in charge of building their e-commerce site. They now have a Web server to host the Web site along with an application server to support the sales of bowling balls and accessories over the Internet. Francesca's boyfriend, Moon Doggy, a brutally handsome, extraordinarily intelligent fellow graduate and surfer, has a degree in business intelligence applications with a minor in boogie boards. He convinced Billy Boy that they absolutely have to have a data mart to support the Web site. From this mart, Moon Doggy can mine the *clickstream* to increase Internet sales.

At this point, Billy Boy's head is spinning. He has all sorts of clients talking to all sorts of servers. His CIO, Clarence, is telling him that they have an absolute mess on their hands. There are no organizational standards for any of these systems, and department managers are going off and developing systems with no regard for how to share information across the enterprise. There are a ton of servers, each running its own operating system. Unfortunately, the only server with which Billy Boy is familiar is Eunice down at the local coffee shop.

In Chapter 5, we will try to lend Billy Boy a hand. We will examine the different architectures in place in many organizations today. We will see that many organizations use mainframes, UNIX servers, and low-level network servers. Each environment has its own set of applications, each with its own benefits. At times, the distinction between the different systems has blurred. At other times, nonexistent divisions have been raised. In addition, there is confusion about the role played by each in IEBI.

We will begin our study of servers with the mainframe. Many have decried the server as dead technology. Some suggest that the mainframe hasn't a place in IEBI. While there are challenges to integrating this technology into an Internet-enabled architecture; the mainframe is *not quite dead yet*. Many organizations are finding new life for the mainframe, front-ending these systems with Web and application servers in an attempt at integration. We will discuss what role these processing powerhouses can play in IEBI. At the same time, we must realize that these days are not all happy times and pass the soda crackers for the mainframe. Although these systems have significant capacity, they also have some considerable challenges. We shall discuss the inflexibility of these systems as well as the obstacles to maintaining them.

Our discussion of the mainframe will lead us into an examination of the forces that gave rise to a new architecture: client/server. As we shall see, department managers grew frustrated with the control Information Technology (IT) departments had over information. In an attempt to have more control over their own information, these managers seized the technological advances that made client/server environments possible. They began to develop their own systems that were free from the repressive control of the IT department. We can see this represented within Billy Boy Bowling Balls as well. Manufacturing, shipping, sales, and administration each has its own LAN. The managers of these departments became their own mini-CIOs. As each manager independently developed his or her separate information infrastructure, each independently faced the same set of problems. They also came up with their own sets of answers, fracturing the information infrastructure. The nervous system of these organizations became diseased. Parts of the nervous system were cut off from the others.

This client/server architecture was just the beginning of something; it was a new way of thinking that would enable the current Internet age. Many of the concepts and technologies that have made the Internet possible could not have occurred without client/server architecture. As we shall see in Chapter 5, an Internet-enabled application is another step in the evolution of the client/server model. While this may be blasphemy to some, as we come to understand the true meaning of client/server, we shall see that the Internet cannot be anything but this next step. We can see this by simply looking at the terminology of the Internet. We have thin *clients* speaking to Web *servers* and application *servers*.

We may be tempted to classify the Internet as simply another client/server architecture, and in a sense we would be correct. There is an important distinction between an Internet application and traditional client/server, however. An Internet application uses a very specific set of technologies for its implementation and adheres to certain principles of openness. Rather than describing an Internet application as just another implementation of client/server, we should describe it as a very specific implementation of client/server, an implementation that is the next phase of client/server's evolution. This of course means the ultimate demise of what has become known as client/server. Homo sapiens are the descendents of homo erectus in the same sense that the Internet application is the descendent of client/server. Unfortunately for client/server, homo erectus is an extinct species. This is reminiscent of a Florida congressional election in which the conservative candidate accused his opponent of having a brother who is a homo sapiens and a sister who is a known thespian. Not being able to deny such a charge, the liberal lost.

Homo erectus died out because homo sapiens were superior. Such is the case with an Internet-enabled application. The benefits of an Internet-enabled application make it markedly superior to its client/server ancestor. Software vendors are able to develop software on one platform, the Internet. They are now able to write one version of the software that runs on any client that is able to support a browser. This is also a benefit to the end user. Rather than supporting applications on a variety of different platforms, there is now one application that executes in a single environment.

What is perhaps the greatest benefit is the centralization of the system. As we can see with Billy Boy Bowling Balls, the client/server world in which each department manager develops systems specifically for his or her own needs fractures the organization's information infrastructure. There is no way for Billy Boy to gather all this information together in one place. Administration and shipping are connected to one another, but manufacturing is out there by itself. It doesn't interface to any of the other systems. This is the chief benefit of the Internet-enabled information infrastructure: All the systems are integrated into one. We can now have an information infrastructure in which all of the systems are able to contribute to the centralized data warehouse. Through this centralization, decision makers are able to get a single view of the organization.

To achieve this objective, however, we must have a common means of communication. As we discussed in Chapter 2, one of the major steps forward in the evolution of the Internet is the development of a standard networking protocol. It would be inappropriate to discuss IEBI without examining the Internet itself. In Chapter 6, we will discuss how the Internet works.

We will begin our discussion about the Internet with an introduction to the standards bodies that have contributed to developing standard networking protocols. These groups include the International Organization of Standards, the Institute of Electronics and Electrical Engineers, and the International Telecommunications Union. These standards bodies are responsible for the development of networking models and standards that have allowed the communications world to move from proprietary networking protocols to a standard method of communication.

We shall see that the Transmission Control Protocol/Internet Protocol (TCP/IP) and Ethernet became the predominate protocol and network architecture of the Internet. In Chapter 6, therefore, we will review how each protocol provides for communication over the Internet. In our study, we will examine how a Web site like *www.bowlingwithbilly.com* establishes a connection with a computer system on the other side of the planet.

# Chapter 5

# SERVERS: THE HEART OF IEBI

*Unlike historians, those of us living through a crisis lack the luxury of assigning clever names to disagreeable events. Years from now the situation that I label "the disconnect" may well be known by a different term. The shorthand we use is irrelevant. The consequences we endure are not. By whatever designation, the disconnect that has evolved over the past 30 years between corporate executives and the managers of the information technology resource represents an enormous drain on the productivity and competitiveness of the United States. The disconnect has profound and sweeping implications for both you and your organization.*

*—Charles B. Wang*
Techno Vision[1]

Charles Wang's book *Techno Vision* was published in 1994, the dawn of e-commerce. In this work he describes a disconnect between those who use information and those who maintain it. In this chapter we will examine some of the causes of this disconnect as well as its implications. Of course, we have an advantage over Charles Wang: We can look back. We are not in the heat of the situation. We can see not only the disconnect, but how it has been one of the catalysts for the integration of the Internet into the information infrastructure of many organizations.

---

[1] Wang, Charles, *Techno Vision*, McGraw Hill, 1994. Used by permission.

In Chapter 2, we described the birth of the Internet as the point at which we established communication between two systems. In these early days, systems residing on a network were peer to peer; they were relatively equal in their responsibilities on the network. As the Internet developed, this changed. We moved from a peer-to-peer network to architectures that divided the responsibilities for certain tasks between systems. This gave rise to the server.

In this chapter, we examine the heart of the network, the server. We begin our study with a look at the mainframe and how it fits into the Internet-enabled world. As we shall see, the shortcomings of the mainframe gave rise to a new paradigm, client/server. While giving users greater access to information, client/server architectures have issues of their own. The next step in the evolution of information systems, the Internet-enabled application, provides a solution to many of the challenges offered by client/server.

## 5.1 The Server

In Chapter 3, we discussed the IEBI loop. At the heart of this loop is the data warehouse. This *centralized* repository of information broadens the view of the IEBI system beyond the borders of our organization to span the breadth of the entire value chain. The system supporting this repository is a database server. This server is one of many in the IEBI loop. There are in fact multiple servers performing a variety of functions. The selection of which architecture we use for which function is a critical factor in the success of our implementation. In this section, we shall examine three architectures: mainframes, client/server, and Internet-enabled.

You might wonder about the relevance of such a discussion. After all, haven't we already agreed that we are implementing *Internet* Enabled Business Intelligence? Well, actually, the story isn't as simple as that. No single architecture sits in isolation of others. Simply taking into consideration the systems already in place within the organization makes this discussion necessary. The examination of these structures has relevance to which architectures we choose to employ in our implementation.

## 5.2 The Mainframe

"Reports of my demise are greatly exaggerated." When I think of mainframes, I think of Mark Twain's well-known quote. Today, when people discuss mainframes and mainframe applications, they use the term *legacy*. This has the connotation of something old, something thrust upon us that would not be our first choice. A legacy applicant to a fraternity is one whose family has a history of membership and who therefore receives special consideration. Perhaps without this consideration, the applicant would not pass muster. Is this really the state of the mainframe market today? Do mainframes have a place in the IEBI?

To answer these questions, we must first understand what a mainframe is. When I sat down to write this chapter, I thought I could easily put this into words. Surprisingly, I couldn't. As a Supreme Court justice once said of pornography, "I know what it is when I see it." Coming up with a definition is a bit more difficult. A mainframe is a big computer system, a really big computer system. How's that? As technology advances system capabilities, the lines between the mainframe and a large server have blurred, making it more difficult to compose a simple definition distinguishing the two. The very technologies upon which these systems are based have merged as well. Mainframes are replacing ECL (Emitter-Coupler Logic) components with CMOS (Complementary Metal-Oxide Semiconductor), resulting in more compute power in smaller spaces. We can see that at least as far as hardware is concerned, the mainframe is far from a musty old beast sent out to graze. These systems are excellent when processing large volumes of data, especially in a batch mode. In addition to huge processing power, they also have tremendous Input/Output (I/O) capabilities. But, what about the software?

Two years ago people were predicting the end of the world. The Y2K bug was going to bring about not only the end of the world, but also the second coming of Christ. (I say this not to be flip; I actually knew people who sincerely believed this.) The media-engendered hysteria, however, entirely missed the point. The date problem that became known as a bug, wasn't. It was not the result of poor programming, but of good! I actually remember sitting in a COBOL class in the late 1970s and being told by the instructor to only use two digits. He made the offhand remark that no one would be using these programs in the year 2000, so why worry about it. We all expected our code to be scrapped long ago. The problem was that the code worked *too well*. There was no need to change something that was doing the job. Such is the case with most mainframe software.

There is a very real downside. While many organizations that have mainframes as part of their information infrastructures are still spending substantial sums on upgrading their systems, most of the money is spent in maintaining the existing systems. Hence the mainframe's legacy reputation. We have noted how the term *legacy* connotes something handed down from previous generations. Such is the case with mainframes today; they still host applications built a generation ago by programmers who have long since hung up their flowcharting templates. Many of the investments in upgrading the applications themselves, such as providing Internet access, are merely putting a new coat of paint on an old barn. The legacy applications remain at the heart of these systems. These applications are not rolling stones—they do gather moss. The lack of documentation and staff intimately familiar with the already existing software leads to functions being re-created over and over again. This results in redundant applications and code scraps, both of which ultimately increase system costs. In addition, the very nature of the implementation makes it cumbersome to modify the business logic in applications.

The biggest challenge faced by the mainframe is not really technology. It is more of a matter of perception. The mainframe is like a tank—a big, bulky monster that moves forward with great deliberation. The thing about tanks is that they are sure handy on a battlefield. They aren't, however, terribly sexy. Next time you're at an IT cocktail party, tell the new blonde-haired, blue-eyed programmer who just graduated from Malibu State College with a B.S. in computer science and surfboard waxing that you are a COBOL programmer. See what kind of reaction you get. This is the problem: Mainframes have lost their sizzle. We aren't impressed anymore by banks of blinking lights, dip switches, and spinning tape drives. Fewer people are interested in the technology. This makes it even more difficult to find talented technical staff in an already tight market.

Can the mainframe pass muster? Certainly, but as time passes, it will become increasingly more difficult to do so. In Chapter 2, we discussed that one of the factors leading to the success of the American industrial revolution was the lack of an infrastructure that needed to be replaced. The early Americans simply implemented a new solution to the production problem. Since there was no *old* solution already in place, there wasn't any hindrance to this new approach.

The complexity of the software along with the dwindling supply of programming talent creates a downward spiral. It begins when parts of the organization approach the IT department requesting reports or modifications to existing applications. Since these changes are complex and there are fewer programmers to make them, these changes take time even under the best circumstances. Managers who are not familiar with the causes of the delay grow frustrated and view IT as resistant or, worse yet, incompetent. More than once, I have attended meetings to discuss changes to a large mainframe-based application, and production managers were there with their same old complaint: "Why can't you guys get your act together? My son-in-law wrote a program for me on his PC that does the same thing in just a week." Any explanation of the differences between a PC-based, single-user database program and a mainframe enterprise application was lost on them. In many instances, however, perception becomes reality. The perception was that IT was slow and resistant. IT developed a siege mentality, thus becoming slow and resistant. In the mind of the user, IT saw themselves as the high priests of information. Users, as supplicants, paid homage to the lords of silicon and their representatives, the IT department. IT in turn passed judgment on which requests were worthy of consideration.

This set the stage for the client/server revolution. Client/server systems *empowered* users, giving them unprecedented access to their systems and applications. Individual department managers became mini-CIOs, each implementing solutions that met their specific needs. While mainframes were islands of information, client/server dispersed information throughout the organization. Claudius Caesar said that within every lie, there is a truth, and within every truth, there is a lie. There are points on both sides of this issue that are correct and points that are somewhat exaggerated. To understand this more fully, let's try to dispel some of the myths around client/server.

## 5.3  Client/Server Architecture: The Upstart Crow

The client/server architecture is perhaps the *upstart crow* of computer architectures. The term comes from a quote of Robert Greene about Shakespeare: "For there is an upstart crow, beautified with our feathers, that with his tiger's heart wrapped in a players hide, supposes he is as well able to bumbast out a blank verse as the best of you: and being an absolute *Iohannes fac totum*, is in his own conceit the only Shake-scene in a country." The irony is that the upstart crow, Shakespeare, is a long-remembered staple of English literature, while the others are long forgotten.[2] After all, who in Hollywood is planning to make the film *Greene In Love*?

In our industry, the upstart crow is the client/server architecture. There is, however, a general misunderstanding of the term client/server. In the minds of most people, client/server means a somewhat powerful system on an individual's desktop, connected over a LAN to a much more powerful backroom system that runs some database or other application. The desktop system runs an application and does most of the computing. The client makes requests of the backroom system, the server, for data upon which it will perform some operation. While this may be a particular implementation of client/server, it is just that: a specific implementation. It is not a description of the client/server architecture. This misconception has tremendous implications not only for the Internet-enabled infrastructure, but for IEBI as well.

Figure 5.1 presents the client/server architecture. A client/server architecture is composed of client and server processes. Both the client and the server are processes; they are not necessarily discrete systems. A client/server application really is a multiprocess application, as shown in the figure. It is composed of two general types of processes. The first is the client process. The client process is *proactive*; it generates requests that are then passed to the server. The server is *reactive*. Its only reason for existence is to process the requests sent to it by clients. Given this scheme, the server process is a constant. It runs, theoretically, forever. This background process is the heart of the system; if the server process goes down, the entire system is down. Who in the business world today at one point or another has not suffered from a crashed server? The client process is different. The client process has a limited life span. It executes only as long as the user has need of it. If a client process goes down, it does not affect the entire system, simply the individual user.

---

[2] I suppose there are people who are aware of Christopher Marlowe, that other guy who got stabbed in the eye in a bar fight, but they would be hard pressed to connect his name with the "Jew of Malta." Actually, one of the few things Hollywood got right in the film *Shakespeare in Love* was Marlowe's death; apparently, the thespians of Shakespeare's time were similar to the rappers of our own.

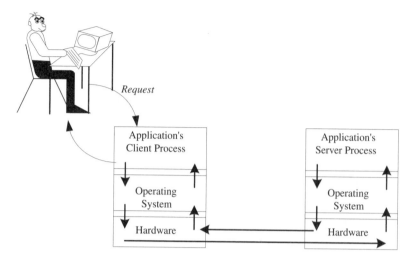

**FIGURE 5.1** The client/server architecture.

Note that this architectural layout is a conceptual design. As such, it does not define specific implementation details, such as hardware or software requirements. Those details are best left to the detailed design phase. There is nothing inherent to the client/server architecture requiring these processes to run on separate systems. We show this in more detail in Figure 5.2. Let's take Oracle's SQL Plus as an example. This is a tool on the user's system through which the user writes SQL commands to access data in the database. The tool can access any database on the network, whether it is on the same system as SQL Plus or on some backend server. If I were to run SQL Plus on the user's system and the database on another, there would be little disagreement that I have a client/server application. Basically, this is the layout shown in Figure 5.1. Suppose we run the client process on the same system as the server process. Is it still a client/server application? Has anything in the application, with the possible exception of a few initialization parameters, changed at all? Of course not; it is the exact same application! Nothing has changed. We are simply running the different parts of the client/server application on the same box, which is an implementation detail and *not* something inherent to the design of the system.

Let's take this analysis one step further. The architecture does not mandate any specifics on which requests are generated by the client or who initiates the request. Referring to Figure 5.3, we see that this has some interesting implications for the application designer. There are times when a client is actually a server, and there are other times when the server is actually a client. When a user logs on to an application, the first thing that the application does is validate the user. The application server submits a request to the access server for validation of the user. At that point, the application server is a client of the access server. Once the user has been validated, he or she will begin to process transactions or perform data analysis. The application server then begins to make requests of the database server. Again, we see that the application server is a client to the database server. Some database servers' only clients are intermediary servers, such as an application or Web server.

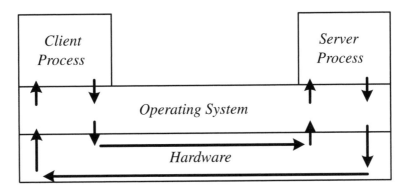

**FIGURE 5.2**  Single-system client/server implementations.

In Figure 5.1 we see what is described as a *two-tier* architecture: The client is the first tier and the server is the second. Figure 5.3 shows a *three-tier* architecture, where the middle tier is an application server. We could almost look at the processes that reside on these intermediate tiers as *server/client processes*—at times they are servers and at other times they are clients. Typically, these processes are referred to as servers, since this is their main function. In many environments, we have simply stopped counting the tiers and now refer to them as *n-tier* implementations.

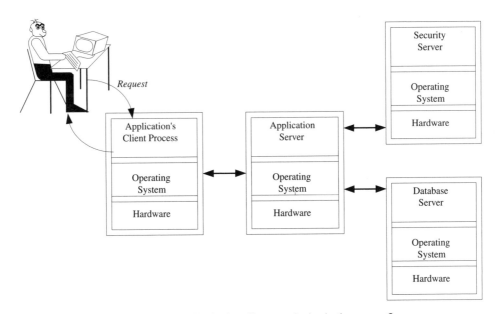

**FIGURE 5.3**  Who is the client, and who is the server?

Generally, we see the client process as the part that interacts with the user. Although it is not a requirement, we usually see clients implement a Graphical User Interface (GUI) for accepting commands and data from the user. The client, therefore, manages the mouse clicks, keyboard entries, and data validation. The client must also deal with error recovery. This is especially true with IEBI. The client must not lose *context* if an error occurs in the midst of a drill-down or rotation. When possible, the system needs to recover and continue processing.

Just as the client process has certain requirements, so too does the server. Theoretically, the server has one specific function. Perhaps the server is an access server, as shown in Figure 5.3, or a database server. This is a theoretic view of the server, however. There are times when the system architect for implementation considerations may combine multiple functions in one server. In either case, the server must maintain service. As we noted earlier, if the server dies, the entire system is dead.

The level of uptime is based on how critical the application is to the operation of the organization. The highest level of system availability is a *fault-tolerant system* in which there is 99.999 percent system uptime. This is also referred to as five 9s. This works out to a downtime of approximately 5.25 minutes per year. If our server processes orders for our Web store, we would probably want to maintain this level of system availability. Other applications may require a *high availability system,* where system uptime is only 99.9 percent. A high availability system can be down roughly 9 hours per year. When considering how critical a system is to the operation of your organization, do not be too quick to label it as nonessential. It wasn't that long ago that email was considered a luxury; now many organizations are stopped dead in their tracks without it.

### 5.3.1 BENEFITS OF CLIENT/SERVER COMPUTING

There were several driving forces behind the adoption of client/server architectures. Some of these forces were technological, some economic, and others political. Client/server architectures were touted as delivering innumerable benefits in each area. Again, quoting our good friend Claudius, "Within every lie, there is a truth, and within every truth, there is a lie." Quite often the enthusiasm to fulfill political needs drove managers to find technological and economic benefits that may not have actually existed.

The technological drive behind client/server was, simply stated, that we could do it. Technology up to that point did not make client/server a reasonable alternative for most applications. The dawn of the PC was the first step in making client/server a reality. The PC gave us a platform upon which we could run the client process. This may seem in conflict with what we stressed earlier, that client/server does not necessarily mean a PC for the client and a separate system for the server processes. This isn't really the case. The PC simply made the solution more practical, which is perhaps the origin of the misconception behind the nature of client/server.

Consider the alternatives for implementing a client prior to the PC. The first alternative was to create separate processes on the same system, such as a mainframe. In most, if not all, cases this simply did not make sense. Why go through the additional development complexity? There would have to be additional processes to manage the multiple clients and the server process. An easier solution was to create one process that did everything.

A second alternative was to use minicomputers and distribute the processing across these systems. Actually, some of the first client/server applications were implemented using this technology, although they may not have been referred to as such. The first client/server system in which I was involved was back in 1978. At that time, we used minicomputers as our clients. The communications protocol was proprietary, and much of the interaction between the client and server processes had to be custom developed.

We continued developing applications like this until the mid-1980s. They were large and expensive, which was great for consultants like me. In 1993, I met a systems analyst for a large aerospace company in southern California. He received a very large bonus because he had recognized the expense behind a system I had developed in 1988. It seems that he was able to replace these expensive minicomputers with low-end UNIX workstations. The costs of the new systems were less than the annual maintenance costs for minicomputers.

It is more than just the PC that has provided new client alternatives. It is also the rate at which the power of the PC has increased over the years. It wasn't that long ago that a system with a 100-MHz CPU, 64MB RAM, and a 4-GB hard drive was a hefty system. Today we discuss systems with a 2-GHz CPU and 80 GB of disk space. As the power increases, so too does the functionality that we can build into the client-side applications.

In 1980, on a small ranch outside Ojai California, I had dinner with a forward-thinking system designer. We had met to plan a way to start a company. We weren't quite sure what it was we wanted to do, but we wanted to do something. I was especially excited about the then burgeoning field of computer graphics. During the course of the evening, he kept repeating the same line: "You don't get it, Bill. Stop thinking of graphics as the output and start thinking of it as the input." He was right on both counts. Initially, most PC application interfaces were character-based, as were their mainframe and mini predecessors. In the mid-1980s, however, we saw the rise of the GUI. Graphics were now the input as well as the output. Client/server applications took advantage of this new way of interacting with the system.

In the Character User Interface (CUI) world, users interacted with the system in one of three ways: by command, by menu, or by function keys. The output of these systems was equally uninteresting. The GUI changed how we work with systems. At first, this was not as readily accepted as you might think. The argument was that a true typist never took his or her hands off the keyboard. A GUI forced you to go to a mouse. Forget the fact that most of us aren't *true typists*—a well-designed GUI didn't force you to reach for the mouse. Most continued to employ the use of function keys. Eventually, the obvious benefits of a GUI won out. It provided a richer means of working with applications. A GUI is more than just icons and images. It gives the user a means to visualize not only the data but also the flow of an application. While the benefits of visualization could fill a chapter in and of itself, suffice it to say that visualization is a more powerful means of communicating thoughts and ideas. A visual image leaves a much more lasting impression than mere text. As the old adage goes, a picture is worth a thousand words.

The GUI is key for IEBI. One of the most important aspects of any well-designed BI application is that the decision maker is able to interact with the data. Consider for a moment the *old* way of doing things. A decision maker would ask for a report from IT. In anywhere from a week to a month, he or she would get the report. The report in turn would possibly generate additional questions. The answers to these questions may be embedded in the report in such a way that it would require the analyst to make hand calculations. In many instances, the answers would not be in the report at all, generating a need to request additional reports. There was no way for the IT department to anticipate what additional questions may be asked by the decision maker. With the high turnaround time for reports, the numbers were often stale, and the critical window for the business issue to be resolved had closed.

For IEBI to work well, the decision maker needs the ability to interact with the data. In BI, it is easy to visualize what it means to *interact with the data*. When the decision maker looks at a set of numbers, he or she has an understanding of the significance of those numbers that a software engineer or programmer does not have. When decision makers interact with the data, they can take a number and drill down into the source of that number. They can rotate and aggregate the data to put the number in a different context. Once the numbers are viewed in that new context, the decision maker may gain a new perspective on their significance. He or she might decide to pull in additional information via an ad hoc report. If we look back at the old way of doing things, described in the previous paragraph, this interaction would never have been possible. This is the power of a GUI in an IEBI environment. It provides the decision maker with a means to truly explore the data describing the business environment.

The PC, however, was not enough. There was also the development of standard communications protocols. This was an important innovation for the progress of client/server. Prior to standardized protocols, client/server systems custom built their own communications. This meant the development of low-level communications libraries for each new system. This task was further complicated when establishing communications between systems running different operating systems. Standardized communications protocols, such as TCP/IP, made it possible to share information between many varied systems. Developers can easily take advantage of these standardized protocols by integrating standard API (Application Program Interface) calls into their applications, simplifying the process of communicating between systems.

Standardized communications freed the system architect to choose from a larger variety of servers. They were no longer limited to a particular vendor or a particular operating system. There was no reason a server running one operating system could not support clients of another. The server, the thing in the back room that no one saw, became a commodity. This was the dawn of the *open systems environment*.

These technological benefits purportedly led to economic benefits. The move from propriety mainframes to standards-based commodity servers drove down the cost of the systems. The price per millions of instructions per second (MIP) for a desktop client was also much less than that of the mainframe. These cost-per-MIP comparisons, while interesting to some, were not very compelling outside the IT department. The large, absolute capital cost savings, however, were compelling to the folks in finance. The initial outlay for a mainframe was far greater than for a UNIX-based system, for example.

Cynics might look at this line of reasoning and ask about the cost of the client. Shouldn't the cost of the client be added into the system cost as well? True, but in the interest of consistency, the cost of the client must be amortized over multiple applications. This not only reduces the cost of the client to the new system, but in most cases eliminates it. If the client system is already on the user's desktop, it is inappropriate to burden the cost of the new system with the entire cost of that PC. We are only concerned with the incremental costs.

In addition, the move from a proprietary to a more open systems environment was believed to reduce overall system costs. In the proprietary environment, the systems were held hostage by the vendor. The cost of porting an application to another environment was simply too high. Once a vendor had a system installed, the vendor owned the account. In an open systems world, this is not the case. Although moving from one UNIX server to another wasn't always as simple as the proponents of open systems claimed, it was still significantly easier to switch between them. With low change over costs, there is increased competition, which in turn lowers prices. Prices have dropped to such an extent that we now have an open-source market with access to free high-quality software such as LINUX.

A final economic benefit is what some call a *soft* number, not something directly reflected on a balance sheet. This is productivity. Control is taken away from the IT department and delivered to the individual users. They can now perform tasks on their own. More importantly, they are also able to perform tasks in their way. They are freed from the burden of communicating, and at times justifying, their needs to an IT department. An example of this in the IEBI world is the decision maker's ability to interact with the data. The decision maker is now more productive, since he or she has the necessary data when needed. Decision makers are more effective and ultimately more productive.

Again we hear that old refrain, within every lie, there is a truth, and within every truth, there is a lie. As stated earlier, the real driving force behind client/server was neither technological nor economic. The true force behind the proliferation of client/server technology was political. The key for this political motivation is described in Bernard Liautaud's book *e-Business Intelligence*.[3] Liautaud describes the relationship between *information dictatorships, information anarchy,* and *information democracy.* Figure 5.4 shows the distinction between these information models. As we see in this figure, an organization's *information governance* is determined as a function of information control to information access.

Liautaud cites three models of information governance. The first is *information dictatorship.* In this model, there is a high degree of control, yet limited access to information. These environments are reminiscent of the mainframe heyday, when requestors of the data approached IT departments as supplicants who petition the

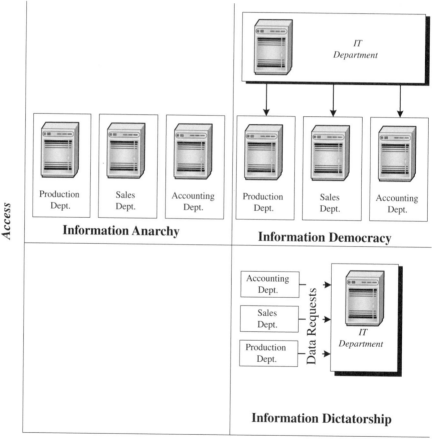

**FIGURE 5.4**  Information governance.

---

[3] Liautaud, Bernard, and Hammond, Mark, *e-Business Intelligence: Turning Information into Knowledge into Profit,* McGraw Hill, 2000.

high priest of data for the blessings of information. The second model of information governance is *information anarchy*. In this model, there is a great deal of access to information, yet little if any control. Taken to the extreme, every department has its own server and standards. Applications and metadata vary from organization to organization. While every department has control over its own data, there is little if any sharing of information, making it difficult, if not impossible, to share data between departments. It is often a substantial challenge to glean an enterprise-wide view of the organization from the detritus of information anarchies. The ultimate environment, of course, is one in which there is open access to controlled information. These information governance models are *information democracies.*

In addition to accurately describing the state of many information infrastructures, these models also demonstrate the evolution of information systems. As stated earlier, the true driving force behind the client/server architectures was political. Department managers were tired of struggling with IT to get at the information. There was a coup to overthrow the information dictatorships. Many revolutions in history promised a glorious new world of equality, liberty, and fraternity, but instead led to anarchy. Such was the case with the revolution of information systems. The plethora of departmental point solutions led organizations into information anarchy.

It is important to consider the distinction between these different models and the effect they have on the value of an organization's information systems. In Chapter 2, we discussed Bob Metcalfe's description of the value of a network as the number of people on that network squared. Kevin Kelly maintains in *New Rules for the New Economy*[4] that in the Internet age, multiple simultaneous connections can be made. In such environments, the value of the network increases not by squaring the number of people on the network but by raising the number of people on the network to the power of that number. The key to all this value, however, is the ability to share information. Moving from an information dictatorship to an information anarchy still limits the overall value of the network. In anarchy, while there may be a way to send an electronic signal from one department to another, the ability to share meaningful information is still inhibited. Differing applications and metadata limit the practical sharing of information. This, of course, is all the more critical for IEBI, where the data from these many differing systems is consolidated into one centralized data repository.

The ultimate objective of IEBI is to share information across the entire value chain. If the value of information increases with the number of people who share it, what of the value of IEBI? It is like putting wood on a fire—the more wood you add, the hotter the fire. With IEBI, the more information you add, the more valuable the IEBI system.

Whether the increase is squared or exponential, the value of the IEBI system is a function of the scope of the data contained within it. If we have a simple data mart whose scope is manufacturing, there is value delivered to the organization. If

---

[4] Kelly, Keven, *New Rules for the New Economy*, Penguin Books, 1999.

distribution is added to the scope of the data mart, its value increases. The expanded scope allows analyses that span both manufacturing and distribution. Manufacturing is able to understand both how distribution affects manufacturing and how manufacturing affects distribution. The understanding becomes a two-way street. The same holds true for the distribution department. Each department is better able to understand how its internal processes affect and are affected by other departments. As the IEBI system expands to include all departments throughout the organization, the two-way street evolves into a complex weave of connections between departments. The value of the network begins to rise exponentially. The question with which we are faced, however, is how to evolve the organization from an information anarchy to an information democracy. How do we establish control while providing open access to data throughout our organization?

## 5.4 The Internet

The solution to the problem of distributing information throughout the organization while providing centralized control is the Internet. All Internet-enabled applications, however, are not created equal. There are Internet applications, and then again, there are Internet applications. In Chapter 2, we discussed Tim Berners-Lee's proposal for a hypertext markup language and how that proposal served as a basis for the first browser, MOSAIC, written by students at the NCSA in Urbana-Champaign, Illinois.

Back then the delivery of information over the Web, while simple, was very limited. As shown in the Figure 5.5, the browser communicated with the Web server using HTTP, the HyperText Transfer Protocol. The browser would make requests of the server that in turn passed back HTML, HyperText Markup Language, pages. There wasn't much to an HTML page; it contained a mix of text, the specification for the display of that text, graphics, and links to other HTML pages. The client in this environment simply served as a means to display the data and communicate with the server. This of course limited the capabilities of an IEBI application.

The first challenge to delivering an IEBI application was to maintain *state*. HTTP is stateless. This means that each request received by the server from the client is treated as separate and unique. There is no association between one request and any previous or subsequent requests. When creating HTTP, the objective was to deliver data over the Internet. Establishing a state was much more complex and was unnecessary to meet the design objectives. If the file didn't make it to its destination, that was fine; a new request could be submitted. There was no long-term damage to an application because of a break in communications.

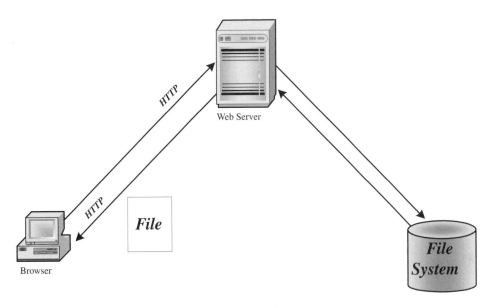

**FIGURE 5.5**   Basic Web application.

In a client/server environment, we must maintain state. If, for example, we wish to select a particular data item and drill down on that item, it is a simple matter for the client/server application to send a more specific request to the server. In a stateless environment, where the client is used as means to display the data, it is difficult for the server to maintain state; or the context in which the client is making the request. This limitation to HTTP not only limits the capability of the decision maker to perform analyses, but as we shall see in later chapters, it also limits our ability to analyze activities on our Web site.

There is yet another complication to this scenario: The data must be in the form of an HTML page. Data could not be pulled directly to the browser from a database or an application to fulfill a request. If it wasn't in an HTML page, it was inaccessible. There was no way for the user to truly interact with an application. This, of course, brought us back to the days of the mainframe when there was no such thing as ad hoc reporting. It didn't take developers long to realize this shortcoming. In fact, the interval between the two was so short that one could almost consider them commensurate. To remedy this situation, an interface was developed between the Web server and the application. Figure 5.6 presents this solution.

The Common Gateway Interface (CGI) defines a way to communicate with the Web server. As shown in the figure, the user makes a request via a browser. Typically, the request is in an HTML form. Upon receiving a request, the Web server initiates a CGI process. The information in the HTML form is used by the Web server to build a packet, which ultimately is passed to the CGI program. This packet contains whatever information is necessary for the processing of the request by the CGI program. For example, the request may require a query to a database, in which case the CGI program establishes a connection to the database. It then builds and issues the query. Upon receipt of a response from the application, the CGI pro-

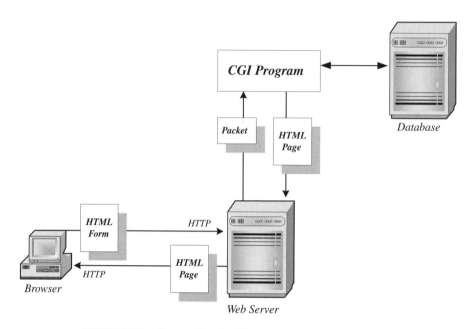

**FIGURE 5.6** Connecting the Web server to the application.

gram formats the data into an HTML page and passes the page back to the Web server. Once the data is passed back to the Web server, the work of the CGI program is completed and the process terminates. The Web server in turn passes the HTML page back to the requesting browser.

For IEBI applications, CGI was certainly a step in the right direction. As we said earlier, the Web server only understands HTTP, a stateless protocol. Within the Web server itself, there is nothing we would consider application logic. It receives requests for specific files and passes them back to the requesting browser. There is no continuity between one request and the next. Multiple requests made from one browser are treated no differently than multiple browsers each making a request. CGI, however, provides us with two methods of establishing a *pseudo-stateful* connection.

To establish state, we need to establish a bridge between one request and the next. Figure 5.7 demonstrates the first method of establishing such a connection. In this scenario, we use the fact that the CGI application constructs the Web page to our advantage. Let's say that we are an online bookstore. In this store, we have set up personalized pages for repeat customers. On these personalized pages, we have recommended reading lists. One day, user A at browser A enters our Web site from her personal page. She sees on the recommended reading list *Object-Oriented Data Warehouse Design: Building the Star Schema* by William A. Giovinazzo and decides to investigate this title further by clicking on the link to that page. The CGI application passes the page back to browser A via the Web server, but prior to doing so, embeds a tag in the HTML page. This tag identifies the session in which this request was made. The CGI program then terminates.

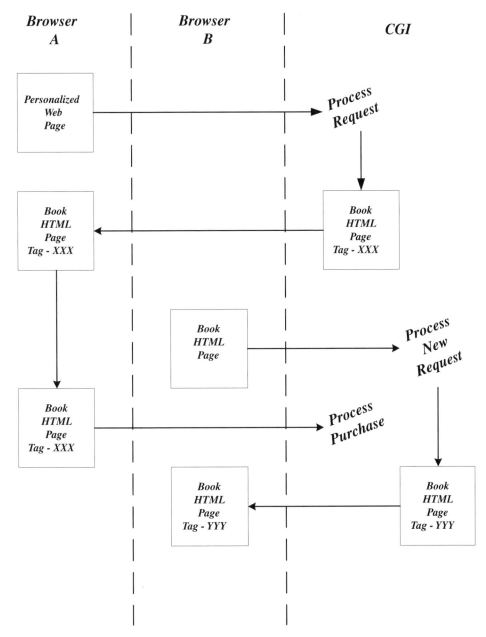

**FIGURE 5.7**  Establishing state with CGI.

At the same time, user B receives an email from a friend recommending the same book. The friend included in the email the Uniform Resource Locator (URL) for the book. User B clicks on the link and immediately goes to the page for the book. The Web server starts another CGI process to generate a new page with a completely different tag. Meanwhile, user A reviews the Web page and decides that she must have this insightful, unique book to truly understand star schema design methodologies. She orders the book. When she submits her request to purchase the book, the CGI program receives the HTML page with the embedded tag and determines that the purchase is part of the user A's session. User B, however, not recognizing the brilliance of the author, decides to terminate the session in order to watch championship wrestling.

While we can see that this method is useful in simulating a state to our sessions, there is a problem. Every time we process a request, we need to reconstruct our Web page. In addition, this is only good for one session; there is no persistence. If the user terminates the session and returns at a later time, there is no continuity between the two. To resolve these issues, Netscape developed a solution that is elegant in its simplicity: cookies. YUM! (Personally, I feel that chocolate-chip is overrated. Give me a good oatmeal raisin with a glass of milk any day.) Rather than modify the HTML pages in response to a request, the CGI application requests the browser to create a simple block of text. This text uniquely identifies the browser from other browsers accessing the Web site. Figure 5.8 shows how this works.

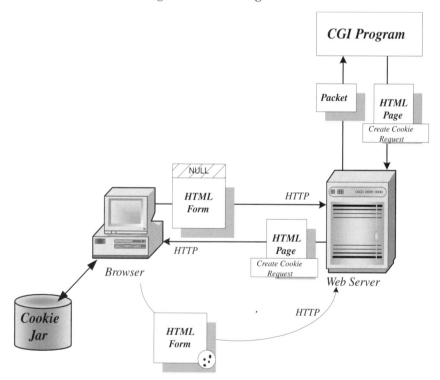

**FIGURE 5.8**   C is for cookies. That's good enough for CGI.

As we can see, the browser makes its initial request of the Web server. The server, as we described earlier, builds a packet of information and starts the CGI process. If the application does not find a cookie in the packet passed to it from the Web server, it assumes that this is the first visit to this site from this browser. The application therefore adds a request for the browser to create a cookie on the client's local system (in some cases, the user may set the browser to not allow cookies). If it accepts the cookie, the text string is saved in the browser's memory. This text string, the cookie, is passed to the Web site with any subsequent requests. When the CGI application receives the cookie, it will know that this is a returning user. When the browser terminates, the cookies in its memory are written to disk and retrieved later, when the browser is restarted.

We can employ these cookies the same as we did with HTML tags. The difference is that continuity can be maintained even beyond individual sessions. In the example presented in Figure 5.7, we noted that the user ended the session to go watch championship wrestling. Let's say that after a time, he comes to his senses and realizes his dire need for the book *Object-Oriented Data Warehouse Design: Building the Star Schema*. When he returns to the Web site using browser B, the cookie will be passed along with the request and the application identifies the browser as having visited this page before.

Establishing state provides IEBI systems with two very important capabilities. First, we are able analyze how a user travels through our site. As we watch where a user goes on our site, we gain a better understanding of his or her behavior. Customer behavior becomes input to our IEBI system. Based on these behaviors, we are able to customize or personalize users' experiences on our site. Second, we can provide better support for the decision maker. By establishing continuity, the decision support system can maintain the context in which the decision maker is functioning. Since we now understand where they are and where they've been, we can more easily accommodate what they would like to do. For example, we can provide drill-down, rollup, and rotate capabilities when performing multidimensional analysis. So, establishing state provides IEBI with both better input and better output. In Chapter 13, we will discuss how to use cookies to better understand customer behavior.

CGI was not, however, a panacea for the data warehouse architect designing a client interface. The first challenge, of course, is that we are still working with a stateless connection. Although CGI could be used by a talented programmer to maintain the notion of a session, it wasn't a simple process. It is important to stress that while CGI allowed us to simulate state, the connection between the browser and the application remained stateless. Every request to the Web server generated a new CGI process. CGI did not provide for reentrant code or for sharing code between processes. Consequently, each request required that a new connection be established with the application. Consider what this means in terms of processing requirements. Each request means that an HTML page is sent to the Web server. A new process is initiated and a new connection is made to the database. As you can well gather, in addition to being slow, this consumed a great deal of resources. The resolution to this problem was the application server, presented in Figure 5.9.

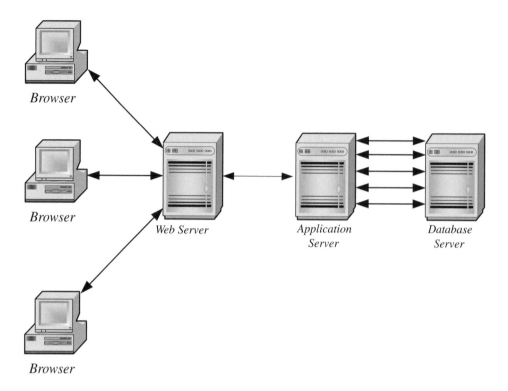

**FIGURE 5.9** The application server.

We could characterize an application server as *stateful* CGI, but such a characterization can be misleading. As we can see in the figure, an application server is a server process that sits between the Web server and the backend database. Recall the definition of a server process: It is a reactive process running virtually forever. The CGI program is similar to the server in that it responds to user requests. It differs in that there is a one-to-one correspondence between each user request and the CGI program, continually starting and stopping with each request. The application server is persistent. Where the CGI program is designed to service one request for its entire processing life, the application server is designed to repeatedly process many simultaneous requests. The browser clients are clients of the application server, which is itself the client of the database server. This in effect abstracts the connection between the client and the database. The application server is now responsible to establish communication with the database server and make efficient use of its resources.

Since the application server process is persistent, we can now maintain a true state for our clients. Just as with CGI, we provide a cookie to the client process to identify an individual browser. When the user at that browser begins a session, we establish and maintain a state for that particular client. The CGI program, in stopping after processing the user request, loses its context. When a subsequent request is received from that client, the state must be retrieved before processing can continue. The persistence of the application server means that it does not loose context between client requests. As new requests are received from the client, the application server maintains the state for each client within its own persistence engine. Users can terminate from these sessions as easily as they can from more traditional client/server or mainframe applications. Inactive sessions or sessions for browsers that have lost connection can be timed out by the application server. The application server can simply terminate these sessions. It can also save their state for retrieval later.

The maintenance of state is just part of the story. While important, the application server also optimizes the utilization of resources. Since the application server is designed to serve many requests at one time, requests share resources. As shown in Figure 5.9, the application server supports its own data cache. The basic principle with caching is that you store data in memory as closely as you can to the user. The application server stores in its memory data it has retrieved from the database server. Subsequent requests from clients requiring the same data can be serviced directly from the application server's cache rather than querying the database. Because data is pulled directly from memory, this improves system response time and reduces the number of queries to the database, ultimately reducing the load on the database server.

Consider the effects of caching on IEBI, perhaps in our organization we have a BI portal, as described in Chapter 3. As part of this portal, we may have a standard set of graphs and reports that are referenced by the C-level executives within our organization. These Web pages are retrieved directly from the application server's cache. As the user drills down for more detail, the application server caches the new pages as well.

Connection pooling is another optimization technique of the application server. As shown in Figure 5.10, pooling allows the application server to service more clients than connections to the database. Again, this is due to the persistent nature of the application server. As we stated, there is a one-to-one relationship between the client and CGI process. Since GCI processes cannot share resources, there is a separate connection to the database for every client request, each connection being reestablished with every new request to the database. The application server opens a set of connections to the database and shares them between the clients. Remember that the application server is the client of the database server. As such, the application server sends requests to the database server over whichever connection is available.

For example, a request is sent from browser 1. The application server may send that request by using a database connection. While the response is being sent back to the client, the application server may receive a request from browser 2 and submit a query for that request over connection A as well. While the request for browser 2 is being processed, browser 1 may send a subsequent request that is processed via connection B. Which browser sends the request has nothing to do with

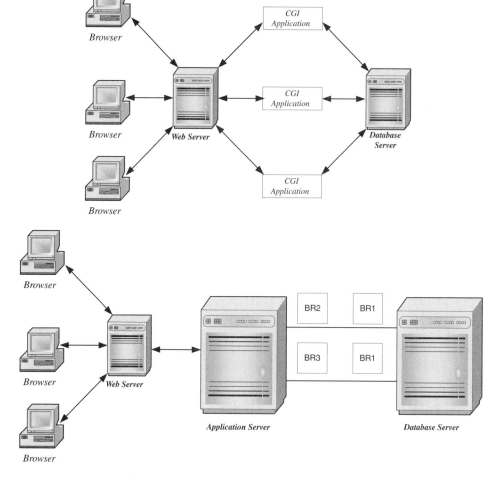

**FIGURE 5.10**   Application server resource sharing.

which connection is used to service the request. Connection pooling also allows the application server to establish fewer database connections than clients accessing the system. If, for example, the application server on average has 100 clients accessing the database 30 percent of the time, the system need only establish 30 connections to the database. Another alternative is to establish as few as 20 connections for the typical load, with the option of creating up to 35 to address peak requests.

Going forward, we expect to see two types of application servers. The first will be general-purpose application servers. These will be more or less *platforms*—servers upon which application developers will be able to develop their own Internet-enabled applications. Examples of these application servers are the Oracle 9iAS and BEA Web Logic. The second category of application servers will come from the application vendors themselves. While these systems will be extensible, their primary focus will be to act as an application server for that vendor's particular set of functionality.

### 5.4.1 THE INTERNET-ENABLED APPLICATION: A NEW AGE FOR CLIENT/SERVER

In reviewing these architectures, we need to consider an important point. We often hear discussions of client/server versus Internet-enabled or Web-enabled applications as if the two were to distinct solutions from which the data warehouse architect has to make a selection. A Web-enabled application, however, is not something different—it is merely the next phase in the evolution of client/server.

We defined client/server as an architecture in which there are two sets of processes. The first is the server, which is reactive. It runs virtually forever and responds to requests sent to it from the client. The client, the second process type in the architecture, is just the opposite. It is proactive and runs for the duration of the user session. Apply this definition to the Web-enabled application shown in Figure 5.5. We can easily see that the Web-enabled application fits this model. The client browser proactively makes requests of a middle tier, a Web server, that processes the requests and passes them on to some backend server.

As we compare Figure 5.9 to Figures 5.1 and 5.3, we see that Web-enabled applications are simply a specific implementation, or an evolution of client/server applications. Web-based applications are further down the evolutionary chain than client/server. There couldn't have been a Web without the development of client/server concepts. The basic principles of multiple processes communicating with one another to share the workload were first developed in the client/server world.

There is, however, a distinction between a Web-enabled or Internet-enabled application and traditional client/server architecture. Traditional client/server systems have a large server in the background that is *front-ended* by a smart or *fat* client. The fat client carries out most of the processing locally. The Web-enabled application has a *thin* client front-ending a middle tier that is composed of a Web server, an application server, or both. A thin client is a client that has a limited scope; it merely acts as a front end to the background system. The background servers provide the functionality.

### 5.4.2 THE BENEFITS OF WEB-ENABLED APPLICATIONS

The same technological, financial, and political forces that brought about the shift from mainframe systems to client/server are causing a shift from client/server to Web-enabled applications. These benefits become even more profound in the context of IEBI. As we expand the scope of our IEBI system, the value of the system quickly increases. The Internet allows for the expansion of this scope to extend throughout the entire organization and beyond. No longer bound by the four walls of our organization, the Internet provides for the integration of partner and supplier information systems.

To parallel our discussion of client/server benefits, we begin with the technological benefits. In the client/server era, we had a diverse set of clients. Since a major part of the application ran on the client software, developers would develop software for every major operating system, or at least every profitable one. In addition to the expense of developing multiple versions of the same software, client/server vendors were also challenged with varying degrees of system capabilities. Where one operating system provided capabilities that made certain functionality simple, other systems were more restrictive. These more restrictive systems either limited the functionality of the client or required more of the software developers.

The benefit of a Web-enabled application is a pervasive client. There is one client to which all applications are written: the browser. Figure 5.11 demonstrates this environment. The browser acts as an envelope in which the client operates. As clients are developed, they are written against a standard browser. The browser abstracts the network and operating system functionality. When the client requires these services, such as receiving input from the user or communicating with the server, requests are made via the browser. While not all browsers are created equal, they are close. In a client/server environment, we have a specific client. To distribute our application to a user outside the organization, someone would have to physically install the client on that user's system. Since we are writing to a browser, we assume that everyone has the browser and we can easily distribute the application across our value chain. The browser in turn makes whatever requests are necessary to the operating system. The benefit is that the browser developer, not the software developer, deals with the differences between the different operating systems.

This gives rise to another technological benefit, the portal. Consider what the portal does. It takes the interface to separate applications and combines them into one Web page. From one Web page, a user can access email, reports, external Web sites, and internal applications. Most important, the user is not aware of moving between *applications*, but is simply linking to another page on the Web site. This is extraordinarily important to the designer of IEBI systems. Consider the average decision maker. These are management types, not technicians. The IEBI system must be as simple as possible, not because of any lack of intelligence on the part of the decision maker, but because of a lack of interest. The decision maker wants to get to the point. What's the bottom line? Anything more than a few steps will cause him or her to delegate the task to a subordinate, thus diminishing the value of the IEBI system.

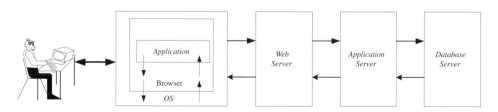

**FIGURE 5.11**   Client–browser–server relationship.

These technological benefits lead directly to financial benefits. First, we see that a pervasive client has significant cost savings. The application is written to one environment. This means one set of code to write and maintain. The implication of this, of course, is one programming staff, which is perhaps the most expensive software development resource.

The second financial benefit is a higher return on investment. Earlier, we stated that an information portal makes a simple interface from which the decision maker can easily gather information from a number of sources. We also noted that without such an interface, there is a high probability that the decision maker would gladly delegate the gathering of this information to a subordinate. We need to reemphasize a point made earlier: It is important to the value of the IEBI system that the primary user be the decision maker. Why? One of the shortcomings of IEBI in the mainframe era was that the decision maker had to go through an intermediary to gather data. In the Internet age, why would we settle for creating an intermediary in order to gather data from the system? In effect, we would be returning to the days of mainframes when the consumer of the data and the person who generated it were two separate people. The establishment of a portal gives the decision maker easy access to BI. This ease of access means that the decision maker is the primary user, thus increasing the overall system value. This portal into the business environment creates a single consolidated view of the business. This leads us to the final and perhaps the most important force leading to the development of IEBI: the political force.

We can see how the Internet has satisfied the desires of the major political factions within an organization by returning to our earlier discussion of information governances. We noted that there are three types: dictatorship, anarchy, and democracy. Information dictatorship forced the decision maker to go to a third party for information. We just discussed how such an environment reduces the value of IEBI. In the age of information anarchy, while each department may have been empowered with its own systems, there were significant barriers to establishing an enterprise-wide view of the organization. The decision maker could not get a consolidated view of the entire organization. IEBI moves us from anarchy to democracy. It provides us with the ultimate solution for decision maker.

IEBI threads the eye of the proverbial needle. On the one hand, we have centralized control of information. Rather than a plethora of independent data marts, we have a central data warehouse. Should the need arise for a separate data mart, we establish a dependent data mart. At the same time, the Internet provides us with universal access to this central repository. Universal access has the connotation of access to output, but it is only part of the story. Universal access also means the ability to provide input from any system within the organization as well.

How does this create a political force that moved organizations to Internet enablement? Let's begin by understanding that individual department managers didn't care. Voltaire noted how little one individual is truly concerned with another; it is only when an individual's needs are threatened that one develops a true concern. Basically, what's in it for me? While this is a very pessimistic view of human nature, one cannot help to see a good deal of truth in this sentiment. Department managers weren't concerned. They had their own little information fiefdoms that were meeting their needs. Centralization was the last thing on their minds. If the individual department manager wasn't concerned, then who was? Where did the political force originate? The political force behind centralization of information came from the people who were most affected, the C-level executive, the center of the corporate structure.

While a fragmented information infrastructure may have served the needs of the individual departments, it in no way met the needs of central management. There was no enterprise-wide view. How many C-level executives are challenged with the question, Who are my top ten customers? Only a centralized information infrastructure could answer this question with any amount of certainty. Second, each department built its own independent mini-IT departments. These redundant departments generated greater cost to the organization. In short, these organizations had higher cost and lower effectiveness. The C-level executive, desiring an enterprise-wide view of the organization, drove the organization to developing a centralized information infrastructure.

## 5.5  The Oracle 9 Internet Application Server

The Oracle 9iAS is an excellent example of both an application server that is available to developers to develop their own applications and a platform for Oracle applications. The Oracle 9iAS is designed to be an environment in which multiple applications can be integrated into one *portal*. Users are able to access data from browsers or wireless devices to view both unstructured and structured data. Figure 5.12 presents the structure of the Oracle 9iAS.

### 5.5.1  APPLICATION SERVER CACHE

Let's begin by relating the features of the Oracle 9iAS with the discussion in the previous section. In Figure 5.12 we note that there is not only a cache between the application server and the database, but between the Web server and the client. In a sense, the application server is *surrounded* by cache. The Web cache stores both static and dynamic HTML pages. If a page requested by a user is in the Web cache, it is sent directly from the Web cache. Of course, the Web cache cannot store all the pages for a particular Web site. The cache must be cleared of old or outdated pages.

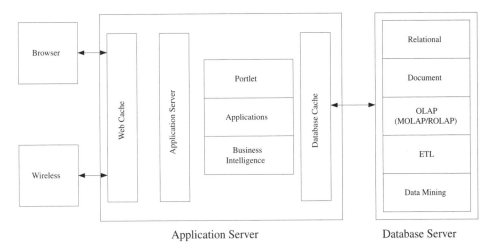

Application Server             Database Server

**FIGURE 5.12** Oracle 9iAS.

The Oracle 9iAS uses a heuristic algorithm to determine which pages need to be refreshed from the Web server. The algorithm uses two variables for every page. The first is a priority variable to establish how important any change may be to a Web page. The second is a validity flag to signal when the data is outdated or invalid and needs refreshing. The first may indicate a cosmetic change, such as a graphic image, font, or color layout. While these changes are nice, they are not critical to the correctness of the data on the page. Consequently, we may give these pages a low priority. We would like to see the change, but it is not critical that it occur immediately. The second flag, when checked, notes that the data on the Web page is no longer valid and must to be updated. For example, we may have a Web site that provides information about our organization along with our price list. At some point in time, we change our company logo along with several prices in the price list. When a user comes to our Web site, we would not want the entire cache purged and repopulated from the Web server. This could quite possibly bring down the Web server. Instead, when a page is accessed, we check to see if the page is valid. If the current cache page is invalid, it is deleted from cache and a newer, valid page is requested from the Web server. If the page is valid, but has a low update priority, the activity on the Web server is checked to see if there are pages being downloaded that are of a higher priority. If the Web server is too busy, the current cached page is sent to the client. If the Web server is available, a new page is retrieved.

Consider what this means in relation to IEBI. The application server builds user-requested pages, storing them in the Web cache upon creation. As the user drills down, the new pages are also loaded into the cache. As we proceed back up through the aggregated data, as users quite often do, the cached pages are sent to the user, eliminating the need to access the Web server.

The application server also maintains a database cache, which sits between the application and database servers and maintains complete database tables so that queries can be processed completely on the application server. This is very important to IEBI. For example, Oracle provides pre-aggregation of data through materialized views and summation tables. We can cache the materialized views in the database cache on the application server. The majority of queries are fulfilled by the application server, freeing the data warehouse server resources to meet requests that are more demanding. Only when the user requests data that is down to the deepest level of detail do we need to perform a query against the actual data warehouse database.

## 5.5.2  CUSTOMIZABLE PORTAL PAGES

Another important aspect of the Oracle9iAS is the ability to create an information portal. We discussed the concept of information anarchy, an environment where there is an explosion of information systems and no centralized control of the data. We see symptoms of that anarchy in the Internet-enabled information infrastructure of many of today's organizations. There is a multitude of Web sites and Internet applications throughout the organization. Finding a specific piece of information is near impossible because each department has its own site. Even when you know where to find the information, every time you go to a different Web site, you have to log on to yet another system.

Now consider the needs of the decision maker. He or she may require reports on a daily basis. Perhaps the decision maker uses a multidimensional analysis tool. In addition, the C-level executive may be interested in viewing the company's Balanced Scorecard. A manufacturing executive may be interested in analyzing production costs using the Activity Based Management tools or in doing profitability analysis on a particular region or product line. Even in the best of situations, where the Web sites to access these applications are bookmarked in the user's browser, they would still require separate logons.

This is where the portal comes into play. The term portal is freely bantered about in the marketplace. A portal establishes a single, personalized Web site from which the user can access any number of applications. The Oracle9iAS provides an extensible framework for bringing together applications and business information into a single personalized Web page; it is in effect a single point of access to information. Note that from this one page the strategist has access to a balanced scorecard application, reports, alerts, email, multidimensional analysis tools, and activity-based management systems.

What is important about this environment is that to the user, this is simply his or her Web page. The fact that he or she is accessing multiple applications in different parts of the world is invisible to the user. He or she may have no concept of which applications are providing which information. It is all one integrated environment. How does the Oracle9iAS make this happen? *Portlets!*

As we noted, the portal is a framework. Into this framework fit the portlets, reusable interface components that provide access to Web-based resources. These resources can include any Web page, application, BI report, syndicated content feed, hosted software service, or resource. Companies can create their own portlets or acquire third-party portlets from such companies as Cognos and Business Objects. What is key is that the user is provided a seamless environment or console from which the organization's environment can be analyzed.

We need to emphasize this point, not only in relation to the Oracle9iAS, but to IEBI in general. It is critical to the success of IEBI that the decision makers interact with the data. It is up to the architect of the IEBI system to lower whatever barriers there are between decision makers and the strategic information they need to do their jobs. With the IEBI portal, the decision maker has the complete complement of BI tools at his or her disposal.

If we were to play this out in a typical business scenario, the decision maker may note on his site that a key performance indicator in the balanced scorecard is out of range. Perhaps profitability for a particular product is down. From this page, the decision maker goes into the activity-based management tool and determines that the cost to manufacture the product has risen dramatically. In tracing through the activity costs, he notes that the capacity of a particular manufacturing facility has been exceeded, forcing production to run an additional shift. The decision maker then refers to the multidimensional analysis tool, where he discovers excess capacity at another nearby facility. He then sends an email to the production manager concerning what has been discovered. As far as the user is concerned, this was all done from one application, the IEBI portal. In reality, the decision maker has accessed five different applications. The important part is that we have given the decision maker a way to interact with the data.

## 5.6 Conclusion

In this chapter, we discussed three different types of architectures: mainframes, client/server, and the Internet. We learned how the inaccessibility of data within the mainframe gave rise to client/server computing and how client/server evolved into Internet-enabled computing. Rather than seeing the Internet as something new and different, we have come to see the Internet-enabled application as the next step in the evolution of client/server. The server takes on more of the processing, leaving the client primarily to manage the user interface.

We should make no mistake about the mainframe: These systems aren't quite dead yet. They will continue to serve as sources of legacy information and in some instances as repositories of information for IEBI systems. In these latter cases, the mainframe will be surrounded by middle-tier applications that provide Internet capabilities. Moving forward, we will see the mainframe playing a dwindling role. The lack of accessibility to data and the inflexibility of the system will bring about its ultimate demise. Many have made this prediction, and mainframe supporters quickly point out how wrong they have been. In the long run, the shrinking mainframe market will reduce investment in the technology to the point where it will fall so far behind that it will no longer be a viable alternative.

# Chapter 6

# THE INTERNET NETWORK

*It is a fact or I have dreamt it – that by means of electricity, the world of matter has become a great nerve, vibrating thousands of miles in a breathless point of time?*
—*Nathaniel Hawthorne*
The House of Seven Gables

Did you know that the size of the booster rockets for the space shuttle was determined by the size of a horse's backside? You see, the length of a wagon axle was based on the width of the horses pulling the wagon. As the wagons traveled along the roads, they would wear ruts into the road, making it difficult for wagons whose axle length was something other than the standard. Soon, everyone was making all their axles the same length. When trains came along, they of course made the axles for the railroad cars the standard length. This in turn determined the space between the rails. The tunnels that trains went through were based on the standard width of railroad cars. Since the booster rockets for the space shuttle were transported by train, it could be no larger than a train tunnel's opening. So, the width of the space shuttle's booster rockets is based on the size of a horse's backside.

So what about Hawthorne's great nerve? The national information infrastructure as described by Don Tapscott in *The Digital Economy* becomes *the means by which the world of matter* develops this nerve. As companies integrate their information systems into the national information infrastructure, we develop the one nervous system that creates the one virtual organization. We have been saying this right along. So what are the pieces that make up that infrastructure? How do the pieces work together, and why do they work that way? In order for all these pieces to work together, somewhere along the way, someone had to establish a single standard. Where is the backside of the Internet's horse? (I can't believe I wrote that.)

Internet standards did happen by design, and not just by accident. In this chapter, we discuss some of the organizations that defined these standards and how these standards are involved in the workings of the Internet.

This chapter discusses how the Internet works. So often, we spend time discussing the Internet and this global network that we forget it is, in its own way, a work of art. This is not hyperbole. The technical aspects of the Internet, two systems on opposite sides of the planet speaking with one another, are truly fascinating. To some this may be basic networking concepts, but if we are going to talk about Internet Enabled Business Intelligence (IEBI), we should at least ensure that we are certain of how the Internet functions.

## 6.1 Standards Bodies

A variety of standards bodies govern the exchange of information over networks. Some are established by government agencies, such as the Department of Defense and the National Bureau of Standards, an agency of the United States Department of Commerce. Other standards organizations have more of an international scope, such as the Institute of Electronics and Electrical Engineers (IEEE), the International Telecommunications Union (ITU), and the International Organization for Standardization (ISO). Each organization has had its input into establishing a standard for network communications.

Perhaps one of the most interesting of these organizations is the International Organization for Standardization. It has been in existence since 1947 and is a non-governmental organization dedicated to promoting standards. Its mission is to develop an international set of standards to facilitate the trade of goods and services.

You have to love this organization—it is always thinking. You may notice that we refer to this organization as ISO, and not IOS. The group realized that the acronym IOS wouldn't translate well. After all, the translation for standardization into Italian or German may not start with an S, and who's to say that the ordering of the words would even be the same. Instead, it chose ISO from the Greek *isos*, meaning equal. Through standardization, we establish equality. All vendors are free to compete in an open, nonproprietary market. ISO is a standards organization that began by standardizing its name.

ISO is well known for standards in a variety of industries. ISO standards include film speed code; telephone and banking cards; standardized freight containers; safety wire ropes; international codes for country names, currencies, and languages; and paper sizes. ISO has even established a standard for the size of screw threads. In some industries, they are best known for the ISO 9000, a standard methodology for quality management and quality assurance.

ISO is a member of the International Telecommunications Union, which was established in 1865 and later became an agency of the United Nations. This organization's scope is a bit narrower than that of ISO. The ITU's focus is on international treaties, regulations, and standards for telecommunications. Prior to 1992, standardization was managed by a subgroup known as the Consultative Committee for International Telegraphy and Telephony (CCITT). As of 1992, however, CCITT ceased to exist as a separate subgroup.

Organizations such as ISO and ITU are critical to the future of the Internet. The Internet is a communications medium that spans the globe. The charter of the ITU is to establish international cooperation and develop technical facilities so that all nations can benefit from improved communications. ITU is also tasked with providing technical assistance to developing nations. We need to stop and consider the benefits of such a mission. We discussed how the Internet benefits the individual organization or company trying to compete in a global economy. The same holds true for entire countries. In fact, the benefits are multiplied. As developing nations come online, they have greater access to markets where they can sell their goods and services. They also have greater access to information, providing them with the technical knowledge to improve the processes used to manufacture and deliver. Ultimately, this benefits everyone. Industrialized nations benefit as well. They gain new trading partners. As they gain new sources of goods and services, they develop markets within those emerging nations—entire new populations ready for our goods and services.

The final organization we will discuss is the IEEE. Back in my undergraduate days, when I had a lot less experience and a lot more hair, IEEE was the first professional organization of which I became a member. The organization is a leader in such areas as telecommunications, aerospace, computer engineering, and biomedical technology. It is composed of 36 *societies,* or subgroups, and four technical councils. In addition to technical publishing and conferences, the organization is also responsible for creating a number of consensus-based standards.

The remainder of this chapter examines the standards that were developed by each of these organizations. We will discuss the Open Systems Interconnection (OSI) reference model developed by ISO. We will compare the Transmission Control Protocol/Internet Protocol (TCP/IP) to this model. We will then use the model to examine the technology used to build the Internet.

## 6.2   The ISO/OSI Reference Model

How do you swallow an elephant? A bite at a time. This is the methodology used by ISO in developing a reference model for network communications. The OSI reference model is a guideline for the functionality of networking standards and protocols. Figure 6.1 presents the structure of this reference model. It divides the problem of communicating between systems into individual, bite-sized tasks. These subtasks are represented as layers in the reference model. It then solves each subtask. The stacks in the figure each reside on a separate system. An individual layer in the stack on one system communicates with that same layer on the other system. Communications between the two layers is carried out indirectly through the lower levels of the model.

For example, an application in one system wishes to communicate with an application in another. To carry out this communication, the application communicates to the presentation layer that in turn communicates with the session layer. This process repeats until the message passes between the two systems over the physical layer. The message then makes its way up the stack to the presentation layer on the destination system.

In Chapter 5, we showed how Internet-enabled applications interact with the browser. The browser in turn invokes the operating system. We can see how the communication proceeds down from the application layer of one system, across the network, and back up the stack to the destination application. In reviewing the model, we should note that this is a *reference model*; it is not a specification for a particular protocol or implementation. We use this reference model as a way to understand and organize other protocols and standards.

To understand this model more fully, let's review the function of each layer.

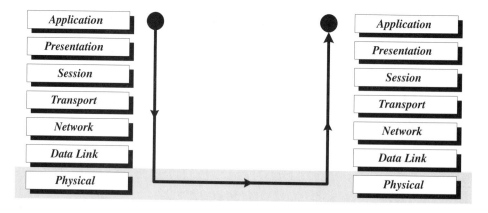

**FIGURE 6.1**   ISO/OSI reference model.

1. **Physical**—Defines the actual hardware connection between systems. Physical specifications include specification of the connector type. Is it a USB port, RS-232, or RJ-49? These are all different types of connectors. The physical layer also describes the electrical specification between systems. Is the network analog or digital? It describes something about that actual physical connection between systems.

2. **Data Link**—Organizes the stream of bits it receives from the physical layer into *frames*. A frame is composed of a header and trailer that contain control information. The data link layer, in addition to detecting errors in the data, controls the flow of information between the systems.

3. **Network**—This layer's task is to move information across the network. The network layer examines the network layer address of a packet of information and passes it on to the next subnetwork within the Internet via a router.

4. **Transport**—This layer provides reliable delivery of data across the network. Note that there is a significant difference between *ensuring reliable delivery* and *guaranteeing delivery* of data. The transport layer will detect when a message is not acknowledged as having been received by the destination system. It then informs the session layer and allows the upper layers to take whatever action may be necessary.

5. **Session**—This layer controls the flow of information between the systems. It manages the dialog between the systems that are communicating with one another.

6. **Presentation**—The presentation layer converts the bits into something meaningful. It is at the presentation layer that the data is compressed or encrypted.

7. **Application**—The final layer, the application layer, manages the communication between the user or application and the network. The application layer includes virtual terminals and mail transfer services.

As information proceeds down through the ISO/OSI reference model, each layer may add a header and in some cases a trailer to the data. This additional information is used to communicate to the corresponding layer on the destination system. For example, the data link layer, which is responsible for detecting errors in the data, might add parity bits to the message as it passes from the network layer to the physical layer. The data link layer on the destination system will take the data it receives from the physical layer and reconstruct the header built on the originating system. It is then able to use this header information to detect errors and possibly correct them.

Let's look at one more example to demonstrate this point. We noted that a cookie is a block of text. An application may generate a message containing a cookie. This message is composed of the cookie itself and some control information contained in the message header. The presentation layer encrypts the entire message, including the header created by the application layer. Once the message is encrypted, the presentation layer adds its own headers and trailer. The presentation layer on the destination system uses this to unscrambled the encrypted message. The session level receives the message from the presentation layer, complete with the presentation layer header, and passes it on to the transport layer. The transport layer adds its own set of headers and trailers to create a segment. The segment is passed to the network layer, which constructs a datagram by adding its own headers and trailer. The data link builds a frame, which is passed to the physical layer, where the frame is passed to the destination system as a stream of bits.

The destination system performs the same functions in reverse. The stream of bits is used to construct a frame. The control information in the header and trailer of the frame tells the data link layer how to process the data contained in the frame. The cookie proceeds up the ISO/OSI stack, with each layer peeling off the associated header. Finally, the cookie arrives at the application layer, where it is received by the destination application. We will discuss the concept of packets again later in this chapter.

## 6.3    IEEE 802 Specifications

As we noted in the previous section, the ISO/OSI reference model is not a specification for a network protocol. The ISO standards body instead developed a model, or a framework, for components of a network protocol. The IEEE, however, did define such a specification with the IEEE Project 802. This specification addressed the two lower layers of the ISO/OSI model, the physical and data link layers. The following is a list of some of the IEEE 802 standards specifications:

802.1    System Management & Internetworking

802.2    Logical Link Control

802.3    Media Access Control/Ethernet

802.4    Token Bus

802.5    Token Ring

802.6    Metropolitan Area Networks

802.7    Broadband

802.8    Fiber Optic

802.9    Integrated Voice & Data

802.10  LAN Security

We will not examine these standards in any detail here. Later, when discussing how we communicate over the Internet, we will review the relevant standards. The rest have been included here so that we can understand the context in which they reside.

## 6.4  TCP/IP

Let's revisit the purpose of a communications protocol. The intent is to provide a means by which two systems can communicate with one another. To establish this communication, they must both agree on a common language and syntax. The objective of the ISO/OSI reference model is to identify the pieces of the communication upon which agreement must be made. The protocol itself is the language and syntax that fits within that reference model. The protocol that has become the lingua franca of the Internet is TCP/IP.

TCP/IP was defined by the Networking Working Group in 1971 and integrated into the UNIX operating system shortly thereafter. The specifics of a TCP/IP implementation are defined in *Request For Comments* (RFCs). As the name implies, these documents invite users and concerned parties to make proposals and recommendations for new protocols and improvements to existing ones.

Figure 6.2 presents TCP/IP's alignment with the ISO/OSI reference model. The TCP/IP suite is composed of four layers, each of which corresponds to one or more layers of the ISO/OSI reference model. The process/application layer corresponds to the application, presentation, and session layers. Within this layer, we find the different applications that are part of the TCP/IP suite, such as the File Transfer Protocol (FTP), the Trivial File Transfer Protocol (TFTP), Telnet, and the Simple Mail Transfer Protocol (SMTP). FTP is described by RFC 959, TFTP by RFC 1350, Telnet by RFC 854, and SMTP by RFC 2821.

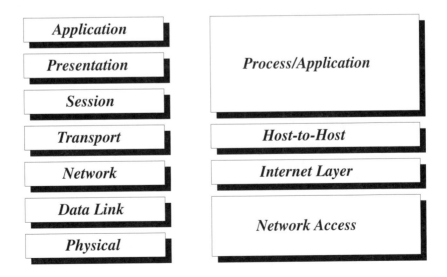

**FIGURE 6.2**  TCP/IP.

The next layer in the suite is the Host-to-Host layer that corresponds to the Transport layer of the ISO/OSI reference model. The TCP of TCP/IP resides at this layer in the protocol suite. Recall that the Transport layer is responsible for reliable delivery of data across the network. This is the job of TCP. It creates the packets and ensures that they are acknowledged by the destination system. RFC 793 describes this protocol in detail. Another protocol residing at the Host-to-Host layer in the TCP/IP suite is the User Defined Protocol (UDP), as described in RFC 768. UDP differs from TCP in that it does not require an acknowledgment on the part of the destination system.

The Internet layer of the TCP/IP suite corresponds to the Network layer of the ISO/OSI reference model. Again, thinking back to the ISO/OSI discussion, we see that this layer's task is to move information across the network. The network layer examines the network layer address of a packet of information and passes it on to the next subnetwork via a router. It is at the Internet layer that we find the Internet Protocol (IP). IP fragments the packets into datagrams, routes them to the destination system, and reassembles inbound datagrams into packets.

The final layer of the TCP/IP suite is the Network Access layer. This layer corresponds to the Data Link and Physical layers of the ISO/OSI reference model. The Network Access layer establishes the physical connection between the networked systems. The IEEE standards we discussed in the previous section described the different network topologies that establish this connection. The IEEE 802.3 standard describes the Ethernet bus topology, while IEEE 802.4 describes a token bus and IEEE 802.5 describes a token ring.

## 6.5 Talking Over the Internet

We now know that a communications protocol establishes the way in which two systems communicate with one another over a network. We also know that TCP/IP is a standard protocol that has become the lingua franca of the Internet. So, what does this mean to us? How does TCP/IP enable us to use something like *www.bowlingwithbilly.com* to access another system on the network? The answer is something quite amazing—amazing that it works. There are three basic elements that we use to accomplish this communication: the hardware address, the TCP/IP address, and the domain name. We will examine each of these in more detail in the following subsections.

### 6.5.1 HARDWARE ADDRESS

When we start sending messages around the world, common sense tells us that we need a way to identify the destination of each message. This is the destination address. One would think that the URL above would be sufficient for communication. While text strings work well for people, they really aren't very efficient for systems. We need a way to uniquely identify everything that is sitting on our network. This is where it starts to get amazing. *Burned* into every Network Interface Card (NIC) is a 6-byte address. The first 3 bytes of that address is the identification number of the manufacturer of the card. Figure 6.3 gives a graphical representation of where hardware addresses fit into this scheme. If we were to remove this card from System A and put it in System B, the hardware address moves with the card. This is true for no matter where we go in the world. If we were to move a system from the San Diego office to the Sydney, Australia, office, the system keeps the same hardware address. How does our protocol use this address to communicate?

The TCP/IP passes frames between systems. Each frame contains the hardware address of the destination system. Figure 6.4 demonstrates the construction of a TCP/IP frame. The data is passed by the application to the Host-to-Host layer, which in the case of this example is TCP. If we were transferring a file using TFTP, we would be using UDP. TCP adds a TCP header and passes a message to the Internet layer using IP. The Internet layer adds an IP header to the message, creating a packet that is passed to the Network Access layer. Note that the IP Header contains the IP address of the source and destination system. This layer builds a frame that contains the destination and source addresses of the frame. In addition, the Network Access layer adds some control information. By adding this hardware address in the frame, we have identified specifically which NIC on the entire face of the earth is to receive this frame of data.

We now have the two ends of the spectrum. On the one end, we have the hardware address, which is convenient for the computer. The trouble is that the hardware address is not so friendly to people. On the other end, we have a name, like *www.bowlingwithbilly.com*, something with which people like to deal, but isn't very convenient for computer systems. The next step, therefore, is for us to find a way to map between the two.

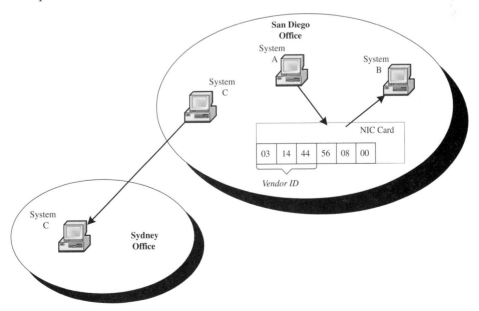

**FIGURE 6.3** Hardware address.

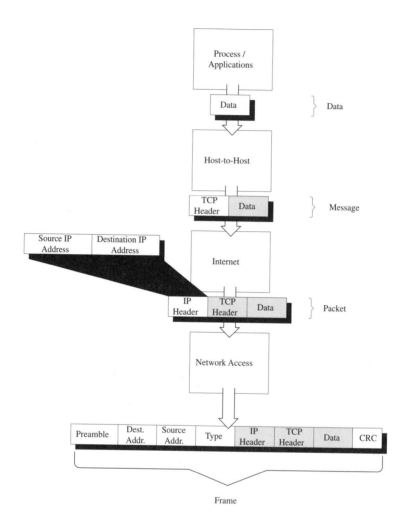

**FIGURE 6.4** TCP/IP frame construction.

## 6.5.2 DOMAIN NAME SYSTEM (DNS)

When we request a file through a Web browser, we're asking for a specific file on a specific computer somewhere on the Internet. To understand this more fully, let's look at an example. Summer is on the way and we want to check out the latest in suntan oil. Naturally, we turn to our dear old alma mater for advice by entering the Uniform Resource Locator (URL) *http://oil.tanning.malibu.edu/products/ study.html* in our browser. While it may read like another intimidating piece of computer-ese, compared to a hardware address, the URL has greatly simplified the way we find information on the Internet. The core technology behind the URL is the Domain Name System (DNS), that magical entity that allows us to find a specific computer on the Internet by simply typing its name.

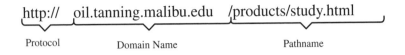

http://  oil.tanning.malibu.edu  /products/study.html

Protocol        Domain Name              Pathname

**FIGURE 6.5**  Uniform resource locator.

The three main components of a URL are shown in Figure 6.5. The first is the protocol. This specifies the protocol we will use when accessing the file on the remote system. The most commonly used protocols are HTTP, HTTPS (HTTP Secure), and FTP. Next is the domain name, which identifies the specific system we wish to access on the Internet. Finally, we have the pathname to the file on that system we wish to access. We can look at this URL and see that we plan to use the HTTP protocol to access the file *products/study.html* on the computer *oil.tanning.malibu.edu*.

Notice that .edu is appended to the end of the system name; this is the *generic domain name*. The DNS uses this extension to locate the desired computer on the Internet. The DNS is a hierarchy of systems. Figure 6.6 shows the structure of this hierarchy. Each node in the hierarchy is identified by a label that can be up to 63 characters long; names are formed from the bottom up to the root. In our example, we have our alma mater Malibu State. We can see that there are three departments at the school: surfing, computer science, and tanning. The tanning department has two computers, bambi and oil. The computer science department has a database server named data and a computer for business intelligence applications named bi. A *fully qualified name* is unique throughout the entire Internet and ends with a period. The fully qualified names for these systems would therefore be *bambi.tanning.malibu.edu., oil.tanning.malibu.edu., bi.cs.malibu.edu.,* and *data.cs.malibu.edu.*

Names that do not end with a "." are *relative domain names* and are converted to fully qualified domain names by appending the local domain information. It is unusual to see the "." at the end of a URL. Typically, we end domain names with

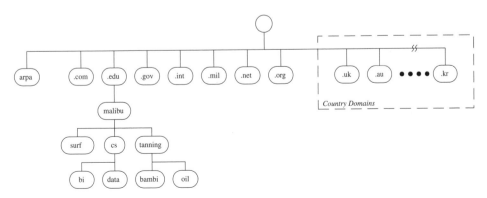

**FIGURE 6.6**  DNS hierarchy.

the generic domain name and the "." is implied. Since the only node in the DNS hierarchy above a generic domain name is the root node, there is little real meaningful difference between the two.

We refer to *malibu.edu* as the *domain,* the name under which all of Malibu State's computers are registered. The various departments divide the domain into *subdomains.* Subdomains allow Malibu to have two computers with the same name (remember, we're computer geeks—half of our computers are named after *Star Trek* characters), yet still be identified by different fully qualified names.

As we look across this hierarchy, we see the top-level domains displayed under the root node. There are two categories of top-level domains. The first are the *generic* or *organizational* domains, such as .com and .edu. These domains, listed in Table 6.1, are also referred to as the U.S. domains. They form the foundation on which all United States-based domain names are built (although some, such as .com, are truly international).

**TABLE 6.1**  Generic Domains

| Domain | Description |
| --- | --- |
| .com | Commercial organizations |
| .edu | Educational organizations |
| .gov | Agencies of the U.S. government |
| .int | International organizations |
| .mil | United States military |
| .net | Networks |
| .org | Miscellaneous organizations |
| .biz | Newer versions of .com |
| .info | Miscellaneous domains |
| .name | Personal sites |

The second group is composed of the geographic domains, such as .uk and .kr (the United Kingdom and Korea respectively). They serve to organize the names of computers residing in the rest of the world. You may note that there is no .US domain. You may also note that we use certain terms interchangeably. In fact, every domain is also a subdomain relative to the top-level domains, and even they are subdomains relative to the root. Fully qualified names are also considered a kind of domain name, except that rather than organizing a network, they designate a computer.

As one could therefore imagine, the number of domain names is rather large. Remember, these names include not only the names of all the Web sites on the World Wide Web, but the names of all the computers that are linked to the Internet. If we were to take into consideration just the servers in all the universities in the United States, the number of domain names would be enormous. The solution, of course, is to delegate the administration of parts of the DNS hierarchy. The Internet Corporation for Assigned Names and Numbers (ICANN) accredits companies who in turn are charged with maintaining the top portion of the hierarchy. These registrars are responsible for distributing unique domain names under their assigned top-level domains. A domain may be comprised of a single university, such as Malibu State, or a commercial entity such as *bowlingwithbilly.com*. Once the domain name is registered, it is the owner's responsibility to create any desired subdomains.

To understand how domains are administered, let's refer to Figure 6.7. The administration of a domain requires that a *primary name server* and one or more *secondary name servers* be established for the domain. The role of the primary domain server is to maintain a database of host (i.e., computer) names and the IP address of each system identified by those names. These servers receive requests for the IP address of a system with a particular domain name through a domain query. Browsers, for example, generate domain queries to locate Web sites. When the name server receives a query for an IP address, it searches its local database for the domain name. If the server has the IP address, it passes the result back to the requestor.

Often, the name server is unable to satisfy the request by itself. Each name server in the Internet knows the location of the *root* or *top-level* name servers. A root name server contains the name and location of each second-level domain server. For example, the root name server for .edu contains the address of the name server(s) for the *malibu.edu* domain. When a name server receives a request for a domain name that is not in its database, that name server makes a request of a root name server. The root name server returns the location of a second-level name server. The original name server then queries the second-level name server. This continues for each subdomain (*malibu.edu* to *tanning.malibu.edu*) until the IP address associated with the fully qualified name is found. The local name server then caches the domain name along with its associated IP address in its local database. In this way, the next request for this name or for any of the subdomains it encountered along the way can be resolved more quickly.

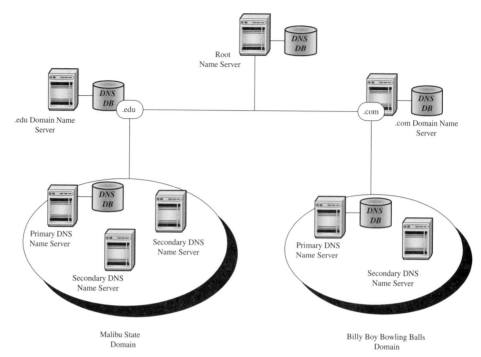

**FIGURE 6.7**   Domain administration.

### 6.5.3   THE IP ADDRESS

Although we have an address for the computer with which we wish to communicate, we do not have the address we need. There is the natural tendency to wonder why, if we are able to map the fully qualified name to an IP address, don't we cut out the "middle man" and simply map the name to the hardware address. The problem with a hardware address is that it is based on the individual NIC card; there is no relationship between the hardware address and where the system sits on the network. Remember, we can move these systems around at will. The hardware address does nothing to help us locate our destination system.

The IP address of a system is a logical address divided into 4 bytes. Anyone who has ever configured a system for network communication is familiar with IP addresses. Typically, we see the IP addresses written in *dotted decimal notation,* where the IP address is represented as a set of four decimal numbers between 0 and 255. Each decimal number is separated by a period. An IP address might be something like 128.204.122.098.

Figure 6.8 shows the structure of an IP address. There are three classes of IP addresses. A zero in the first *bit* of the 4-byte string indicates a Class A IP address. The first byte of a Class A IP address contains a network address and the remaining three bytes contain the address of a node on that network. Class B addresses

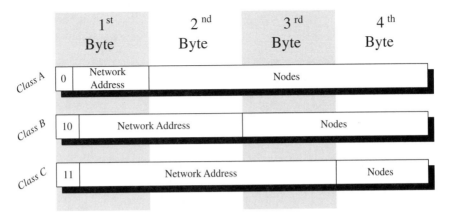

**FIGURE 6.8** IP addressing.

are indicated by 10 in the first two bits of the IP address. Class B network addresses are 14-bit long (bits 3 through 8 of byte 1 plus byte 2). The last two bytes of a Class B network contain the node address. Class C addresses are indicated by 11 in the first two bits. The remaining bits in the first byte, plus bytes 2 and 3 contain the network address, with the last byte reserved for the node address.

The IP address now gives us a way to locate the destination system. We can see how IP addresses are used to locate systems on the Internet in Figure 6.9. Let us assume that the user on the system with the IP address 201.109.103.211 would like to FTP a file to the user on the system with the IP address 201.109.103.212. As the message containing the data is passed from TCP in the Host-to-Host layer to the Internet layer, IP adds the IP header with the destination system's IP address. The Internet layer then uses the Address Resolution Protocol (ARP) to map the IP address to the hardware address on the destination system's NIC.

ARP maintains a table that maps IP addresses to hardware addresses. When a message is composed with an unknown IP address, a broadcast is sent to all the nodes on the network, requesting that they identify themselves. The hardware address of both the source and destination systems are added to the frame header, and the message is sent to the destination system.

This is rather simple if we are all residing on the same network. The challenge occurs when we attempt to communicate with a system on another network. Let's say that now instead of sending the file to a system on the same network, our user wishes to FTP that same file to the server with the IP address 221.120.221.102. Of course, our user identifies the server using its name. DNS provides IP with the IP address of the destination server, which is added to the IP header of the packet. Since the network address of the destination is different than that of the source, we know that we have to send the data through a router.

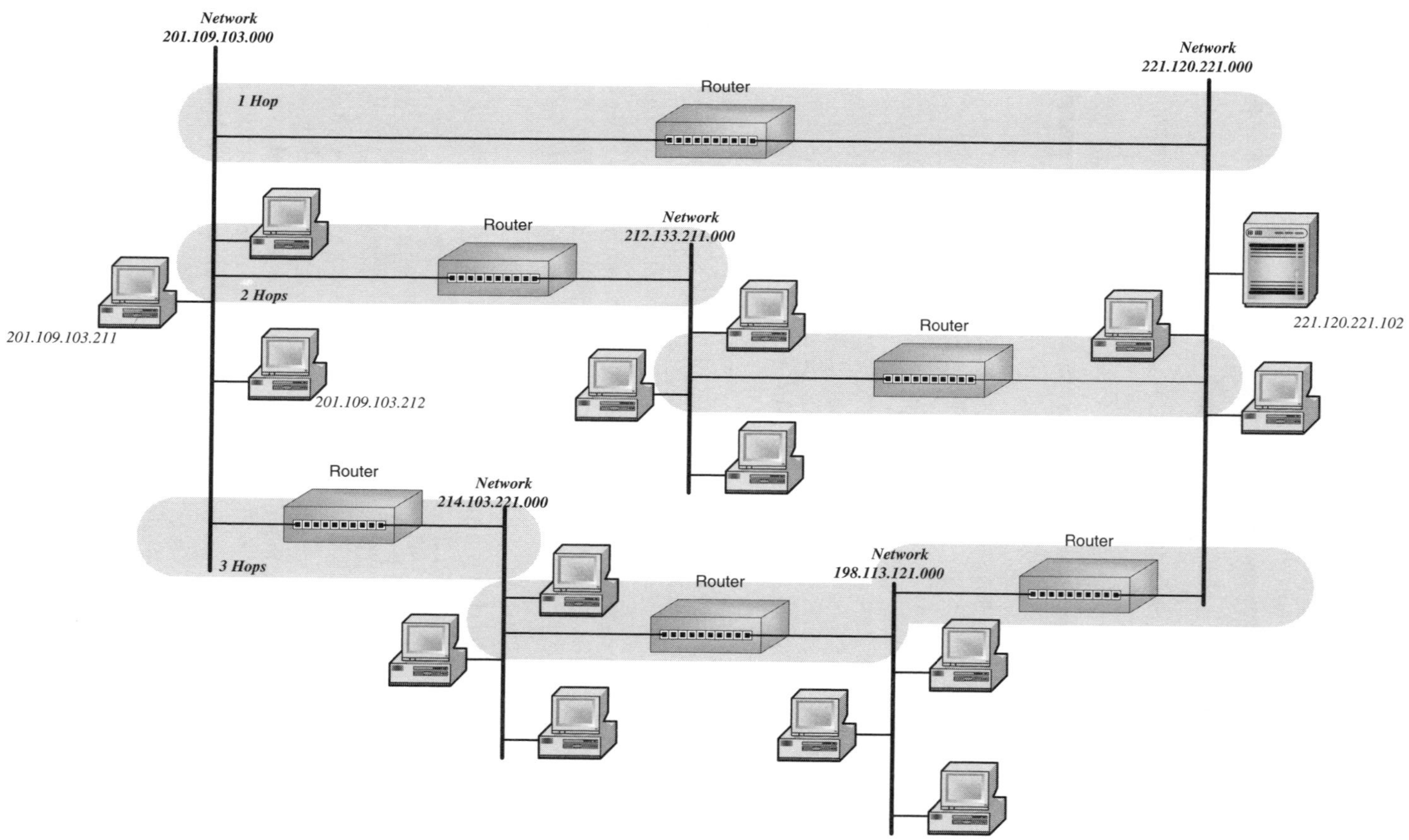

**FIGURE 6.9** Frame routing.

Network
221.120.221.000

221.120.221.102

Router

Network
198.113.121.000

Router

Router

Network
212.133.211.000

Router

Network
214.103.221.000

Router

Router

Network
201.109.103.000

1 Hop

2 Hops

201.109.103.212

3 Hops

201.109.103.211

134

Routers use the Routing Information Protocol (RIP) to keep informed of the different networks to which it is connected. This information is contained within the router's routing table. In addition, the routing table includes the number of *hops* it takes to get to a particular network. The number of hops indicates how many networks through which the data must pass to reach its ultimate destination. We see in the preceding figure that the message has three alternative routes.

After determining the best route for the message, ARP determines the hardware address of the router, which is then placed in the frame header's destination address. When the router receives the frame, it examines the destination address in the IP header to determine the destination. It then creates a new frame with its own hardware address as the source address of the frame. The frame is then passed on to its destination.

## 6.6  Dynamic Host Configuration Protocol

If you have a desktop system that stays in the same office, it makes sense to give the system ownership of its own IP address. In other environments, this could be quite cumbersome. Anyone who has ever worked for a large corporation and had to travel from office to office with a laptop has experienced this. Typically, the first thing you have to do is find someone, a network administrator, who can give you an available IP address on that particular subnet. You then configure your system with the new parameters and hope that you didn't accidentally grab an IP address the administrator didn't know was used.

Dynamic Host Configuration Protocol (DHCP) simplifies this entire process. DHCP centralizes the process of distributing IP addresses. In addition to improving the lives of traveling tube-heads such as myself, DHCP simplifies the process of network administration. No longer is it necessary for administrators to maintain lists of available IP addresses. The DHCP server manages these numbers. The DHCP server also reduces the total number of required IP addresses. Although a particular network may have a potential 200 or 300 servers and laptops, only those servers connected at that point in time require an actual IP address. Depending on the nature of the office, the difference between the potential and the actual number of systems can be quite significant. In a sales or consulting office, the majority of users will typically be out of the office.

Figure 6.10 shows how DHCP provides this service. When users boot their systems, the network initialization procedure begins by searching for the DHCP server. Once the DHCP server is found, a request is made for an IP address. The server contains all the information necessary for the client's network configuration, including a pool of available addresses. After retrieving a valid IP address from the pool, the DHCP passes back to the client the IP address, the network configuration parameters, and a lease. The lease defines the duration for which the parameters are valid.

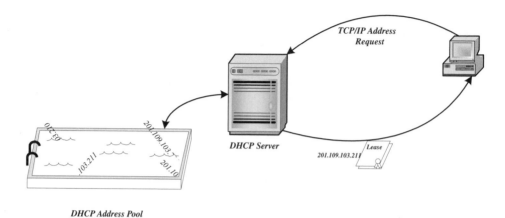

DHCP Address Pool

**FIGURE 6.10**  Dynamic host configuration protocol.

## 6.7 Conclusion

In this chapter, we learned how different organizations have come together to define standards for the Internet. ISO has developed the OSI reference model to provide a structure to define the different steps within a protocol. We also learned how the IEEE has defined the TCP/IP, which has become the common backbone of the Internet.

In our discussion on networking, we reviewed how all the pieces of the TCP/IP suite work together. We begin with the name of the resource we wish to access. Then, using DNS, we are able to find the IP address of any public resource anywhere on the Internet. The IP address tells us specifically to which network the resource belongs. For resources on our own network, we are able to use ARP to acquire the hardware address of the resource. Using the hardware address, we are able to communicate with the other system.

In the event that the resource resides on another network, the message is passed through a router. Using RIP, the router determines the most efficient path to the remote system. The router for this path communicates with the remote network on behalf of the client.

How smoothly the different pieces of the Internet work together, how well we can establish communication to distant systems, is wondrous. As we go forward in our discussion of IEBI, we should keep this in mind. We should be vitally aware of how such a complex and technical system functions with such reliability.

# Part 3

# The Software of the Internet

# Chapter 7

# Empowering the Internet-Enabled Information Infrastructure

*The galling thing about the generally poor quality of much current software is that there is no extrinsic reason for it; perfection is, in principle, possible....*

*It is only our own human frailties that limit the quality of software. We humans are not particularly adept at dealing with extremely complex situations. On the surface it may appear that large programs are rather like small ones—only bigger. Nothing, however, could be further from the truth. The complexity of programs grows at least as the square of their size. It doesn't take a very large program to be beyond our human limitations.*

—*William A. Wulf*

*Comments on "Current Practice"*

Research Directions in Software Technology[1]

---

[1] Wegner, Peter (Ed.), *Research Directions in Software Technology,* The Massachusetts Institute of Technology, 1979. Used by permission.

Software, that's what it's all about. The fastest, most advanced computer hardware in the world won't do you a bit of good without the software to drive it. While this may seem obvious, for a very long time people simply did not get it. Many still don't.

In my first programming position, I wrote software to run on a Data General computer. At the time, the company had its own proprietary operating system, a pretty darn good operating system at that. The system was so good that several companies attempted to purchase just the operating system. No big deal today, right? Back then, Data General refused to sell the operating system without the hardware. It was so adamant in its opposition that it fought and won a lawsuit in which it was accused of restraining trade.

Several years later I worked for a company that was founded by several Data General engineers. When the company's market began to flounder, I discussed with several of the marketing organizations the idea of attacking the database server market. This was back in the late 1980s when there was no clear leader in that market. At the time, the company was too focused on delivering a system based on a newer chip set to be bothered. After all, I was talking about using the old hardware to go after a market with nothing more than new software.

About 2 years ago, Data General was purchased by EMC. The server line, which eventually moved to UNIX, is now dead. My second company has faded into history. The company went belly up in the early 1990s, reduced to an imperceptible blip in the evolution of information technology. Both companies missed the point. Hardware no longer drives our industry. Instead, we are driven by the functionality of the software. The hardware has become little more than a commodity.

There is a very old, very dumb joke. A man, after 30 years of marriage, is rummaging around in his wife's closet and finds an odd-looking box. In the box he discovers two ears of corn and $300,000 in cash. He confronts his wife with his discovery. She explains that every time she had been unfaithful to him, she saved an ear of corn. Taking this in stride, he reasons that while not pleased with the discovery in the grand scheme of things, two indiscretions in the course of 30 years is not as terrible as it could be. He presses her, however, to explain the $300,000. "Well dear," she replies, "that's from trading in corn commodities."

A commodity is something in which there is little distinction, such as the corn in our story. I know farmers who can discuss at great length and in great detail the differences in corn. For most people, though, corn is corn. The distinctions made by a connoisseur are lost on us. The same is true with hardware. While the IT department may be interested in the difference between one hardware platform and another, to most end users, there is little difference.

Simple economics is engendering a process of commoditization in the computer industry. Examine the application technology stack presented in Figure 7.1. As each layer in the stack becomes standardized, the layers beneath become more of a commodity. It began with the hardware, or perhaps more accurately, with the

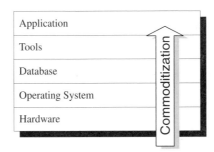

**FIGURE 7.1** Commoditization of applications.

operating system layer. At one time, hardware was the main consideration in choosing an application. The selection of one vendor or another drove an entire list of subsequent decisions. Certain applications were simply unavailable on certain platforms. With the rise of UNIX and the independence delivered by open systems, the gulf between hardware platforms narrowed. Hardware is much less of a driving force than it once was.

The same is happening with all the layers of this stack. Applications deliver the solution, not the hardware or the operating system. The applications abstract the layers beneath. Few people outside of the IT department are concerned with what lies beneath the applications. Soon, these layers will become as much of a commodity as the hardware. As a particular layer develops into a commodity, it becomes less and less restrictive of the ultimate solution.

We discussed the IEBI solution as a solution in which there are three main ingredients: the organization, the Internet, and Business Intelligence (BI). By bringing them all together in one solution, each is transformed by the others. We also discussed the hardware of the Internet. We reviewed the hardware systems and the connections between these systems that create the Internet. Upon which server the application is executing as well as where the server is physically located is irrelevant to the system user. Quite often, a single application will execute across multiple servers.

There is a very practical implication to the abstraction of these lower layers. When the hardware, operating system, and even the database become abstracted, we move closer to the goal of establishing a truly integrated information infrastructure. The abstraction of these lower layers removes the barrier that once separated applications running on different platforms. Applications hosted on one server can interact with applications on another. The interfaces to these applications can be tiered together into one common portal. One may argue that this was certainly possible in traditional two-tier client/server technology, where the level of abstraction was not nearly as high up the application technology stack. While this *may* be true, we must wonder at what cost. It may have been possible, but was it really practical? Was it really seamless? Internet enablement of the application moves the abstraction of the application technology stack to a level at which we can achieve this seamless integration.

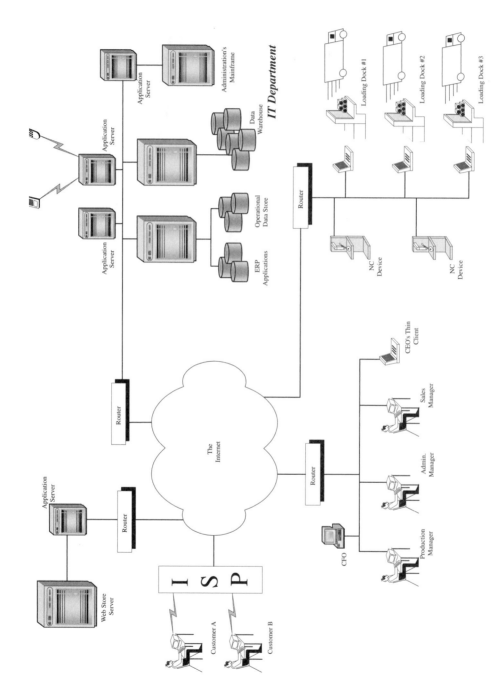

**FIGURE 7.2** Billy Boy's Internet-enabled information infrastructure.

Let's return to our good friend Billy Boy of Billy Boy Bowling Balls. The good news is that Billy has made some pretty good progress since our last visit. Realizing that his systems were a mess, he hired the world renowned CIO Miles Mody. Figure 7.2 presents the overhaul of Billy Boy Bowling Balls' information infrastructure. As we can see in the figure, all systems were centralized in the IT department. This created an information democracy, enabling individual departments to develop their own customer applications while giving IT the control required to maintain a cohesive enterprise environment.

With the exception of the administrative applications running on the mainframe, all of the applications are running on one server in the IT department. It was decided that, at the present time, the administrative mainframe applications were too expensive to replace. They were front-ended with an application server instead. This freed Billy Boy to replace the desktop systems in many departments with lower cost thin clients. This is done only when the older systems have reached the end of their useful life and need replacing. Billy Boy continues to buy laptops when managers or employees need to have a system with them when they leave the office.

The same server that supports the Enterprise Resource Planning (ERP) system also supports a class II Operational Data Store (ODS). The ODS provides management with reports that update throughout the day. A separate data warehouse has been implemented that provides long-term analysis and reporting. The data warehouse also supports the organizational data mining and personalization applications.

Billy Boy has also tied his numerically controlled devices into the information infrastructure. The devices are able to provide real-time updates on the status of production. This data is included in the daily reports supported by the ODS. It is also incorporated into the data warehouse for the more long-term analyses. Where in the past the production environment was isolated from the rest of the information infrastructure, it has now been fully integrated into the rest of the organization.

This is still all hardware. Without the appropriate applications to run in this environment, Billy Boy is not much better off than he was with the old infrastructure. If we succeed in creating a software architecture that maps to this Internet-enabled infrastructure, we will succeed in achieving what we discussed at the beginning of this chapter. The underlying hardware is abstracted. The practical effects of this abstraction means that we have a truly integrated information infrastructure. Systems are able to interact with one another regardless of which server is hosting them.

In this section we investigate the software that will provide for this integration. We begin by examining Java. Java is described as "a simple, object-oriented, network savvy, robust, secure, architecture-neutral, portable, high-performance, multithreaded, interpreted, dynamic language."[2] It is a language specifically designed for the Internet. Java is more than just a language; it is also a platform for the development of Internet-enabled applications. Developers can now develop true IEBI systems with both the Java language and environment.

There are two primary areas where Java's object orientation comes into play. First, the language provides for the abstraction of such BI functions as data mining and On-Line Analytical Processing (OLAP). Through this abstraction, the underlying OLAP, data mining, and database applications become invisible to developers. This enables applications to move more easily from platform to platform. Independent Software Vendors (ISV's) can now develop applications once and have them execute on many different platforms. Second, with Java's object orientation, we can create components that can be later assembled into complete applications. We will examine how these objects, JavaBeans, are used specifically within the area of BI.

As we noted, Java is more than just a language. It is a platform for the development of Internet-enabled applications. The Java platform addresses the architectural characteristics of a multitier environment, leveraging the middle tier servers for greater system flexibility and capacity. Another important aspect of this platform is that it is able to address the variety of clients present in an Internet-enabled environment. Using the Java platform, IEBI system developers are able to provide access to wireless devices. Decision makers are now able to access their Decision Support Systems (DSS) virtually anywhere in the world.

The Java language and platform provide a means of creating a process, which is only part of the story of Internet-enabling an application. The other part is the data used by the process. The data part of the IEBI solution is the eXtensible Markup Language (XML), which is a mechanism for sharing information between systems across the Internet. In many ways it is just as flexible and architecturally neutral as Java. In Chapter 9 we explore how XML can be used in conjunction with the eXtensible Stylesheet Language (XSL) to distribute strategic information to virtually any client used by a decision maker.

In Chapter 8 we discuss the process—Java—and in Chapter 9 we discuss data—XML. In Chapter 10 we discuss how the two are brought together through metadata. Metadata flows through the system with the actual data. This mandates that any means of communicating the metadata must be as flexible and platform-independent as the data itself. One solution to the metadata issue is the Common Warehouse Metadata Interchange (CWMI) standard. We will conclude this section with a review of CWMI.

---

[2] http://java.sun.com/java2/whatis/

# Chapter 8

# JAVA

*All hail, great master, grave Sir, Hail! I come*
*To answer thy best pleasure; be't to fly,*
*To swim, to dive into the fire, to ride*
*On the curl'd clouds. To thy strong bidding, Task*
*Ariel, and all his quality.*

*William Shakespeare*
The Tempest

No book on Internet Enabled Business Intelligence is complete without a discussion of Java. This chapter opens with a quote from the Tempest. Ariel, *an airy spirit,* is willing to span the globe at Prospero's command. The spirit is willing to dive into fire, to ride upon clouds, to be put to the test in order to fulfill Prospero's request. In the same way Java is able to reach across the globe, to virtually any system on the Internet.

Java was first introduced by Sun Microsystems in May 1996. It is owned by Sun, which is actually a very good thing for achieving Java's objectives. We all know that an elephant is a mouse designed by a committee. If Java were in the control of some committee or industrial group, it would quickly lose its relevance. It would be buried under an avalanche of competing interests. While Sun has in place the appropriate mechanisms to grow Java to meet the evolving needs of industry, Sun has been successful in keeping Java on track, focusing on fulfilling the needs of Internet application developers.

I am a strong supporter of Java and where Sun is taking the environment. The basis for this enthusiasm is what Java does for the IEBI system developer. Java is described as "a simple, object-oriented, network-savvy, robust, secure, architecture-neutral, portable, high-performance, multithreaded, interpreted, dynamic language."[1] Java achieves this objective and provides us with the tools necessary to achieve our goals.

As discussed, the Internet has greatly expanded the scope of BI. No longer do the four walls that bind our organization define the scope of our system. IEBI extends back to our suppliers. It reaches forward through our distributors to the end user, to the ultimate consumer. Suppliers, distributors, and end users all benefit from IEBI; all are direct users of IEBI. Two-tier client/server architectures, while they may have had their moment in the sun, are no longer sufficient to meet the needs of an Internet-enabled environment. We have moved on to a new stage in the evolution of information systems, an Internet-enabled stage.

If this is true of the underlying hardware architecture, it is all the more so for the software applications that execute on that architecture. Languages and environments that were designed initially for client/server, or worse yet, for mainframe environments, are no longer sufficient to meet the needs of the Internet age. This is the importance of Java. Although a major part of Java is the language itself, it is more than just a language. It is also an environment, a platform upon which we develop Internet-enabled applications. The design of both the Java language and the Java environment map directly onto the Internet architecture we described in Chapter 5. We now have both the language and the environment that enables us to develop true Internet-enabled applications. This is critical to the IEBI systems designer. Java provides both the language and the environment to develop an IEBI system that stretches across the entire value chain.

In this chapter, we begin by discussing the basic concepts of object-oriented programming. This is the basis of Java as well as of many of the concepts we will explore in this chapter. Much has been written about object-oriented programming. In this chapter, we explore these concepts from unique perspective—a perspective that I hope will prod all of us into thinking a bit differently about object orientation.

We move from our discussion on object orientation to exploring the Java language itself. What are its design objectives? How do those objectives affect IEBI? We examine the Java platform and how it can support IEBI applications, then explore some of the proposed standards for how Java can be applied to IEBI. Specifically, we look at the Java Data Mining (JDM) API and the Java OLAP API. We conclude this chapter with an example of how Oracle uses JavaBeans to simplify the development of IEBI systems.

---

[1] http://java.sun.com/java2/whatis/

## 8.1   Object Orientation

In the bad old days, when programmers such as myself wore our flow charting templates with pride, software was pretty much written according to a process flow. The flow of control began at the first line of code and continued to the last line, with a few loops, if statements, and subroutines in between. Most of the time, we were left on our own to develop an entire application from scratch, continually reinventing the wheel by rewriting the same set of functions. In addition, some parts of this code were better written than others. It was common to have a newly written function corrupt a file or reduce system performance.

To improve both productivity of the staff and the integrity of the system, managers began to develop libraries of functions within an application to support the various resources. When a program accessed a file, for example, it would do so through the common library functions. Some might consider this approach the predecessor to object-oriented software development. In a sense, these libraries *objectified* system resources. The application began to see the resource as an entity and surrounded it with a set of functions.

One could argue that object-oriented programming began almost 400 years ago. John Locke, an English philosopher born in 1632, developed a new way of looking at the universe. He believed that everything in the human mind was an *idea*. When he used the term idea, he was referring not only to thoughts, but to everything in our heads. This included sensory input, pain, and emotions. Everything. Everything we know, think, perceive, or feel is an idea. Consequently, we do not have a direct connection to the universe; we can only work with the ideas in our own heads. This book is a simple example. You know that you have this book in front of you because you are receiving sensory input. You see it because it reflects light and your eyes perceive that light. The perception of this light is an idea. If you are holding the book, you feel its weight and the texture of the cover. Both the weight and the feel of the book are sensory input, ideas. The book itself, however, is more than an image, weight, or texture. The book is beyond the things that we perceive. It is beyond our ideas.

Philosophers describe this as the difference between *immediate* and *mediate*. There are things as we experience them, the immediate, and then there are things as they are unto themselves, the mediate. If you were to meet me, you would probably experience me as a brutally handsome, highly intelligent fellow with a rapier sense of wit and keen insights. Nevertheless, is that who I truly am? These are only your perceptions of me. Every human being is much more than who he or she appears to others to be. There is an entire internal aspect to every person. We may perceive a person as angry and hostile. We don't necessarily see or understand the internal forces that drive those actions, which are an outward manifestation of the internal feelings.

Figure 8.1 demonstrates the difference between the mediate and the immediate. The immediate can be broken down into two categories: attributes and behaviors. Attributes are the characteristics of the object. A person's attributes are his or her height, weight, eye color, and hair color. Behaviors are actions. A person may run, walk, laugh, or cry. These are all things that we can observe. While an emotion, a mediate, may manifest itself in the immediate, it is still mediate. A person may feel sad, and cry. The behavior is crying, which is immediate. The emotion, sadness, remains mediate.

We can only perceive what we can perceive. This means that our understanding of anything in the world around us is limited to our perceptions. Objects become *abstractions* of their actual existence. That is, we focus our attention only on the relevant aspects of an object, ignoring those aspects that do not relate to the current interactions. We ignore the unperceived and focus only on the perceived attributes of an object that relate specifically to us. We may abstract an individual based on the way he or she interacts with us. We may label this abstraction as a nice guy or a good sport because those terms are indicative of their behavior. We infer the mediate from the immediate. Internally, the reason a person is a good sport may be that he or she lacks the courage to express the hostility he or she may feel at losing. Since we have no perception of the fear or the suppressed hostility, the inference or conclusion we draw about the internal may be quite incorrect. The mediate may be something altogether different.

In a sense, this is how the object-oriented world experiences its environment. In the bad old days of programming, every interaction between the external world and the program was separate and independent. There were no structures within the language that abstracted the entities. Object-oriented programming changed

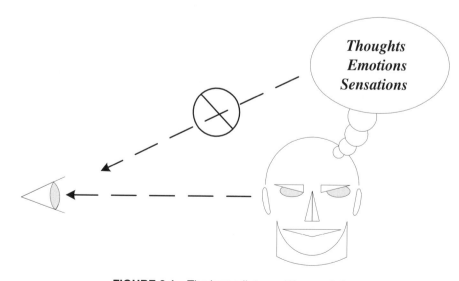

**FIGURE 8.1**   The immediate and the mediate.

this view. We see this in Figure 8.2. Programs now work with objects that are abstractions of things within the environment. The immediate characteristics of the object, both attributes and behaviors, are *public*. They are seen from outside the object. The mediate behaviors and attributes of the object are private, accessible only to the functions that are internal to the object.

A relational database demonstrates the difference between public and private. Public behaviors of the database can include open, close, read, and write. The database also has attributes that reflect the state of the database, such as opened or closed. When our application wishes to establish a connection to the database, it can invoke the database open behavior. The application can then retrieve data by invoking the read behavior. These are actions carried out by the object. Objects also have attributes. These may include the state of the database or an output queue. For example, our application may check the state of the database to determine if it is open. The state is an attribute of the database.

The database object also has attributes and behaviors that are private to the database itself. Programs outside of the database cannot see them. For example, the database may have an archive log for database recovery. Without going into the details of an archive log, functions within the database write and read from this log, but it is not accessible to the program invoking the database object. We may also have attributes that are exclusively internal to the database, such as block size. While functions within the database may need to know the block size, applications accessing the database need not.

We now move from Locke to Hume. Hume discussed causality, how one state causes or brings about another. Hume noted how we draw conclusions about cause and effect based on our observations. For example, let us assume that a child, for the first two years of his life, experiences only spherical objects that are rubber balls—balls of all sorts of shapes, sizes, and textures. Then one day his uncle comes

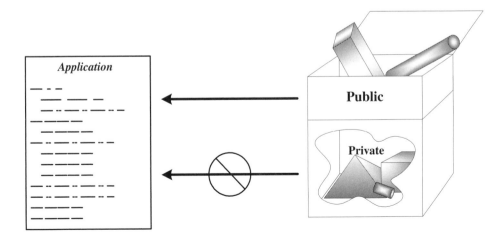

**FIGURE 8.2** Object structure.

to visit and gives him a ceramic ball, perhaps it is a globe. The child immediately takes it and slams it to the ground. Of course, not having experienced a sphere other than those made of rubber, the child had no idea that it would shatter. He naturally assumed that the ceramic ball would behave as all other spherical objects in his life behaved. He thought it would bounce. This brings us to the another aspect of object-oriented programming: *classification.*

What the child did was something we all do. He extended his past experience and projected it onto the new object. In real life each time we encounter an object, we don't treat it as if it is the first time we encountered such an object. When we get in a car, we know from our experience with other cars how the steering wheel, brakes, and transmission work. There is no need to retrain ourselves with the new car. We do the same with object-oriented programming. We take the objects that are similar and create a class. The class describes the attributes and behaviors common to the objects in that class. The child created in his mind a class of objects called balls to which he ascribed certain attributes. First, all balls had a spherical shape. Second, they had a range of textures and colors. Certainly, the attributes of the globe fit these criteria. Balls also have certain behaviors. Balls, as well as globes, roll. Balls bounce. The child quickly learned that ceramic spheres do not share the bouncing behavior with balls.

In object-oriented programming, the objects within a class have similar attributes and behaviors. In our example, we can have the class `balls` and another class `globes`. We might even have a class called `fruit`. In each class, we specify the attributes and behaviors that are common to the objects within that class. When describing a `balls` class, we would give it the attribute `spherical` and the behavior `bounce`. For the `globes`, we would assign the attribute `spherical` and the behavior `shatter`.

This would work well in some situations, but we can do better. Rather than create a single class for each type of object, we create a hierarchy of classes. We present such a hierarchy of classes in Figure 8.3. `Spheres`, the topmost node in the hierarchy, is a *superclass*. The classes beneath the sphere are its descendents. The superclass contains behaviors and attributes common to the descendents. The descendents *inherit* these from the superclass. The `balls`, `fruit`, and `globes` classes are also superclasses. They contain the behaviors and attributes that are specific to them and their descendents. A ball may have the behavior `bounce`, while the fruit may have the behaviors `ripen` and `taste`. We push the behaviors and attributes down a level because they are not common to all spheres. A ball may have the behavior `bounce`, but `ripen` is meaningless to it.

We know that not all balls bounce the same. While a golf, tennis, and baseball all may bounce, they do so in very different ways. The different ways in which a subclass carries out a behavior is a *method.* If we bounce a tennis ball, the characteristics of how that ball bounces is its method. The way in which a baseball bounces is very different. Rather than discussing balls and spheres, think for a moment how we might apply this to an application. We might have an application that writes to

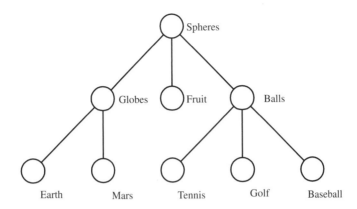

**FIGURE 8.3** Class structures.

several output devices. In some cases, the device is a printer, while in others it is a terminal. The way we write to each will differ; these differences are the different methods. The behavior is the same, writing to an output device.

We should make an important distinction between a class and an object. A class describes a type of object, not an actual instance of an object. When we define a balls class, we do not have an instance of a ball. This is actually something quite common to most programming languages. Data types such as integers, floating-point numbers, and characters do not actually create an instance of a variable. They are just types, not the actual variables that hold values. When we write our program, we need to create a variable that is an actual instance, a data type. Similarly, when we create an object class, we are only establishing the class type, not an instance.

A class with actual instances is a *concrete class*. A class in which there are no instances is an *abstract class*. In our example, we may specify that a sphere must be one of the three subclasses. A ball, however, can be a general, nondescript ball. In this case, the spheres class is an abstract class. There are no actual sphere instances. The balls class and all its subclasses do have instances, which makes the balls class a concrete class.

In creating these class structures, we are able to manipulate groups of objects at one time. This is inherent to an object-oriented programming environment. The remainder of this chapter discusses Java. As we explore both the Java language and its environment, we shall see how we can use this object orientation to develop IEBI applications.

## 8.2    The Java Programming Language

The Java programming language is described as "a simple, object-oriented, net-work-savvy, robust, secure, architecture-neutral, portable, high-performance, multithreaded, interpreted, dynamic language."[2] Also, with the appropriate peripherals, it will wash your car and baby-sit your kids. Okay, I threw in that last part, but with all the claims that are made concerning Java, it is almost believable. Let's take a moment to understand some of these claims and how they relate to IEBI.

### 8.2.1    SIMPLE

When we first approach the Java language, we note its simplicity. As we consider the complexities of other object-oriented languages, such as C++ and Smalltalk, we wonder how an object-oriented language could be simple. Isn't the basic method-ology complex? Both Smalltalk and C++ are very much like the first video camera I ever bought. Prior to purchasing it, I went out and read all the reports on video cameras. I soon learned there were certain features that were absolute necessities. First, I had to have the ability to add scrolling titles. Second, I desperately required the ability to focus in on objects as tiny as a ladybug. When it finally came time to buy the camera, I selected the model with the highest rating and the most features. Oh, it was a marvel of modern recording devices. Visions of mini-epics danced through my mind the night I bought that camera. In years to come, my children would bless me for documenting their childhood so well and so creatively. You could probably guess where this story is going. In the end, I took the basic home movies: my children's first steps, birthday parties, and Christmas mornings. The only feature I used at all was the fade-in/fade-out; it was the only one I could fig-ure out. Today, that particular camera sits inoperable in the back of a closet, and a new one with fewer features has taken its place. This is what is happening with programming languages, at least in the Internet-enabled world.

Both Smalltalk and C++ have a rich programming environment with all sorts of features and functions. Unfortunately, a good number of these functions are not necessary to the majority of applications, or they simply don't make sense. Consid-er some of the things we can do with C++: operator overloading, multiple inherit-ance, and automatic coercions. (Automatic coercion! I have relatives doing time for this!) Is this functionality necessary?

Every good engineer knows *KISS,* Keep It Simple, Stupid. Simplicity, howev-er, is even more important in an IEBI implementation. Time and quality are critical success factors. As we noted earlier, Business Intelligence 101 tells us that we sell IEBI to the C-level executives. The trouble with this rule is that their attention span

---

[2] http://java.sun.com/java2/whatis/

is short. Do not expect to walk away with their buy-off on an IEBI system and return 16 months later with the beginnings of what you sold them. They will pull the plug on such a project long before you deliver; I have the battle scars to prove this is true. We need to get the C-level executives some basic level of functionality as soon as possible to insure continued support for the project. Java's simplicity allows us to get something developed quickly.

Rather than provide an extensive syntax in which the language implements every conceivable function, Java is a simple, straightforward language. IEBI is difficult enough; adding a complex language into the mix does not make it any easier. While the language is simple, the power to develop very complex applications is great. We shall see how we can easily develop complex applications with Oracle's BI JavaBeans later in this chapter.

### 8.2.2  ROBUST AND SECURE

Robust is one of those words like "nice"—overused to such an extent that it tends to lack real meaning. We talk of environments being robust, but it is typically a term used by marketing when searching for a nondescript adjective or beefing up a presentation. The dictionary defines robust as "powerfully built" or "sturdy."

While simplicity is beneficial, are we sacrificing the ability to build *robust* applications? Actually, Java's simplicity contributes to the robustness of the language. Both Smalltalk and C++ are like a chainsaw—they could easily cut through most objects with little resistance. That is the good thing about chainsaws. The not so good thing about chainsaws is that they cut through most things with little resistance. Slicing off an arm or a hand is a simple process that occurs far too often. Although a handsaw might not be able to cut through a redwood, when was the last time you heard of someone accidentally cutting off his or her arm with a handsaw? True, Smalltalk and C++ give you a lot of power, but with that power you can easily hurt yourself.

One of the features of the C language, and later C++, is the ability to point at specific memory locations through pointer data types. In C, a program can easily step outside the memory boundaries of an application. If we are lucky, the operating system will pick this up and we'll get an error. In a less lucky environment, the program will be allowed to access memory and possibly cause a more devastating error. Java's memory management model is much simpler, which makes it much more robust. We work in an object-oriented environment, which means that everything we do is in terms of objects. When we create a new object, we do so with the new operator. There is no such thing as a programmer-defined memory pointer type. Everything we do in memory is within the context of objects.

Robustness entails more than simplicity. Java helps to insure robustness by catching errors *before* the application is deployed, a novel concept in the application development world. One way it does this is by applying strict compile-time and runtime checking. C++, on the other hand, allows the *implicit* declaration of methods and functions. Java *requires explicit* declarations.

### 8.2.3 ARCHITECTURE-NEUTRAL, PORTABLE

In Chapter 5, we discussed the features of the Internet and the importance of a pervasive client, a single, consistent environment for every client that desires access to the system. The importance of this is that the application developer can now write to a single platform. He or she need not develop separate versions of the software to accommodate for the nuances of the variety of platforms that will act as clients. Java extends this capability.

With most other high-level languages, applications are compiled to generate *machine code,* the binary instructions that cause the system to perform the tasks described in the source code of the program. One of the problems with this approach is that each system has its own machine code. Any application developed in this manner is dependent on the underlying system. A Java compiler, however, generates *bytecodes.* These are high-level, machine-independent codes.

Sitting between the Java application and the actual system is the *Java virtual machine (JVM).* Figure 8.4 shows this structure. This platform *abstracts* the specific hardware and operating system. Recall our definition of abstraction from earlier in the chapter; with abstraction, we focus our attention only on the relevant aspects of an object, ignoring those aspects that do not relate. The JVM hides the specifics of the hardware and operating system. Instead, it creates a standard virtual machine across all systems, providing Java applications with a single environment in which to execute. Where traditional compilers generate machine code that runs on the specific system, the bytecodes generated by the Java compiler run on the virtual machine.

One would assume that architectural independence would be synonymous with portability. While the two are closely related, they are not the same. Portability drills down a step. In the bad old days when I was a programmer and we had steam-powered computers, we would joke about memory pages. A page of memory isn't a term you hear that often these days. Back then, the page size would vary from one system to another. The joke was that when someone would move code from one system to another, they would ask, "How big is a page?" The answer was, "Oh, typically eight and a half by eleven." This may not be funny to you, but we were programmers and everyone knows how funny programmers are. The point of the story is that memory varied from system to system. The length of an integer, floating-point number, or character changed from system to system as well. Specifications for languages such as Fortran, C, and C++ designated the size of these data types as *implementation-dependent.* Java did not make this mistake. As we can see in Table 8.1, the arithmetic functions and the primitive data types used by these functions are all defined by the Java specification. The data types have specific, defined lengths regardless of the system.

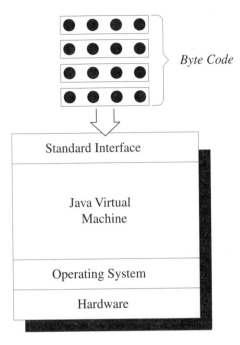

**FIGURE 8.4**   The JVM.

Most platforms are capable of supporting arithmetic in each of these formats. By implementing the Java language with these specifications, the data types become standard across all platforms. This enhances the portability of the programming language by eliminating a possible implementation dependency.

**TABLE 8.1**   Java Data Types

| Data Type | Length |
| --- | --- |
| Byte | 8-bit two's complement |
| Short | 16-bit two's complement |
| Integer | 32-bit two's complement |
| Long | 64-bit two's complement |
| Float | 32-bit IEEE 754 floating point |
| Double | 64-bit IEEE 754 floating point |
| Character | 16-bit Unicode Character |

### 8.2.4  HIGH-PERFORMANCE

You may wonder how the overall performance of the application is affected when intervening layers of software are added. After all, we have bytecodes executing on a virtual machine that is sitting on top of an actual system.

For most applications, this environment delivers sufficient performance. There are, however, instances where better performance is necessary. In such cases, the bytecodes can be transformed at runtime into the machine code that is native to the system upon which the application is executing. This provides for performance that is equal to, if not greater than, the performance of other high-level languages such as C and C++. This is referred to as just-in-time (JIT) compilation.

### 8.2.5  MULTITHREADED

Multithreading, as the name implies, allows multiple parallel streams or threads of control to flow through the application. One of the challenges of parallel processing is making sure that we don't step on one another's toes. When two processes are competing for the same resource, there needs to be some method of arbitration to allow one process to gain and maintain control of that resource. In short, threads need to learn to do what we all tell our children to do: *share*.

In the past, parallel processing was more at the mercy of the underlying operating system. High-level programming languages did not provide specifications for parallel processing. These specifications were again considered implementation-dependent, which left the implementation of these functions to vendor-supplied libraries. This is contrary to Java's design goals. First, it is complex. It is not a trivial task to share resources between different threads of control. Locks must be acquired and released appropriately. The applications also need to contend with how to handle abnormal termination. Each vendor has its own way of dealing with these issues, which leads us to the second issue, portability. We have discussed how Java's design is architecture-independent and portable. Implementation of multithreading through vendor-specified libraries defeats this design goal.

The Java THREAD class provides built-in support for multithreading. This built-in support overcomes the shortcomings we described earlier. For example, within the THREAD class is a set of methods used to start, stop, and check the status of threads. This makes the process of developing multithreaded applications much simpler and more portable. Java threads are preemptive; threads of a higher priority are able to take control of the processor from threads of a lower priority. Java threads may also be time-sliced when the underlying system supports it. By implementing multithreading at the language level, a method within a class can be declared as *synchronized*. This synchronization uses a *monitor* and *condition variable* strategy to ensure that variables maintain their integrity.

The point of multithreading is to be able to do more than one thing at a time. This is especially beneficial to IEBI. When doing multidimensional analysis, for example, data for a view can be displayed by one thread, while another thread prepares another view. Another possible use is the ability to *predrill* the data. The next level down in detail can be retrieved by one thread while other threads retrieve data at a deeper level of aggregation.

### 8.2.6  SUMMATION

We began this section with a description of the Java language: "a simple, object-oriented, network-savvy, robust, secure, architecture neutral, portable, high-performance, multithreaded, interpreted, dynamic language."[3] Table 8.2 summarizes the benefits Java delivers to IEBI.

**TABLE 8.2**   The IEBI Benefits of Java

| Feature | IEBI Benefit |
| --- | --- |
| Simple | Reduces software development cost and time to delivery. |
| Robust | Provides a solid, reliable environment in which to develop software. |
| Secure | Memory protection protects system from inadvertent or intentional system corruption. |
| Architecture-Neutral | Provides a consistent environment across all platforms for applications to execute. |
| Portable | Applications are written once and can execute on any platform. |
| High Performance | Applications can be compiled to machine code to deliver better performance. |
| Multithreaded | Multiple tasks can be executed in parallel, improving overall system performance. |

As you will note, we have not discussed several of the features of Java, such as network-savvy, interpreted, and dynamic. We will look at them as we discuss the Java environment.

## 8.3   Introduction to the Java Platform

In Chapter 5, we discussed a multitier architecture from the hardware perspective. In such an environment, we moved the application logic, which had in the two-tier world been supported on a *fat client*, to the middle tier. On the front end is the interface, the part of the application that communicates with the user. This is the proactive portion of the application. Through this interface, the user ini-

---

[3] http://java.sun.com/java2/whatis/

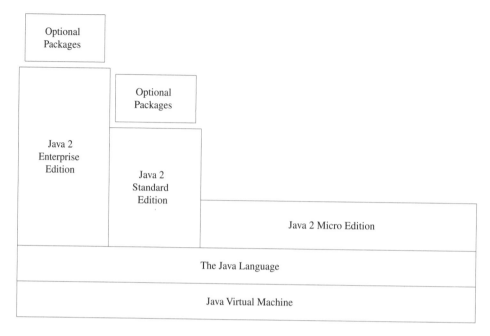

**FIGURE 8.5** The Java platform.

tiates the requests for the various services provided by the system. These processes are short-lived, starting and stopping at the request of the user. On the back end are the systems services, such as database management systems. These services are totally reactive and long-lived, theoretically running forever. We can see how this adds a level of complexity to the development of our application. In the two-tier environment, we had a simple many-to-one relationship in which many clients communicated to the one server process in the background. In a multitier environment, we have a many-to-many relationship in which multiple clients communicate with multiple middle-tier servers, which in turn communicate with many back-end services.

The Java platform maps directly onto this multitier architecture. Both the front and back ends of the application are abstracted, leaving the middle tier free to focus on the application's business logic. There are a wide variety of client devices. To meet the needs of these different platforms, there are three different editions of Java. Figure 8.5 presents the relationship between these different editions.

### 8.3.1 THE JVM

The JVM is that part of the Java environment that makes a Java system independent. It is an abstraction of the underlying system. As shown in Figure 8.4, the JVM sits between the system and the application or applet and acts as a *virtual* system. The application does not see the underlying system; it sees only the JVM. The

JVM in turn takes what it receives from the application and executes it on the system. The JVM can run on top of most operating systems. Figure 8.6 pulls back the covers on the how applications and applets execute on the JVM.

The process begins with Java language source code. This code is saved in Java files, <YY>.*java*, where <YY> is the filename and *.java* is the filename extension. These files are compiled by the Java compiler into Java bytecodes, which are then stored as Java class files. These files are named <XX>.*class*, where <XX> is the filename and *.class* is the filename extension. Class files are machine-independent, allowing the output of the Java compiler to be sent to virtually any system.

Prior to the JVM receiving these files as input, the *Java Class Loader* and *bytecode verifier* load the bytecodes into memory and verify them for security. The bytecode verifier is an important element in creating a robust Java environment. The Java code could have originated from any source. It is the job of the verifier to insure that the code does not corrupt the JVM. In examining the bytecodes, the verifier establishes the type information and checks the types of parameters that are passed to the bytecode instructions. Once the class file passes through the verifier, we know that there are no stack overflows, bytecodes are receiving appropriate parameters, and the object field accesses are legal.

As we see in the figure, once the code has been received by the JVM, it can take one of two paths. The first path is through the interpreter. The interpreter takes the byte codes and runs them in the Java Runtime System. The runtime system is the piece of the JVM that interfaces with the actual operating system. The concept of *linking* a program as in some other high-level languages is not really performed within the JVM. When we look at loading a program in the object-oriented world, we are really talking about loading new classes. Older high-level languages do this in a *static* fashion. Once the source has been compiled, the output is linked.

Bytecodes are different than object code; they are symbolic. The indices and offsets to methods are symbolic names. When a method is first invoked, the JVM searches a table of method names. Once found, the offset to the method is used to access the method for quicker access. This has the advantage that new methods can be added during runtime. Classes loaded from the Java Class Libraries are dynamically loaded as they are needed.

### 8.3.2  JAVA APPLETS AND APPLICATIONS

Note in Figure 8.6 the difference between an applet and an application. Often, an applet is defined as a lightweight application; this is only partially correct. While applets are typically characterized as somewhat smaller applications, this is more of a function of how they are invoked, not a technical requirement.

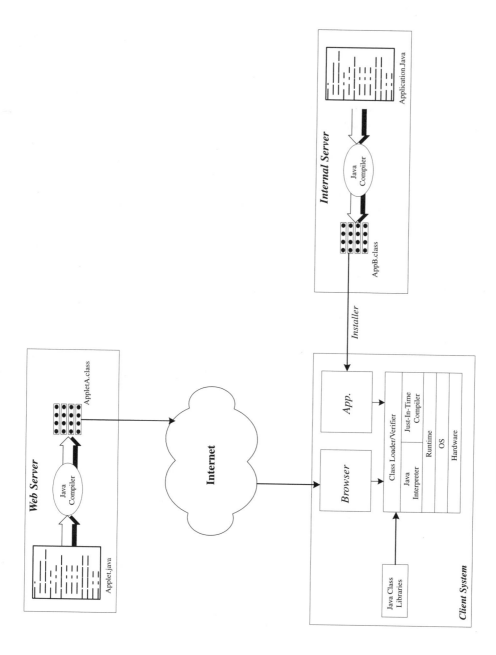

**FIGURE 8.6** Executing applets and applications on a JVM.

Applets are invoked differently than applications. An applet is invoked when the browser loads a Web page with an applet tag. When the browser encounters the tag, the program automatically downloads the applet from the server and runs it on the client. Since the program, or applet, downloads from the server, it is typically small in order to avoid lengthy download times. Also, note that applets are invoked when a browser downloads a Web page containing the applet's tag. This means that applets require a browser to run.

Java applications are full-fledged applications. They are invoked and executed like any other type of program. Java applications, however, require that the Java platform be present. Currently, there are some functional differences between an applet and an application. The applet is less secure than an application, since it can come from just about any Web server on the Internet. Applets do not necessarily originate from a trusted environment. Applets are therefore restricted from reading or writing to any file system other than the server from which they came.

### 8.3.3 JAVA PLATFORM EDITIONS

In Figure 8.5, there are three versions of the Java platform: Java 2 Micro Edition (J2ME), Java 2 Standard Edition (J2SE), and Java 2 Enterprise Edition (J2EE). Each Java platform edition is designed to address a different segment of the market. J2ME addresses devices such as cell phones, pagers, and PDAs—typically, the needs of small, mobile clients. J2SE is the next step up, addressing the development requirements for applets and applications. To address the development needs of the enterprise server-side applications, use J2EE. Across all of these environments, we have the Java language itself.

As we look at the J2EE environment, we can see the developer has the option of either presenting services directly to a browser using Java Server Pages (JSPs), or providing those services to the browser via applets and JavaBeans. Figure 8.7 presents each alternative. On the one hand, we can support applications through HTML-based clients. Using JSPs, the application server dynamically generates HTML pages, which are sent directly to the client system's browser. Developers can combine static page templates with dynamic content. The structure of a JSP includes tags that invoke JavaBeans components to implement complex functionality. The alternative to the method described above is to build an applet that communicates directly with a mid-tier application. This moves the responsibility of formatting and often processing the data to the client-side applet. In many ways, this mimics the traditional two-tier client server model.

As we can see, the Java platform provides application developers with a foundation upon which they can build multitier applications. Through the use of J2ME, these applications can be deployed on a variety of devices, extending the reach of the IEBI system beyond the physical walls of the organization. The next step is to examine how the Java language has been extended to specifically address IEBI system requirements.

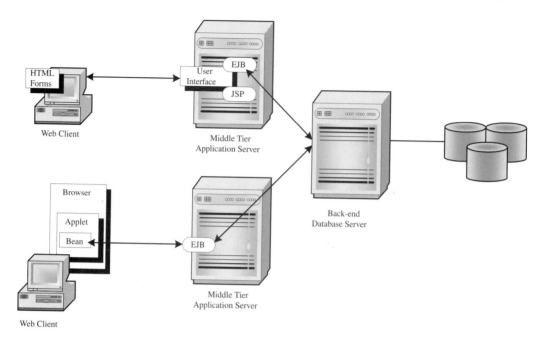

**FIGURE 8.7** Implementing multitier applications with Java.

## 8.4 Java Specification Request (JSR)

All languages, with one glaring exception, have their dialects. When I was an undergraduate, it took me several years to decide what I wanted to do with my life. (Oh no, here comes another story!) During that time, I took a variety of classes, one of which was Italian. My mother was Sicilian and my father's family was from Calabria. The Italian spoken in our home consequently was a combination of the two dialects. When I went to school, we were taught the Florentine dialect, a variation that lacked, in my opinion, the passion and flare of the more southern tongues to which I had grown accustomed. In many cases, the two were so different that they were barely recognizable as the same language. While they both started with a common language, they were separated enough that their speech evolved in different ways.

Languages such as Cobol, C, Smalltalk, and even Fortran, all have their own dialects. Programming languages, just as human speech, change and evolve as people use them. The way one vendor or operating system implements C++ deviates from another. At times, these deviations are referred to as *extensions*. Roughly defined, extensions are a vendor's way of taking something standard and making it specific to its own environment. Software developers are locked into a particular platform. This is the antithesis of all Java's objectives.

Java is the one glaring exception to this rule of language. The reason for this is Sun Microsystems. Wisely, Sun has stated quite simply to the market, "Java is ours and this is how it works." There are no *extensions* to the language. Java, the Popeye of programming languages, is what it is and that is all that it is. Now, I said Sun was wise in this decision, and this isn't because I am looking to get a job from Scott McNealy. Rather, it avoids the problems associated with different vendors modifying the language to the extent that it loses its portability and platform-independence. While the need for control is recognized, there is also a realization that environments, situations, and attitudes change. A word or phrase in one generation may have one meaning, while in another have a completely different connotation. Programming languages evolve in the same way. The original definition of a language could not possibly anticipate environmental changes or new applications. JSRs are the way in which the language can grow to meet changing conditions.

A JSR is a formal request to extend the Java specification to include new functionality within the language. A JSR is adopted through the Java Community Process (JCP). The JCP is composed of the following steps:

1. **JSR Review**—Community members define a specification, which is approved by the Executive Committee (EC). The EC is composed of stakeholders and members of the Java community. Currently there are two executive committees; one responsible for desktop/server technologies and one responsible for consumer/embedded technologies.
2. **Public Review**—The JSR draft is reviewed by the public at large. An Expert Group further revises the JSR based on the response from the public.
3. **Proposed Final Draft**—A final draft is composed based on the revisions from the public review. This serves as the basis for the Reference Implementation (RI) and the Technology Compatibility Kit (TCK). The RI is a proof of concept prototype that demonstrates the capabilities of the specification. The TCK is a package that assists in testing whether a specific implementation is compliant with the specification.
4. **Final Release**—The RI and the TCK are completed, and the specification is sent to the EC for approval.
5. **Maintenance Review**—During this phase, the RI and the TCK are updated to meet enhancements, revisions, and requests for clarification and interpretation.

The importance of this process is that it controls what is and isn't Java. By having a central committee, the controlled evolution of Java maintains the design objectives of the language. In the following subsections, we discuss two JSRs specifically related to IEBI. Since these JSRs are not yet in final release, this discussion merely serves as an introduction to what is being proposed, without delving into the details of the implementations.

## 8.4.1  JSR-73: THE JAVA DATA MINING API

In Chapter 3, we discussed data mining and the different types of data mining applications. To date, the interfaces to these applications have been vendor-dependent, which is contrary to Java's objective of platform-independence. To maintain this independence, the Java community is in the process of establishing a standard Application Program Interface (API) for data mining systems that is freed from any specific implementation. Although not yet finalized, JSR-73 defines the JDM API. Client applications written against this single API run against any back-end system that supports the standard. Although the standard has a required baseline functionality, there are optional packages within the standard. For example, some vendors may support classification models using decision tree-based algorithms, while others support only clustering using the k-means algorithm. As one can well imagine, the breadth of data mining functions and algorithms would require this type of approach. How an individual vendor implements the API is at the discretion of the vendor. A vendor can implement JDM as an API native to the application or develop a driver/adapter scheme. In the latter, the driver/adapter mediates between the JDM layer and multiple vendor products.

We begin the data mining process by preparing the data used to build a model. The validity of the conclusions we draw from the data mining operation, the quality of the output, is a function of the quality of the data that goes into the model. For this reason, the preparation of the data is perhaps the most critical step in the process. We have seen this when discussing the data warehouse: The majority of the work in building a data warehouse is the piece that prepares that data—the extraction, transformation, cleansing, and loading. The same is true for data mining. Generally, about 80 percent of the work in data mining involves preparation of the data. Just as we do in data warehousing, we need to cleanse and normalize that data. In some instances, we may need to define new attributes that are functions or combination of others.

The next step is to build a model. A model is a scaled down version, or representation, of something else. Because it is a simplification of the actual thing, we are able to analyze and work with the model more easily than with the modeled object. Whatever we learn from the model, we can then apply to the actual thing.

I have to believe that every American male spent a good deal of his adolescence building models. Oh those sweet afternoons spent with nothing more than a box of plastic pieces, a few toothpicks and a tube of model glue. (This was in the days before sniffing.) It was sheer delight to watch those odd shapes form various hot rods, airplanes, and battleships. The only problem was that I wasn't getting my homework done. Sister Robert Francis was quick to point out that I was probably never going to amount to anything by frittering away my time. Then again, she never put together a 1969 Corvette complete with windows that really rolled down!

One year, for Christmas, my older brother did it. He gave me the veritable Mona Lisa of models, the Mount Everest of miniatures. He gave me the "Visible V-8"! It was truly the model that all other models hoped to be. When finished, the engine would run like a real V-8. The pistons would move up and down; the lifts would lift; the fan would fan; the crankshaft would crank. What made this model special was the clear plastic engine block that allowed you to see all the parts working together. Of course, it didn't run on gasoline. Instead, a small electronic motor turned the crankshaft and made it look like the engine was running. How astounded my family and friends would be when, once the V-8 was assembled, they could watch for hours the workings of an internal combustion engine. How they would marvel at my skill and expertise. Women would want me! Men would want to be like me!! Mothers would want their daughters marry me!!! I'd show Sister Francis. All I needed to do was to figure out how to put the thing together.

By modeling a V-8, I grew to understand how an engine works. I couldn't have very well put together a real V-8 engine in my room when I was 11, although some in my neighborhood who tried it in their garages. So I took something else, something that was a representation of that engine, a model. I learned from that model how an engine works. I also learned that I didn't want to be an auto mechanic.

Models are similar in the data mining world. The models we built as children were, in a sense, a compact representation of something. Through this representation, I discovered something about the real world. In this way they are similar. Note that there is a difference in how these two types of models take us through this process of discovery. The child's model reduces reality, yet it still is very much like the real-world object. Data mining, however, creates fully transformed, reduced versions of the data that may look nothing like the actual data. Consider the decision trees we discussed in Chapter 3. We extracted from the data a series of *if-then* rules that created our tree structure. This is more than just a simplification of the data. Looking at the actual data would give us no insight into the knowledge hidden within the complexity of the data.

While we can see that both a child's model and a data mining model seek to describe something, they do so in very different ways. Yet, this is still only one type of data mining model: descriptive. Data mining models can be descriptive, predictive, or both. The descriptive model assists us in understanding the complexities found in the data. The predictive model helps us look into the future and predict some future result. We will see this come into play in later chapters when we discuss the use of data mining in the personalization of our Web site. The data mining model describes the behavior of certain customers and customer types. Based on this description, we will attempt to predict their behavior.

As we can see, the data mining model is very different from the child's model. The child's model is *constructed*; the data mining model is *discovered*. The actual process of discovering this model is data mining. Data mining is very different from most applications. In most applications, we create a process that models the real world, the purchasing of a product or the servicing of a customer request, and run data of specific occurrences of these events through the model. In these environments, the data is dynamic and the model is static. In data mining, we reverse this: The data is static and the model is dynamic. We take the static data and from that derive a model. If the data changes to reflect a change in behavior, our model changes.

We can see this process of discovery as we look at the JDM process. We specify *function settings* that describe the type of problem we are trying to solve. Is it a classification problem or a clustering situation? We then define a task that builds the model using the input data and function settings. The output of the task, the discovery process, is the model itself. Models learn in two ways. The first, *supervised learning,* requires a known value to be predicted, referred to as the target. The second is *unsupervised learning,* which uses no such target. Examples of unsupervised learning include clustering and association rules.

To insure that the model is truly predicting results and has not merely learned the input data set, we test the model with other known data sets. This gives us a sense of the accuracy of the model. Supervised models and some unsupervised models, such as clustering, can be applied to data to predict target values or make assignments to categories or clusters.

### 8.4.1.1 Model Building

The first step in the data mining process is for the client to build a model. As we have discussed throughout this chapter, Java is object-oriented. We take advantage of this approach in the construction of our model. We define function settings as noted above. Function settings are built through a series of objects whose attributes are set and methods invoked. In a sense, we *objectify* the data mining process.

If we think of the data mining process as a group of objects working in conjunction with one another, the first object we encounter is the process, or data mining task, itself. We therefore begin the process with the creation of a *data mining task* object. When we do this, we define the physical data, mining function settings, algorithm settings, and finally the task. In some instances, we may wish to define map attributes. This is the object that is the embodiment of our data mining process. Envision it as the tool by which we manipulate the data mining process. We use this object to specify the asynchronous processing of tasks. As you can well imagine, data mining tasks can be quite lengthy. It is beneficial, therefore, to be able to run these tasks asynchronously. We can also use this object to terminate or interrupt tasks that are currently processing. The data mining task object also receives the input parameters to the data mining process. There are different kinds of tasks: build, test, apply, import, and export.

The data mining task object receives two forms of input. The first type of input received by the data mining task is the data to be mined. The *physical data* object defines the layout of the data. Note that the JDM API allows the inclusion of table and multirecord data types. A table is a simple table in which each record contains a case. Each table column contains a specific variable of the analysis, such as age, gender, or income. In a multirecord data type, the columns of the record assume a specific role. Columns that assume a role contain such elements as customer IDs, sequence numbers, or item names.

The second type of input the task object receives is the commands, or settings, that define how we are going to mine the data. The settings fall into two groups: function settings and algorithm settings. Function settings are the high-level specification for the construction of a model. These are defined by the *function settings* object. The function settings are high-level enough that the client can identify the type of results that are desired without having to specify a particular type of algorithm. A client can specify functions of classification, approximation, attribute importance, association rules, and clustering models. Some parameters for function settings are optional. Omitted parameters or specific algorithms are automatically selected by the back-end data mining process that best supports the task defined by the client's input parameters. Algorithm settings provide specifications for the specific algorithm that is to be used by the model. These are defined in the *algorithm settings* object.

The JDM API, as of this writing, recognizes four data mining functions or algorithms. Each function has its own distinct strengths and weaknesses. The JDM API data mining functions are as follows:

1. **Association**—Used extensively in marketing for situations such as market basket analysis. This type of data mining operation finds an association between data items. There is the old example of a high correlation between the purchase of disposable diapers and beer. Association rules are a form of unsupervised learning.

2. **Classification**—Used extensively in customer segmentation and credit analysis. This type of data mining places a record in specified groups. Classification is a form of supervised learning.

3. **Approximation**—A method used to predict the difference between predicted data and actual data sets. This method is based on the concept of a regression towards a mean, which was first introduced by Francis Galton approximately 100 years ago. Approximation is a form of supervised learning.

4. **Clustering**—Used in retailing when retailers would like to understand similarities in a customer base, such as customer churn. In this function, subjects that share common behaviors and characteristics are grouped together. Clustering is a form of unsupervised learning.

As we can see, these data mining functions fall into two basic categories. The first is descriptive; the data mining method attempts to provide an insight into the characteristics of the data in a more concise manner. The second is predictive. This type of mining predicts some future behavior.

The separation of the algorithm settings from the mining function settings provides for two types of users. One might wonder about the need for two types of settings. The JDM API provides for the needs of many types of users and clients. The function settings provide for the needs of the majority of users. More advanced users, users with greater knowledge of the data mining process, can fine-tune data mining tasks with the algorithm settings.

### 8.4.1.2 Model Testing

The next step in the data mining process is to test the model we have built. Note that testing is applicable to supervised models, those models that have a target. It is not a required step, but helps assess the accuracy of the model. The testing phase evaluates how well the model predicts outcomes. It is important to perform the test with a known data set that is different from the data used to construct the model. We need to understand the predictive qualities of our model. If we test the model with the same data set we used to build the model, we could have a model that has simply *memorized* the data used in construction. When testing the model with a second known data set, we are performing an *out-of-sample* test. An out-of-sample test tells us how well the model is able to predict against an unknown data set.

With the JDM API, the mining task accepts as input mining data and the mining model. The format of the input data is the same as the input to the model during the construction phase. The results of the test are stored in the *test result* object. The format of the output is dependent on the type of mining model used. This makes sense. One would not expect the output of an approximation, for example, to be in the same format as the output of a classification model.

### 8.4.1.3 Applying the Model to Data (Scoring)

The final step in the data mining process is to apply the model to the actual data. Typically, applying is not used for association rules. The data to which we apply the model is possibly a previously unseen data set. This is the actual data for which we intend to make predictions. As such, the data must be preprocessed in the same or a similar way as the build data. By similar, we mean that the data must contain, at a minimum, the same set of attributes used to build the model. For example, if we built a model that uses gender, age, and income to perform a prediction, then the actual data to which the model is applied must contain gender, age, and income. The main emphasis is on the preprocessing. In other words, we need to use the same statistics from the build data transformations on the score and test data.

The results of the data mining operation are stored in the location specified by the data mining task object. They are typically comprised of one result per test case. For example, we may use classification to predict whether a particular type of individual belongs to one political party or another. In another instance, we may be interested in the probability of a particular household to purchase a product or service. In this case, the data mining operation returns a probability for an entire household, not for a particular individual. In either case, the JDM API allows the user to specify the content of the results returned by the data mining process.

### 8.4.2 JSR-69: THE JAVA OLAP API

As of this writing, JSR-69 has not been fully described. The OLAP Council's Multidimensional API (MDAPI), however, approximates what we expect to see. The MDAPI provides clients with an object-oriented interface to multidimensional databases. Through this interface, client applications are able to connect to a multidimensional database and query its metadata and data. In keeping with the objectives of the Java language, the MDAPI hides the idiosyncrasies of the underlying database, providing portability and system-independence. In Chapter 3, we discussed OLAP and multidimensionality, so we will not go into the basic principles here. In this section, we specifically discuss the OLAP Council's MDAPI.

We noted how Java abstracts the underlying platform, hiding the variations between platforms. The MDAPI, in the same way, uses an object-oriented approach to abstract the implementation details of the underlying multidimensional database. The application manipulates the objects that are part of the API. There are four basic types of objects in the MDAPI: session, metadata, queries, and drivers. The individual vendors implement objects, but their specification is defined by the OLAP Council. The only exception to this rule is the session object, which is implemented by the OLAP Council. Figure 8.8 presents the relationship between the objects in the MDAPI.

Understand that the MDAPI is not a piece of software or a thing purchased from the OLAP Council. The MDAPI is primarily a specification. The OLAP Council publishes the specification, and the OLAP vendors provide the implementation. As part of this implementation, vendors are allowed to extend the MDAPI to

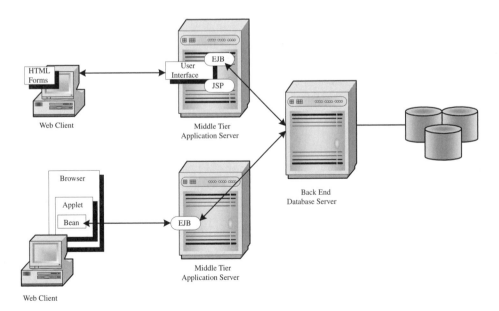

**FIGURE 8.8** MDAPI data model.

include special database features and functions. At first glance, this may seem to be contrary to the basic portability functions of Java. The objects in the interface, however, are implemented as Java interfaces. By specifying the MDAPI as a set of interfaces, the OLAP Council provides vendors flexibility in implementing the underlying methods.

In a typical OLAP session, an application establishes a connection to a database and retrieves the metadata to understand the analysis space represented by the multidimensional database. The application then requests some data, performs some analysis, and possibly queries more data. Each action is performed by the application with a specific MDAPI object.

We establish a connection to the database via the session object. In Figure 8.8, we see that the session object is the root of the MDAPI. It is through this object that applications access the multidimensional database. As we said above, this is the only object that is actually implemented by the OLAP Council and is therefore vendor-independent. The session object is the first MDAPI object to be installed on a platform; subsequent installations of MDAPI objects register with the session object. In this way, the session object is cognizant of all MDAPI instances on a system. This enables the session object to load any driver installed on the system.

The session object method *getDriverByName* returns an instance of the driver object specified by the driver name. The driver class is the vendor's specific implementation of the MDAPI. It is through the driver that we establish a connection to the database. The connection remains open until it is specifically closed. Since the connection is subordinate to the session, the connection will also be closed if the session terminates. As shown in Figure 8.8, a single session can support zero to many simultaneous connections to a single multidimensional database. The connection object is the object through which the application interacts with the multidimensional database. It provides for metadata navigation, description of the data source capabilities and policies, and the maintenance of the connection itself.

We create multidimensional analysis spaces, or hypercubes, with the MDAPI via the connection object. We could in fact think of the connection object as a hypercube. It is composed of dimensions of which one and only one is a measures dimension. Each cell contains values identified by *value descriptors* and defined by a combination of one *member* from each of the dimensions. To query this cube, we create *member queries*.

To understand a member query a bit better, let's stop and consider a dimension. A dimension binds an analysis space and is represented, when drawn, by an axis. The axis represents a scale, which can be either a nominal scale or an interval scale. All possible values of this scale are the domain of dimension values. In forming a member query, we specify a subset of values from this domain to return for each of the dimensions. If we specify a set of members when creating the member query, the results of the query are returned in the order specified. We may also define the ordering of the returned values.

The MDAPI is not JSR-69, although it approximates what we expect to see in the JSR. The MDAPI applies to a variety of languages, not just Java. However, some basic considerations had to be made in establishing the MDAPI to map it to the Java environment. For example, although Java methods may receive zero to many parameters, they return only one value. The MDAPI therefore has been defined so that there are no methods that return multiple output parameters.

In the past, one of the values returned by a procedure was a status code. Java, as well as several other modern languages, provides for raising an exception. An application can build a set of exceptions that provide specific information on the nature of the error, which is passed to the exception handler. The Java MDAPI method will always raise an exception to indicate that an error has occurred.

As we can see in Figure 8.8, there are many instances in which there are one-to-many relationships. Consider for example the relationship between the hierarchy object and the level object. In both cases, the relationship is one-to-many. In such cases, the application has to know which and how many objects there are in the relationship. The Java MDAPI implementation uses a *collection class* to represent these relationships. A collection class is a type of container that holds other objects. It *collects* the other objects. The collection can collect the objects in the one-to-many relationships. Once the objects are contained in the collection, the application can then interact with the objects as necessary.

## 8.5 JavaBeans

We began our introduction to object-oriented programming by describing how years ago project managers would create libraries of common functions. We repeatedly used these functions throughout the project lifecycle, with the aim of increasing both productivity and system integrity. This is one of the aims of object-oriented programming—to increase the reusability of code. This is also one of the aims of Java. Up to this point, however, we have primarily focused on Java's abstraction of the underlying IEBI platform. The Data Mining API provides a means for clients to connect to a back-end data mining engine. The MDAPI provides a means of writing an application with a common set of objects that can be independent of the underlying multidimensional database.

In all of the cases, we still need to sit down and write the application. Wouldn't it be wonderful if we could leverage the reusability given to us by Java's object orientation to develop IEBI systems? Fortunately, the Java language designers have seen this need and provided us with JavaBeans. There are two types of JavaBeans, JavaBeans and Enterprise JavaBeans (EJB). JavaBeans are a specialized class of reusable components. They are self-contained objects assembled to form an application. We can envision these beans as the software entities that implement specific controls and widgets when developing an application. We will see in the subsection to follow, however, that they can be used in the middle tier as well to implement application logic. Developers write the beans according to a set of rules that define how the tools interact with one another. By following these rules, the Java-Beans can be integrated into any Integrated Development Environment (IDE). Tools such as Oracle's Jdeveloper, IBM's Visual Age, Inprise JBuilder, Sybase's PowerJ, and Symantec Visual Café all work with JavaBeans. The IDE is able to inspect the JavaBean and understand its methods and attributes. The tool can then manipulate the bean just as it would any other entity.

Application developers benefit from JavaBeans in two ways. First, organizations can use beans for their internal software development projects. This is similar to what we did in the old FORTRAN days. The first thing a development team does is create a base-level set of beans. These beans can implement such functionality as the User Interface (UI) components or application logic. With standardized beans for the UI, applications have the same look and feel throughout the organization. Beans can also be used in the development of applications. For example, a department may develop beans that read and write to a file according to some specific standard. Application developers use the beans to interact with the file, thus ensuring that the standard is enforced.

Application developers also benefit from the use of prebuilt JavaBeans developed by the Independent Software Vendor (ISV). An ISV may offer a data mining or OLAP tool. Along with the actual software, the ISV may distribute a set of beans that interact with the application. One could assume that since the ISV developed the tool, it will also know how to optimize the beans to use the tools in the most efficient manner. Application developers can then simply take the beans provided by the ISV and plug them into their homegrown application. This of course results in inexpensive, efficient applications specifically tailored to the needs of the organization.

These two benefits combined solve another issue faced by many organizations. We discussed in Chapter 5 the differences between information dictatorships, anarchies, and democracies. We noted how the Internet-enabled structure gives us the benefit of centralized control found in information dictatorships, while giving individual departments the independence found in information anarchies. This led to information democracies. JavaBeans are one of the features of the Internet that enabled us to develop such a democracy.

Departments that wish to develop their own applications often are not concerned with enterprise standards. This causes endless problems on an enterprise-wide scale. When the developer of the department's application disappears, IT is handed the task of supporting it. There are no UI or coding standards, so applications vary greatly from department to department. To resolve this issue, IT can simply release to the departments JavaBeans that meet the corporate standard. The departments can use these beans to develop their individual applications as they see necessary. The IT department is able to enforce its standard, while the department's application development effort is simplified.

The second class of beans we can discuss are EJBs, which address the ability to deploy component-based, distributed applications. The EJB architecture is defined by Sun as "a component architecture for the development and deployment of component-based distributed business applications. Applications written using the Enterprise JavaBeans architecture are scalable, transactional, and multi-user secure. These applications may be written once, and then deployed on any server platform that supports the Enterprise JavaBean specification."[4] We can envision EJB as an application framework for the development of application server components. Where JavaBeans support a component model, EJB support reusable components designed to run in an application server. These application server components are referred to as server components.

At first we might be tempted to look at EJB as an extension of JavaBeans, but this would be incorrect. JavaBeans use `java.beans` defined in the Java API. EJB uses the classes and interfaces in the `javax.ejb` package. JavaBeans define components such as UI interface objects and widgets. EJBs address the management of distributed objects in a multitier environment.

The concept behind EJB is that objects residing on a middle-tier server appear to be residing on the client. The actual location of the object is transparent to the client. Figure 8.9 shows how this works. In this figure, we have a simple distributed object called `OLAPSERVER`. Applications interact with the `OLAPSERVER` object via the `OLAP` interface, which is separate from its implementation. The `OLAPSERVER` object, however, supports the interface, providing to it the actual business logic and state. A stub on the client, in this case `OLAP_STUB`, resides on the client so that it seems as if the `OLAPSERVER` resides on the client. The stub communicates with the skeleton on the server to fulfill requests made by the client.

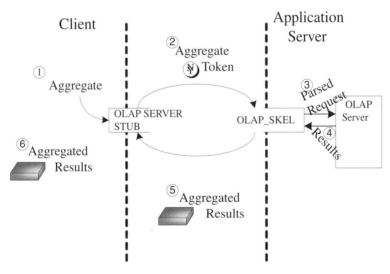

**FIGURE 8.9**   EJB remote method invocation.

---

[4] Sun Microsystems' Enterprise JavaBeans Specification, v1.1, Copyright 1999 by Sun Microsystems, Inc.

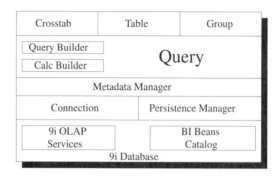

**FIGURE 8.10**   Oracle Business Intelligence Beans architecture.

To understand how this works, let's follow the request demonstrated in Figure 8.9. When a method, such as AGGREGATE, is invoked on the stub, a token is created and sent to the OLAP skeleton, OLAP_SKEL. The skeleton parses the request and invokes the appropriate method on the object. The object in turn passes back the results of the request, in this case the aggregate values. The skeleton passes the results back to the stub, which in turn passes it to the client. As far as the client is concerned, the request was made to and fulfilled by the client stub.

As we discussed in relation to JavaBeans, there are benefits to the use of EJB. Just as with JavaBeans, applications are standardized through out the organization. We can envision ISVs implementing their applications on the middle tier and distributing the appropriate stubs for further development by the user.

We discussed how JavaBeans can help ease the struggle between individual departments within an organization and IT. EJB takes us another step towards this goal. In Chapter 3, we compared IEBI environments in which a central data warehouse supports dependent data marts. Departments resist such centralized system because they want to maintain control of their applications. With EJB, departments are able to integrate their applications into a central system while still maintaining their freedom.

One of the concerns with giving the departments free access to the centralized data warehouse is the integrity of the data coming into the warehouse. In addition, standards need to be maintained for data access. Since the actual implementation of the object is on the server, the central IT department can maintain standards, yet turn over application development to the individual departments.

### 8.5.1   ORACLE 9i BUSINESS INTELLIGENCE BEANS

In this section, we examine the use of JavaBeans in an IEBI environment. Oracle has developed Oracle 9i Business Intelligence Beans, a set of standards-based BI beans that take advantage of the Oracle 9i OLAP. These are exactly what we discussed in the previous section—a set of building blocks upon which developers can quickly and easily build complex BI applications. These beans fall into three basic categories: Presentation, OLAP, and Catalog services. Figure 8.10 shows the architecture in which these beans fit together.

At the topmost level, we have the Presentation beans. Developers can choose to present data in three different modes: graph, table, or crosstab. Graphs provide complete analytical support for drilling, changing the graph layout, and providing data tips. Tables provide the traditional row-oriented data views. Crosstabs offer a multidimensional view of the data, providing such multidimensional capabilities as drilling and pivoting. Presentation beans are either Java-based for users with high-speed connections or HTML-based for users with slower dial-up connections.

Recall from our earlier discussion of object-oriented programming that we can build applications by reusing prebuilt objects. This is part of the motivation for designing Java as an object-oriented language as well as the concept behind Java-Beans. To achieve this objective, JavaBeans must be replicable, able to be used over and over again in different applications, and adaptable, able to be modified to meet the specific needs of the application. This poses a challenge, since the two goals seem to conflict with one another. How do we create objects that we can customize and still maintain repeatability? Oracle 9i Business Intelligence Beans uses presentation beans that provide *customizers* that enable end users to format the presentation of the data. The presentation beans customization allows the end user to modify all the aspects of presentation, such as formatting and filtering of the data.

Again, we see another example of replicability and adaptability in the second type of Oracle 9i Business Intelligence Beans, OLAPBeans. *Out of the box*, as they say, the OLAP Beans support the OLAP features integrated into the Oracle 9i database. Developers, however, are able to adapt the default functionality through a set of APIs. Additional OLAP functionality can be created via the Query Builder and the Calculation Builder. These tools allow the decision maker to create advanced calculations through templates. We discussed in Chapter 3 the importance of creating an environment in which the decision maker can truly interact with the data. These builder tools are important in this regard. They provide simplified access to the advanced OLAP features in Oracle 9i while freeing the decision maker from the necessity of understand the underlying SQL.

The Business Intelligence Beans Catalog manages the metadata definitions of all the developer and user defined BI objects. An XML-based catalog saves the definitions of all reports, graphs, favorite queries, and custom measures. These object definitions are organized into folders with security features that enable users to securely share reports and calculations. All client types, such as Java and HTML, support the definitions within the Business Intelligence Beans Catalog. The application logic can be deployed on any of the different tiers, such as a thin client or Java client, yet all the logic resides on the middle tier.

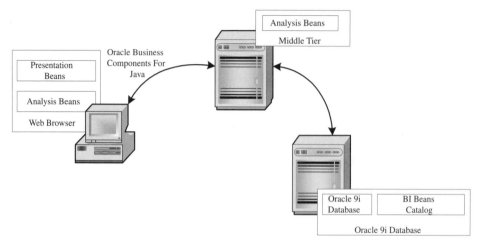

**FIGURE 8.11**   Oracle Business Intelligence Beans.

In Figure 8.11 we see how the Oracle 9i Business Intelligence Beans work together. The presentation beans are downloaded to the client's browser. Proxy objects are also downloaded to the client's browser to provide a *stub* for the OLAP Beans. The actual implementation of the beans occurs on the middle tier. By implementing the objects on the middle tier, applications can be written to support a variety of clients. The proxy object communicates with the middle tier via the Oracle Business Components for Java, eliminating the need for the developer to deal with a CORBA connection.

Oracle 9i Business Intelligence Beans demonstrate two important features of Java and JavaBeans. They have been able to successfully leverage the object-oriented aspects of Java to provide a scalable, portable BI environment over the Internet. They have also shown how software providers can use beans to extend the functionality of their products. Since it is Oracle, they are able to develop beans that are more fully integrated into the underlying OLAP engine. This of course results in better performance, greater functionality, and a higher level of integration. As other software vendors follow suit, the benefits of JavaBeans and EJB will become more pronounced in the general software industry as well as in the world of IEBI.

## 8.6   Conclusion

In this chapter, we explored the Java language and platform. Java is of course important to anyone developing an Internet-enabled application, but it is especially important to those of us developing IEBI systems. Its implementation simplifies the development of applications that extend across the entire value chain.

Throughout this chapter, we discussed the features of Java and how they might be applied to IEBI. We traveled through the forest, examining the trees. Let us now pause on the hilltop overlooking the forest. Let us now look at Java as a complete entity. What we see is an environment rich in resources. The Java platform, in its various editions, digs down deeply into the very systems upon which the Internet is built, providing us with the ability to extend IEBI to such systems as servers, desktops, and even wireless devices. It also reaches up into the very top of our applications, providing us with JavaBeans and APIs to implement our IEBI systems. All of this is built in an object-oriented environment that abstracts the underlying structures, giving us the advantages of an architecturally neutral, portable, development environment.

Years ago, when I was a very young programmer, I was briefly employed at the Jet Propulsions Laboratories in Pasadena, California, working on the Deep Space Network. It was an interesting assignment, to say the least. While there, I witnessed the volume of coffee consumed by the staff who worked so long and diligently to develop these advanced systems. This was in the days long before boutique coffee shops and gingerbread latte. Back then, coffee was coffee: hot, black, strong, and quite often thick. Since then, I have often thought that man would never have made it to the moon if it weren't for the coffee. That was a long time ago—the first foray into the New Frontier. We now have Java. One can only imagine where that will lead.

# Chapter 9

# eXtensible Markup Language

*And the whole earth was of one language, and of one speech. And it came to pass, as they journeyed from the east that they found a plain in the land of Shinar; and they dwelt there. And they said one to another, Go to, let us make brick, and burn them thoroughly. And they had brick for stone, and slime had they for mortar. And they said, Go to, let us build us a city and a tower, whose top may reach unto heaven; and let us make us a name, lest we be scattered abroad upon the face of the whole earth. And the Lord came down to see the city and the tower, which the children of men builded. And the Lord said, Behold, the people is one, and they have all one language; and this they begin to do: and now nothing will be restrained from them, which they have imagined to do. Go to, let us go down and confound their language, that they may not understand one another's speech. So the Lord scattered them abroad from thence upon the face of all the earth: and they left off to build the city. Therefore is the name of it called Babel; because the Lord did there confound the language of all the earth.*

*Genesis 11:1–9*

In the preceding chapters, when we looked at the information infrastructure as a complete entity, we included such devices as cell phones, pagers, and Personal Digital Assistants (PDAs). Including these devices in the organization's information infrastructure provides decision makers with instantaneous access to strategic information no matter where he or she might be. Consider how we might tie these devices into an information infrastructure. A Balanced Scorecard application, for example, can send notifications to a decision maker's cell phone when Key Performance Indicators (KPIs) fall out of range. C-level executives can query decision support systems from their PDAs, whether they are in a car on the way to the airport or in a meeting in a partner's conference room.

These devices allow us to extend the reach of IEBI beyond the four walls of our organization to locations that may not be conveniently wired for Internet access. In reviewing the wireless option of Oracle's Application Server, 9iAS, we noted how it enabled the distribution of information to these devices using eXtensible Markup Language (XML). The Java platform J2ME is dedicated to developing applications that can be supported by these devices. J2ME can employ XML to distribute data to various wireless devices. The dissemination of information to an ever-expanding set of wireless devices, however, is just one use of XML. It exemplifies the ability of the markup language to act as a common language in the communication of data as well as in the structure in which the data resides.

The universal delivery of information, both within the corporation as well as to its partners, requires system and device independence. The need, therefore, is to devise a common language for the communication of data while maintaining the structure and context of that data. The solution is a *metalanguage*, a language whose primary function is to express the metadata surrounding data. In Chapter 10, we discuss metadata in detail. For now, we can rely on the trite definition, that metadata is data about data. It defines for us the structure, format, and characteristics of the data. Typically, metalanguages are referred to as markup languages, but as we shall see, the markup aspects of a metalanguage are just one of many characteristics.

Markup languages are not exclusive to the world of the Internet or even technology. The origins of all markup languages lie back in antiquity—that is to say, in the days of hardcopy. The squiggly lines and circles editors use to make corrections in manuscripts are an example of markup languages. These marks tell a compositor or typist how a particular section of text is to be presented. To see one form of markup language, simply view the hidden characters in a word processing document. These characters are all part of the markup language for that word processor. In the Internet age, we have extended this concept to develop a language that describes how data is to be displayed while allowing the device itself to decide the specifics on how to display it. The creator of the information is able to describe the format of the document while maintaining device-independence. The device displaying the document, however, can use the markup information to display the document in a way most appropriate to its own environment. In short, while the document is defined independently, it is displayed dependently.

This chapter focuses on XML. This metalanguage combines a wide breadth of functionality while maintaining its simplicity. We begin this introduction with a brief view of its origin and history to provide a contrast to other markup languages and develop an appreciation for the simplicity and strength of the language. We then explore the details of XML and how to use it. Once we understand how it works we look at XML in action by reviewing the application of XML in the BI space.

## 9.1 The Origins of XML

XML is more than YAML (Yet Another Markup Language). Figure 9.1 presents the XML family tree. The XML standard shares the same heritage as HyperText Markup Language (HTML); both are descendents of the Standard Generalized Markup Language (SGML). XML, while combining many features of both its parent and sibling, overcomes their drawbacks. Where SGML is complex, XML is simple. Where HTML is limited, XML is powerful. To understand this difference, let's begin our examination of XML by looking at the entire family.

SGML became an international standard in 1986. It is described in ISO (International Standard Organization) 8879. You may recall from Chapter 6 that ISO is one of our friendly standards bodies. Like other markup languages, document designers use SGML to define their own format for documents independent of the destination device or system. The strength of SGML is that it can be used to format large, complex documents or vast repositories of information. It does more than simply describe a visual image. It actually creates a structure for the document. This makes the standard ideal for large mission-critical systems. Companies that produced large documents are able to take advantage of SGML's power and flexibility. The disadvantage is that the ability to handle these large complex documents and repositories has made the SGML standard itself large and complex.

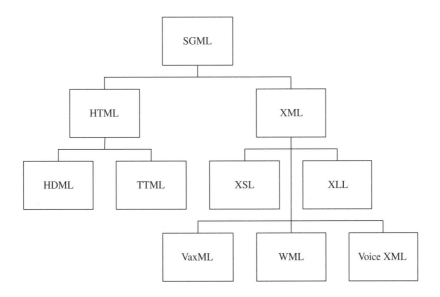

**FIGURE 9.1** Markup languages family tree.

As we have seen, cost is typically a by-product of complexity. The complexity of SGML made the standard the language of large corporations. The required initial investment for SGML document processing was too large for smaller organizations. The issue, therefore, remained: How do companies, especially smaller organizations, deliver information over the Web, an environment with a plethora of destination system types? The easiest solution to this problem was to create a subset of SGML specifically designed for the World Wide Web. This subset should be simple yet flexible enough to display the information in an independent manner. This was the birth of HTML.

Tim Berners-Lee at CERN first developed the HTML in 1989. The greatest difference between HTML and SGML was its objective. HTML simply created a way to express how documents' text and images were to be displayed. It did not provide a structure to the document, as did SGML. Note that HTTP is concerned with the transmission of not only documents, but also of *hypertext* documents. These are documents with links to other parts of the document as well as to other documents.

This simplicity made HTML inexpensive enough for any organization to create and transmit hypertext documents. A hypertext document was not all that different from a word processing document with embedded tags. This simplification also had its liabilities. HTML, while simple, lacked structure. Without the ability to distinguish between the different parts of a document, systems were unable to manipulate the subsections. Simple tasks such as numbering section headings or locating section titles in a document became much more difficult. As we shall see later, this lack of structure created other issues that could not be resolved by HTML. While one might be tempted to call this a deficiency of the language, it must be remembered that structure was not necessary to HTML's objectives.

As we can see in Figure 9.1, the XML standard is not a replacement for SGML or HTML but a complement to it. The objectives of the XML metalanguage recognize SGML's complexity and structure as well as HTML's simplicity and lack of structure. XML defined three simple objectives: extensibility, structure, and validation. One might call the XML standard the Goldilocks of markup languages. SGML is too complex. HTML is too simple, but XML is just right.

As the name implies, XML is an extensible markup language. HTML has a fixed set of tags and attributes, which are defined by the World Wide Web Consortium (W3C). XML, on the other hand, allows the definition of tags. Document authors can create new tags and attribute names as they see fit. This empowers XML designers to create sets of tags that address specific needs. Examples of such extensions include the Chemical Markup Language (CML) for the chemical industry and the Mathematical Markup Language (MML) that provides tags and attributes for the representation of math formulas. There are also extensions that range from the Resource Description Framework (RDF) that provides the integration of metadata to the eXtensible User interface Language (XUL) that provides the customization of user interfaces.

The second objective of XML is that of structure. Eskimos have hundreds of different words for snow, but none for palm trees. The simplicity of HTML makes it wonderful for the construction of Web pages, which is the intent of the language. Web pages, however, don't necessarily require any real structure. Structure to HTML is like a palm tree to an Eskimo. XML makes it possible to support structures such as hierarchies and data associations. We shall see in Chapter 10 how XML is used by the Common Warehouse Metadata Interchange (CWMI) to provide such a structure for the exchange of metadata.

Structure allows a document to be divided into its component parts, making it much easier to process. Consider a book, for example. It is composed of sections, chapters, paragraphs, and diagrams. Breaking these apart for storage into a database becomes a much simpler task if the structure of the document is understood. It is also possible to take parts of a document and process them differently. Perhaps a report designer would like to send the executive summary to the information portals of the organization's C-level executives, with a link to the actual report stored somewhere else on the Web. It may be desirable to store the contents of the report in a database, where specific parts, such as the executive summary or conclusions, can be viewed periodically and all the detail archived elsewhere. If we assume that the report is generated frequently, the task becomes burdensome in an unstructured document. In a structured environment, the component parts of the report can be distributed as the author sees fit. This structure also allows the author to store these component parts into a database.

The third objective in the design of XML is that of validation. HTML does not have a way for the application working with the HTML document to validate the syntax of the document it receives. When we think about it, this makes sense. HTML has no need for validation. HTML documents are either valid HTML documents or they are not. The originating author should be able to easily validate the document. XML, however, is extensible. The author of an XML document can extend XML to fit his or her particular needs. As such, the application receiving the XML document must be able to validate the document.

There are two levels of validation. The first is what is known as simply a *well-formed* document. A valid document defines itself. This is the case where the author has defined his or her own set of tags, which are used within the document. The second level of validation is that of being *valid*. A valid document strictly complies with the markup and syntax of a particular environment. Although it is possible for the definition of this environment to be defined within the document, as we shall see in the next section, it is not necessary to do so. While this may seem a bit nebulous, we will elaborate on document validation later in this chapter.

## 9.2  XML as a Medium of Exchange

While XML may be an improvement over both SGML and HTML in general, we are concerned with specifically how XML helps the data warehouse architect. As we shall see in this section, the objectives of XML (extensibility, structure, and validation) make it especially well suited for BI applications. The Internet expands the scope of IEBI, providing additional sources of data as well as new channels for the distribution of information. This is shown in Figure 9.2. In this diagram, we see that XML can serve as the main interface for the exchange of data between systems that are both internal and external to the organization. These systems can be both the source of data feeding our IEBI system as well as the destination of the IEBI system's output.

Let's begin by examining the source side of the equation. One of the challenges in IEBI is the integration of data from heterogeneous systems. XML simplifies this task. In Figure 9.3, receiving XML data is compared with receiving a standard ASCII file. At the heart of receiving the standard ASCII file is an application that makes sense out of the file. This application parses that data, validates it according to some set of business rules, and loads it into memory. On the XML side, a Docu-

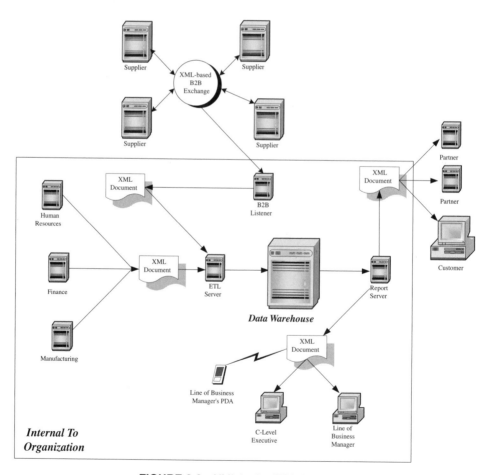

**FIGURE 9.2**  XML in the IEBI data flow.

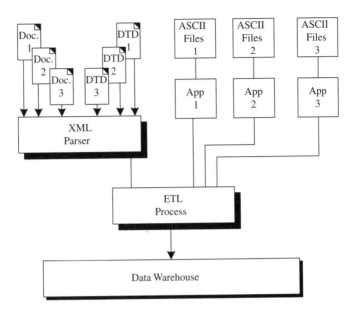

**FIGURE 9.3** XML ASCII input comparison.

ment Type Definition (DTD) describes the structure of the XML document that contains the input data. A standard XML parser receives as input both the XML document and the DTD. It then parses the document according to the description in the DTD. The data is then passed to the ETL process, which incorporates it into the data warehouse.

In the ASCII environment, as the business rules change or as the additional file types are added to the input stream, the parsing application must be updated. This of course requires regeneration of code as well as testing and integration of the new code into the existing system. In the XML environment, the DTD reflects changes in the structure of the input as well as changes in the business rules. As the environment changes, so does the DTD. The process that actually performs the parsing remains the same. We will see later in this chapter that it is far simpler to maintain a DTD than an actual application.

Quite often the structure of the input may vary with the source. Perhaps there are multiple suppliers, each using their own ASCII file structure. In such cases, either a single, very complex application is written to process each of the file types or multiple parsing programs are maintained for each file type. Both solutions increase the complexity of the IEBI system. On the XML side, a separate DTD is maintained for each file type. The parsing program simply parses the input XML document, validating it against its DTD.

We can now apply this XML data integration process to our XML-based B2B exchange. Referring to Figure 9.2, we can see how to use XML to monitor activities on our XML-based B2B exchange. Information is passed between participants in the exchange via XML documents. A listener monitors the activities between the participants of the exchange, copying the XML documents. These documents are then incorporated into the data warehouse, where they are merged with data from other parts of the organization.

Figure 9.2 also shows how XML can be used in the distribution of data. Just as we expect partners to share their strategic information with us for their benefit, we in turn benefit by sharing our own strategic information with them. We can of course do this using an XML report server. The data is generated once. Then, using the XML structure, it is divided and distributed to both partners and customers based on their specific needs. While each partner gets a copy of the same report, the data they receive is tailored to their specific needs. Customers, on the other hand, receive a completely different set of reports. All of this information is divided using XML structures.

We can see that using XML allows us to provide different views of the same data. As shown in Figure 9.2, the reports server performs that actual extraction of the data from the data warehouse. The data is stored in the reports server in an XML document. The data is then distributed to the individual users from the reports server. The content and structure of the data is based on the needs of the individual user. For example, C-level executives may receive aggregated data of the performance of all regions, while regional managers receive detailed information on the performance of their individual region.

Another benefit of the XML structure is the ability to send a complete structure to an individual PC or workstation and push the processing of that structure down to that workstation. For example, we have a multidimensional structure that an analyst may wish to manipulate. We can send the entire structure to the analyst, who can then take the structure and perform whichever multidimensional operations he or she may choose locally. This has the advantage of allowing the analyst to work on the data when he or she is unable to connect to the Internet.

We can see in Figure 9.2 that there are several areas where IEBI can leverage the capabilities of XML. These capabilities can be summarized as

1. The validation and extensibility aspects of XML make it useful in bringing together data from many independent systems.
2. The structure capabilities make it possible to generate a report once while tailoring the final output of that report to the specific user's needs.

The structure capabilities also enable much of the processing to be offloaded from the central data warehouse to the middle-tier servers.

## 9.3    The All-Powerful Wizard of XML

The previous sections describe the *wonderfulness* that is XML. Actually, there is a problem with XML. The problem is that XML is very simple. In fact, it is so simple that people like me have a difficult time writing substantive books on it. How do you fill 700 pages with something as easy to understand as XML? Well, in this section, we will show you how to put together an XML document. Now, there are many very good books on XML that provide all sorts of information relating to the markup language, but to understand the guts of XML, the real substantive parts, takes just a few pages. We'll prove it by doing so here.

As we have already stated several times in this chapter, XML provides a means to create a structure into which you place your document. There are three simple syntactical rules to follow to create this structure. The tree consists of a root with elements, attributes, and text. The structure begins at the root from which extends branches, which are the elements. These branches can lead to other branches or leaves, which ultimately contain the data. The rules to create the structure are as follows:

1. Everything is based on one and only one root.
2. Any tag that is opened must also be closed.
3. Attributes must be quoted.

The simplicity of these rules provides almost limitless variations. We may wish, for example, to create a structure that defines an address. In Figure 9.4, we have diagrammed the address structure and shown the XML that describes this structure. This is a simple structure composed of one tag, address. To create this structure, we open a tag and then close it. The tag is opened with the angle brackets: *<tag name>*. The tag is then closed with angle brackets as well, but with a slash preceding the tag name: *</tag name>*. This tag creates the components of the structure. In our example, we have just one component, address. All the data for the address is within this one structure. In some cases, this would be fine, but what if we were interested in the components of the address? We are no better off with this structure than if we had simply created the address with free-formatted text.

In order to access the components of the address, we can define a more elaborate structure. This is shown in Figure 9.5. Here we see a complete layout of the address with each component fully expanded. In this example, we have a tree-like structure where *Address* is the root. From this root the tree expands to the different branches of Name, House, and Locality. Each branch expands to the individual data elements, or leaves.

```
<address>
Alfred E Newman
1313 Mocking Bird Lane
Pine Falls MN 52523
</address>
```

**FIGURE 9.4** Simple address structure.

By simply parsing this XML document, we can create the structure of the address. This structure of course makes it much simpler to extract the individual elements of the address. If, for example, we wish to extract the city or zip code from the address, we can do so easily. This gives us a great advantage over simple text

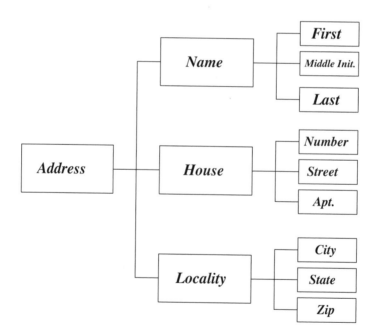

```
<address>
   <name>
      <first>Alfred</first><mid-init>E</mid-init><last>Newman</last>
   </name>
   <house>
      <number>1313</number><street>Mocking Bird Lane</street><apt></apt>
   </house>
   <locality>
      <city>Pine Falls</city><state>MN</state><zip>52523</zip>
   <locality>
</address>
```

**FIGURE 9.5** A complete address.

blocks or even the previous XML address structure. No longer are we dealing with one amorphous blob of ASCII data, but with a well-defined structure whose individual components have a distinct beginning, middle, and end. Applications working with this document can easily parse the document correctly. Once the document is parsed, the receiving application can apply the appropriate style sheets or embed any desired link.

This document is described as *valid*—that is, it meets all the syntactical XML requirements. First, the structure of the document has one root, *Address*. Second, every tag that has been opened is also closed (unless I made a syntactical error that proofreading did not catch.) The third rule concerning attributes at this point is inapplicable, since the address does not have any attributes. Note that valid is the base level for XML documents. A valid document creates a tree-like structure. Documents that are not valid do not create this structure and cannot be considered an XML document.

In reviewing the example, we see that there is really no way with a valid document to verify the structure itself. The example does not include the country of the address. This may be correct, but then again, it may not be. There is no structure arbitrator in a well-formed document to mandate what should and shouldn't be included in a structure. The receiving application assumes that a well-formed XML document is correct.

A *well-formed* document is a valid document whose structure is defined in a DTD. The question of whether the developer requires XML documents to be valid or well-formed is up to the individual. As with all design issues, the system architect needs to determine the need, as well as the cost, for meeting the higher standard. If the cost of dealing with invalid yet valid documents is less than the cost of requiring well-formedness, then it is probably not worth enforcing the higher standard.

The DTD provides a definition of our document's structure. It enables a *parser* to understand the structural pieces of the document and make them available to the receiving application. In Figure 9.6, we see the DTD for an annual report.

```
<!ELEMENT report    (header, unit, corp-sum)>
<!ATTLIST year_qtr NUMBER #REQUIRED>
<!ELEMENT header    (rpt_title, date, executive-sum)>
<!ELEMENT rpt_title(#PCDATA)>
<!ELEMENT date      (#PCDATA)>
<!ELEMENT exec-sum (title, paragraph+)>
<!ELEMENT paragraph(#PCDATA)>
<!ELEMENT unit      (title, overview, table)>
<!ELEMENT overview (paragraph+)>
<!ELEMENT table     (head-row, data-row+)>
<!ELEMENT head-row (item-col, data-col)>
<!ELEMENT item-col (CDATA)>
<!ELEMENT data-col (CDATA)>
<!ELEMENT data-row (item-name, data-value)>
<!ELEMENT title     (#PCDATA)>
<!ELEMENT item-name(CDATA)>
<!ELEMENT data-value (CDATA)>
<!ELEMENT corp-sum (title, overview)>
```

**FIGURE 9.6**  DTD of an annual report.

We see in the figure above how to declare the document and the structures that comprise the document. Each of these lines follows the same basic format.

```
<!ELEMENT name (content specification)>
```

where

❏ `<!ELEMENT`—Key phrase specifying that this is an element type declaration.

❏ Name—The name of the element being declared.

❏ (content specification)—Specifies the content of the element. An element can contain

  • Other Elements—In this case, the name of the element is enclosed in the parentheses. Multiple elements are delimited by commas. This is demonstrated in the first line of the example with the declaration of the book element.

  • EMPTY—Signifies that the element is empty.

  • CDATA—Signifies that the element contains character data.

  • #PCDATA—Signifies that the element contains parsed character data.

❏ Content specification+—A plus sign signifies that there can be multiple occurrences of the content. This can be seen in the specification of the executive summary element that allows for multiple paragraphs to be included within the executive summary.

❏ >— Closes the element specification.

We also see in this DTD a specification for an attribute. The following statement specifies the attribute:

```
<!ATTLIST year_qtr   NUMBER #REQUIRED>
```

The attribute allows the developer to add explanatory notes to the document—in effect, metadata. The attribute is not part of the content of the element, but a way of providing descriptive information about the XML document or the specific element. In this particular example, the attribute `year_qtr` provides information on the fiscal year and quarter of the report. Often, the attributes provide hyperlinks to other data elements.

The DTD, however, simply describes the structure of the document. Figure 9.7 charts this structure. It does not provide the content. The structure tells us what components are expected and where they fit together. The content of this structure is something else completely. We present content of the quarterly report in Figure 9.8. We can see part of the appeal of XML. This annual report can be easily archived within a database. Later, applications can compare individual components of this report with past reports. It may be desirable to break up the report and distribute just the corporate summary along with the individual departments' results. The point here is that we now have a structure with which we can work.

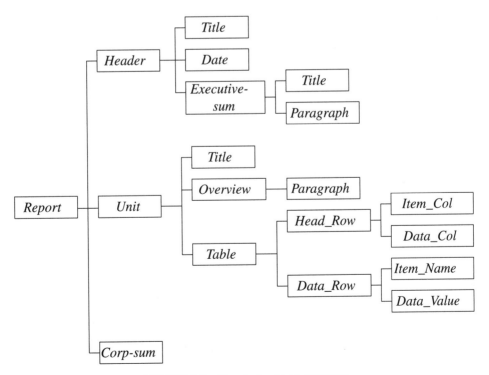

**FIGURE 9.7**  Quarterly report structure.

The DTD provides a means for the application receiving the document to determine if the structure is complete. In order for a document to be well-formed, it must conform to its DTD. Documents can, however, meet the standard of valid without a DTD. Each has its purpose. Often, when working over the Internet, an application may not have access to a DTD. There may be nothing wrong with the actual document or with the XML structure it describes—it simply may not have an associated DTD. In such cases, meeting the valid standard may suffice.

```
<report>
<header>
<rpt_title>Big Time Corporation Third Quarter
    Report</rpt_title>
<date>March 17, 2001</date>
<executive-sum>
<title>Another Record Breaking Quarter</title>
<paragraph>This had been a really terrific..
    </paragraph>
..more paragraphs..
</executive-sum>
</header>
<year_qtr = "2001">
<unit>
<title>Western Sales Region</title>
<overview>..The west is wild with sales ..</overview>
<table>
<head-row>
<item-col>Products</item-col><data-col>Units
    Sold</data-col>
</head-row>
<data-row>
<item-name>Tapioca</item-name><4000>
</data-row>
..more data rows..
</table>
</unit>
..more business units..
<corp-sum>
<title>A Healthy Outlook</title>
<overview>..This has been a very good quarter
    ..</overview>
</corp-sum>
</report>
```

**FIGURE 9.8** Quarterly report.

We discussed how the XML standard can be extended for specific industries and applications. The creation of a DTD is how we achieve this extension. Organizations wishing to create a standard by which applications can communicate over the Internet create and distribute the DTD for that standard. Documents are passed and validated against this DTD. For example, if we wish to establish an electronic data interchange (EDI) standard so that we can communicate more easily to both customers and suppliers, we simply create a DTD that describes the documents we expect to receive and transmit. We now have a common language by which our organizations can communicate with one another.

## 9.4    Parsers: Nothing Happens Until Someone Sells Something

I have a favorite business expression: Nothing happens until someone sells something. A corollary to this is that when all is said and done, there is more said than done. Well, that's enough for clever and witty sayings. The point is that there needs to be some practical implementation to all solutions. In business, all the lovely products in the world don't mean a gosh darn thing until some one goes out and sells the stuff. In planning, all the *nice* ideas are great, but there needs to be some implementation. In the world of XML, it is great to have all these nicely structured files flying around the ether space, but there needs to be a way for the software to practically take advantage of them. We discussed how nicely XML structures documents. We discussed how important that is to the application, but the question of how we access and work with this structure remains.

This is where parsers come into play. Parsers are that interface between the application and the XML document. The concept of a parser is actually quite common. For many years, compilers worked in two basic phases. The first phase grouped characters into tokens and words. In the second phase, parsers identified the constructs made by these words. These constructs were the basis for generating executable code. Parsers in the world of XML perform the same function; they break a document down into its component parts. This decomposition provides the developer with two capabilities: the verification of the structure of the document access to the component parts of the XML document.

The first use of a parser, to verify the structure of the XML document, requires that the parser be able to verify documents at both the valid level and the well-formed level. Remember that validity is the less stringent of the two. We discussed in the previous section the three simple rules required for a document to be valid. The parser checks the documents to insure that it meets these criteria. We made the point in the previous section that valid is the base level. A document that is not valid cannot be considered an XML document. A parser should also be able to recognize the higher XML standard, well-formedness. A well-formed document is one whose structure is verified against a DTD. The parser should be able to take as input both the DTD and the XML document and validate the XML document against the DTD.

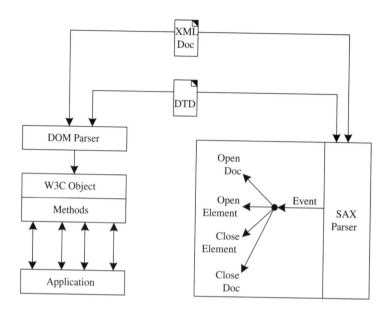

**FIGURE 9.9** DOM versus SAX.

The second function of a parser is to extract the data from the XML document. Earlier in this chapter, we compared receiving XML documents with standard ASCII files. We noted that the main difference between the two is that as documents evolve or as new types of documents are added, there is no need to rewrite the transformation program to accept these changes. In the XML world, we simply pass the parser a DTD that has incorporated these changes. Used in this manner, parsers are the software component that transforms the XML document into data in memory. The application can then work with the data, whether it is storing it in a database, displaying it, or simply using it in some calculation.

Of course, to work with the parser, the application needs some means by which it can invoke its functionality. While the number of parsers continues to grow, there is a move to standardize the parser interfaces. One standard is the Document Object Model (DOM) which employs, as the name implies, an object-oriented approach. The parser builds a document object in memory. The second method is an event-based approach. This method is employed by the SAX (Simple API for XML) standard, where the application events are driven by the XML document. Figure 9.9 contrasts the two types of parser interfaces.

There are three basic DOM levels. A first level DOM parser, DOM Level 0, receives a structured document and generates a W3C-compliant document object. The entire document is stored in memory as an object. The details of the object are hidden within the object. The application uses DOM methods and interfaces to extract the data from the object.

Level 1, the second level DOM, is separated into two parts: CORE and HTML. The CORE defines low-level interfaces that represent *any* structured document. These core interfaces therefore provide a means by which applications can access HTML as well as XML documents. The core also contains extended interfaces for XML that are not required by the standard if the parser is designed specifically for HTML documents. The second part of DOM Level 1 defines higher level interfaces for the HTML documents. DOM level 2, as with the previous levels, specifies a platform-independent and language-independent interface. This standard defines an interface for the access and update of the content and structure of documents. The basis of DOM level 2 is DOM level 1 core.

SAX standardizes the interface details for an event-based callback interface. The design of SAX overcomes what proponents feel are drawbacks to DOM. For example, DOM loads the entire document into memory. While this may enhance performance, it can be a challenge, particularly when working with very large documents. Since SAX abandons the object approach, it doesn't encounter memory or performance problems that can sometime plague object-oriented implementations. The challenge with SAX, however, is that the programming paradigm is somewhat different from what most programmers are accustomed to.

Actually, SAX is somewhat reminiscent of real-time programming. Real-time applications sit and listen for an interrupt. Then, depending on the interrupt level, a particular interrupt handler is invoked. With SAX, as the application moves through the XML document, different software units are activated. This may sound a bit unusual at first, but it is really rather simple. Since all valid XML documents contain a basic tree structure, we can be certain of encountering certain events as we traverse an XML document. For example, we know that we can expect a start and an end to the document. We also know that we will encounter a beginning and an end element. Perhaps we receive several different types of files, as in a B2B exchange. When we encounter a document beginning, we can open the necessary files for processing that document type. As we work our way through the document, we may write records to the database at the end of each element. Once we encounter a document end, we may terminate our application.

## 9.5   XSL: The Internet's Rosetta Stone

In 1799 near the lower Egyptian town of Rosetta, French troops discovered a black basalt slab that turned out to be of great importance in understanding ancient cultures. The stone, known today as the Rosetta Stone, bore three different scripts: hieroglyphic, demotic, and Greek. The scripts each told the same story. In 1822, French Egyptologist Jean Francois Champollion was able to decipher this stone, making it possible to translate papyri and other stones. This translation identified the clues essential in deciphering all ancient Egyptian inscriptions.

Today we are in a new age. Information is no longer etched in stone but sent electronically through wires and fiber optic cables. Throughout this chapter, we have discussed how XML can be used as a means of providing structure to this data so that it is more easily communicated. We have not discussed, however, the weightier matter of how this XML translation occurs. Of course, we are always left with the alternative of translating this data programmatically. While this is certainly an option, it defeats the purpose of XML being a simple way to communicate information between systems.

The solution, as one can no doubt surmise from the title of this section, is XSL, eXtensible Stylesheet Language. XSL turns out to be the Rosetta Stone of the Internet age. It contains two XML applications, which operate independently of one another: one to transform the documents and one to format the resultant output. It is important to note the independent aspects of the two applications. In many environments, the representation or format of the data is not relevant. We have seen this in the B2B space, where XML is used merely to translate the data from one system's format to another. There is no human review of the data, so formatting is unnecessary.

Eventually, the data needs to be displayed; this is especially the case in the BI arena. XSL therefore deals with the display of information, providing transformations to HTML as well as XML. Transformations to XML documents are not restricted to the original set of tags established in the original document's DTD. Transformations can generate completely new sets of tags in the resultant XML or HTML document.

The transformation can occur on either the server or the client. The transformation can be performed in advance and stored on the server. We will see an example of this when reviewing a real-world use of XML in an IEBI environment. The transformation can also occur when requested on the client. Figure 9.10 presents the simplicity of an XSL transformation. As shown in the diagram, the transformation receives as input the XSL style sheet, the input document, and optionally the DTD of the input document. The input document can be of any markup language that is a descendent of XML. The transformation process requires that the input document contain a tree structure. This means that all input documents must meet the XML validity requirement. Whether the input is XML, HTML, or SGML, all must be valid.

The second input is actually a specific type of XML document, an XSL style sheet. This style sheet contains a series of transformation rules referred to as a *template*. Each rule is a *template element* containing a pattern and a description of the output. The pattern is the *match attribute* of the template element. The value of this pattern is compared with the nodes of the input XML document. Nodes matching the pattern described in the XSL template elements are formatted according to the content of that template element. The output is then put into an XSL transformation output tree. XSL's use of the input tree structure is what necessitates the input document's compliance to XML's validity requirement.

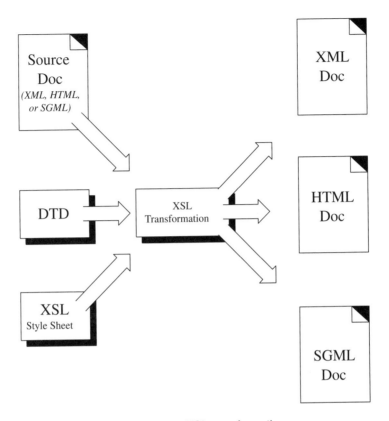

**FIGURE 9.10** XSL transformation.

While this explanation may seem a bit nebulous, let's look to our annual report for clarification. Let us say that we want to take the annual report and display it on our Web site. Of course, we would want to highlight the executive summary on a page of its own. Figure 9.11 presents the XSL style sheet for extracting the executive summary from the XML document to create an HTML file.

We now have the basic XSL template. The next step in the process is to use this template to generate an HTML file. The XSL process works with the input tree structure. It works its way through this structure, comparing each node in the structure with the elements of the template. To visualize this process a bit more clearly, we present the structure of the quarterly report in Figure 9.12. The XSL transformation process begins with the root node of the XML input document. It compares this node with all the template rules in the style sheet. We see that this matches the pattern of the first node in our XSL document. The output of this element is the opening HTML. This opening tag is written to the output document. We also see that the element directs the transformation to `apply-templates`. This causes the transformation to process the children of the current node.

```
<xsl:stylesheet>

  <xsl:template match="/">
    <html>
      <xsl:apply-templates/>
    </html>
  </xsl:template>

  <xsl:template match="header">
    <xsl:apply-templates/>
  </xsl:template>

  <xsl:template match="rpt_title">
    <head>
      <xsl:apply-templates select="rpt_title"/>
    </head>
  </xsl:template>

  <xsl:template match="executive_sum">
    <body>
      <xsl:apply-templates/>
    </body>
  </xsl:template>

  <xsl:template match="title">
    <b>
    <xsl:value-of select="title"/>
    </b>
  </xsl:template>

  <xsl:template match="paragraph">
    <xsl:value-of select="paragraph">
  </xsl:template>

</xsl:stylesheet>
```

**FIGURE 9.11**  XSL style sheet.

The next child in the structure is the header node. This also happens to match the next element in our XSL template. The content of this element is `apply-templates`, which causes the transformation to process the children of this node. The next node in the input XML document is the report title, which is contained in the `rpt_title` node. This node matches the next element of the XSL template. The content of the element outputs the report title to the header of the HTML page. It then directs the transformation to proceed to the next node in the XML structure with the `apply-templates` command.

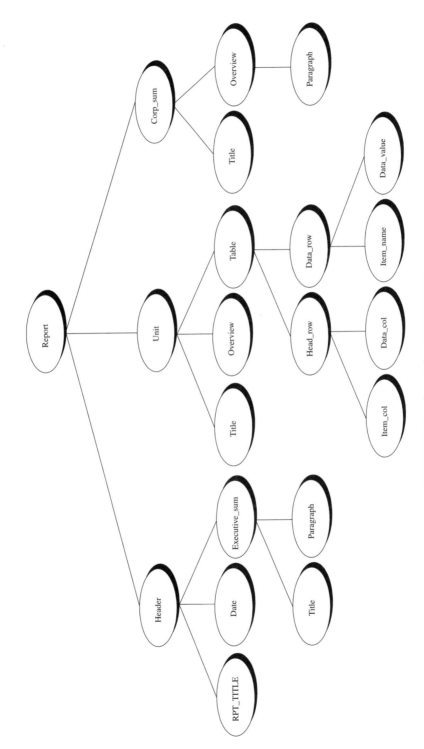

**FIGURE 9.12** Quarterly report structure.

```
<html>
   <head>
   BIG TIME CORPORATION THIRD QUARTER REPORT
   </head>
   <body>
   <b> Another Record Breaking Quarter </b>
   … … … more paragraphs … … …
   </body>
</html>
```

**FIGURE 9.13**  HTML version of quarterly report.

The next node in the header branch of the quarterly report is the executive summary. As we move into the `executive_summary` branch, the tag `body_text` is inserted into the HTML document. Nested within this insertion is another statement to apply the templates, which drives us down into the children nodes in the structure. The next child node is the `title` node that conveniently matches the pattern for the next element in the XSL template. This element's output causes the text "Another Record-Breaking Quarter" to be written out, surrounded by HTML bold tags, `<b>  </b>`. The template element is applied to the `paragraph` node within the executive summary. The difference is that the only output that is generated is the text within the original XML document. Figure 9.13 presents the results of the transformation process.

In reviewing Figure 9.13, we see that we have easily transformed an XML document into an HTML file. This process can be repeated for the rest of the quarterly report. Using attributes where appropriate, we can insert links between pages. As each quarterly report is generated, it is automatically posted to the corporate Web site, where employees, investors, market analysts, and even competitors can view it.

In this example, we placed a quarterly report on a Web site. Big deal, eh? What's this have to do with business intelligence? Well, let's not miss the vision because of this simplified example. In Figure 9.14 we show how we might be able to take advantage of XML in an Internet-enabled data warehouse. Think of what we can do with such a transformation process when applying it to BI. We discussed at the beginning of this chapter how the use of XML in a B2B exchange can simplify the extraction of the data from the daily transaction. We also showed that one of the advantages of XML is that we can take two documents, an XML document and a DTD, and easily convert them to a memory structure. This is presented in Figure 9.14. When we wish to convert different types of documents or make modifications to the current document, we change not the conversion process but the input to that process.

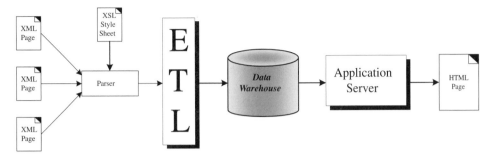

**FIGURE 9.14** XML in an Internet-enabled data warehouse.

Now, consider the nature of an exchange. It is still a transaction-oriented system where the structure and format of its data is to facilitate the processing of individual transactions, no different from any other source system. If the transactions are based on XML, however, the ETL process is greatly simplified. First, we know the structure of the XML documents flowing through the exchange, since we probably have the DTDs of these documents. If we don't, how can our exchange deal with them? We then use XSL to extract from these files the data we need for our data warehouse. The XSL transformation process goes through the document, searching for the nodes that are of interest, and writes them to the output XML document.

## 9.6 XML in the Real World

We have discussed the importance of XML and its ability to bring structure to documents as well as its ability to act as a common language across the Internet. We conclude our discussion of XML by examining a real-world example of its use in IEBI. In Chapter 5, we discussed Oracle 9i Application Server; in this chapter, we expand this discussion to show the mobile features that Oracle 9iAS Wireless uses to distribute information to various wireless devices. We also examine how this can be used in a real-world situation by an IEBI system.

In discussing the development of Internet-enabled applications, we noted the importance of moving much of the functionality of the application to the middle tier. The Java platform, discussed in Chapter 8, moves much of the business logic to the middle tier, leaving the client side free to maintain the user interface. This also frees the back-end server to focus on processing requests received from the middle. The application server supports the processing in this tier. Oracle 9iAS Wireless continues this strategy, moving the processing into the middle tier.

Figure 9.15 presents the architecture of Oracle 9iAS Wireless: Content flows from the data warehouse through the middle-tier application server to the client system. The key is that the content, which is the real asset to the data warehouse,

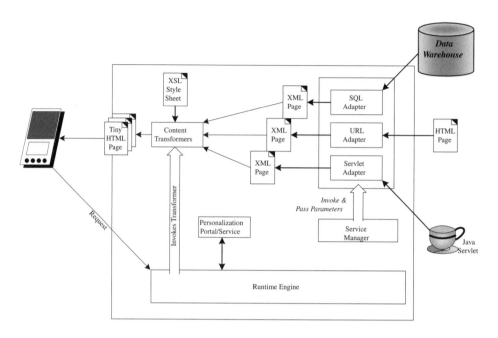

**FIGURE 9.15**   Oracle 9iAS Wireless architecture.

remains the same. It is adapted in the middle tier by the application server so that it can be easily displayed by the client device. The application server accepts input from a variety of sources: Web Pages (HTML), database applications, Java servlets, Java Server Pages (JSPs), and email. The *Content Adapters* and *Services Manager* components interact with the content services to provide Web services. These components abstract the content they receive by transforming it into XML. The XML is passed to the Oracle 9iAS Wireless *Content Transformers* and *PersonalizationService/Portal* components that transform the XML to the appropriate markup language for the user's specific device. The interaction between two sets of components is managed by the Oracle 9iAS Wireless runtime engine.

Let's take a more detailed look at how these components interact with one another. We begin with the Content Adapter. As the name implies, the Content Adapter gathers the data from the data source and adapts it, which means that it transforms it into an XML document. Now that we have the content in XML, we can distribute it to virtually any client device we wish. When we wish to provide a service through Oracle 9iAS Wireless, we must create a new Content Adapter. There are a number of prebuilt Content Adapters that include an SQL adapter, a Java servlet adapter, and a URL adapter to provide access to HTML pages.

The Service Manager that receives the request for the Web service via the run-time engine invokes the appropriate Content Adapter. The Service Manager demonstrates what we discussed theoretically in Chapter 5. We noted that part of the power of an application server is its ability to provide connection pooling. This is what the Service Manager does. When it receives a request from the Runtime Engine for a particular service, it invokes the appropriate service, passing the parameters required to service the request. The Content Adapter, however, is loaded only once, and the Service Manager pools the requests to the various adapters.

On the other side of the application server is the data out piece, the part of the application server that pushes the information out to the user. This is managed by the Content Transformer and Personalization Service/Portal Component. The Content Transformer transforms the XML document generated by the Content Adapter into the markup language that is appropriate for the user's device. The Content Transformer uses a device-specific XSL style sheet to perform the appropriate transformation. The selection of the style sheet is based on the context of the user's session. This context as well as personalization of the services provided to the user are managed through the Personalization Service/Portal.

As we have said time and again, BI needs to permeate the entire organization. We must no longer bind ourselves to the four walls that define the physical boundaries of our organization—we must look across the entire value chain. Oracle 9iAS Wireless does this using XML and many of the concepts discussed in this chapter. To see this in action, we return to our good friend Billy Boy of Billy Boy Bowling Balls. It's Monday morning and time for Billy to meet with one of his distributors, KingPin, to negotiate the contracts for the coming year. The agenda for the meeting indicates that KingPin will lay out their road map for the upcoming year. Based on that road map, the two organizations will coordinate their strategic plans.

Billy Boy, being the smart boy that he is, has implemented an IEBI system using Oracle 9iAS Wireless. As he prepared for the meeting, he reviewed the state of Billy Boy Bowling Balls' relationship with KingPin using his IEBI system. The system showed that the distributor has a commanding share of the market in the eastern and central United States. It also showed that while KingPin was one of their chief customers for low-margin standard balls, it was one of the lowest distributors of custom balls. Billy Boy of course came equipped with this information.

During the course of the distributor's presentation, KingPin noted that it was poised to establish offices in each of the major western markets. While it saw an across-the-board increase in sales, it also predicted tighter margins in the western region. If Billy Boy Bowling Balls wanted to continue to be KingPin's main supplier of standard bowling balls, KingPin would have to receive better discounts on standard bowling balls.

During the break, Billy Boy flipped open his PDA and connected to his IEBI portal. The first thing he did was check the company's Balanced Scorecard to see how the organization was performing in the west. It was quickly apparent that they were a number two or quite possibly a number three player in that market.

He then verified the margins on each of the different lines of bowling balls. This profitability analysis used activity-based costing to determine cost for each bowling ball line. He then returned to the meeting and proposed that he would agree to a deeper discount in the standard line of bowling balls if KingPin agreed to a significant increase in custom bowling balls. After some negotiation, the concept was accepted by both parties. The only question that remained was how much of an increase in custom balls Billy Boy would ask for how much of a discount in standard balls.

So what happened? How was Billy Boy supplied information by the IEBI system? Through the Personalization Service/Portal, Billy Boy was able to determine which services he was able to access through his PDA. Through this component, the link between the data content sources and the individual users is established. When Billy Boy establishes an HTTPS session, the Runtime Request Manager authenticates the user and recognizes the user's logical device. The runtime engine then sets up the environment for the user to start making requests. Based on the user's personalization information, the runtime engine loads a Content Transformer for the user's device and the Content Adapters for the desired services.

Billy Boy's first request is to the company's balanced scorecard. The scorecard is produced on an HTML Web page. When Billy Boy's request is received by the runtime engine, the request is passed to the Request Manager which in turn passes the request to the HTML Content Adapter. The adapter retrieves the information from the scorecard application and passes it back to the HTML Content Adapter, where it is converted into an XML document. The Content Transformer then takes that XML document along with the XSL Style Sheet for Billy Boy's PDA and converts it to a TinyHTML. The TinyHTML is then passed to Billy Boy's PDA.

One may wonder why we bother with this intermediate step of converting to XML from HTML. Couldn't we use an XSL style sheet to convert directly from HTML to TinyHTML? We could, but then all we could send out would be TinyHTML pages without another request to the back-end server. While Billy Boy is in negotiations with KingPin, his COO happens to be on vacation in Bora Bora. As a dedicated employee, he wants to make sure that everything is going well back home. Using a wireless connection to the Internet, he uses his pocket PC to review the company's balanced scorecard. Rather than making another request of the server, Oracle 9iAS Wireless takes that cached XML document and transforms the content for the COO's pocket PC.

Billy Boy also checked the margins on the different lines of bowling balls. The content source for this data is a Java servlet. In a manner similar to the balanced scorecard's Web page, the request was passed to the content source via the content adapter. The adapter converted this data to XML, which was then transformed to a TinyHTML Web page and passed to Billy Boy's PDA.

## 9.7   Conclusion

What is important about XML? Actually, why does IEBI care about XML? As we have repeated many times throughout this text, IEBI is significantly different from BI. It extends across the entire breadth of the value chain, reaching back through our suppliers to the very beginnings of the value chain. It also looks forward all the way to the end user. IEBI is also deeper than traditional BI. While some have seen BI as the purview of the C-level executive and top-level decision makers, IEBI reaches down to the depths of the organization. It permeates all processes and all activities.

The Internet has created the actual physical connections, however circuitous, between systems throughout the world. Through these connections, we can establish the electronic means of communications of the participants in our value chain. We need more than that, though. We need a means to create applications that can execute across this structure. We need the software that can run across this environment. Java fills this role: Java is a programming language and platform for the development of applications across the Internet. It has enabled us to reach across the Internet to connect with our suppliers. It has also enabled us, with its various editions, to reach down into our organization to provide support for the plethora of devices that are now able to connect to the Internet.

Having the hardware and the software is only part of the picture. We still need data. After all, both hardware and software exist for one purpose: to deliver data to the decision maker. In the old days, when we were all running in proprietary environments, we each had our own way to represent data: EBCDIC and ASCII. Even in the two-tier client/server days, it was still pretty simple. The output devices all had relatively the same characteristics, and we all spoke ASCII.

Today we are in a brave new world, a world in which we use many different types of devices with many different characteristics. XML provides the common language for the representation of the data across these many systems. With XML, we can communicate not only the actual content of the data, but its structure as well. We can use this common language to distribute our data to these many devices.

We can see where XML sits in the IEBI *structure*. At the base, we have the hardware that provides the connection between system. The applications sit on top of this hardware—this is Java. The applications provide the processing. The data is expressed in XML, and XSL provides the translation of the data for the various devices. It tops off the stack.

# Chapter 10

# COMMON WAREHOUSE
# METADATA

*"And only* one *for birthday presents, you know. There's glory for you!"*
*"I don't know what you mean by* glory," *Alice said.*

*Humpty Dumpty smiled contemptuously. "Of course you don't—till I tell you. I meant* there's a nice knock-down argument for you!"

*"But glory doesn't mean* a nice knock-down argument," *Alice objected.*

*"When* I *use a word," Humpty Dumpty said in rather a scornful tone, "it means just what* I *choose it to mean—neither more nor less."*

*"The question is," said Alice, "whether you* can *make words mean so many different things."*

*"The question is," said Humpty Dumpty, "which is to be master—that's all."*

—*Lewis Carroll*
Alice in Wonderland

Words and their meanings—consider how important they are to communication. The discussion between Alice and Humpty Dumpty is an especially poignant scene in literature. What does a particular word mean? Humpty Dumpty apparently sees himself as the arbiter of which words have which meanings. Many people today are just like Humpty Dumpy: They select words based on what may sound pleasing regardless of the meaning. Many marketers and politicians use words that are pleasing to the ear: If the way in which their words are used doesn't quite fit their meaning, they don't worry about it—most people won't notice or at least won't challenge them on it.

Words are powerful. Words are the handles by which we grasp concepts. When we think, we use words. When we wish to communicate a concept, we use words. I grasp a concept by its handle, the word that describes it. I communicate this same concept by handing the person to whom I am communicating that handle, that word. The words we choose and the meanings of those words, both the connotative and demonstrative meanings, are critically important. George Orwell, in the fabulous book *1984*,[1] demonstrated the power of words. He wrote of an entire ministry of the government dedicated to the reduction of words. Its objective was to reduce the vocabulary and eliminate words. Good, excellent, and great were reduced to good, double-good, and double-plus-good just as bad, terrible, and horrible were reduced to bad, double-bad, and double-plus-bad. As words were eliminated, concepts were eliminated. If no word for freedom or liberty existed, the concepts of freedom and liberty were hindered, for people had no way to communicate those concepts. In Orwell's world, the government controlled the minds of the masses—their thoughts—by controlling their speech.

Words and their meanings are data and metadata. As you read this book, I am communicating data to you. The meaning of the words you are reading is the metadata. Unlike Humpty Dumpty, we have all agreed on the metadata. If we encounter a piece of data with which we are unfamiliar, such as esymplastic, we look it up in a dictionary. The dictionary is our central metadata repository. *The Professor and the Madman*,[2] by Simon Winchester, is an excellent case study on the compilation of this metadata.

While what we have discussed to this point is the usual use of metadata, typical discussions of metadata are in the context of technology. In this chapter, we discuss metadata in its typical context, how it is used in relation to technology, specifically IEBI. We begin this discussion with a definition of metadata and its importance in relation to IEBI. We then discuss the different types of metadata and its storage in the central metadata repository. We conclude with a review of the Common Warehouse Metadata Interchange (CWMI). CWMI is an eXtensible Markup Language (XML)-based standard used for communicating metadata between systems. We discuss how this standard is implemented and how it can be used by IEBI systems.

---

[1]Orwell, George, *1984*, New American Library Classics, Reissued 1990.

[2] Winchester, Simon, *The Professor and the Madman*, Harper Perennial, 1999.

## 10.1 What Is Metadata?

Metadata is important. No organization knows this better than NASA; they learned the hard way. The second Martian Explorer crashed because of metadata. It seems that the development team was working with the English system of measures and the flight team was working with metric. When it came time to land, the flight team fired the engines at the wrong time and the probe crashed. The story goes to prove that numbers in and of themselves are meaningless.

Quite often we discuss numbers so freely that we forget that numbers are like words. They are merely representations of a concept. The numbers are not reality; they simply allow us to express reality. One reason so many children don't understand math is because it is taught as a language without meaning. We run them through multiplication tables and drill them on the operation of the language. At the bottom of the page, we throw a couple of word problems at them to show how to use the numbers in real life. Yet we don't emphasize the meaning behind the language. Then we wonder why children don't get it. For example, 31,536,000. Does this number mean anything to you? Can you do anything with it? Sure you can do some operations on the number, but the results of those operations are no more meaningful to you than the actual number. The number actually represents the number of seconds in a year. Now you can do something meaningful with the number.

I gave you the metadata of the number 31,536,000. The traditional definition of metadata is "data about data." I have never found this definition useful, so let's drill down a bit. The prefix *meta* in the original Greek meant "what comes after." The term metaphysics, for example, came from the original publication of Aristotle's work. The editor put the subject we now call metaphysics in the book after physics, so he named the book metaphysics, the book that comes after physics. We have come to use the prefix *meta* to mean something that goes beyond. Metaphysics goes beyond normal physics. In the same sense, we can look at the term metadata as something that is the next thing to data, or something that goes beyond the mere data.

The novice to metadata typically sees it as little more than formatting information. How are the numbers formatted? Is the data floating-point or integer? If we are working with text data, we concern ourselves with the number of characters in a field. As we can see by the previous example, the presentation of the numeric data provided us with all the information we needed concerning the format of the data. Formatting is only one type of metadata. There is a plethora of metadata on any single piece of data.

We can describe metadata as going beyond data in the sense that it provides the data with context. It provides the frame of reference that the simple data lacks. The previous example of 31,536,000 demonstrated the need for context. A number is just a number unless we put something around it to give it meaning. Numbers are just one type of data; text data also needs a frame of reference. Consider the following two pieces of data: Balebail and Prakash. Here we have text data that most assuredly means something, but without the metadata, the meaning of the data is lost. Most readers probably don't recognize this data as a name. In this example, we have both a first name, Prakash, and a last name, Balebail. Without the metadata, this meaning is lost. We can conclude that metadata transcends data. It describes, or provides the context for, the data.

## 10.2  Metadata and IEBI

Given that metadata provides meaning to data, we can certainly understand that metadata is used throughout the entire life cycle of any system, from analysis and design through construction and implementation. Ultimately, metadata comes into play in the day-to-day use of the system. The nature of IEBI gives an added importance to metadata. As we have said throughout this book, IEBI systems are distinct in their nature from traditional Enterprise Resource Planning (ERP) systems. This difference amplifies the need for quality metadata. If we were to place metadata importance on a scale of 1 to 10, in a traditional ERP system we might give it a 6 or 7. Sure, metadata is important, but it wasn't necessarily critical in ERP systems. The metadata may not have been of the best quality, if it was present at all, yet these systems operated just fine. The lack of metadata was really a burden on the shoulders of those maintaining the system. In IEBI, however, metadata would rate a 9 or 10. Metadata is important to the designers and developers as well as to those who use the system on a daily basis.

Figure 10.1 presents the flow of data through an IEBI system. This data flow differs from the data flows presented in previous chapters. In this figure we have added the flow of metadata through the system. In examining this data flow, we

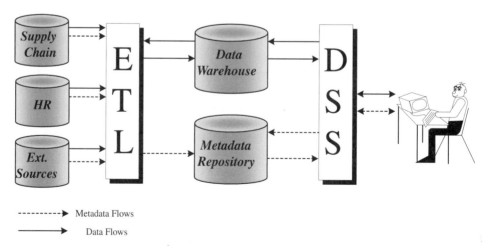

FIGURE 10.1   Metadata in IEBI.

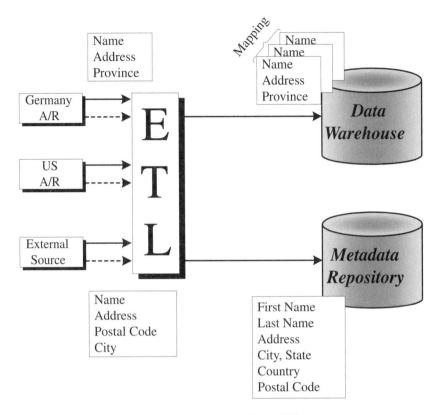

**FIGURE 10.2**   Metadata use in the ETL process.

see how metadata is used in the flow of information from the operational system to the business strategist. Most of this is what we would expect to see. Metadata is the basis for the Extraction, Transformation, and Loading (ETL) processes that incorporate the operational data into the data warehouse. It defines the mapping of the data from the source to the target. The transformation of the data also uses metadata to define the domain of values for a particular field in both the source and target systems.

What is unique about IEBI? Why is metadata so much more important to the data warehouse? One might argue that every system receives input. Is it simply that the data warehouse input comes from *another* information system? Actually, it is that the data comes for *many* other systems. Figure 10.1 shows the incorporation of more than mere data into the data warehouse. Metadata is also brought into the data warehouse to form a central metadata repository. Even in the best of situations, where we have a single instance upon which the operational system is based, we still have to deal with conflicting metadata. Figure 10.2 illustrates this point. The figure presents an international organization in which the data warehouse derives customer data from Accounts Receivable (A/R) from both Germany and the United States. The system also receives customer information from an external source, let us say a system that provides demographic data. It should be a simple matter to compile all this data into one system. Note the difference, though, in the address. In Germany, the address is composed of a province rather than a state. The domain of valid provinces is different from those of valid states. We can also see that the way in which the address is stored for the external system is different from the addresses received from the A/R system.

These issues are resolved within the metadata. It is within the metadata that we devise a consensus on the meaning of the data. Ultimately, the various definitions from each separate system, along with the mapping of the source to the target, are stored in the central metadata repository.

Metadata is also of critical importance to another IEBI system user: the business strategist. In traditional operational environments, the user may have little or no concern for metadata. He or she is probably satisfied with knowing the format of the data and the domain of acceptable values. The business strategist, however, is often just as concerned with the metadata as with the data itself. While the strategist may not describe his or her needs as being metadata, he or she typically asks questions answered only by metadata. What is the source of the data? When was this data collected? What elements does this data include? This is all metadata. If we think about it, we can see that metadata is used in the very construction of the reports and analyses developed by the business strategist.

The strategist selects data from the data warehouse by specifying the parameters of the report or query. These parameters are metadata. In addition to drilling into the data itself, the strategist may also be interested in drilling into the metadata. He or she might drill to the source of the data displayed on the screen or when it was extracted from the source system. In Chapter 2, I referred to a time when I had to justify the cost of a BI system to a board of directors. During the presentation, I put up my matrices of data showing the cost of the current system and the remarkable savings incurred through implementation of its replacement. As I stood up there sweating in front of them (this *was* the culmination of 10 months' work), I was grilled by the CEO. "Where did you get these numbers?" "How was that computed?" He was asking for the metadata. Imagine if I had this displayed in some ad hoc query tool. With each question, I would be able to simply select the data item and drill down into the data's metadata. Imagine the strength of the data if right then and there I was able to validate the data on the screen. In addition to showing the actual numbers, I could present the way in which the numbers were calculated as well as the history of the data, such as its source and age.

## 10.3   Types of Metadata

The example above raises an interesting point. If a number is a price, commission, or salary, we have a certain understanding of the context. We fill this in on our own. In the business world, much of the data's context is often left undocumented. It is assumed that the user will understand what is meant by the data. Often, system engineers and administrators content themselves with only a partial description of the data, the format. If we truly want to capture the context of the data contained within a system, be it a data warehouse or an operational system, we need to expand our view. Figure 10.3 presents a mapping of the many different types of metadata required for a complete view of the data's context.

The following list provides a more complete description of each metadata type:

❏  **Static**
   - Name—Provides the name by which the data element is known to the system. For example, Employee_Name, Customer_Name, and Customer_ID.
   - Description—Provides a full text description of the data element.
   - Format—Provides the data presentation rules.
   - Data Type—Defines the data that is stored within the data element. For example, integer, floating-point, and Boolean.
   - Relation—Defines the relationships between objects within the system. For example, Customers buy product.
   - Domain—Provides the domain or range of valid values.
   - Business Rules—Provides the rules of the organization that govern the data element.

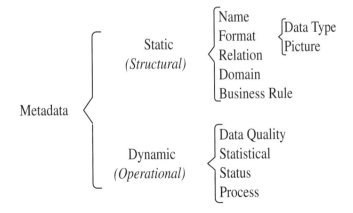

**FIGURE 10.3**   Types of metadata.

❏ **Dynamic**

- Quality—Describes the quality of the data within the system, such as the accuracy, completeness, consistency, and validity. An example of quality metadata within the data warehouse is the extraction log, which is discussed in Chapter 3. This log provides statistics on the data loaded into the data warehouse;
- Statistical—Describes usage and administrative characteristics of the system. Maintaining statistics on which data is most frequently accessed or the types of analysis performed on the data is extremely useful to systems developers in enhancing the performance of the system. It is also common to keep statistics on which users access the system, how often it is accessed, and for how long;
- Status—This metadata keeps track of the general health of the system. It is also beneficial to keep a record of backup statistics such as when a backup was last performed, how long the backup took, and what errors occurred. It is also helpful to keep track of disk utilization, system failures, Mean Time Between Failure (MTBF) and Mean Time To Repair (MTTR).

Figure 10.3 shows that there are two basic types of metadata: static and dynamic. Static metadata describes the structure that contains the data, and dynamic metadata describes the overall status of that structure. One of the most critical, yet least documented, static metadata types is the business rules. It is often assumed these rules are known by the user. With business rules, however, even the most obvious data elements are not always clear. What is a car? What distinguishes one car from another? Looking at two different cars, you could distinguish between car A and B. What if I take parts from car B and use them as replacement parts for car A? How many parts moved from A to B will it take to make A into B? This may look like a ridiculous example, but this question goes back to the time of Socrates. He asked these very same questions of a boat. If we continually replace the parts of a boat, when does the old boat become a new one? It is a very real issue. In the case of a car, the business rule is simple: The car's serial number is attached to the dashboard under the windshield. To whatever car A's dashboard is attached is car A. Although the rule is simple, it is not necessarily known unless documented.

Obviously, there will be changes to business rules, so one might object to the inclusion of business rules as static metadata. Static does not mean to imply the metadata never changes, but simply that it changes less frequently than dynamic metadata. The dynamic metadata primarily relates to the state and use of the data. Dynamic metadata has an operational flavor. It reflects the changing state of the system. Consider the different types of dynamic metadata. Dynamic metadata refers to such data as backup, data usage, space usage, and user access. All of this data is constantly changing.

## 10.4   The Central Metadata Repository

As we can see, there is a need for accurate and reliable metadata throughout the entire organization. This need extends from the data warehouse architect all the way to the business strategist. Figure 10.4 shows the different groups that require metadata. Each group shown in this diagram has its own unique metadata needs. At first glance, one might not consider end users to be interested in metadata. When we consider our definition of metadata—that it provides the context for the data—we see that users are the ultimate consumers of metadata. Metadata, especially in a BI environment, is critical to the end users. When the user is looking at a particular data element, the metadata provides the meaning. The reverse is true as well: When the user knows what data he or she wants, the metadata tells the user where to find it.

As seen in Figure 10.4, the end user is different from the other users of metadata. The end user consumes metadata but does not have direct input into the metadata repository. The data warehouse architect, system engineers, and administrators all provide input into the repository. The following lists some of the interactions with the metadata repository:

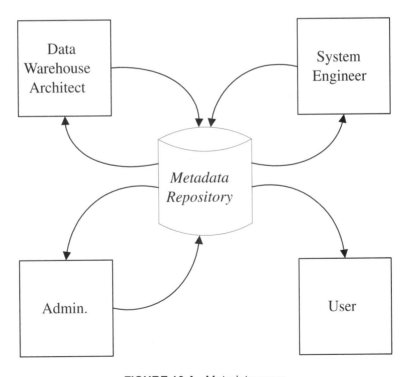

**FIGURE 10.4**   Metadata users.

❏ **Data Warehouse Architects** define the basic structure of the system.

❏ **System Engineers** enhance the environment that changes the metadata. For example, a review of the data utilization may show that users are consistently asking for certain sets of aggregations. The system engineers may decide to precompile these aggregations. The metadata repository is updated to reflect this change.

❏ **System Administrators** review performance statistics such as disk and CPU utilization. Administrators modify the environment to improve system performance.

❏ **Database Administrators** review data utilization statistics and modify the environment to improve performance as well. Database Administrators do such things as build indexes or rebuild fragmented tables.

❏ **Data Administrators** have perhaps the most interesting interaction with the metadata repository. One might even consider the data administrator the *owner* of the metadata. The data administrator monitors the quality of the data and detects changes in metadata. It is the responsibility of the data administrator to maintain the quality of not only the data, but of the metadata as well. For example, the data administrator reviews the extraction log. This log detects when the metadata for the operational environment is not synchronized with the data warehouse. The data administrator is responsible for updating the warehouse to allow for proper data loading.

The central metadata repository is critical to the success of not only the data warehouse but of the entire organization. As such, the scope of the repository should extend to the entire enterprise. This enterprise-level view is contained within the Enterprise Data Model (EDM). While the EDM is not strictly part of the data warehouse project, we will address it due to its effects on the warehouse.

## 10.5  Enterprise Data Model

The central metadata repository contains an enterprise-wide view of the data. The repository organizes this metadata into a data model whose scope encompasses the entire organization. We call this the EDM. The EDM provides a schema or blueprint of the organization's business. In the previous section, we discussed how metadata provides the context for data. When the context encompasses the entire organization, it describes the organization's business. To achieve this end, the EDM is a compilation of metadata from all systems within the organization. This is shown in Figure 10.5.

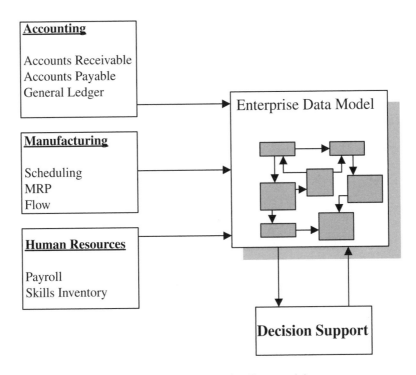

**FIGURE 10.5**   Enterprise data model.

As shown in the diagram, each department provides its own input into the EDM. The departments need to provide complete metadata for each system. The data administrator integrates this information into the EDM. The challenge for any system that spans departments is reaching a consensus. There will be disagreements concerning the data's definition, attributes, and business rules. Virtually all the metadata elements have the potential of becoming hotly contested issues. The only real blessing for the data warehouse architect is that this is not his or her responsibility. It is the responsibility of the data administrator.

Actually, in shifting the responsibility to the data administrator, I am only half joking. Strictly speaking, the EDM is not part of the data warehouse project any more than it is for the implementation of any other system. It is often confused as being part of the warehouse because the warehouse is the first system that truly attempts to integrate the data from the disparate operational systems. As shown in the diagram, the data warehouse not only contributes to the EDM, but receives input from it as well. While in a perfect world new systems would be designed with consistent metadata, in reality this is rarely the case. Most often, departments purchase systems from multiple vendors by selecting the best of breed. As of this writing, vendors have not done us the courtesy of providing a standard set of metadata.

While the EDM is not part of the data warehouse, it is most definitely part of the IEBI system. Understanding the need for quality metadata in an IEBI environment places the EDM squarely in the center of IEBI. As such, we need to understand the necessity to construct a central metadata repository that has as complete a view of the entire organization as is practically possible.

## 10.6 OMG & OMA

Nature hates a vacuum and will always seek to fill it. Just as in nature, the business environment hates a need and will form a committee to fill it. Despite reports that an elephant is a mouse built by committee, some committees actually do accomplish something useful. The need to share metadata within an information infrastructure has been addressed by the Object Management Group (OMG). The OMG is a software consortium established in 1989. It is the world's largest consortium, composed of more than 700 vendors, developers, and end users. The mission of the OMG is to promote the theory and practice of Object Technology for the development of distributed computing systems.

For an Internet-enabled world, the OMG needed to develop a specification for distributed objects. This specification would define a standardized object-oriented architectural framework within which developers could create software. In keeping with the objectives of object orientation, the specification would need to address object reusability. The Internet establishes an environment in which many types of applications run on a variety of platforms. The OMG specification would therefore also be required to address portability issues. This same environment also requires that these various applications running on these many platforms interact with one another, requiring the specification to address object interoperability. Ultimately, the OMG defined the *Object Management Architecture* (OMA).

The OMA is described in the *Object Management Architecture Guide (OMAG)*. This guide provides both the *OMG Object Model* and the *OMA Reference Model*. Every object in an object-oriented environment has attributes that are visible to the outside world. The OMG Object Model specifies an implementation-independent way of defining these attributes. The OMA Reference Model is just that: a model to which developers can refer to understand the components, interfaces, and protocols that make up the OMA.

In order to complete the OMA, the OMG must provide detailed specifications for each object in the architecture. The specification of each object within the OMA is generated through a Request For Proposal (RFP) process. The process starts when a task force within an OMG Technology Committee generates an RFP. Responses to the RFP are evaluated for compliance with the OMA by this same task force. The task force recommends specifications to the Technology Committee, which votes to determine whether a specification should be recommended by the OMG board of directors for adoption. There is also a business committee that addresses the commercial viability of a particular specification. Based on this input, the OMG board of directors votes on the adoption of a specification on behalf of the overall OMG.

The progress the OMG has made on OMA includes the *Meta-Object Facility (MOF)* that defines the *meta-metamodel*. I think we have gone a meta too far. Be that as it may, the MOF specifies the semantics to describe metamodels in a variety of domains. In addition to the MOF, the OMG has also defined an *Object Analysis & Design (OA&D) Facility*, which specifies the *Unified Modeling Language* (UML) as a common metamodel. UML also provides a set of interfaces for the support of dynamic construction and traversal of user models.

## 10.7   Common Warehouse Metadata Interchange

In most environments, IEBI is implemented with a variety of tools drawing data from a variety of sources. We have discussed how IEBI distributes data throughout the organization. Often, this information is delivered to many different decision support tools on various platforms. In today's environment, the traditional wisdom is that it is possible for a single metadata repository to implement a single metamodel to meet all the needs of an organization. The OMG chose instead to provide a single standard for the interchange of warehouse metadata. This single interchange is the CWMI, which is compliant with both MOF and UML notation.

CWMI is a complete specification in that it provides a complete description of the semantics and syntax for IEBI tools and applications to exchange metadata. The specification defines a common warehouse metamodel, APIs, and interchange formats. Application and tools conforming to these specifications can exchange warehouse metadata. The specification actually consists of several elements that are based on the OMA. CWMI uses the MOF as the meta-metamodel, the UML as the graphical notation, and XML as the medium of information exchange between systems.

As we can see in Figure 10.6, there is a relationship between each structure that we have discussed within the OMA. The entire structure is designed to represent metadata. Metadata is data, albeit a different type of data than what most people normally encounter. Being data, it requires its own metadata: meta-metadata. The model representing this meta-metadata is contained within the MOF, which is the meta-metamodel. This is the base of the entire structure. At the levels above the MOF, we see parallels between the data warehousing world and the other objects within the OMA. The UML is the common OA&D metamodel. In the same way, the Common Warehouse Metamodel is the common metamodel for the warehouse model.

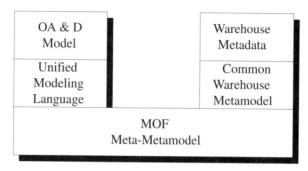

**FIGURE 10.6**   Relationships between CWMI, UML, and MOF.

By basing CWMI on the UML and MOF, the OMG achieved several important objectives. First, these are proven technologies. Common Object Request Broker Architecture (CORBA), which is the specification for the programming interfaces to the OMA Object Request Broker, is just one example of a successful application of OMA. By using a proven technology, CWMI can create a stable, enterprise-level environment that is generic and independent of any specific data warehouse implementation. This implementation-independence allows CWMI to be portable and usable on any computer system.

The intent of the OMG was to define an interface rather than attempt a specification for a common metadata repository. While this may be the case with the actual specification, it does not preclude the data warehouse architect from establishing this central metadata repository on his or her own. As a common metadata interface, CWMI enables the establishment of such a central repository. Figure 10.7 demonstrates the relationship between CWMI and the central repository. In the diagram, we see that there is one central repository. ETL and decision support tools can contribute and extract metadata via CWMI.

The importance of a central metadata repository cannot be overemphasized. The repository is the source of the truth. In an environment where there is no such repository, there is no definitive source of the metadata. In an environment with such a repository, the metadata contained within the central repository is *the* metadata. Any metadata conflicting with this central system is by definition ignored. In such a role, the repository becomes the center of the IEBI system; all other systems within this information infrastructure will need to read and write from this repository. To fulfill the requirements driven by such an environment, we can use standard database technology to maintain this repository. This is of course what the repository is—a database. It just happens to be a database of metadata.

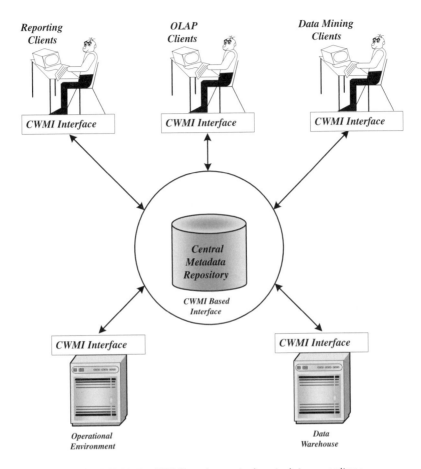

**FIGURE 10.7**  CWMI and a central metadata repository.

## 10.8  The CWMI Architecture

CWMI is an IEBI metadata framework. To provide for all the components of an IEBI system, this includes more than just the metadata concerning the target data structures. It also includes the metadata for the data warehouse processes and the data sources. The data warehouse processes addressed by CWMI deal with the creation and management of the data. Again, the goal of CWMI is to provide a means of metadata interchange among analytical tools. To meet this variety of needs, CWMI consists of a number of submetamodels, as shown in Figure 10.8.

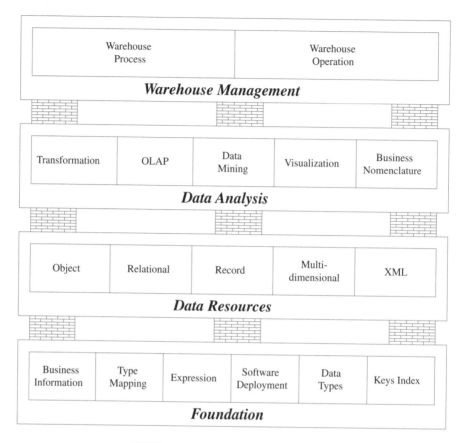

**FIGURE 10.8** The CWMI metamodel.

❑ **Foundation**—Metamodels for the representation of model elements representing shared concepts and structures.

❑ **Data Resources**—Metamodels for the representation of object-oriented, relational, record, multidimensional, and XML data sources.

❑ **Data Analysis**—Metamodels for the representation of data transformation, OLAP, data mining, visualization, and business nomenclature.

❑ **Warehouse Management**—Metamodels for the representation of data warehouse processes, including the representation of the results of the operations.

CWMI uses *packages*. Packages are a mechanism by which we can control the complexity of CWMI by creating logical groupings of interrelated classes. The developer can then focus attention on the individual metamodel packages, using them independently of the others. Although the packages are independent, by virtue of their integration into the overall CWMI architecture, they can share a common purpose. In the sections that follow, we explore each submetamodel and its contribution to the overall CWMI architecture.

### 10.8.1   CWMI FOUNDATION

The CWMI Foundation layer contains the metamodels of concepts and structures that are common to the other CWMI packages. The Foundation metamodels sit between the more general world of the object model and the IEBI-specific metamodels of other CWMI packages. The object models at the very base of this structure are general metamodels that can be applied to any number of diverse areas. The Foundation metamodels, however, act as the basis for the entire CWMI architecture. The other CWMI metamodels can extend the Foundation metamodels to meet a specific need. As a result the packages within this layer are less specific to IEBI and have a more general flavor than the metamodels in the other categories. Let's examine each in a bit more detail.

#### 10.8.1.1   Business Information

The Business Information metamodel is meant to provide a means to define business-oriented information. Some metadata relates not to the things represented within the IEBI system, but to the IEBI system itself. The Business Information metamodel represents this type of data. This is not the representation of a complete IEBI metamodel, but of the business information around the data warehouse and IEBI system.

In the Business Information metamodel, we find the classes Document, ResponsibleParty, and Description. The ResponsibleParty class contains information pertaining to the parties responsible for the IEBI system, including who they are and how they might be contacted. Likewise, the Document metamodel provides information pertaining to the documentation of the IEBI system itself, while the Description class provides general information describing the system.

#### 10.8.1.2   Data Types

In establishing a metamodel for data types, we again encounter the challenge that the diversity of IEBI tools present. Since there are so many different IEBI tools, it would be difficult to establish in advance the data types necessary to meet all their needs. The reasons these tools are incompatible are as varied as the tools themselves. In some instances, it may be as simple as an ISV attempting to differentiate itself in the market. In other cases, dependencies on hardware or implementation language may contribute to the variation. The Foundation metamodel therefore does not define a specific set of data types.

There is a recognized need to define data types that may be specific to a particular environment. The desire for the exchange of data between systems of differing types is also recognized. To meet these needs, the Foundation metamodel first provides the definition of several generally common data types, which are included more to serve as an example in the appropriate use of the metamodel than anything else. Second, the Foundation metamodel contains data types that are necessary for the exchange of information among diverse tools and systems.

### 10.8.1.3 Expression

The Expression metamodel provides a means for the other packages with CWMI as well as IEBI tools to define expressions in a common form. By describing expressions in a common form, the expression can be exchanged between systems. This makes it possible for systems to share transformations and mappings as well as how data elements within the system are derived. Another important aspect is the ability to provide lineage tracking. If we are going to use a particular transformation or equation in our system, we would like to know its source. The CWMI model, by storing the data in a common form, provides this capability.

What is interesting about the Expression metamodel is that it defines all expressions in terms of expression trees. Take the simple expression $X + B$. We can rephrase this to be $sum(X + B)$. We can then construct a hierarchy from this expression similar to the one shown in Figure 10.9 ($a$), or we can create an even deeper structure using this same hierarchical approach. As an example, let's look at one of my personal favorite expressions, $y = mx + b$. We could rephrase this to be $sum(multiply(m,x),b)$, in which case we would have a tree structure similar to the one shown in Figure 10.9 ($b$). By the way, for those of you not familiar with this equation, this is the equation of a line. I used it extensively in the days when I wrote computer graphics programs.

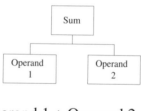

Operand 1 + Operand 2

(a)

Sum

Multiply    B

m    x

m * x + B

(b)

**FIGURE 10.9**  Expression trees.

### 10.8.1.4   Keys Indexes

The Keys Indexes metamodel describes keys and indexes. Okay, I know you're shocked. The term *keys* here applies to the data elements that specify a particular instance of an object. An index is the means by which these elements are sorted. We are still in the Foundation layer, so this metamodel simply defines expressions of base concepts, such as unique constraints and relationships. The other packages within the CWMI structure or other IEBI tools build on these base elements.

The Keys Indexes metamodel is of great importance to the data warehouse architect. My previous book, *Object-Oriented Data Warehouse Design,* discusses the importance of keys and establishing abstract keys in the data warehouse. At the same time, we do not wish to lose the keys that are part of the system of record. The decision maker would like to have the ability to drill down to the atomic level of the data. In some instances, he or she might even desire to trace the data back to the system of record. This makes it important for the data warehouse architect to bring the keys over with the original data. As we established earlier, we need more than just the data. We need the metadata as well. The Keys Index metamodel is the basis by which we can communicate this data.

### 10.8.1.5   Type Mapping

The Type Mapping metamodel is used when different systems have data types that are not quite the same. The Type Mapping metamodel provides a means by which these differing types can be mapped between systems. The data between these systems can then be exchanged. The metamodel provides the data warehouse architect with the ability to create multiple mappings between two data types and to specify which of the two is preferred.

### 10.8.1.6   Software Deployment

The Software Deployment metamodel describes how software is used within the IEBI system. As we examine the metamodel, we see such objects as Deployment Components, Machine Objects, Data Managers, and Data Providers. All of these objects work together to provide a complete picture of how and where the software is being used.

Let's look at this a bit more closely. The Deployed Component Object defines a specific component on a specific computer within the IEBI system. If, for example, we are working in an environment with multiple dependent data marts, we might have the same multidimensional analysis tool operating on two different systems. Each instance of the tool will have a separate deployed component. The systems upon which these separate instances are running will each be described by their own instance of the Machine object.

There are multiple Deployed Component subclasses. A database management system (DBMS) is a Data Manager. These objects are associated with data *containers*—entities such as schemas, relational catalogs, and files that provide access to data. Another subclass of Deployed Component is a Data Provider. Providers are the means by which data within the Data Manager is accessed. We would expect a Data Provider to incorporate Java Database Connectivity (JDBC), which provides a client with access to the database.

Using the Software Deployment metamodel as a base, we can see how a complete environment can be described within the system. Again, we need to remind ourselves that we are not just working with a BI system, but with an IEBI system in an environment with multiple systems operating in conjunction with one another. Such an environment is much more complex than a transaction-processing system, where one system operates within clearly defined parameters. It is even more complex than simple BI, where the BI system does not reach outside of the organization. IEBI is a system of many diverse systems that may or may not reside within the same organization. We all know the theme of this chapter by now: Where there is data, there is metadata. The Software Deployment metamodel provides the structure for this metadata.

### 10.8.2   CWMI DATA RESOURCE

The Data Resource layer includes metamodels for the definition of data resources: relational, record, object-oriented, and multidimensional. These are all base-level data resources from which we draw our data. As we progress up the CWMI framework, we progress from the general to the specific. The Foundation layer is very general; it simply provides a basis for the construction of other objects. The Data Resource layer provides us with a metamodel for the description of our data source. In the following subsections, we examine each metamodel within this layer.

#### 10.8.2.1   Object Model

The Object Model contains the features, and only those features, of UML that are necessary for the creation of CWMI metamodel classes. Other CWMI packages use the Object Model for the creation of their own metamodel classes. By making the Object Model a subset of the UML, the CWMI packages can take advantage of the benefits of the UML without being encumbered by the weight of its full breadth and scope.

The Object Model attempts to thread the eye of the proverbial needle, providing simplicity while sharing a common functionality. It is divided into four subpackages: Core, Behavioral, Instance, and Relationship. The Core package acts as the basis for the other packages, providing the elements necessary for the common functionality. The other three packages are based on the Core package. The functionality of the packages are independent of one another, so the implementation of one, such as the Instance, does not require the implementation of another, such as the Behavioral.

Each package within the Object Model collects classes and associations that describe some subset of CWMI types. The behavioral metamodel, for example, collects the classes and associations that describe the behavior. It acts as a foundation for recording the invocation of defined behaviors. In like manner, the Relationship metamodel collects the classes and associations for the description of relationships between the objects within the CWMI repository. The Instance metamodel provides for the inclusion of an actual instance of the data with the metadata.

The Instance metamodel may be a bit confusing without an example, so let's take a moment to look at this more closely. The Instance metamodel is useful in situations like the one shown in Figure 10.10. My previous book, *Object Oriented Data Warehouse Design*, discusses the use of a self-referencing data structure to represent corporate structures. The structure shows two companies related to one another. The company has two ends, the parent company and the child. Each instance of the Corporate Structure association has a sting-value attribute describing the relationship. This relationship can be shown as CWMI Object Model metaclasses: Class, Attribute, Data Type Association, and Association End.

### 10.8.2.2  Relational

The Relational package deals with relational data resources. It describes data sources from which data is retrieved via Structured Query Language (SQL), Open Data Base Connectivity (ODBC), or JDBC. The top-level container of the Relational package is the Catalog, the unit managed by a data resource. Inside are the catalog schemas, which are composed of tables. These tables are comprised of columns of specific data types. The Relational package also addresses indexing, primary keys, and foreign keys. As we see throughout the higher levels of the CWMI architecture, the Relational package extends the structures established in both the Foundation layer and Object packages.

### 10.8.2.3  Record

The Record metamodel is part of the Data Resource Layer. Its purpose, along with the other packages within this layer, is to describe a data resource. One such resource type can be a record. The CWMI model uses the Record metamodel to cover a great many different types of data resources. A record can include a variety of structures and is not limited to what one might traditionally think of as a record. These resources can extend beyond what is found in files and databases to include structured data types within languages or documents. The Record metamodel can be used to describe any structure that has a hierarchical nature. The only exception to what is included within a record type are structures whose only use is in a specific language. Such structures or record types are best addressed in an extension to the CWMI architecture.

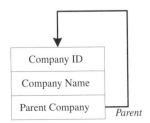

**FIGURE 10.10**  Instance metamodel.

#### 10.8.2.4   Multidimensional

Just as we have a Relational metamodel to represent Relational data resources, we also have a metamodel for multidimensional data resources. These are used to represent multidimensional resources that are actually represented by Multidimensional database systems (MDBS). The MDBS world differs greatly from its relational database management systems (RDBMS) cousin. In the relational world, we are used to certain standards and constructs. Unfortunately, this is not the case with MDBS. Such OLAP concepts as dimensions and hierarchies are implemented within the MDBS engine. These engines are proprietary, and there is no published standard on the representation of multidimensional databases. The metamodel is therefore general in nature. Extensions can be made to provide for the specific OLAP tools.

#### 10.8.2.5   XML

The final data resource, while not *yet* the most important data resource, is certainly growing in significance. In Chapter 9, we discussed the importance of XML in the exchange of information. It is quickly being accepted by many as the standard language of exchange between systems. As such, XML is an important data resource for IEBI. The XML metamodel describes XML data resources. While the version of the metamodel is based on XML 1.0, the XML metamodel will be revised as modifications to XML are adopted by the W3C.

The XML metamodel is composed of a *schema*. An XML schema is composed of *element types*. Element types are definitions and declarations of XML *attributes* and *content models*. A specific element type definition can define an attribute, content model, or both. An attribute can have a default of *required, implied, default,* or *fixed,* while content models can be either *empty, any, mixed,* or *element.* A content model of the type *element* consists of specified element type references, element content models, or both. Mixed content models are composed of character data and element type references. Finally, content models of the type *any* can consist of any element types.

### 10.8.3   DATA ANALYSIS

The Data Analysis layer of the CWMI packages deals with the use of the data. Whereas the Data Resources layer dealt with the source of the data, the Data Analysis layer deals with what is done with the data once it is extracted from this source. In the layer, we see metamodel packages for the representation of the data transformations, OLAP, data mining, information visualization, and business nomenclature. Each is concerned with the use of the data as it comes from a data source.

### 10.8.3.1  Transformation

As we discussed in Chapter 3, the first step in the BI loop is the ETL of the data. Transformation is the process that converts the format and content of the data to be consistent with the data warehouse. As one can well imagine, the transformation process is a core function of the BI loop. We must be able to share the metadata concerning this process between systems.

The Transformation metamodel provides the mechanism for the exchange of metadata concerning the transformation process. The Transformation metamodel associates a transformation with the data sources and targets. The sources and targets can be object-oriented or relational data types. The granularity of the data can be a class, attribute, table, or column. We relate the source and target data through the transformation. The relationship can happen at a coarse level, or high level, of granularity where the specifics of how one data element relates to another is unknown. This is known as a *black box* transformation. We can also be more specific in the description of the relationship and define how a specific piece of data relates to another. In this case, the specific mapping of the data is described. This is referred to as a *white box* transformation.

### 10.8.3.2  OLAP

The OLAP metamodel package is used to described the features most common to OLAP systems. First and foremost, the metamodel must include a means to describe a multidimensional view of the data. The OLAP metamodel must also support time-series and what-if scenario analyses. The metamodel must also support the ability to drill down and roll up data along a hierarchy. The OLAP metamodel provides for a mapping of these structures onto an actual implementation, as described in the CWMI Relational and Multidimensional packages.

### 10.8.3.3  Data Mining

As we discussed in Chapter 3, data mining is the process of finding patterns that are hidden in the data. Perhaps we search for the demographics of the people who visit our Web site that are most likely to buy. We discover these patterns by examining a known data set, such as the demographics of people who actually purchased products. We then search data with unknown results for those patterns. The Data Mining metamodel provides the structure for the metadata that describes this process.

In previous chapters, we noted that the data mining process entails the construction of a model that is controlled by settings. The model is associated with its own set of attributes. Within CWMI the Data Mining model is defined by the MiningModel. The settings for this model are defined by ModelSettings, and the attributes are defined by the ApplicationInputSpecification. The MiningModelResult defines the metadata for the results of the data mining operation.

### 10.8.3.4  Information Visualization

Ultimately, we need to get the data out of the system. Information Visualization is concerned with data output—the Decision Support System (DSS) level of the BI loop, which is presented in Chapter 3. DSS is a very broad category with systems ranging from simple reporting to graphics tools that display information from a variety of viewpoints. Since visualization is such a diverse category, the Information Visualization package is generic, with container-like structures.

### 10.8.3.5  Business Nomenclature

In section 10.3, we discussed the different types of metadata. Up to this point we have been discussing mainly what is traditionally thought of as metadata, data structure, and format. The Business Nomenclature metamodel looks at the data from the business perspective. It is concerned with how the data was derived, from which data sources it was derived, as well as the DSS tools used to examine the data.

The objective of CWMI is to provide for the exchange of metadata. To the business strategist, this form of metadata is perhaps the most critical. Key to understanding the validity of a piece of data is to know the origin of the data. "Where did you get your numbers?" As data moves from the source systems through the data warehouse to the business strategist, the business metadata travels with it. The Business Nomenclature metamodel provides the vehicle for the exchange of this data by each system in this process.

## 10.8.4  WAREHOUSE MANAGEMENT

The final layer of metamodel packages is the Warehouse Management layer, which is the topmost layer in the CWMI architecture. It represents the warehouse processes as well as the results of these operations.

### 10.8.4.1  Warehouse Process Package

The Warehouse Process package defines the processes within a transformation. A Warehouse Process object relates a transformation and the events used to trigger the transformation. The transformation process itself can be viewed as either a complete process using the TransformationActivity object or at a more granular level with the TransformationSteps object. The WarehouseProcess object is either of the subtype WarehouseActivity for the representation of TransformationActivity or of the subtype WarehouseStep for TransformationStep.

The WarehouseProcess that represents the transformation process is related to one or more events identified by WarehouseEvents. There are three types of Warehouse events. A Schedule event occurs at specific points in time or at regular intervals, such as every two days. Events can also be external events, which are events that occur outside of the data warehouse. Internal events are events that occur within the data warehouse.

### 10.8.4.2  Warehouse Operation

The Warehouse Operations metamodel package deals with the daily operations of the data warehouse. The data contained within this metamodel deals with not the structure of the warehouse or the data contained within it, but with the operation of the warehouse itself. We see in this package such operational considerations as Transformation Executions, Measurements, and Change Requests.

The Transformation Execution package describes the most recent executions of transformation. This data is used to determine the timeliness of the data within the data warehouse. It also can be used to record the history of the data warehouse. The history of the warehouse includes a record of when data was incorporated into the warehouse, the transformation processes, and the originating system. The measurement package provides for the application of measurements to model objects. This could include such things as the anticipated or planned size of the object. The Changes Request package provides for the recording of proposed changes to the data warehouse. Data warehouse architects can also use this metamodel to keep a record of which changes were actually made to the data warehouse and which were rejected.

## 10.9   XML Metadata Interchange

A recurring theme throughout this chapter is that CWMI is used to exchange metadata between systems. The question is how it does this. What are the mechanics of the exchange? How do we actually transfer the metadata information from one system to the next? In Chapter 9, we discussed XML and how it is used to exchange structured documents between systems. Since CWMI has a structure, it is only natural to apply XML and use that structure as the medium of metadata exchange. This is the XML Metadata Interchange (XMI).

XMI is the method by which data warehouse metadata that conforms to the CWMI metamodel is communicated. XML is particularly attractive for exchanging metadata. XMI format becomes independent of any specific middleware technology. It enables CWMI to become truly open. Any tool or application can read and generate an XML document. This of course makes it possible for them to read and generate XMI documents, which in turn makes it possible for any tool to communicate with any other tool via XMI.

We can view CWMI metadata as just another source of data for XML. This is a huge benefit for XMI. Standard tools for the composition and validation of XML documents are available for XMI. Using the *XML Document DTD Production Rules,* the tools can communicate the metamodel between systems. As we discussed in Chapter 9, the DTD describes the structure of the document. The *XMI* DTD describes the structure of the metadata. XMI then generates an XMI document containing the metadata using *XML Document Production Rules.*

Just as CWMI can serve as another source for XML, it also acts as a destination. The target system receives both the XMI DTD and the XMI document. Again, we can employ the use of standard XML tools. These tools, using the DTD, decode the XMI document and reconstruct the metadata.

## 10.10  Summary

In this chapter, we defined metadata as the data that goes beyond data and it extends the data to give it meaning. This is especially important in the area of IEBI, an environment in which many disparate systems must communicate. All of these systems need to establish a way to communicate.

Communication is more than just establishing a connection between two entities. We do that all day long on the Internet. It is also more than sending and receiving data in an understandable and reliable format. That is provided through TCP/IP. Communication occurs when all parties involved agree on the meaning of the data being communicated. The meaning of the data is contained within the metadata.

Just as with the data, we need to establish a means to communicate the metadata. When communicating with human language, we have a dictionary with an established format and structure. In the IEBI environment, we have the Common Warehouse Metadata Interchange. With an agreed-upon format and structure, systems use CWMI to communicate the metadata. While valuable, CWMI is not the panacea that some would have us believe. CWMI is simply a standard for the structure and format of communicating metadata; it does not guarantee communication.

The real star of this chapter is not metadata, or even CWMI. The real star, the lynchpin of metadata, is the data administrator. Metadata and CWMI are important. We need to keep in mind, though, that metadata is only data and CWMI is the structure in which it resides. We can have all the systems in the world sharing metadata through CWMI, but if it isn't correct, it doesn't amount to the proverbial hill of beans.

Consider the common dictionary. Generally, dictionaries agree on the meaning and use of words. That's what makes them valuable. But what if they didn't? What if my dictionary defined the word *coffee* as a "a reptile with a scaly, elongated body, movable eyelids, four legs, and a tapering tail"? You would probably ask me for a cup of coffee once before we came to some agreement on the metadata for the word coffee. If this is true of the metadata of human language, what about IEBI metadata? Do we need to wait for the disagreement in metadata to cause such a fatal error that we are forced to come to some agreement?

The data administrator is the individual responsible for the metadata. The importance of his or her role is directly correlated to the importance of metadata. Data validation, be it data or metadata, cannot be automated. It requires a human element. Just as in the dictionary example, while the structure can be perfect, the content can be flat out wrong. Not only is the quality of the data itself the responsibility of the data administrator, but so is the quality of the metadata. The data administrator is ultimately responsible for communication between systems, which is essential to IEBI.

# Part 4

# Building Relationships Over the Internet

# Chapter 11

# LOOK OUTWARD ANGEL

*There are many companies that have a 1 percent share of an enormous market and have spent millions trying to get to 2 percent. It's perfectly acceptable if you're not the market share leader. Not every company can be. But businesses of all sizes—from the corner store to a global conglomerate—can and should look at sales from a customer perspective. The investment required to find, convince, and ultimately acquire new customers can be significant. Adopting a customer share strategy requires that you look at your prospects and customers along a continuum, where the marketer methodically develops an ever-increasing level of loyalty.*

*—Tom Osenton*

Customer Share Marketing[1]

Earlier, we discussed the IEBI solution and its elements. We saw that as the Internet evolved, it caused organizations to change and affected business intelligence (BI). We then examined the Internet at the hardware level. We learned that by moving from single, monolithic systems to multitiered architectures, we change information dictatorships to information democracies. These structures enabled IEBI to reach deeply into the organization while expanding the entire value chain. We also examined the software of the Internet. We reviewed how Java is structured for the Internet and multitier architectures and how XML can be used as a means of exchanging both data and metadata. We discussed all the pieces of IEBI, from the applications to how they are brought together in a single information infrastructure. Now, let's look at IEBI in its entirety.

---

[1] Osenton, Tom, *Customer Share Marketing*, Prentice Hall, 2002. Used by permission.

Let's return to our good friend Billy Boy of Billy Boy Bowling Balls to see this in action. When we last visited with Billy Boy, his CIO, Miles Mody, had implemented a new information infrastructure. Figure 11.1 presents the applications that run on this structure. As we saw in Chapter 7, all of the main servers are maintained by the IT department. One server is dedicated to supporting the Enterprise Resource Planning (ERP) applications as well as real-time OLAP analyses and reporting. A second dedicated data warehouse server is responsible for the company's balanced scorecard application, activity-based costing, OLAP and data mining. Both of these servers are front-ended by an application server. Both the ERP/Operational Data Store (ODS) system and the data warehouse are based on the same database technology. The ETL process uses database procedures to transfer the data from one system to the other.

The legacy mainframe, responsible for the administrative applications, is also front-ended by an application server. In addition to supplying an interface to the various users, the application server is responsible for the Extraction, Translation, and Loading (ETL) of data for both the ODS and data warehouse. As new data is entered into the administrative system, the application server generates an XML document, which is passed to the ODS. Each night, the data is extracted in batch mode from the administrative system and sent to the data warehouse, again in the form of an XML document.

Also, note the production department. J2ME processes drive the numerically controlled devices. In addition to controlling production, these applications report back status to the ODS and data warehouse. The data is then incorporated into the company's strategic reports and BI applications. The shipping department has fewer information processing requirements. Billy has opted, therefore, to supply this department with thin clients. Running on these thin clients are Java applets. The applets provide shipping information as well as data supporting entry by the dispatcher and loading dock supervisors.

Each of Billy Boy's managers is provided with an IEBI portal. The content of each portal is dependent on the role of the manager. The portals are also *customizable,* allowing the manager to modify the portal to fit his or her individual needs and taste. An example of one such portal is presented in Figure 11.2. Each window in this portal is an application *portlet.* The portlet is a window on the Web page that provides information from a specific application. In the upper right-hand corner of the portal is an email portlet. To receive a particular email message, the manager simply selects the message. The portlet brings the manager into that specific application where he or she can review the email. The other portlets work in the same way. To go into the balanced score card application, the user selects which perspective within the scorecard he or she would like to review.

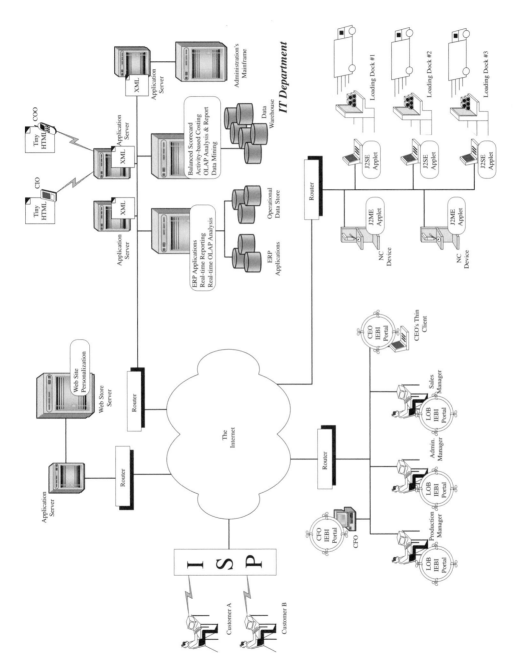

**FIGURE 11.1** Billy Boy Bowling Balls revised information infrastructure.

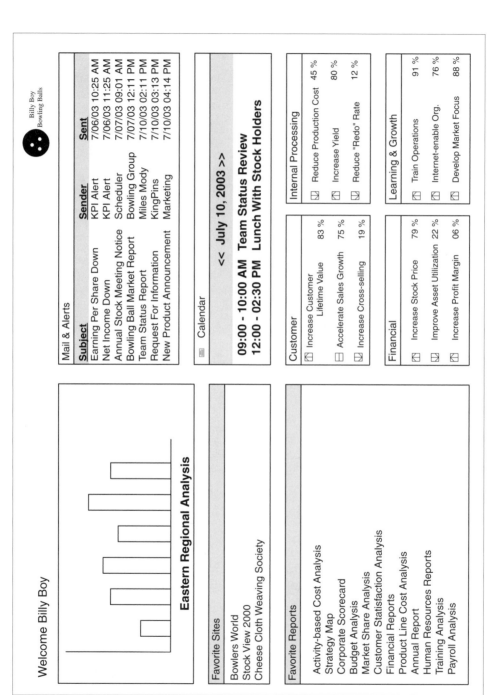

**FIGURE 11.2** Billy Boy Bowling Balls IEBI portal.

Notice how this one Web page brings together all the information needed by the manager. From this portal (or window), the user can view the state of the organization. If properly designed, this window becomes the decision maker's standard system interface. The decision maker can easily move from one application to the next in one integrated environment. Quite often, he or she need never know which application is supporting the queries; as far as the decision maker is concerned, this one portal *is* the information system. In Chapter 7 we discussed the abstraction of the different layers of the application stack. The IEBI portal abstracts the entire stack. Each application stack layer, from the hardware to the application itself, is abstracted by the portal.

Billy Boy Bowling Balls' decision makers can now focus on what is important: the strategy of the organization. Let's imagine what this means in a very real and practical sense. On Monday morning, Billy Boy comes into the office and the first thing he does is log on to the system. Immediately, the IEBI portal in Figure 11.2 is displayed on his thin client. Among the various items on his screen, he notices that Earnings Per Share (EPS) is not increasing at the desired rate. He realizes there is a problem, but he is not certain of the cause. Billy Boy decides to examine the components of EPS to better understand what is causing this problem.

He looks down the screen to examine the Key Performance Indicators (KPIs) of his organization. Each KPI is displayed in one of scorecard perspectives. The financial perspective confirms what he has seen in the graph above: Overall profitability is down. He also sees in this perspective that while the company has been doing well in reducing expenses, it has done a poor job in increasing sales. Billy decides that he wants to look at his strategy to understand what is happening with sales. He selects *View Strategy Map* from the list of business reports. The system displays the strategy map presented in Figure 11.3.

It doesn't take Billy Boy long to understand what is happening. The reduction in cost has been successful because they have delivered on their strategy. The IT department has implemented an ABC system and trained the managers of the production department on its use. He has seen how his production staff has used this system for budgeting and expense control. The program has been very successful. The other half of the picture is not bright; not all this stuff about developing a customer-driven culture and increasing customer lifetime value has really taken shape. Returning to the IEBI portal, Billy Boy sends an email to Miles Mody and the head of sales. He points to the reports he just reviewed and wants a plan of action from them by the end of the day.

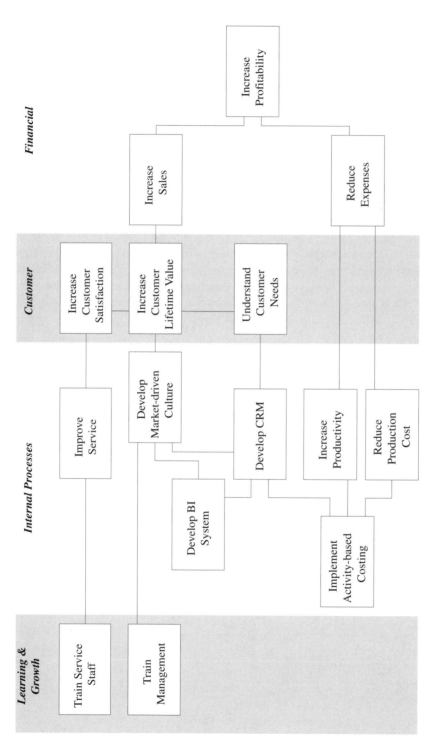

**FIGURE 11.3** Billy Boy Bowling Balls strategy map.

What do customer satisfaction, customer lifetime value, and customer-driven culture mean in an Internet age? These expressions weren't always snappy marketing clichés. There was a time when no one thought about *customer lifetime value* or being a *customer-driven organization*. No one thought about it because it was just an accepted way of doing business. If you were a tailor or grocer, you never thought about creating a mutually beneficial relationship. You knew Mrs. Barretta down the street. She was the one who made that great Bagne di San Giuseppe. You knew Mr. Barretta would stop in every night on his way home for a fresh loaf of bread. You could set your watch by it. When a nice shipment of peppers came in, or artichokes came in season, you would put some aside for her. You knew she would want them.

The world changed, though. Somewhere along the way, we got the idea that antiseptic, homogenized warehouses of prepackaged industrial slop could somehow replace good ol' Mr. Piasentino and his counter of nickel candy. Part of this change was that the relationship between the company and the customer was lost. We turned to selling product in mass to leverage economies of scale. When dealing on such a large scale, we lost the ability to deal with individuals one on one. Chapter 12 discusses this situation in more detail as well as how the Internet can assist us in solving this problem.

The key to building this better relationship is developing a better understanding of the customer. The old-time grocer knew us, which meant he knew our needs, wants, and behaviors. The Internet gives us the ability to develop this understanding of our customers again. In the old days, the corner grocer watched when you came into the store. He knew you and remembered what you did. In the big warehouse stores, they may be able to know what you bought, but they can't track what you put back on the shelf. They can't analyze which products you may have seen but decided not to buy. Chapter 13 discusses how, with the Internet, we can do this type of analysis. We look at how we can collect data to perform clickstream analysis.

Once we have all this data, what do we do with it? In Chapter 3, we discussed data mining, and in Chapter 8, we discussed data mining with Java. In Chapter 14, we discuss how to apply data mining to the clickstream data to better understand customer behavior. Based on this behavior, we can help guide our customers through our site, enhancing their shopping experience. *Enhancing their shopping experience*—doesn't that sound like a slick marketing phrase? While this may sound like fluff, there is substance behind it. We mean by this that we will help them fulfill their needs and desires. We will assist them in finding what they want and what they need. We will not try to cram a bunch of stuff down their throats or sell them products or services just to get their money. We will work with them so that they come to accept our company not just as a vendor, but as a trusted advisor. When we achieve this goal, we have truly developed an *enormous* strategic competitive advantage.

# Chapter 12

# CRM IN THE INTERNET AGE

*Customer-driven competition is what we call one-to-one marketing, a form of marketing that was prohibitively expensive, and therefore nearly inconceivable, to the traditional marketer just a few years ago. Today, as we enter the Interactive Age and microchip-controlled products, it has become a prerequisite for competitive success.*

*—Don Peppers and Martha Rogers*
Enterprise One-to-One[1]

Years ago I heard a comic being interviewed about a trip to southern California. He said that he made the trip to see the barnacle migration. The interviewer pressed him further. What did he mean by *barnacle migration*? The interviewer had never heard of such a thing. "Oh," the comic replied, "most people think it's a whale migration. It's really the barnacles migrating, and whales are going along for the ride." In a way, he had a pretty good point. Who is really doing the migrating: the whales or the barnacles? Just as with many other things in life, it is a matter of perspective. Two people can look at the same thing and draw completely different conclusions.

I was in a conversation recently that revealed a similar difference in perspective concerning Business Intelligence (BI). We have described BI as a three step process: acquire, analysis, and action. We collect data, analyze it, and take some action based on that analysis. When I see a process or a system that performs these steps, I see a BI system. Recently, I was discussing Customer Relationship Management (CRM) with a friend. I made the point that CRM is really a vertical of BI, that

---

[1]Peppers, Don, and Rogers, Martha, *Enterprise One-to-One,* Random House, 1999. Used by permission.

it is BI applied to a specific area. After his head exploded, I quickly came to realize that we had a huge difference in perspective. Is BI a barnacle or a whale? Is CRM migrating, or is BI?

We discuss in this chapter how the strategy of many organizations focuses inward. We will also see that this inward focus ultimately leads to the company's downfall. The chapter also shows that the only successful strategy looks outward. It is driven by customers, by their needs and wants. We have consistently described BI as a strategic system. It provides decision makers with the information necessary to both formulate a strategy and measure the performance of the organization in delivering on it. It is not critical to the BI system itself if that strategy is inward or outward facing.

There are two aspects to CRM: analytical and operational. The analytical portion collects and aggregates the data. It then provides a means for the decision maker to analyze this data so that he or she can better understand the organization's customers. The operational aspects of CRM are those areas that are customer-facing, such as the electronic storefront and Web-based helpdesk. These operational functions are driven by the analytical aspect of CRM. In the end, we see that CRM does what BI does: collects, analyzes, and acts.

Don Peppers and Martha Rogers describe an outward facing strategy as customer-driven, a one-to-one marketing perspective. They also note that in light of recent technological developments, we are able to do today what was inconceivable a few short years ago. So what has changed? Well, the answer to that question was provided in the first section of this book. What has changed is IEBI. We will see in this chapter that the Internet enables us to truly develop a custom, one-to-one approach to each and every customer. We shall see that CRM in the Internet age is IEBI.

## 12.1 The Customer-Driven Organization

There are three basic types of organizations in the world: engineering-driven, sales-driven, and customer-driven. Figure 12.1 presents the differences between these types of companies. The first, the engineering-driven company, sells what it knows how to make. The second, the sales-driven company, makes what it knows how to sell. In both cases, the focus of the organization is internal; they look at what *they* can do or what *they* know. Both are recipes for failure. The only corporate structure that promises long-term success is the customer-driven organization. The focus of such organizations is outward. They look at what the customer needs and wants.

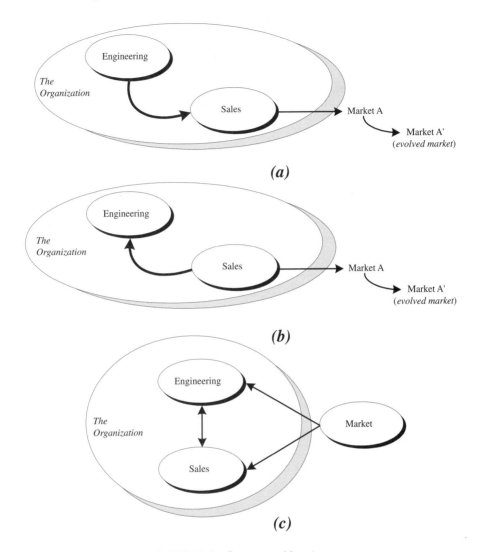

**FIGURE 12.1**   Company driver types.

As we can see in Figure 12.1 (a), the flow of information in the *engineering-driven* organization is from engineering out to the market by way of the sales force. This is typical of high-technology organizations. They have the mistaken belief that technology can sell itself. These companies are successful as long as the market has a need for the product. When the market evolves to something new, as seen in the figure where there is an evolution from A to A', the company misses the change and wonders what happened to its market share. This is part of the reason for the burst of the dotcom bubble. Dotcoms focused not on what the customer needed, but on what they could build. At the peak of dotcom mania, companies looked at what they could sell over the Internet. Sure, we had the technology to create *icecubes.com*, but does anyone really *want* to buy ice cubes over the Internet?

The second type of organization is *sales-driven*, as shown in Figure 12.1 (b). In this type of organization, communication is still from the inside out. The driving department is sales. The focus is not on the customer, but on what can be sold. Here, too, the organization misses the change in the evolution of the market. One might assume when looking at the sales organization that sales would be most in touch with customer needs. Unfortunately, the focus is usually on making quota for the quarter. These organizations are driven by short-term gains, not by a long-term strategy.

The sales-driven organization brings to mind a documentary I once saw on elephants. At one point, a female elephant died. Her mate, not understanding that she was dead, tried everything he could to rouse her. It was obviously to no avail. She just lay there, a huge dead carcass. This reminds me of sales-driven organizations. A sales-driven organization, just as with the engineering-driven organization, lacks a strategic view of its market. Sales is a lagging indicator. If you depend on it to tell you if you are doing things right, you won't know that something is sick until it is dead. I have seen this happen time and again. Sales start to slump, so management puts more pressure on the sales force. This doesn't work, because the market has shifted. Customers are no longer interested in the products, but management doesn't see the change. They have no insight into the market. They just don't understand why they can't sell this stuff anymore. They try everything they can to revive the corpse, but it just lies there, a big stinking carcass.

The only type of company that succeeds in the long term is the *customer-driven* organization. Figure 12.1(c) shows the flow of information for customer-driven companies. In this scenario, the organization actually listens to the customer it intends to serve. As the market changes and evolves, the company changes with it. It builds what the customer wants. If it doesn't know how to build what the customer wants, it learns how to build it. If it doesn't know how to sell what the customer wants, it hires the talent to sell it. It changes to fit the market.

Notice how this corresponds to our description of BI in Chapter 3. Organizations with low-level intelligence are reactionary; these are the sales-driven organizations. Other low-level organizations are emotional; these are the engineering-driven organizations that fall in love with their own technology. Both lack data and the appropriate mechanisms to analyze the data. They have no insight into their customers. When they *do* gather data, it is used to validate a decision that has already been reached. Customer-driven organizations, on the other hand, gather data concerning the characteristics of their market. They analyze the data and use this for the basis of their decisions.

## 12.2 The Ultimate in Customer-Driven

Let's take a trip into the future to see what the ultimate customer-driven organization might be like. In this future, we manufacture a device that sits in a convenient corner of a customer's home or office. Whenever our customer opens the front door of the device, the thing that would most satisfy his or her need at that moment appears. The customer doesn't even have to say what it is that he or she may want. The product simply appears. In the morning, the perfect breakfast is prepared exactly the way he or she likes it. As the customer dresses to leave for the office, his or her clothes, perfectly matched and tailored, are already laid out. That night after dinner, the customer opens the door to find a book. The author and genre are new to the customer, but the book turns out to be one of the best he or she has read in a long time. What makes this machine even more wonderful is that the price is exactly what the customer would want to pay, not a penny more. The breakfast, clothing, and book were acquired at a price that the customer feels was a pretty darn good deal.

If it were possible to develop such a device, we would easily eliminate all competitors. We would perfectly fulfill the wants and desires of all our customers. They would soon learn that there is no need for them to turn to any other vendor. They would establish a relationship with us in which they are dependent upon this one device to meet all their needs. Unfortunately, such technology does not exist, at least not at this point in time. It does demonstrate, however, the ultimate objective of the customer-driven organization.

The customer-driven organization creates a relationship with the customer, a *mutually beneficial relationship* in which the customer sees the organization as a trusted advisor. The organization undergoes a transformation as well. It no longer views the market as some nebulous cloud into which it dumps its products and services. We understand that the market is not monolithic, but comprises diverse sets of individuals who have their own needs and wants. In such an environment, we must develop a relationship with each individual—a relationship in which they communicate their desires to us and we fulfill them. Establishing and maintaining this relationship is a specialized area of BI known as *Customer Relationship Management* (CRM).

## 12.3   CRM in the Internet Age

CRM enthusiasts typically howl when I say that CRM is, in effect, a vertical within BI. Again, let us refer to the BI loop: BI extracts data from the operational environment and stores the data in some structure that is distinct from the operational system. The extraction process transforms and cleanses the data to be consistent with the data in this other structure. The Decision Support System (DSS) delivers this data to the decision maker, who uses it to formulate some plan of action.

BI is a necessary component for any business process. In processes where the consumer is the target of the analysis, BI can create significant differentiation. Most other BI endeavors create internal efficiencies that indirectly enhance value to the customer. CRM performs this same process. CRM takes the data from the operational environment and stores it in the CRM system. It then provides this data to the decision maker, who uses it for managing the relationship with the customer. Figure 12.2 presents this flow of information.

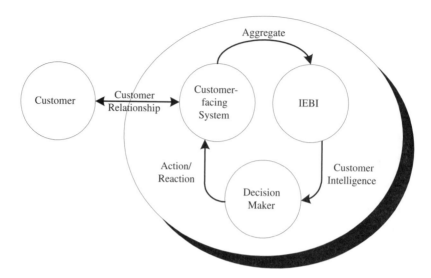

**FIGURE 12.2** BI-enabled e-commerce = CRM.

The loop shown in Figure 12.2 is similar to the BI loop presented in Chapters 1 and 3. In this loop, the operational systems from which we extract data are the systems that record the interactions with the customer. These *customer-facing* systems can include Point-Of-Sale (POS) systems that record purchases made by customers, customer support systems that record post sales activities, and especially Web sites that record Internet-based communication with customers. All of these systems are possible source systems for our IEBI/CRM solution.

As we can see in this figure, the IEBI system aggregates the data from the customer-facing system to provide customer intelligence. The customer intelligence provides a complete picture of the customer, a 360-degree view. This complete picture is in terms of the individual as well as in the context of his or her demographic groups. It shows the individual customer and, where appropriate, the household to which the customer belongs. This complete view also presents an analysis of past behaviors to predict future actions.

The decision maker uses this data to guide future interactions with the customer. These interactions may be both reactive and proactive. We discuss each type of interaction later in this chapter. For now, we need to understand that CRM is not a separate system that sits outside of IEBI. CRM is as essential an ingredient in the IEBI solution as the Balanced Scorecard (BSC) and Activity Based Management (ABM). The balanced scorecard applies IEBI to the management and formulation of strategy. ABM applies IEBI to the management of cost. CRM applies IEBI to the management of customer relationships.

While IEBI/CRM is an IEBI solution, it is a solution with an additional ingredient, a solution with its own unique flavor. It is the difference between marinara and Bolognese. In the next few sections, we look at how this additional ingredient transforms the other elements of our solution. We look at how adding meat—CRM—to our sauce has changed its flavor.

### 12.3.1 THE VALUE OF THE CUSTOMER RELATIONSHIP

The first ingredient of the IEBI/CRM solution is the meat itself, the customer. It is, in effect, the base of our sauce. One of the major benefits to being a customer-driven organization is that as the market changes, so does the organization. Think of this in terms of our solution. If we use beef as the base of our sauce, we have a sauce that is different from one with a pork base. The market, or customer, is the base of the solution. As its flavor changes, so too does the flavor of our solution.

This change in perspective focuses on the nature of the relationship we have with our customer. CRM is about *relationships*. The engineering-driven organization sees them as users, those pesky people who never truly appreciate our genius. They tolerate them because they perform a service. The sales-driven organization sees them as a *one-night stand*. They buy them dinner, hold their hand, and tell them they love them. Then, once they *close the deal*, it is on to the next sucker with money. To describe the quality of the relationship in both these situations as poor is an understatement.

In the customer-driven organization, the thing that is of real value to the organization is not its technology or the individual sale. The greatest asset to the customer-driven organization is the relationship established with the customer. In this type of relationship, we are concerned with providing for the needs and wants of the customers. We exist to serve them, to make their plight better. Through the continued delivery of quality service, we create customers who remain loyal to our company.

It has long been maintained that it is 10 times more expensive to find a new customer than it is to keep an old one. About 2 years ago, I was returning from Chicago from a speaking engagement. I arrived at the airport very early and spent about 2 hours waiting for my flight. Then, 15 minutes after our scheduled boarding time, we were told our flight had been cancelled. This made me angry, since this just *happened* to be 20 minutes after the departure of a competing airline's flight to the same destination. I was not in the most pleasant of moods. After a heated exchange with the airline representative, I turned to walk away. Then, just barely loud enough for me to hear, he said "If you don't like it fly another airline." As I waited for my next flight, I used my cell phone to call his CEO. I informed the CEO's office that I planned to take the employee's advice and that they would not see me on another flight. In a sense, we broke up. I terminated the relationship.

Consider what this one statement by the employee cost the airline. On average, I make one round trip a week. With that one statement, the employee shifted all of that revenue from his employee-owned airline to his biggest competitor. What will it take to move that many customers from the competitor to their own airline? How much of a discount will it have to give? What promotions will it have to run? The airline lost not just one but 50 flights annually. Let's explore the difference between these two.

We can view the customer relationship as an annuity. When properly maintained, that relationship provides an ongoing revenue stream to the organization. This is known as the customer's *LifeTime Value* (LTV). Just as we can determine the present value of an annuity, we can determine the present value of a relationship with a particular customer. The current LTV of a customer is a summation of the profit for each year times the *Present Value Interest Factor* (PVIF).

Before we look at a specific example, let's take a moment to understand what we mean by PVIF. The present value of something in future is how much we would need to invest today to have that value at a given point in time in the future. For example, if I have an account that gives a 6 percent annual return on my investment, and in 5 years I want to have $200 in that account, I would have to put $149.46 in that account today. The PVIF is the factor we apply to that future amount to put it in today's terms. The PVIF for 5 years at 6 percent is .7473.

Figure 12.3 illustrates how to apply this calculation to LTV. In the figure, we see that a particular customer is expected to initially generate $100 profit in the first year. The present value of this profit at a 6 percent interest rate is $94.34. We apply this same procedure for the expected profits from this customer for the remaining years of the expected life of the customer relationship. Summing these values gives us an expected LTV of $1,413.24.

As we can see, the customer's LTV is calculated for the entire length of the relationship. What determines the length of the relationship is the strength of that customer's loyalty. In our futuristic story, customer loyalty was built through understanding customer needs and wants. The better we are able to meet these desires, the more loyal they are to us.

There are two important points concerning customer LTV. First, a customer's LTV is a summation discounted value. Since LTV is a discounted value, the duration of that lifetime is not relevant to the comparison. All LTVs are comparable. If customer A has an LTV of $10,000 and customer B has an LTV of $8,000, customer A is the more valuable, even if customer A's relationship spans 20 years and customer B's spans 10. The LTV is the present value of the relationship.

The second point is that an LTV is a prediction. In the examples we have used in this section, our level of precision is down to the penny. This risks giving a false impression concerning how well we can predict LTV. While it may be correct to use this precision when calculating an annuity where all future cash flows are known, this is not the case with customer LTV. Customer LTV is a prediction based on statistical analysis. The level of accuracy of any statistical analysis is a function of the deviation about the mean. In short, we may be able to be close in our predictions, but very rarely, if ever, will we be able to predict with 100 percent accuracy. In addition, the prediction of an event becomes less accurate the further out in time the event occurs. Therefore, as time increases, so does the risk of our prediction being incorrect.

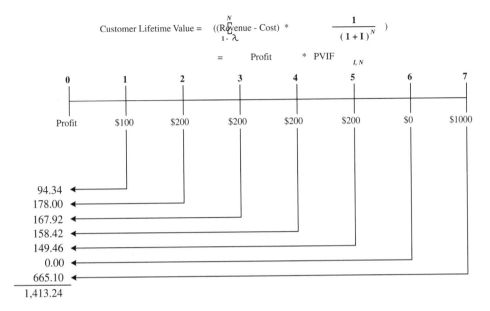

**FIGURE 12.3**  Calculating customer LTV.

To compensate for an increased risk over time, we make the following change to our PVIF equation:

$$\text{Customer Life Time Value with Risk} = \sum_{1-\lambda}^{N} \left( (\text{Revenue} - \text{Cost}) * \frac{1}{(1 + I + R)^N} \right)$$

In this revision of the equation, we have added a risk value, $R$, to the denominator of the PVIF. As time, $N$, increases, so does the effect of the risk factor reducing the present value of the profit. We have demonstrated how this affects customer LTV in Table 12.1. Compare the present value of customers with no risk to those whose risk is 5 percent and 7 percent. Although the cash flows over the same period of time are the same, as risk increases the present value of those cash flows decrease.

**TABLE 12.1**  Customer LTV with Risk Compensation

| Period | Future Value | 0% Risk PVIF | 5% Risk PVIF | 7% Risk PVIF | Present Value with 0% Risk | Present Value with 5% Risk | Present Value with 7% Risk |
|--------|--------------|--------------|--------------|--------------|----------------------------|----------------------------|----------------------------|
| 1 | 100.00 | 0.9434 | 0.9009 | 0.8850 | $ 94.34 | $ 90.09 | $ 88.50 |
| 2 | 100.00 | 0.8900 | 0.8116 | 0.7831 | $ 89.00 | $ 81.16 | $ 78.31 |
| 3 | 100.00 | 0.8396 | 0.7312 | 0.6931 | $ 83.96 | $ 73.12 | $ 69.31 |
| 4 | 100.00 | 0.7921 | 0.6587 | 0.6133 | $ 79.21 | $ 65.87 | $ 61.33 |
| 5 | 100.00 | 0.7473 | 0.5935 | 0.5428 | $ 74.73 | $ 59.35 | $ 54.28 |
| 6 | 100.00 | 0.7050 | 0.5346 | 0.4803 | $ 70.50 | $ 53.46 | $ 48.03 |
| 7 | 100.00 | 0.6651 | 0.4817 | 0.4251 | $ 66.51 | $ 48.17 | $ 42.51 |
| | | | | Totals = | $ 558.24 | $ 471.22 | $ 442.26 |

Ultimately, the greater we are at risk of losing a customer, the less valuable that customer is to our organizations. Compare the LTV of the three customers described in the table. A customer with a 7 percent chance of terminating the relationship is much less valuable than a customer from whom the organization can depend on a steady revenue stream.

### 12.3.2  CHANGING THE ORGANIZATION'S PERSPECTIVE

This brings us to the second ingredient in the IEBI/CRM solution, the organization. If we are to truly be a customer-centric organization, we must pay more than lip service to making the customer relationship the thing that drives the organization. In a very tangible way, we must change the way we do things. The question of course is how. How do we structure our organization so that the customer relationship drives what we do? How do we take all these nice platitudes and turn them into real business processes?

To understand customer loyalty, we need to look at the relationship from the customer's point of view, not ours. Several years ago, I was in a meeting in which a new marketing campaign was being developed for yet another company. They came up with the brilliant idea of not trying to *sell* to customers any longer, but to switch to a total self-service model. The customers would simply go to the company's Web site for all their needs. Dissenters in the organization pointed out that its competitors would continue to try *selling* its customers products. The party line was that our vastly superior technology would drive the customers to our Web site. It was like saying "I am so attractive, everyone will simply have to date me." Well, you can guess what happened. The campaign failed miserably. Customers left in droves and the company lost market share.

The obvious, and might I add extraordinarily stupid, mistake was that the company was approaching the market based on its internal needs, not on those of the customers. It wanted the world to work in a particular manner so desperately that it sat in the corner with furrowed brow, attempting to recreate the world with sheer mental force. In the end, all it got out of it was a headache and a reduced stock price. A purely Web-based service model did not meet the needs of the customers. As we said earlier in this chapter, not all products and services are adaptable to the Web. We need to understand the needs of the customers in those markets.

Part of the mistake this organization made was that it believed it had a lock on the market, which it didn't. Even if it had, this would have been a poor strategy. We mustn't confuse the lack of choice with loyalty. Customers with a choice will remain loyal as long as the organization meets their needs. Customers with no choice will remain loyal only until another choice is available. When another choice is available, the exodus will be even greater from the resentment that has accumulated while there was no alternative. We have seen this happen many times in our own industry. After building control over a particular market, the hardware or software company grows fat and happy. They become less competitive and start to produce inferior products. Eventually, their complacency causes them to miss the inevitable shift in technology. While they may maintain a command over a particular market, that market becomes less and less relevant. This has happened in the shift from mainframes to minicomputers, from minicomputers to workstations, from workstations to Internet enablement.

Organizations are faced with a significant challenge. If markets were monolithic, if there were little diversity between customers, meeting market demand would be simple. The unfortunate truth is that markets aren't that simple. Different customers have different needs at different times. In the auto industry, a customer's transportation needs and wants are highly dependent on many demographic characteristics working in unison. There is the obvious difference between the 30-something soccer mom and the 20-year-old mountain biking MBA student. Even within these demographics, there is a difference in transportation wants. The soccer mom from south Texas whose household income is above $100,000 may be more interested in the big, burly SUV than the mom from a New York suburb with an annual household income in the $80,000 range. Each additional demographic variable can greatly vary the predicted results. So, how does the organization meet these many different needs in an ever-changing market place? How is the organization transformed by the IEBI/CRM solution?

Figure 12.4 presents the information infrastructure of a customer-driven organization. The structure reflects the organization's strategy. The strategy of the organization centers on the development and maintenance of customer relationships; the center of the information infrastructure is the IEBI/CRM system. It acts as the hub, driving and directing the other parts of the company. We can see how this figure is a more detailed view of Figure 12.3. In the earlier figure, the information flows from the customer-facing system to the IEBI/CRM system. Customer intelligence then flows to the decision maker. Figure 12.4 shows some of the many paths that the customer intelligence travels to reach the decision maker.

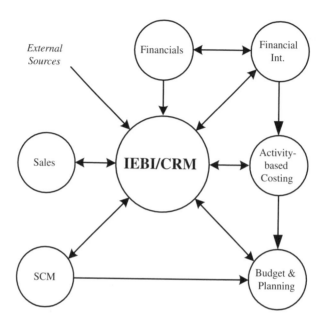

**FIGURE 12.4** A market-driven information architecture.

The entire process begins with the customer-facing system. The IEBI/CRM system aggregates and integrates data from the customer-facing system along with financial and external data. This data is used as the basis for our customer intelligence, which in turn drives the IEBI/CRM system. To quote John Donne, "No man is an island entire of itself; every man is a piece of the continent." The same is true of IEBI/CRM: It is not an island entire of itself. It is part of an integrated system of applications, each of which exchanges information.

In the previous section, we discussed how a customer's lifetime value to the organization is a function of profit. The values used to calculate profit and customer LTV come from two different systems: Activity-Based Costing (ABC) and financial intelligence. ABC gives us a more accurate understanding of our costs. We need to understand the advantages of ABC over the traditional GAAP (Generally Accepted Accounting Principles) method of cost accounting. As shown in Figure 12.5, GAAP reports costs along organizational structures. It is well suited to financial reporting, understanding what departments and divisions are spending. We can see specifically what we spent on marketing *or* procurement. Unfortunately, this type of reporting doesn't tell us too much about the cost of manufacturing or servicing an individual product. What we can't see with GAAP is what we spent on marketing *and* procurement for a *specific* product.

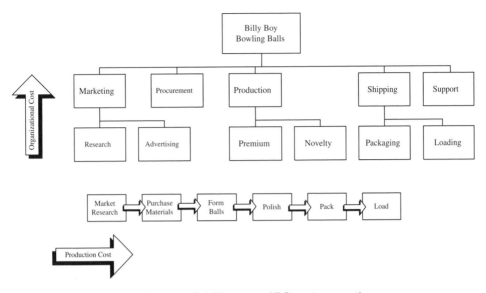

**FIGURE 12.5** GAAP versus ABC cost accounting.

The problem is that the cost of a product doesn't flow up organizational structures. Its costs flow across the organization. A particular product incurs costs from development, marketing, sales, manufacturing, and logistics. For example, we may manufacture watches, hundreds of different types of watches. Marketing may announce a new idea for a watch that costs $100 to produce. We then sell 1,000 of them for $120. We also have a watch that costs $90 to produce and we sell it for $100. Which of the two watches is more profitable? Well, we can't really tell from the information we have here. We discussed what it cost to manufacture, but what about the marketing cost for each product? What about the cost of different distribution channels? Marketing may have spent $20,000 on research and development for the first watch. The distribution channel for the first watch may also be more expensive than the second. GAAP is not able to provide this detailed cost analysis, but ABC can. ABC can tell us specifically the cost of a product with variations in supplier, distribution channels, and manufacturing processes. ABC considers all of these factors when calculating product costs.

Figure 12.4 shows the financial intelligence system receiving the cost information from the ABC system. It combines this information with other financial data, such as revenue, to determine the profitability for specific products, customers, and customer types. This financial data is then passed to the CRM system.

We have several plates spinning on very thin sticks. We discussed customer LTV, ABC, financial intelligence, and IEBI. Let us now step back and look at how these elements together drive the customer-driven organization. Figure 12.6 presents this flow of information between.

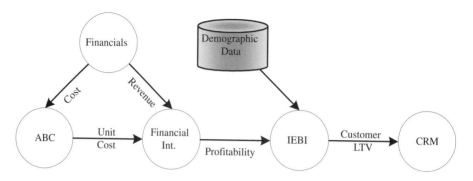

**FIGURE 12.6**   Calculating customer LTV.

The first step in being a customer-driven organization is to understand the LTV of our customers. From the financial system, we extract the cost data and calculate cost object-unit cost for our products and services. The financial intelligence system combines this information with revenue to determine the profitability of each item. The IEBI/CRM system then applies data mining techniques to determine the buying patterns of the different groups of customers. This is the analytical side of IEBI/CRM. Based on these patterns, the system can project the LTV of each customer group. Using these numbers, we can then plot the value of those relationships. Figure 12.7 is an example of such a graph.

The x-axis of the graph represents the profitability of the customer's LTV. The y-axis is the revenue dollars generated by the customer over the life of the relationship. Note that there is a difference in the volume of revenue dollars generated by a customer and the profitability of those dollars. We can divide this graph into four basic quadrants. Quadrants 1 (low-profit, low-volume) and 3 (high-profit, high-volume) reflect what we would expect to see in the graph. Some of our most profitable customers have the highest dollar volume, while our least profitable have the lowest volume. The graph, however, shows some other interesting customer groups. We see that in quadrant 3, there are customers who, based on their volume, should be highly profitable, but aren't. These customers may have special requirements that reduce their profitability or require a great deal of service. In quadrant 2, we see just the opposite effect: highly profitable customers who have a low volume. Perhaps these customers purchase products with large margins and require little service.

As we discussed in Chapter 3, data mining is the process of finding patterns hidden in the data. Once we have plotted each different group, we can mine the customer data to understand the different characteristics of the customers in each quadrant. By answering customer-related questions, we can better manage our relationships with those customers. For example, what is the difference between our low-volume, high-profit customers and our high-volume, high-profit customers? With this understanding, we can develop strategies to move every customer to quadrant 4.

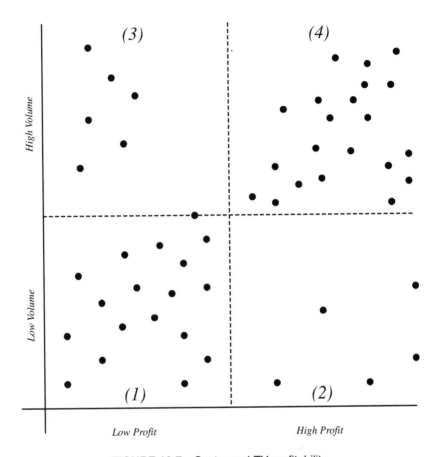

**FIGURE 12.7**  Customer LTV profitability.

   Notice the benefit of the customer profitability and LTV perspective. A sales-driven organization would only look at one line on this graph, the revenue volume. It would have no insight into the costs. Customers that appear to be profitable because of a high revenue volume can in fact be very costly. All the sales-driven company would see is large sales. The engineering-driven organization would have no greater insight into customer profitability. It wouldn't even look at this graph. It may even see the customers in quadrant 1 as just marvelous. These customers may purchase one, possibly two, systems and develop software that did something that is technically astounding. The engineering company would be thrilled. The problem is that they wouldn't be very profitable. After purchasing that one system, the customer would disappear.

### 12.3.3 PUTTING CUSTOMERS BEHIND THE WHEEL

So far we have examined how we can use IEBI/CRM to better understand our customer relationships. What do we do once we have this understanding? Being customer-driven is having our customers drive the direction of the organization. In this section, we examine how we use CRM to drive the organization. Let's look at an example to see how this works.

We may be a click-and-mortar company, interacting with our customers both over the Web and through local retail outlets. Our catalog contains memory cards for digital cameras and MP3 players. In doing a financial analysis, we discover that selling these products over the Internet is not as profitable as sales through our traditional outlets. Internet sales require additional packaging and handling, increasing their delivery cost. The problem is that these are very popular items. We need to decide how to reduce our cost while providing the customer with better service.

Using IEBI/CRM, we can develop a 360-degree view of the customer and develop a better understanding of the dynamics of different groups of customers. Using the IEBI/CRM system, we could can look for common characteristics in customers. When we do this for the groups that purchase memory cards, we see no real distinction that is related to our problem. As we probe the data further, we see that the customers who purchase memory cards in rural areas typically do so in conjunction with other items. We see that the rural customer typically buys a memory card when he or she buys the camera or a photo-quality printer. We could speculate that rural customers, accustomed to purchasing products through mail-order or over the Internet, group their purchases for efficiency. In any event, the grouping of the items amortizes the shipping and handling cost over all the items and maintains the profitability of the memory card.

On the other hand, urban customers, who typically purchase the memory card by itself, are within easy driving distance of a retail outlet. To remedy the situation, we could first suggest that urban customers who purchase the product over the Internet pick up the item at the store instead. We point out that they will receive the product much more quickly this way. If this does not reduce the number of individual memory card orders, we offer customers an incentive to either group the product with other orders or to pick up the memory card at the outlet.

This example does more than address the issue of increasing the profitability of memory cards. It shows how, using profitability analysis, we can develop a more mutually beneficial relationship with our customers. The rural customers buy in volume and are more profitable. In addition to purchasing memory cards from our Web site, they typically buy multiple items at one time. We are doing well with these customers.

Our strategy with our urban customers moves them from low-volume, low-profit to at least low-volume, high-profit or even possibly to high-volume, high-profit. Let us assume that for some urban customers, we succeed in getting them to pick up the memory card at the local outlet. We have increased their profitability, possibly moving them to a low-volume, high-profit customer. The campaign gives the customer a new option for interaction with our company. Their selection of this option indicates that we may be meeting some personal need. For those urban customers who choose to combine their purchases into one shipment, we have increased both their profitability and their volume.

### 12.3.4  THE INTERNET AND CRM

The final ingredient in the IEBI/CRM solution is the Internet. If IEBI/CRM drives the entire customer-driven organization, it will obviously drive how we interact with our customers. In the Internet age, it will drive how we interact with those customers over the Internet. Earlier in the chapter, we described how we can increase customer loyalty by understanding our customers' needs. As we become more responsive to those needs, the customers become more confident in the relationship. Loyalty becomes mutually beneficial.

One way to establish a sense that the company understands a customer is through personalization. For example, we may have a company that sells tools over the Internet. A customer primarily interested in home repair should have a different experience than a customer interested in woodworking. When we projected into the future and discussed a device that would deliver the perfect product for the customer, the device knew without being told what the customer wanted. A customer interested in woodworking would receive different direction than a customer interested in home repair. The device knew. Our Web sites need to get as close to this idealized environment as possible.

The example with which most of us are probably familiar is Amazon.com. Amazon provides returning customers with a personalized home page. Of course, Amazon doesn't call it a home page, but refers to it as "Mary's Store" or "William's Store." This demonstrates how Amazon looks at the experience not from its point of view, but from the customer's. The customer goes to a store to make a purchase. In the case of Amazon.com, the customer's own personal store is tailored to his or her specific needs. At the very top of the page is a welcome message; this is the cyber equivalent of someone greeting you as you walk into your store. Just beneath the greeting is a link to a page of recommended reading.

When recommending products, we should strive to go beyond the obvious. Whether we are recommending books or power tools, the recommendation engine should suggest to the customer things he or she may not normally expect. If we are suggesting books and the customer has rated a particular author highly, it is apparent that he or she would probably be interested in other books by the same author. In some cases, however, such a simple algorithm would get it wrong. Imagine an author such as Isaac Asimov, who has written extensively on areas ranging from science to the Bible to murder mysteries. Is the average reader really interested in that wide a variety of topics?

The recommendation engine should be inventive in what it recommends to customers. Have you ever purchased a product, such as a digital camera or PDA, over the Internet only to have the Web site recommend competing products during subsequent visits? Recently, I purchased a PDA from a Web site, and then a number of competing PDAs were recommended. I wondered, *Is there something wrong with the one you sold me that I don't know about?*

If I buy a sliding-compound-miter saw, don't recommend additional saws. I already have one. *You're not helping.* Instead, think of the things that someone with a sliding-compound-miter saw might want. Why not recommend a measuring tape with a digital readout, an air hammer for finishing nails, or a level? By making the recommendations helpful, things that might not normally be considered by the customer, we demonstrate an understanding of his or her needs. The consumer begins to think of the site as a place to go to receive advice and direction.

Recommendation engines can be both subtle and overt. The previous example demonstrates how a recommendation engine can be used in an overt way. We can also provide recommendations in a more subtle manner. Figure 12.8 presents a Web page with more subtle recommendations. The Web page recommends lists and other books that were of interest to other readers with similar profiles. As we can see, the extraordinarily intelligent readers who rated this book highly also rated these other books highly. Along the right side of the page are lists of books similar to the one in the center of the page.

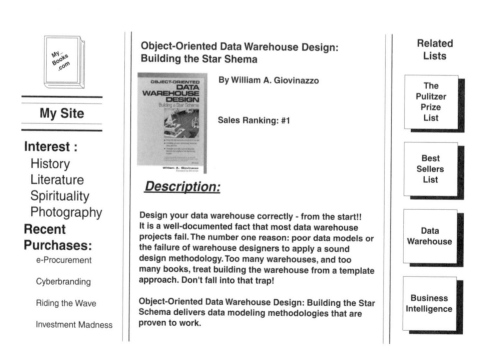

**FIGURE 12.8**  Web page with recommendation.

Our goal is to establish in the mind of the consumer a sense of loyalty, to build a feeling that customers are somehow stakeholders in the organization. Another method is to create a sense of community around the store. When I was very young and actually had hair, I had dreams of being the next Eric Clapton. I had visions of myself up there on stage, jamming with Harrison, Clapton, and the other guys in front of throngs of screaming nubile female fans. It is not at all surprising to discover that there were many of us in my little hometown with the same dream. We all gathered at a little guitar shop on the east side of town. The owner encouraged this community atmosphere. After a few years, the little shop, while still little, had enormous influence. If you were any sort of guitarist in those days, you knew Art, the owner. It was there that you met other guitarists and got advice from Art and the other musicians on how to play as well as what instruments to play. This same sense of community needs to be developed on a company's Web site.

As a site-based community develops, users come to see it as more than a simple store but as a gathering place for like-minded individuals. Again, we see that Amazon has developed this sense of community within its own site. Customers review products and recommend them to other customers; discussion groups are started; customers email one another to ask opinions. Customers are drawn to the site not just for products, but for virtually free information. In the information age, this *is* something for nothing. When we integrate the exchange of information into the purchase process, as we have done here, we are using the Internet specifically as designed, for the exchange of information.

This community approach to sales is integral to a customer-driven strategy. The community becomes another aspect of our customer relationship. As is the goal with the entire relationship, the community aspect of this relationship is mutually beneficial. Not only does the consumer benefit from the relationship, but the supplier does as well. As we monitor the discussions that occur as part of this community, we gain a better understanding of our customers.

Again, look to Amazon as an example of what works. Authors are suppliers; we create a product—books—that is consumed by our customers. The reviews provided on Amazon benefit authors in two important ways. First, when we are researching a topic for a future title, we can examine the reviews of books that already exist. These reviews can tell us where certain books have succeeded and where they might have failed. We can use this research to help shape our own work. Second, these reviews are helpful once the book has been published. We can get a feeling for what our readers did and did not like about our book. When an email address is provided, we can contact that reader directly to probe their comments in more detail. This type of feedback is invaluable to an author.

Most of what we have discussed at this point is reactive. The consumer takes the initial step in the process, and the organization in turn responds. We can also be more proactive in how we deal with our customers. When consumers purchase a product, whether through a traditional outlet or over the Internet, we can simply ask for their email address and permission to send them particular types of information. Consumer can be given the option of receiving news, promotional items, tips and techniques, or industry updates.

For example, I finally go out and buy that sliding-compound-miter saw I have been eyeing for the past 6 months. When I purchase the item, I might be asked if I would like to receive a monthly newsletter on home repair or promotional items such as discount coupons on saw blades. Maybe I will receive copies of *The Baseboard Journal* every 6 weeks. Once I give permission, I have opened a dialog with the company. It can now provide information specific to the product I purchased or even general industry information. It is allowed to proactively communicate with me, the consumer. Through this communication, the company continues to establish a feeling that it is knowledgeable about my needs and there to meet them. The company builds in my mind not only trust, but an understanding that it is customer focused. It is there to support my needs to our mutual benefit.

## 12.4   Conclusion

An outward-facing, customer-driven strategy is key to the long-term success of any organization. The customer-driven organization develops a mutually beneficial relationship with the customer. In changing our view from a discrete customer sale to an ongoing, mutually beneficial relationship, we develop revenue streams. The value of these streams is the LTV of the customer.

One facet of IEBI is CRM, which is that portion of the IEBI system that provides analysis of customer needs, wants, behavior, and value. It is through the IEBI/CRM system that the decision maker is able to predict a customer's LTV. Decision makers are able to optimize this value by understanding the needs and wants implicit in the customer's behavior and providing for them. It is the same old BI loop: collect, analyze, and act.

If organizations are to be successful, they must accept that we are in a new age, the Internet age. As Pepper and Rogers so aptly point out, one-to-one marketing is a prerequisite to remaining competitive. IEBI enables the organization to develop that one-to-one perspective. In Chapter 13, we explore one way in which we can use the Internet to develop this perspective.

# SWIMMING IN THE CLICKSTREAM

*I have often told you that I am that little fish who swims about under a shark and, I believe, lives indelicately on its offal. Anyway, that is the way I am. Life moves over me in a vast black shadow and I swallow whatever it drops with relish, having learned in a very hard school that one cannot be both a parasite and enjoy self-nourishment without moving in worlds too fantastic for even my disordered imagination to people with meaning.*

—Zelda Fitzgerald[1]

A customer-driven organization seeks to establish a mutually beneficial relationship with its customers. It is a symbiotic relationship similar to the relationship between a shark and a remora fish, described by Zelda Fitzgerald. Unfortunately, Zelda got it wrong: The remora fish feeds off the parasites on the shark, not off its offal. In this symbiotic relationship, the shark is cleaned and the remora fish is given a ride with a meal. In the symbiotic relationship between the customer and the company, the customer gets his or her needs and wants satisfied while the company is provided a long-term source of revenue. In the Internet age, we need to become a fish, a remora fish, and learn to swim in the clickstream.

---

[1]From letter to F. Scott Fitzgerald (March 1932.) Reprinted with permission of Scribner, an imprint of Simon & Schuster Adult Publishing Group, from *Zelda Fitzgerald: The Collected Writings*, edited by Matthew J. Bruccoli. Copyright © 1991 by The Trustees under Agreement Dated July 3, 1975. Created by Frances Scott Fitzgerald Smith.

In his book *Customer Share Marketing,* Tom Osenton describes some of the differences between mass-market communications and one-to-one communications. We see in those differences that many of the technologies that make it possible to communicate with our customers were not available a few short years ago. Osenton substantiates Don Peppers and Martha Rogers' statement that one-to-one "was prohibitively expensive, and therefore nearly inconceivable, to the traditional marketer just a few years ago." Thanks to these new technologies, however, we are able to establish this more direct form of communication.

One of the new technologies in the brick-and-mortar world that makes a one-to-one relationship possible is the register scanner. While it is a common part of our lives, this is a relatively new technology. Many may not recall one of the gaffs made by President Bush in the 1992 presidential election. During a visit to a grocery store, the scanners at the checkout impressed him. By that time, scanners were a common part of most people's lives.

From a marketing perspective, scanners made it possible to implement frequent buyer programs. It is common for a grocery or video store chain to issue membership cards that are scanned with every purchase. These programs, while providing the customer with discounts and points towards different rewards, provide the company with a way to track customer behavior. In this chapter, we look at membership programs and their use in tracking customer behavior.

Hey! Wait a minute, I thought this was a book about Internet-enabled business intelligence.

Well, yes, it is. We begin this chapter by talking about membership cards as an example of programs in the brick-and-mortar world. We use this example to show where it is lacking. We then demonstrate how we can overcome these deficiencies in the Internet-enabled world of electronic storefronts. We show how the clickstream records every action performed by customers on our Web site and how we can gather this information for analysis.

We discuss how gathering this information entails more than just parsing a few log files on the server. This chapter explores the problems with *raw* clickstream data. One way to resolve these problems is to employ the use of cookies. Although we briefly described cookies in an earlier chapter, we take a more in-depth look at them here, discussing their creation and use.

## 13.1  The Importance of Customer Identification

One of the conclusions in Chapter 12 is that the customer-driven organization's objective is to develop a long-term, mutually beneficial relationship with the customer. A key element in this relationship is the a sense of confidence on the part of customers, a feeling that the organization both understands and is able to meet their needs and wants. To understand these needs, we must listen to our customers, establishing a dialog with them.

In Chapter 11, we talked about the neighborhood grocer who provided customized service and developed a customer relationship simply by dealing with people as people. The small shop had a small number of customers. The shop owner knew every customer, and they knew the shop owner. As the economy grew and the small specialty outlet was replaced by the mega-superstore, this understanding of the customer was lost.

Today, brick-and-mortar organizations attempt to reestablish this intimacy with the customer base through technology. Although retail outlets cannot record each and every action of the customers as they move through the store, they do have a record of what customers purchased. They can analyze this information to understand customer behavior. We refer to this as *market-basket* analysis. In such analyses, we review what the customer actually purchased and combine that with other information to get an insight to our customer behavior.

My family typically shops at the same grocery store every week. We'll use the name Fred's in place of the store's real name. Every time I stop in, I am asked, "Did you bring your Fred's card?" Heaven help me if I say no. Fred has trained his cashiers to be like commandos when it comes to that card. "You really should have it with you, you know. Would you like to apply for one? Please, it will only take a second." Fred is wise in training his staff to be so diligent. The market-basket analysis that little card enables tells him who you are and identifies your buying habits.

Just recently, I stopped by Fred's to pick up a few things on the way home from the office. There were two people in line in front of me. The man being checked out was buying two six-packs, a bag of chips, and some beef jerky. So much for the myth of Southern California's health food culture. As he was about to pay, the cashier dutifully asked, "Do you have a Fred's card?" He committed the sin of all Fred sins—he tried to check out without a card. The cashier, in her exuberance to serve Fred, insisted that he use a Fred's card whether he had one or not. The second man in line was asked if he would mind allowing the other customer to use his Fred's card, which he readily did. The second man was an older gentleman. His purchases consisted of dental adhesive, fresh fruit, some mothballs, and a fiber laxative. As I looked at the second man's purchases, I realized that the cashier had no idea of the purpose behind those cards. Although it probably did not have enough statistical significance to appreciably skew the market-basket analysis, she was putting bad data into the system. To understand why this creates bad data, let's look at how Fred uses the information.

The Fred's card provides Fred with information that is critical in understanding customer behavior. It tracks my purchases for a particular visit as well as each of my visits. It provides continuity. Without the Fred's card, there is no way to associate a visit to Fred's on Saturday with a visit on Wednesday. This matter is further complicated when Fred has more than one outlet. Let's assume that Fred opens a new store near my office. Instead of stopping by the store on the way home, I walk over to the store near my office and pick up what I need. Without the Fred's card, all Fred would see is a reduction in traffic in the store near my home.

He would have no idea that the new store was cannibalizing business from the older one. One might suggest that we can link visits by credit card numbers. The problem with this method is that it assumes that I have only one credit card, or at least only one that I use for groceries. What happens if I use cash or a personal check? Could we be satisfied with just capturing purchases made by people with credit cards? People with credit cards may have different buying habits than those without.

The market-basket analysis gives Fred an insight into my buying patterns. It tells Fred that I stopped by twice last week to pick up some scotch. It tells him that this week I picked up two more bottles. If I do it again next week, Fred will be calling Alcoholics Anonymous. Fred stores my purchases and my buying patterns in a central system. He then analyzes those purchases to detect buying patterns. One of the things Fred then does is generate a string of coupons on the back of my receipt. These coupons are based on my buying patterns, directing me to products or services that may be of interest to someone in my particular demographic with my particular buying patterns.

As we noted earlier, the customer-driven organization seeks to develop a *mutually* beneficial relationship. The card also tells Fred information that profits him. When my data is aggregated with others, it describes the buying patterns of different demographic groups. Fred can use this information for stocking purposes; stores located in large senior citizen communities may be stocked differently than stores in areas with a large percentage of young families. He may elect to stock based on the ethnicity of the community. Perhaps a store in West Los Angeles, where there is a large Jewish community, is stocked differently in September during Yom Kippur than a similar store in the Ventura Valley, which has a smaller Jewish community. Fred provides better service to his customers by tailoring his service to meet their needs while increasing the profitability of his shelf space.

Let's not forget those coupons that are printed on the back of my receipt. These are also of mutual benefit. The selection of coupons was based on my individual buying patterns. If my purchases included veggie burgers and alfalfa sprouts, it would be probably not be a good idea to print up a discount on a jumbo size bag of pork rinds. The selection can take into consideration which products Fred wishes to move or products that are located in a section of the store where he is trying to increase traffic.

Now consider how the cashier who used the wrong Fred's card corrupted the market-basket analysis. We had a senior citizen who was identified as purchasing beer and salty sack food. In addition, the system shows the customer made two trips to the store that day. What would happen if this was done on a consistent basis? Suddenly, Fred would start pushing beef jerky and beer to geriatrics. Not only would the CDC be less than enthusiastic, so would the customers themselves. They would go to Fred's expecting to find dental adhesive and find instead a two-for-one special on beef jerky with every six-pack of Fred's Brand Ale. What good would a half off coupon on salt-vinegar potato chips do a 76-year-old man with pulmonary edema?

Market-basket analysis does have its limitations. It cannot, for example, tell us what a customer put in a basket and then took out. Nor can it tell us the path that the customer traveled through the store. About 7 years ago, I saw a demonstration of a system that attempted to plot a customer's path. The products in the shopping cart were plotted on the store floor plan. The system then plotted the most logical path from one point to the next. This path was just an approximation. It could not tell with any real surety if the products were purchased in any particular order or whether the path projected by the system was accurate in any way. The store hoped that by aggregating this data, it could discover the least trafficked and most heavily trafficked areas in the store.

## 13.2 Understanding Customer Behavior in the Internet Age

When it comes to understanding customer behavior, we can see that the brick-and-mortar stores have their strengths as well as their weaknesses. This is where the power of the Internet comes into play. As we said above, the Internet gives us a tremendous advantage, because the Web server records everything we do over the Web. The retail brick-and-mortar store could not tell us where the customer went in the store or what may have been in the market-basket that was taken out. Using clickstream analysis, we can observe and record these behaviors.

With e-commerce we are doing more than just mimicking what we have done with brick-and-mortar. To repeat what we have been saying all along, in a solution, the elements of the solution are changed by one another. This is true with analyzing customer behavior. In Chapter 12, we talked about how we could use the Internet to manage our relationships with our customers. Part of that management is the ability to measure our effectiveness in reaching our customers. Let's look at Figure 13.1 to understand the some of the ways in which we can use clickstream analysis to understand customer behavior.

One of the things that market-basket analysis in the brick-and-mortar world could not tell us was how the customer got to our store. We never really knew what drove them to our location, whether it was word-of-mouth or an ad that they may have seen. As seen in Figure 13.1, in the Internet-enabled world, we can track how a particular customer gets to our site. Customer A, for example, is responding to an ad received in an email. In the past, customer A may have purchased a power drill or some accessory related to a drill. Later, when our site is running a special on drill bits, we send an email informing him of the offer. Once he has had a chance to review the products, he may decide that he isn't interested in any of the bits. While visiting the site, however, he decides to purchase a book on woodworking. In this example, we can link a specific sale to a specific campaign.

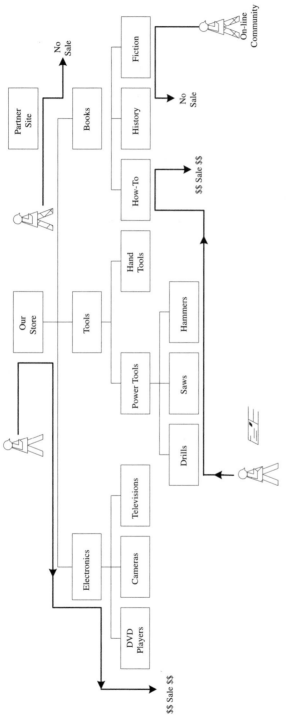

**FIGURE 13.1**  Measuring customer behavior over the Internet.

In the brick-and-mortar world, companies go to great expense in deciding where to put a store. As the saying goes, the three most important things are location, location, location. How are customers finding our site? Are they finding us as the result of a search engine, a banner ad placed out on the Web by the marketing department, or were they referred to our site by a partner? This all speaks to the virtual neighborhood of our site. We can understand our virtual neighborhood by understanding how customers got to our site.

As we look at the types of activities we proposed for reaching out to customers, we see that by using clickstream analysis, we can measure the effectiveness of each. As we consider these, here are some of the analyses we can perform:

- ❏ Are members of online communities purchasing product?
- ❏ Is our top tier of customers members of online communities?
- ❏ Where do most of our customers come from?
- ❏ Are customers being referred to our site by our partners?
- ❏ Are customers coming to our site from search engines?
- ❏ How effective are email promotions?
- ❏ Is a particular promotion profitable?
- ❏ Is our recommendation engine generating sales?
- ❏ Does adding links to sites create sales?
- ❏ Are the answers for questions dependent on a particular product?
- ❏ Are the answers to these questions dependent on demographics of the customers?

The answer to each question is in the clickstream. It is like a prospector panning for gold. As we sift through the data, we can pick out the gold nuggets of information. The remaining sections of this chapter discuss how we do this.

## 13.3  The Clickstream

The Web server records every step of our customer's interaction with our Web site. This means that every time the user goes from one point in our site to the next, the Web server records every file or image that is downloaded, every Web page that is opened. Typically, a Web server uses four logs: transfer, error, referrer, and agent. These are ASCII files whose fields are either tab-, space-, or comma-delimited. Figure 13.2 shows how the server records interactions with the users in each log.

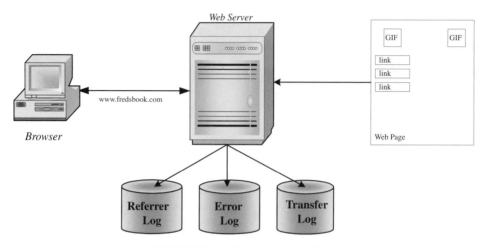

FIGURE 13.2   Web server log files.

The process may not begin at our own site. Perhaps the customer comes to our site from a link on a partner's Web site. The referrer log records this action. When a page is downloaded from the Web server to the customer's browser, the transfer log records a *hit*. A hit is often mistaken for accessing a specific Web page. Hits actually refer to the number of files accessed from a site. In addition to Web pages, graphic images, banner ads, and hyperlinks are hits on a site and are recorded in the transfer log. While this may seem curious at first, consider how the Web server views these objects. Each object—Web page, image, and banner ad—is a file. The Web server does not distinguish between them. When requested, they are all sent to the client via HTTP in the same way. There is no reason for the server to distinguish between them.

The Web server records the status of the transfer in the status log. It also records the type of client making the request of the server in the agent log. Since so much of our clickstream information originates in the transfer log, we examine this log in more detail.

### 13.3.1   TRANSFER LOG FILE

The transfer log file records the transactions between the client and the Web server. This is the main source of clickstream data. From the entries in this log, we can link a domain name or IP address with a request for a specific page on our Web site. The NCSA (National Center for Supercomputing Applications) has described a standard transfer log file format. Figure 13.3 provides a sample transfer log file entry.

**FIGURE 13.3**  Sample transfer log file entry.

The entry presented in the figure is an example of a common log file entry. In addition, an extended format to the log file record includes a referrer and agent field. The following list describes each of the fields in the log file.

❑ **Host**—The IP address or the domain name of the client making the request of the server. In order to log a domain name, the Web server must translate the IP address into a hostname using the Domain Name System (DNS). Refer to Chapter 6 for more details.

❑ **Identification**—The identification field is part of the original RFC (Request for Comment) 931. The field's original purpose was to provide identification of the system making the request. This field is rarely used and is most often a simple dash (-).

❑ **Authuser**—This field is intended to provide authenticated users access to a protected area. When this field is not in use, a simple dash will suffice.

❑ **Time**—This field contains the server's data and time of the request. The format of the time field is

> **DD/MON/YYYY HH:MM:SEC +/- XXXX**
> **Where:**
> **DD/MON/YYYY is the two-digit day, three-character**
> **month, and four-digit year.**
> **HH:MM:SEC is the Greenwich Mean Time (GMT) of the**
> **request.**
> **+/- XXXX is the difference in hours between GMT and the**
> **time local to the server. The difference is expressed as**
> **either plus or minus GMT.**

❑ **Request**—This field contains the request made of the server. The request can be a GET, POST, or HEAD command. The GET command requests the server to get the requested document. The POST command tells the Web server that it is about to transmit data and identifies the program to receive the input. The HEAD command retrieves the HEAD section of an HTML document.

❑ **Status**—The status field records the status of the request. There are a variety of commands (Table 13.1 lists several of the most commonly seen codes). Note that when reviewing these codes, there are certain classes of codes. For example, a status code within the 200 range indicates a successful transfer.

**TABLE 13.1**   Web Server Status Codes

| Code | Description |
|------|-------------|
| **200** | **Successful Transfers** |
| 201 | Created |
| 202 | Accepted |
| 204 | No Content |
| **300** | **Redirected Transfers** |
| 301 | Permanently Moved |
| 302 | Temporarily Moved |
| 304 | No Change |
| **400** | **Failed Transfers** |
| 401 | Unauthorized |
| 403 | Forbidden |
| 404 | Not Found |
| **500** | **Server Errors** |
| 501 | Not Implemented |
| 502 | Bad Gateway |
| 503 | Service Unavailable |

❏ **Bytes**—The number of bytes that were transferred to the client.

❏ **Referrer**—This field is part of the extended common transfer log format. It is a text string that can be optionally sent by the user to indicate origin of the request or link.

❏ **Agent**—This field is part of the extended common transfer log format. This field identifies the client program or browser making the request.

### 13.3.2   MINING THE TRANSFER LOG FILE

Now that we have the transfer log file, let's consider some of the things that we can do with it. Of course, there isn't a great deal of analysis that we can perform on the raw file as it is, so we have to massage it a bit. We start by importing the file into a database and parsing the individual fields into a workable format. The time is parsed into two fields: one for date and one for time. We might also want to transform the time to the time local to the server. The request is broken into two fields as well: one for the command and one for the requested page. We then sort the data

| Host | Date | Time | Command | Page |
|---|---|---|---|---|
| 011.205.201.137 | 10/JUL/2003 | 11:05:23 | Get | ..../...html |
| 011.205.201.137 | 10/JUL/2003 | 11:06:41 | Get | ..../...html |
| 011.205.201.137 | 10/JUL/2003 | 11:09:22 | Get | ..../...gif |
| 011.205.201.137 | 10/JUL/2003 | 11:11:53 | Get | ..../...gif |
| 011.205.201.137 | 10/JUL/2003 | 11:17:19 | Get | ..../...html |
| ● | ● | ● | ● | ● |
| ● | ● | ● | ● | ● |
| ● | ● | ● | ● | ● |
| 011.205.201.137 | 10/JUL/2003 | 12:20:36 | Get | ..../...gif |
| 011.205.201.137 | 10/JUL/2003 | 12:21:27 | Post | ..../...html |
| 011.205.201.137 | 10/JUL/2003 | 12:25:33 | Get | ..../...gif |
| 011.205.201.137 | 10/JUL/2003 | 12:29:59 | Post | ..../...html |
| 011.205.201.101 | 10/JUL/2003 | 11:04:13 | Get | ..../...html |
| 011.205.201.101 | 10/JUL/2003 | 11:07:41 | Get | ..../...html |
| 011.205.201.101 | 10/JUL/2003 | 11:08:22 | Get | ..../...gif |
| 011.205.201.101 | 10/JUL/2003 | 11:13:22 | Get | ..../...gif |

**FIGURE 13.4**   Sorted and parsed transfer log records.

by host, date, and time. This results in a table of data similar to the one shown in Figure 13.4, which presents just a portion of the data that we would expect to see in a transfer log file.

Examining the figure reveals some interesting aspects of trying to interpret customer behavior information from a transfer log. As we follow this stream of data, we see an interesting flow. The same host makes requests of our server. The stream continues somewhat steadily for a period of approximately 15 minutes. There is a gap of roughly an hour before the stream picks up again. When it does make a request, it is for a completely unrelated page. After the user visits this unrelated page, the POST command is sent, which we conclude is a purchase. Shortly after the POST command is another entry in the transaction log that starts another sequence of pages.

From this stream, we can assume that a user did some browsing on our Web site, then for some reason went away for some time. Upon his or her return, the user decided to make a purchase and then do some more browsing. This is one scenario that can be gathered from this clickstream, but not the only one. The trouble with the transaction log is that it only provides us with an IP address, which in the grand scheme of things really doesn't tell us a heck of a lot. An IP address is not a reliable means to identify an individual customer, which means that it is not a reliable mechanism for analyzing customer behavior. Some of the reasons for this are demonstrated in Figure 13.5.

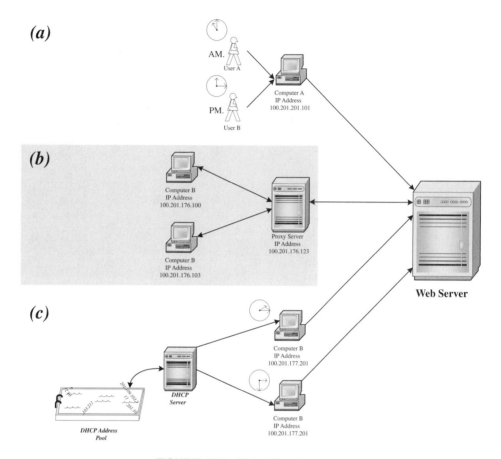

**FIGURE 13.5**  Using IP addresses.

Let's begin by understanding that in the best of all circumstances, an IP address identifies only a specific system. It does not identify a person or even a client application. This is demonstrated in Figure 13.5 (a). We see that computer A at 11:00 is in use by user A. The system may have multiple accounts and multiple users. Later that day, user B works on the same system. In this situation, we have the same IP address and two different users. Typically, we would expect to see this in an office or educational environment in which it is common for different users to use the same system. In such environments, users can have drastically different demographics. Attempting to draw customer behavior information based on IP addresses in these situations would most certainly lead to incorrect conclusions.

An IP address can lead us to false conclusions in other situations as well. Figure 13.5 (b) shows a situation in which clients access the Internet via a proxy server. Businesses and ISPs use proxy servers to reduce Internet traffic as well as control access. For example, filtering software can be hosted on the proxy server to prevent employees from accessing objectionable material. The proxy server will also cache frequently accessed Web pages. This will of course cause the clickstream data miner endless problems in underreporting the number of hits a particular page receives. Nor can we be confident that the IP address reported to the Web server is the address of the system that is actually making the request or that of the proxy server. While it is recommended that the proxy server notify us that a proxy is making the request, there is nothing at present that dictates that this must be the case.

For the data miner, the proxy server means that one IP address will have a mixture of activities. In Figure 13.5 (a), we had just one or two users on the same system. Their behavior was indistinguishable from one another. In the case of the proxy server, we have entire populations of users identified with one IP address. In all likelihood, this population would not have the same demographics. Think of your own work environment. In most cases, there are rather large gender, race, religion, and sexual preference differences as well as differences in income

Finally, we are assuming that IP addresses are static entities. As we can see in Figure 13.5 (c), this is not the case. Quite often, organizations use Dynamic Host Configuration Protocol (DHCP). In these environments, the client system receives its IP address from a DHCP server. The server assigns IP addresses to client systems from a pool of IP addresses during the client's initialization. As we can see in the figure, when the system is first started in the morning, it receives from the DHCP server one IP address. Later that day, for one reason or another, the system is rebooted and is given a completely new IP address by the DHCP server. Meanwhile, the system's previous IP address may be in use by another system.

Any and all of these situations can apply to the clickstream data presented in Figure 13.4. The first group of requests could quite easily have come from a number of different users through a proxy server. We also noted that there was a rather large time gap between the initial browsing of the Web site and the actual purchase. Was this the result of the customer stopping in the middle of the process to have a conversation with someone? Perhaps a husband was discussing a purchase with his wife. We can't be certain. It could just as easily have been one prospective customer deciding that he or she would rather not purchase anything and another customer using the same client to purchase a product. A third alternative is that the original user had a system failure and upon rebooting, received a new IP address, and the record of the purchase is recorded under another IP address.

Each instance is a result of the stateless nature of the Internet. As described in previous chapters, the Web server and the client do not maintain a persistent connection. In a client/server environment, the connection between the client and server has a state. If the client process terminates, the server is aware of that termination. A Web server, since it does not maintain a state, cannot tell one client process from another. If a client process with a specific IP address terminates, the server process is not aware of the termination. If a new client process is initiated with the IP address of the terminated client, the server cannot distinguish between the two. The design of the Internet is such that the server process doesn't care that there is a different client.

## 13.4   Cookies

James Joyce once said that the media could turn a bicycle accident into the fall of western civilization. Something like this happened in the late 1990s. The evening news was all a flurry. The White House was putting files on the computers of people who accessed the White House Web site. They did this to track who visited their site and what they did there! How insidious! How corrupt! How totally appropriate for tracking customer behavior. The Whitehouse was using a tool designed for just that purpose: cookies.

Regardless of the nefarious media spin put on cookies, they are a safe and simple way of maintaining state over the Internet. A cookie is a simple text file stored in either the memory of the browser or on the client system. These files are totally within the control of the user. If you are concerned about privacy, remember that on the Internet you can maintain as much or as little anonymity as you choose.

Cookies are a tool to help us establish an identity for our customers. We can establish this identity both within an individual session as well as between sessions. We can view a cookie as the Internet version of a Fred's card, the example used earlier in the chapter. The cookie provides us with a means to link individual visits by an individual customer to our store, just as the Fred's card did for Fred. Whether the user accesses our Web site via a proxy server, a new IP address, or a system shared with other users, we can link that individual with a specific set of sessions. We can also link that customer with sessions from different clients. We discuss how this works later when we examine the use of cookies.

Cookies also allow us to look at the market basket and beyond. When a customer makes a purchase, we can link all of those purchases together via the cookie. We can also use that same cookie to track the customer's path throughout the Web site and to track which products may have been put into the basket and then removed. This was something we were unable to do in the traditional brick-and-mortar world.

Most important to the customer-driven e-enterprise, we can now associate an identity with demographics and behaviors. The ability to analyze and understand this behavior assists the e-enterprise in better servicing the customer. Ultimately, the consumer profits from the use of cookies. As consumers, we need to recognize that the use of personal information in the hands of a trusted supplier is of great personal benefit. As suppliers, we need to recognize that if customers are loath to provide us with personal information, we have a real problem with our customer relationships. Remember, the point is to develop a mutually beneficial relationship. As with all relationships, if there is no trust, there is no real relationship. Let's take a moment to examine how cookies are used.

### 13.4.1 BAKING COOKIES

Browsers create cookies at the request of a Web server. The cookie resides in memory while the browser is open. When the browser is closed, persistent cookies are written to disk. The Web server requests creation of the cookie with a Set-Cookie HTTP Response Header. The format of the Set-Cookie Response Header is as follows:

```
Set-Cookie: Name=value; expires=date; path=path;
    domain=domain; secure
```

where

- **Name=*value*—**This is the only required attribute of the Set-Cookie command. The name can be any sequence of characters with the exception of semicolons, commas, and white spaces. Cookies can store up to 4K of data, but typically are between 50 and 150 bytes.

- **expires=*date*—**The browser deletes the cookie from the system on this date.

- **path=*path*—**The path tells the browser to which Uniform Resource Locators (URL) the cookie is to be sent. A cookie with the specification *path=/hobbits* will be sent to URLs */hobbits, /hobbits/sam,* and */hobbits/primula/frodo.* This path is relative to the domain described next.

- **domain=*domain*—**The domain identifies for which domain name the cookie is valid. A comparison is first made of the domain name to see if there is a *tail match.* A tail match means the name matches the tail of a fully qualified domain name. For example, we may have *domain=wizards.org* as our specification. This would tail match the domains *gandalf.wizards.org, sauraman.wizards.org,* and *dumbledore.wizards.org.* Only hosts within a domain can specify that domain name. The default domain value is the host name of the server generating the Set-Cookie command.

- **secure—**A secure cookie is sent only over HTTPS (HTTP over SSL) servers. In order for the cookie to be sent, the communications must be secure.

Since there are so few limitations on cookies, Web servers can do a great deal with them. An individual server can send multiple Set-Cookie HTTP Response Headers at one time. However, a few rules apply to sending multiple response headers. Also, note that when sending multiple cookies, you must be careful about the order in which you send them. Cookies with more specific path names should be sent before cookies with less specific names. Cookies with the same path name overwrite one another, with the latest taking priority.

To delete a cookie, the server simply resends the cookie with the expiration date sometime in the past. This does not necessarily mean that the deletion occurs immediately. The browser can delete a cookie whenever it chooses. If the server sends a request for a cookie to be deleted, the browser may delete it at that time or some time thereafter. The browser can also choose to delete a cookie if the total number of cookies exceeds a maximum number. In most cases, the browser deletes the least recently used cookie even if the cookie has not expired. Users can also delete cookies through their browser or in some cases by simply removing the text file from the directory in which the cookies are saved.

Figure 13.6 demonstrates how cookies are created. The process begins when the user queries a Web server site. A CGI script, for example, will detect that the request does not contain a cookie, at which point the server assumes that this is the first visit to this site by the user. The CGI program then sends a Set-Cookie HTTP Response Header to the client. Depending on the setting of the browser, the client may or may not accept the cookie. For our purposes, we assume that the cookie is accepted. When subsequent requests are sent to a matching URL in that domain, the cookie is sent with the request. The Web server receives this cookie and knows with *whom* the server is communicating.

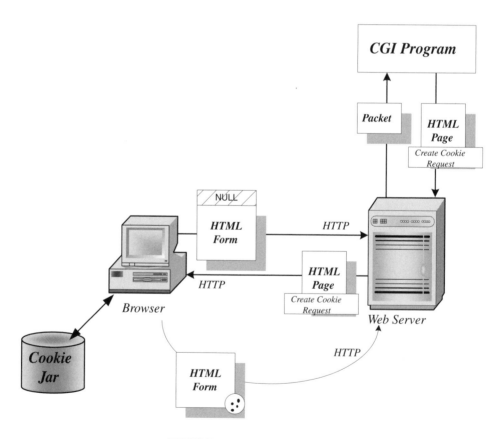

**FIGURE 13.6**   Cookie creation

### 13.4.2  MUNCHING ON COOKIES

Now that we understand how cookies work, let's look at how they solve some of our problems. Let's see how we can turn a cookie into a *Web-based Fred's card*. Let's think back to our discussion of market-basket analysis. First, we want to provide continuity between visits. We want to know when a customer returns to our store. Second, we want to detect patterns in his or her purchases. We would also like to perform some analyses with cookies that we were unable to do with our Fred's card. We want to know the path the customer traveled through our store, how the customer arrived at our store, and what items, if any, he or she put back on the shelf.

Let's see if we can create some sort of identity for the customer. The first step in the process is to create our Set-Cookie HTTP Response Header. In this instance, all we want to do is generate a cookie that assigns a new customer an identity. In our example, a customer, Barney, visits our store, Fred's Books, for the first time. When this happens, we respond with the following Set-Cookie HTTP Response Header:

```
Set-Cookie: user=foo_0710_109; expires=01-Jan-2100;
path=/freds_books; secure
```

Since Barney is a first-time user, we don't know who he is, so we give him a temporary ID of *foo_0710_109*. The temporary ID consists of the date, July 10, and a sequential counter of temporary IDs. This cookie tells us this user is the 109th prospective customer to access our site on July 10. After Barney browses the site for a while, he shuts down his system and leaves the office for the rest of the day.

Later that afternoon, Barney's coworker, Betty, comes into the office to do some market research on her system. Their office uses DHCP, and the server assigns Barney's old IP address to Betty. As she searches the Web, she is referred to Fred's Books by one of Fred's partner sites, Duresly Manufacturing & Drill Supply. This is Betty's first visit to Fred's site, so she receives the following cookie:

```
Set-Cookie: user=foo_0710_146; expires=01-Jan-2100;
path=/freds_books; secure
```

As we can see, another 37 people have visited this site since Barney's visit. Betty browses the recommended pages and decides to purchase what seems to be a very important book, *Object-Oriented Data Warehouse Design: Building the Star Schema* by William A. Giovinazzo. As she makes her purchase, we gather her personal information. We now have an identity linked with the user *foo_0710_146*. At this point, we send her the following cookie:

```
Set-Cookie: user=17898; expires=01-Jan-2100;
path=/freds_books; secure
```

The next time that Betty comes to Fred's Web site, the cookie provides her identification to Fred. Fred's Books is a customer-driven organization. When it sees that Betty is a returning customer, a personalized welcome is put on her home page with a list of recommended books. We may also elect to delete the cookie with the old temporary customer ID by sending a Set-Cookie command with an expiration date in the past.

The following week, Betty sees Barney in the hall and tells him about the fascinating book she bought. Barney is so enthusiastic, he rushes to his system so that he can purchase his own copy from Fred's Books. When he sends his request to the Web server, the cookie that was assigned to him last week is sent with the request. The system immediately recognizes him as a returning customer. When he orders his own copy, we send him the following Set-Cookie HTTP Response Header that identifies him in our system:

```
Set-Cookie: user=18003; expires=01-Jan-2100;
path=/freds_books; secure
```

As did Betty, Barney gets his own identification with Fred's Books. In addition, we link his previous visit to our Web site with his current purchase. Any future purchases he makes are also linked with these visits.

Two weeks later, Barney's wife tells him that he needs to get a birthday gift for his mother-in-law. Being very fond of his mother-in-law, Barney decides to share with her his recent discovery, *Object-Oriented Data Warehouse Design: Building the Star Schema* by William A. Giovinazzo. Using his home system, he returns to Fred's Books. Since this is the first time he has accessed Fred's from his home system, there is no cookie. He goes through the process of being assigned a temporary user cookie. Not only does he purchase the book for his mother-in-law, but he decides to pick up a few things for himself. He quickly decides on *Building the Data Warehouse* by W. H. Inmon and *Convergence Marketing* by Yoram Wind and Vijay Mahajan. When he actually makes his purchase, he is asked if he is a returning customer. Since Fred's Books has a frequent buyer program, Barney gladly identifies himself as a returning customer. The Web server sends his home system a cookie with the same customer identification as his system at work. In the future, if Barney decides to browse from his home or office, all the customer behavior will be associated with his individual account.

Now that we have described the clickstream from the customer perspective, let's examine how we can capture all this information and use it. We can save the cookies in a number of ways, such as with a Perl or CGI script. We can also use a Java program. The simplest method for our purposes is to capture the cookie as part of the transaction log. To do this, we must configure the Web server. Since there are a number of popular Web servers on the market, we will not attempt to define how to perform this configuration.

| Cookie | Date | Time | Host | Command | Page |
|--------|------|------|------|---------|------|
| 18003 | 10/JUL/2003 | 11:05:23 | 011.205.201.137 | Get | ..../...html |
| 18003 | 10/JUL/2003 | 11:06:41 | 011.205.201.137 | Get | ..../...html |
| 18003 | 10/JUL/2003 | 11:09:22 | 011.205.201.137 | Get | ..../...gif |
| 18003 | 10/JUL/2003 | 11:11:53 | 011.205.201.137 | Get | ..../...gif |
| 18003 | 10/JUL/2003 | 11:17:19 | 011.205.201.137 | Get | ..../...html |
| • | • | • | • | • | • |
| • | • | • | • | • | • |
| • | • | • | • | • | • |
| 17898 | 10/JUL/2003 | 12:20:36 | 011.205.201.137 | Get | ..../...gif |
| 17898 | 10/JUL/2003 | 12:21:27 | 011.205.201.137 | Post | ..../...html |
| 17898 | 10/JUL/2003 | 12:25:33 | 011.205.201.137 | Get | ..../...gif |
| 17898 | 10/JUL/2003 | 12:29:59 | 011.205.201.137 | Post | ..../...html |
| 18003 | 10/JUL/2003 | 11:04:13 | 011.205.201.101 | Get | ..../...html |
| 18003 | 10/JUL/2003 | 11:07:41 | 011.205.201.101 | Get | ..../...html |
| 18003 | 10/JUL/2003 | 11:08:22 | 011.205.201.101 | Get | ..../...gif |
| 18003 | 10/JUL/2003 | 11:13:22 | 011.205.201.101 | Get | ..../...gif |

**FIGURE 13.7**  Parsed transaction log with cookies.

Typically, we will see the cookie appended to the transaction log record. Just as we did earlier, we take these log entries, parse them, and load them into our database. The sort we performed on the last clickstream was ordered by IP address, date, and time. Now that we have cookie information, we sort the data according to cookie, date, and time. These results are shown in a table similar to what we see in Figure 13.7. Compare this data with the data provided in Figure 13.4.

Another important action we need to take is to define attributes for the Web pages on our site. As customers travel through our site, we need to know more than the specific pages they visit. We need to understand what types of pages they are visiting. Consider the many types of pages that make up a Web site. There are home pages, personalized home pages, and individual product pages. Some pages are dedicated to product categories such as power tools, music, or electronics. We can drill down from these pages and find even more specific pages: circular saws, classical music, and Personal Digital Assistants (PDAs). Figure 13.8 provides an overview of a typical Web site. We can see that it would be impossible to really understand the type of page the customer visited simply by the location of the page within the Web site's structure.

To solve this problem, we list the attributes of the Web page within the HTML header. We can then extract the page name and its attributes from the Web server for incorporation into the data warehouse. Our data mining tool can then evaluate the effect not only of individual pages on customer behavior, but of entire classes of pages. We can determine if personalized home pages ultimately lead to sales. We can ask which product classifications are more effective than others. We may find that pages listing all types of power tools are more effective than pages listing specific categories of power tools.

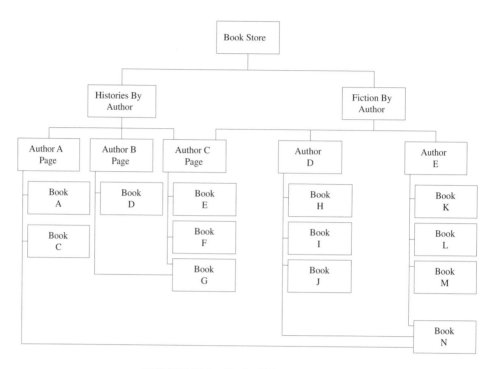

**FIGURE 13.8**  Typical Web site layout.

The actions of Betty and Barney should generate a clickstream similar to the one shown in Figure 13.7. It is also interesting to note that this is the same clickstream data that was presented in Figure 13.4. Adding the cookie dimension to the data provides us with a much clearer image of what has been happening on our Web site. We can now separate the actions of Betty and Barney much more reliably. We can also link the actions of the individual customers to understand their individual behaviors.

One of the first things we want to do with our cookies is to provide a link between visits. Barney demonstrates how, with cookies, we can link multiple visits. The same cookie links his visits from his office and his home. To retrieve all of his visits from our database, we would simply use the key 18003. In addition, using the IDs established by the cookies, we can link the browsing done prior to any visits that resulted in a purchase. All we need do is to include any entries with the cookie *foo_0710_109*.

We would also like to see how the different customers and prospective customers move through our Web site. We can reconstruct the visits made by both Betty and Barney by extracting the clickstream for each and then rebuilding the path according to the time of the page request. In order to derive the path, we must answer some questions. First, when does a visit begin and end? If there is a gap of a day or more between clicks, we could easily assume that these represent separate visits. What if the time span is a matter of hours or minutes? We need to decide the length of inactivity before we call a visit a new visit. We also need to eliminate superfluous entries. As we said earlier, a hit includes many items, such as graphics images and sound files. We need to eliminate these from our clickstream as well.

We can now use this path information to link which pages are most frequently associated with a sale and which are not. By following the path of a particular customer, we can see when the path actually leads to the sale of product. We can also see which pages on our site are least frequently visited—where the dead spots are in the store. We can then explore why certain product pages are dead. Is it that the product is truly unpopular? Can we combine this product with more popular items to help improve sales?

We can also tell the origin of customer visits through the referrer field in the transaction log. We can use this information to find our virtual location on the Web.

As we discussed in the previous section, the use of raw IP addresses can be misleading. The stateless nature of the connection, proxy servers, and dynamic IP address assignments all contribute to the IP address not being a very reliable indicator of the individual user accessing our site. We have proposed that cookies are a preferred method of customer identification. We should note, however, that cookies have their own set of problems.

Cookies identify a particular system, not a person. We noted how Barney purchased products from Fred's Books on his home system. If the next day, Mrs. Barney uses that same system to browse *The Art of Doily Design for Fun and Profit*, the purchase would be attributed to Barney's identification. If she makes a purchase under her husband's account, as far as Fred is concerned, it is the same person. This may not necessarily be a problem. It could be argued that Barney would certainly want to know the types of products in which Mrs. Barney is interested. Being a good husband, if our recommendation engine sent him a notice of a product that is of interest to his wife, he would certainly wish to purchase it. This may or may not be the case. It is really dependent on the individual circumstance. The system designer needs to understand this problem and decide whether it is an issue for his or her analysis.

Users can also actively thwart the system. They may choose to refuse all cookies. They may manually delete their cookies on a regular basis. In other instances, the user may simply not care. In our example, Barney identified himself when he used his home system to browse. He may have chosen not to give us his identity. If he didn't purchase an item, we would not have known that he was a returning customer. He also could have purchased the item using a different credit card, in which case only a house-holding application in our data warehouse would have identified him as the same user.

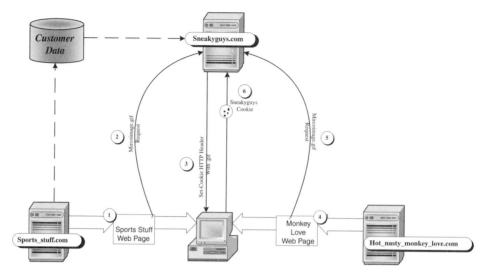

**FIGURE 13.9**   Cross-selling with cookies.

While there is little we can do to prevent users from deleting cookies from their systems, we can certainly understand their concerns. Despite that cookies are limited to one domain, third-party companies can use them to follow an individual's path through the Internet. This is shown in Figure 13.9. As you will recall, a server sends a Set-Cookie HTTP Response Header to a client browser making a request of the server. This request could be for a Web page, a file, or even a Graphics Interchange Format (GIF) file embedded within a Web page. In step 1 of Figure 13.9, we see that a user visits the site *sports_stuff.com*. The page contains the graphic image *microimage.gif* from a completely different server, *sneakyguys.com*.

In step 2, we see that when the browser receives the HTML page, it makes a request to *sneakyguys.com* for the GIF file. Since graphics images can be as small as a single pixel, which is the case in our example, few of even the most observant users would notice the additional request. In step 3, the *sneakyguys.com* server sends a Set-Cookie HTTP Response Header to the client browser along with the GIF file. The browser follows the preferences set by the user and creates the cookie. In our example, when dad decides to buy that new laser range finder he has been eyeing for the past few months, *sports_stuff.com* is able to link his identity with his visits to its Web site. We described this process earlier in the chapter.

Later that day, Junior is left at home unsupervised. Being a 15-year-old, tightly wound sack of raging hormones, he sees his chance while the folks are away and is happily clicking his way to *hot_nasty_monkey_love.com* before the car is barely out of the driveway. He thinks he is getting away with murder. The problem is that he doesn't know about *sneakyguys.com*. In step 4, when he downloads his first page, there it is again: *microimage.gif*. This time, however, the cookie that Dad got when he bought his range finder is sent along with the request for the GIF file. We see this in step 6. *Sneakyguys.com*, however, can't differentiate between Junior and Dad. As far as *sneakguys.com* is concerned, dad is interested in something a bit more nefarious than golf. *Sneakyguys.com* is more than glad to market to dad's seemingly *varied* interest.

You might wonder how we can do this if a cookie applies to a single domain. In our example, the cookie does apply to the single domain. Since a Web page can request images from any and many domains, it is not limited to making requests of servers within its own domain. In this instance, *sneakyguys.com* have agreements with both *sports_stuff* and *hot_nasty_monkey_love* to include its image on their Web pages. Both servers reference a single common server in its own domain.

Both Dad and Junior are unaware of the agreement that *sneakguys.com* has with *sports_stuff.com* to purchase their customer information along with the clickstream data. Two weeks later, Dad starts getting email from the Young Norwegian Hedonist Association inviting him to a clothing-optional golf weekend in the Cayman Islands. Fortunately for *sports_stuff.com*, Dad can't figure out how the heck he got on the mailing list.

The moral of the story? First, as users, we need to be careful which sites we visit. You never know who is watching. My dear sainted Sicilian mother taught me at an early age never to put anything in writing. This is especially true of where you go on the Internet.

Second, as system designers, we need to establish trust with our customers. We discussed how the point of CRM is to establish a mutually beneficial relationship. A critical element of this relationship is trust. One of the ways we can easily lose that trust is to provide customer information to a third party without the customer's expressed consent. Whenever customer data is collected, the policy on the use of that information should be clearly stated on the Web site and stringently followed.

Finally, we also learn a lesson in permission marketing. While our example shows an abuse of collecting customer information, this is not necessarily the case. We could apply these same techniques to cross-selling. The second site could just as easily have been a golf resort or an online ticketing site. We could provide information on local golf courses and golf excursions, cross-selling these additional services. The difference between a campaign being an invasion of privacy or helpful advice is permission.

Before we start any sort of marketing campaign, sending customers an avalanche of emails, it is common courtesy to simply ask their permission. According to Tom Osenton in *Customer Share Marketing*, "capturing a prospect's identity and permission…represents the marketing intersection where mass marketing and direct marketing meet. It is at this level that an ongoing, extremely efficient and relevant permission-granted relationship can begin—one that can uniquely complement the work that mass marketing must continue to do in launching new products in helping to build brand equity and in motivating prospects and customers to take action." As we can see, cookies and their use in capturing a customer's behavior can be an extremely powerful tool if used properly.

## 13.5 Conclusion

We began this chapter with a discussion on the importance of customer identification. We examined how frequent buyer programs, such as the Fred's card, can be used to track customer activities. By analyzing this data, the record of customer activities, we gain insight into the behavior, needs, and wants of our customers. We can use this insight to develop the one-to-one relationship so desired by the customer-driven organization.

Again, we see that the ingredients of a solution transform one another. The inclusion of the Internet in our solution changes how we interact with our customers. It also changes the way in which we are able to track and analyze their behavior. In the Internet age, we have something more powerful than a card to understand customer behavior. We have the ability to distribute cookies to customers and prospects visiting our site.

Cookies in the Internet age are in fact more powerful than the customer identification cards of the brick-and-mortar world. Cookies, in addition to providing market-basket analysis and continuity of customer cards, also provide us with insight into the behaviors of customers while they are in the store and into the activities that comprise the buying process.

In this chapter, we explored how to get the data to perform this analysis. In Chapter 14, we examine how data mining can be applied to this data and how we actually *use* this data to understand and act on customer behavior.

# PERSONALIZATION

*The power to guess the unseen from the seen, to trace the implications of things, to judge the whole piece by the pattern, the condition of feeling life in general so completely that you are well on your way to knowing any particular corner of it—this cluster of gifts may almost be said to constitute experience.*

—Henry James
The Art of Fiction

In Chapter 11, we created a science fictional future in which a device perfectly provided the needs and wants of every consumer. As you may recall, we discussed how this device was conveniently located in the home and office. Without being asked, the system delivered a product specifically tailored to fulfill the consumer's desire at that point in time. In addition to the convenience, the price of the products was considered a bargain. What was compelling about this device, however, wasn't the price or the convenience, but that the device could perfectly fulfill needs and wants. This idealized future is the ultimate in personalization.

If this is our ultimate destination, our goal, how do we get there from here? In the previous chapters, we discussed how we collect and aggregate data. In Chapter 3, we discussed the data warehouse, the central repository of our strategic information. We discussed how our Web sites capture customer behavior in the clickstream. So, what do we do with all this data once we have it? How does it get us closer to our ultimate destination? This chapter answers these questions.

The solution to personalization is data mining. In order to understand how to apply data mining to create a personalized environment, we first need to understand personalization. The discussion begins by defining personalization and contrasting it with customization. We see that we need to come to an understanding of customers. We do this through data mining. We opened this chapter with a quote from Henry James. He described experience as "the power to guess the unseen from the seen, to trace the implication of things, to judge the whole piece by the pattern." This is an apt description of data mining. Through our experience with the customer, we can *guess* the unseen from the seen, to judge the whole piece by a pattern. We shall see how this occurs.

The chapter then examines collaborative filtering and where it falls short in handling such large volumes of information. We see that the only way to adequately analyze this data is through data mining. As we examine the different data mining techniques, we see how methodologies can work together to provide a complete understanding of our customers. Armed with this understanding, we can build a more complete and robust personalized environment.

We conclude this chapter by looking at a real-world example of personalization. We review the Oracle Personalization application and how it can be used by a Web application to provide recommendations to visitors and customers who access our Web site.

## 14.1  Defining Personalization

Personalization is an essential tactic in our IEBI/CRM strategy. As we discussed in Chapter 12, the goal of CRM is to create a mutually beneficial relationship with our customers. It is a symbiotic relationship in which we provide to the customer products and services that fulfill his or her needs and wants. The customer in turn provides a continuous stream of revenue to the company. We establish this relationship through one-to-one marketing, dealing with each customer as an individual. In the brick-and-mortar world, we have certain tools at our disposal that facilitate the creation of this dynamic, such as customer card programs. While many of these technologies are very useful, the data available to the organization limits how far we can take our analysis. We simply cannot answer some questions.

The Internet takes us to the next level of customer interaction. When a customer comes to our Web site, every action that he or she makes on that Web site is recorded. This is the clickstream. We have also seen that while the clickstream is helpful in some respects, it cannot provide us with any degree of confidence an understanding of individual customer behavior. To develop this understanding, we must add cookie data to this stream of information. Cookies, while not foolproof, increase the system's ability to identify an individual customer's activity on our site. With this information, we can create a one-to-one interaction with our customers and a *personalized* experience when they visit our site.

While we can certainly do many things to create a more one-to-one environment for our customers, not all of them should be considered personalization. In some environments, we can create *customized* Web pages. Customers who are primarily interested in books and music can customize their home page to display the most recent releases in their areas of interest. Customers who are primarily interested in quilting and power tools can customize their home page to provide links to companies that provide such products. It may allow them to create *portlets*. A portlet is a portal or Web page embedded within a Web page. Portlets can be used to display the headlines from the latest quilting or power tool magazines. While it does create for the customer a page that is tailored to their specific needs, it does not achieve our ultimate objective. It does not create a relationship with the customer in which we are consulting on his or her needs.

Customization does not convey the feeling that we understand the needs and wants of the customer. Consider a wedding registry. When a couple is about to get married, they register with various stores, listing the products they would like to receive as gifts. These lists reflect the needs and wants of the couple starting a new life together. One would expect to see things like china and silver patterns or sheets and pillowcases. Typically, the bride (any former groom knows he has very little say in the matter) selects something that matches the decor of their new home. Then, when the father of the bride's golfing buddies or business associates need to come up with a gift for the couple, they simply select an item from this registry. While it is certainly generous of them to do so, this doesn't demonstrate any real knowledge of the bride and groom. They told them what they wanted. It isn't as if Rocco the mechanic, who plays poker with the groom's father every third Thursday, noticed a particularly lovely tea set while he was out shopping and thought the bride would just love it. The closest Rocco ever gets to a tea set is a plaid thermos.

The same is true of customization. While it is certainly a good thing for the company to provide, it does not develop a sense that the company has any insights into the individual customer. When customers set up a personal page, they are telling the company what they want. Customization is something that the customer, not the company, does.

Another means of creating a one-to-one environment on our Web site is through the use of *business rules*. Business rules are simplistic in their approach. If I happen to purchase *Nostromo* and *Heart of Darkness* by Conrad, business rules would recommend *Secret Agent*. They might even go recommend *Apocalypse Now* on DVD. This isn't really any more insightful than customization. Isn't it obvious that anyone who is reading through a particular author's work would also be interested in all of the author's work? If I buy a digital camera, is it especially insightful for the vendor to offer me additional lenses or a memory card?

Note that none of these things should be looked at as wrong. We most definitely should provide to our customers the ability to customize their personal home page. We should develop business rules that enable a user to easily find the obvious. While I may be a huge fan of Kurt Vonnegut, I may not be aware of everything he has published. I may discover a new author like Phillip Yancy and want to read all of his books. Sure, I could go look for them on the Web site. It is easy enough to do, but it demonstrates a willingness on the part of the company to assist in the buying process. It is the equivalent in the brick-and-mortar world of a salesperson seeing a customer reaching for an object on a high shelf and saying, "Here, let me get that for you." It is a courtesy that will be appreciated by the customer. It is not, however, personalization.

Personalization goes beyond the obvious. Personalization must be bold and take the consumer to places he or she might not otherwise go. Let's say that like Barney in our earlier example, I buy a copy of *Object-Oriented Data Warehouse Design: Building the Star Schema*. We would expect the recommendation engine to suggest books written by Bill Inmon or Ralph Kimball. We might even expect to see something from Jacobson on object-oriented design. These are all data warehousing- and software-related works. What would be interesting would be books on related topics in other disciplines. Why not recommend Edwin Abbott's *Flatland* or Stephen Hawking's *A Brief History of Time*? Surely, anyone interested in multidimensionality would also find these other topics of interest. In addition, the consumer may not be aware of these other titles. These recommendations both enrich the customer's experience when they visit our site and provide us with a means to market additional products. It demonstrates to the customers that we understand their needs and wants.

Personalization is driven by more than just the current activity reflected in the clickstream. Personalization brings together customers' current and past behaviors to tailor their experiences to meet their individual needs. Figure 14.1 presents the personalization process. The activities of the customer on the Web server are fed into the data mining engine. These activities are defined in the clickstream data. In the event that this is a returning customer, these activities are considered in the context of that customer's demographics. The data mining engine mines similar activities of other customers with similar demographics. Based on this mining process, the data mining engine makes recommendations to the application server. The application server then dynamically composes the Web pages in real time based on these recommendations. The dynamic content of a page can include any number or type of items. Products, banner ads, navigational links, product recommendations, and even product descriptions can be dynamically created.

Personalization is not limited to known customers, but is applicable to anonymous customers, customers whose identity, past behaviors, and demographics are unknown to the server. With personalization, our site can observe the behavior of totally anonymous users and, based on the behavior of other customers, provide recommendations. In our example from Chapter 13, when Barney first came onto our site, he followed a specific path. Other customers, who ultimately purchased products, followed a similar, if not the same, path through our site. The recommendation compares Barney's path through our site with the paths of other customers and recommends the products that were of most interest to these customers.

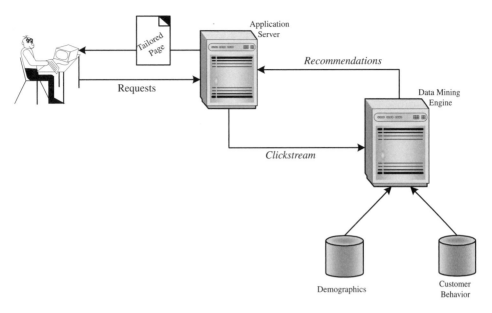

**FIGURE 14.1**    The personalization process.

One method of providing a personalized environment is *collaborative filtering*. We must be careful, however, not to confuse this with data mining. Collaborative filtering creates groups and subgroups of customers and prospects with similar profiles. Recommendations are made on how well the customer fits within a particular group. The difference between collaborative filtering and clustering may not be clear, so let's examine collaborative filtering in a bit more detail.

We can see this strategy at work in Figure 14.2. In the figure, we have represented the customer as a simple square. Each side of this square represents a characteristic, or feature, of the customer. Each feature can have one of three possible values. The smaller squares made up of dotted lines represent a possible value. A customer profile, as represented by the polygon on the left, is created when we fill in a value for each of the four features. We then compare this polygon with the polygons on the left that are the profiles of the groups formed by previous customers. When we locate a group whose profile matches that of the prospective customer, we can provide advice based on the actions of those previous customers. Products and services that were purchased by those customers are recommended to the new prospective customer on the assumption that customers of similar profiles will have similar interest. While the basic reasoning behind collaborative filtering is sound, there are some drawbacks to the method.

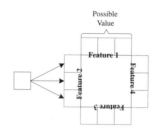

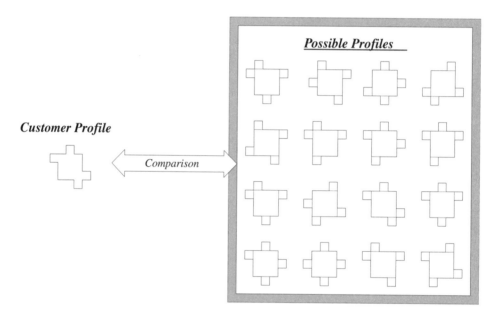

**FIGURE 14.2**   Collaborative filtering.

In our simple example, the customers have only four characteristics, each with three possible values. The number of different profiles shown to the right is a small subset of actual possible combinations. In this particular example, there are 81 different possible combinations, or 3 to the 4 power. The number of possible combinations increases exponentially. If we were to add just one more possible value to each characteristic, we would increase the number of possible combinations to 256. If we had as few as 20 different characteristics with 10 different possible values, we would have 10 trillion possible combinations! This limits the number of different characteristics that can be matched in real time, thus limiting the depth with which we can analyze customer profiles.

As one can well imagine from such an example, even when the possible combination sets are within an acceptable range, collaborative filtering requires a large volume of data. In addition, actually filtering the results is computationally expensive. Just think of the last time you filled out a questionnaire for a free subscription to a trade magazine. There are sometimes 30 to 40 questions on one of those things, with dozens of different answers. Imagine the profile matching task for that many variables!

While customization and business rules are helpful to the customer, they are only part of the story. To develop a mutually beneficial relationship in which we strive to become a trusted advisor to our customers, we need to be proactive, to take the initiative. This initiative is in the form of personalization. While collaborative filtering may provide us with some capabilities in recognizing customer groups, due to its inherent limitations, it is not appropriate for environments in which customer profiles and behaviors are of even a moderate complexity. The only adequate solution for personalization is data mining.

## 14.2 Data Mining

Data mining is at the heart of the recommendation engine. Data mining is a process of discovery. It detects patterns in seemingly random data. We noted how there are different types of data mining: decision trees, genetic modeling, and neural networks. There are situations in which one method may be more appropriate than another. The different data mining methods are not mutually exclusive; rather, they work in concert with one another. In the following subsections, we look at how we can apply these different data mining methods to gain a better understanding of our customers.

### 14.2.1 THE WEB SITE THAT LEARNS

The first data mining method applicable to mining the clickstream is neural networks. These are powerful data mining tools when working with numerical data. As you will recall from Chapter 3, the human brain is a neural network. The brain is composed of neurons, each of which could be thought of as a separate processor. The output of one neuron acts as the input to the next. Figure 14.3 shows the structure of such a network. Each node in the network generates an output, which is a nonlinear function of the node's inputs. The inputs in the structure are weighted according to the pattern recognition formula. During the *training* process, the results generated by the network are compared with the known results, and the input weights are adjusted accordingly. The training teaches the network to learn patterns so that it is able to recognize these same patterns later.

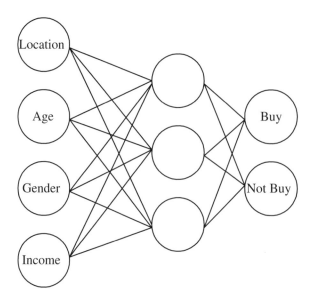

**FIGURE 14.3**  A neural network.

We could imagine a marketing strategist sitting at a terminal watching a user browse our site. Based on his or her experience, the strategist dynamically provides recommendations and influences the prospective customer's path through the store. The trouble with such a scenario is that on the Web we are not looking at one or two customers viewing a handful of products, but at hundreds and thousands of customers viewing hundreds of different products.

Let's look at an example of how this might work. A first-time customer comes to our store from the site of a partner that sells appliances, Friendly Alf's World of Appliances. Within our store we have three departments: kitchen furniture, bed and bath, and formal dining rooms. Our neural network has learned that visitors coming to our site from Friendly Alf's World of Appliances typically come to purchase kitchen furniture. The recommendation engine therefore recommends a variety of kitchen sets that might be of interest to the customer. Instead, the customer visits the bed and bath department, browsing the discount Early American bedroom sets. The customer spends most of her time examining sets with a lighter colored wood stain. The neural network recognizes that the customer may be interested in bedroom sets and recommends low-cost, high-margin bedroom sets. In addition, it changes the kitchen recommendation to include discount kitchen sets.

The customer responds as the recommendation engine predicted and goes to the kitchen area. While there, she proceeds to the higher priced sets and browses several Mission-style dining room sets. The neural network again sees that for a customer who just came from a low-cost bedroom set, such a path will typically not result in a sale. The recommendation engine therefore recommends an inexpensive Mission-style kitchen set. This ultimately leads to a purchase by the customer.

This process involved an anonymous customer, someone who never visited our site before. If this were a returning customer, we may have remembered that he or she had purchased high-priced furniture in the past. We could then have recommended the more expensive items. Perhaps we would have realized that the customer had purchased bedroom furniture from us in the past and we could have recommended lamps that were popular with other customers who purchased that same bedroom set.

### 14.2.2 THE WEB SITE THAT DIFFERENTIATES

Each data mining method has uses that complement one another. As in the previous section, neural networks were well suited to working with numerical data, determining the probability that a customer would or would not buy a particular product based on some path. Decision trees have a different strength. These data mining algorithms work well with demographic data, where each record has many fields and the data sets have large numbers of attributes. There are a number of types of decision trees.

Classification and Regression Trees (CART) are binary, meaning that there are two outputs from every node of the tree. At each node, a variable is tested to see if it is less than or greater than a *split value* to determine if the left or right branch is to be taken. The key obviously is to determine the appropriate split value. The CART algorithm recursively searches the variables to define the most appropriate value for the split. After a tree is fully defined, the algorithm prunes the tree by removing any nodes that reduce the accuracy of the tree.

An alternative method, Chi-Square Automatic Interaction Detection (CHAID), is useful for the categorization. The CHAID decision tree is non-binary and is useful for dealing with categorization. In this case, we would see multiple split values that would encompass the domain of values for a particular variable. Age, for example, could be divided into 10-year increments running from 0 to 120. Figure 14.4 demonstrate the difference between a CART and CHAID decision tree.

In Figure 14.4 (a), we show a CART decision tree based on income. Customers whose annual income exceeds $50,000 have a 67.8 percent probability of purchasing our product, while those whose income is less than $50,000 have only a 25.2 percent probability. CHAID, on the other hand, branches into two or *more* nodes; see Figure 14.4 (b). Using CHAID, we break the income of our customers down into multiple categories, in this case, not just customers with incomes greater than $50,000, but customers whose income is between $75,000 and $100,000.

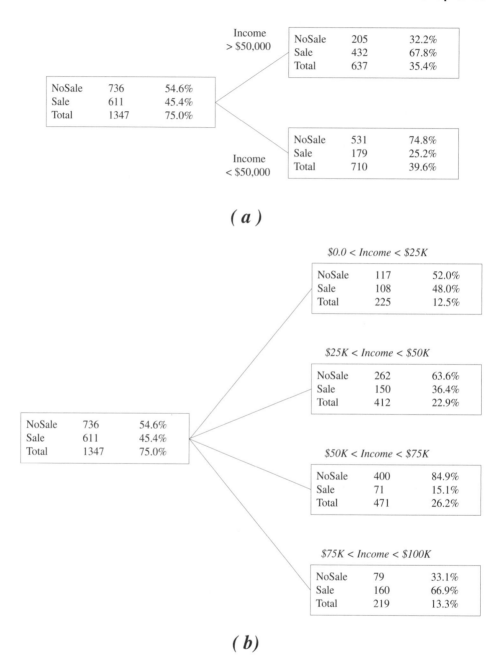

**FIGURE 14.4**   CART and CHAID decision trees.

Human wants and desires are complex and seldom driven by individual motive. We can see that the simple tree structures shown in these examples are not sufficient to fully describe the demographic data analyzed to predict if someone is going to buy or not buy a product. We can, however, create multiple levels to these structures to reflect the different demographic characteristics that come into play when predicting customer behavior. Figure 14.5 presents a more complex decision tree, taking multiple factors into consideration. We have added the variable *gender* to our analysis, giving a more complete description of visitors who are likely to purchase a particular product.

### 14.2.3  THE WEB SITE WITH GENES

The final data mining method we discuss is genetic modeling. The most promising use of this modeling method is in conjunction with other data mining methods to find the *fittest* model. Genetic modeling differs slightly from other data mining algorithms in this regard. While data mining is a process of discovery, genetic modeling optimizes the output of other data mining models. Their discovery is the most optimized model. We often see them used in conjunction with neural networks.

Genetic modeling finds the fittest model through a natural evolution of the models presented to it. The process starts with a genetic pool, a set of possible solutions. The model then *reproduces,* selecting from the genetic pool the *fittest* solutions. The genetic algorithm then takes the fittest solutions and exchanges information between them. This *crossover* process creates solutions with different genetic profiles than the previous generation. This new generation creates new and diverse offspring. *Mutation,* an essential element in evolution, provides a means of creating variation. Where crossover simply creates new genetic combinations, mutation creates new values to be included in these combinations.

Both crossover and mutation create new populations, solutions with new characteristics. The fitness of these new solutions, the subsequent generations, is compared with the previous generations. If the newer solutions are more fit, they replace their predecessors. If they are less fit, they die off. We use this methodology with the solutions derived from the neural network, applying crossover and mutation to the various solutions until we arrive at an optimized solution. The basis of a generation's fitness is how well the data set matches a particular cluster. Remember that genetic algorithms are most useful when clustering data. The fitness of a particular generation is how well the characteristics of that generation match the other data sets within the cluster.

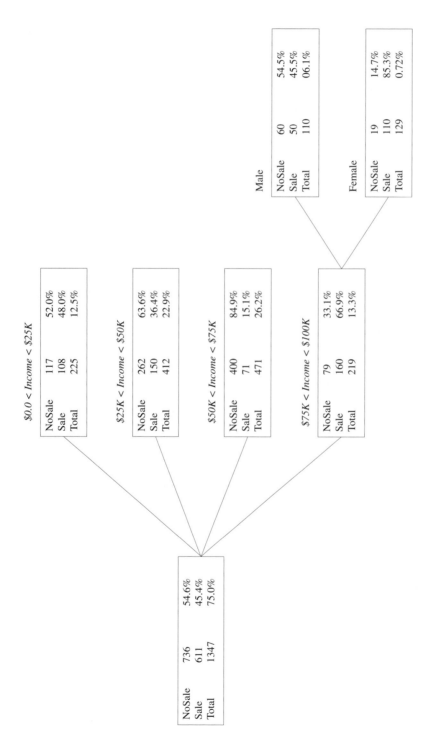

**FIGURE 14.5** CHAID customer segmentation.

## 14.3   The Data Mining Process

Neural networks, decision trees, and genetic modeling are all different types of data mining algorithms. They are not data mining. Look at it this way: Years ago, every computer science student had a copy of the book *Fundamental Algorithms*. It contained many of the basic algorithms we used when writing computer programs. If we wanted to sort data, we simply went to the book and found various ways to sort data. The algorithms weren't programs. They didn't tell us how to collect the data or what data to sort. These questions were up to the programmer to answer. In a very similar way, the data mining algorithms we have described are just that—algorithms. They do not tell us how to collect the data or how to mine the data. That is up to us to decide.

We have described the IEBI process as a three-step iterative loop in which we acquire the data, analyze the data, and act based on the data. As we can see in Figure 14.6, the data mining process is the same basic iterative loop. The first step in the process, acquiring the data, is composed of several subtasks. Before we start to collect data, we must understand the purpose of our search. How can we collect data unless we know the purpose of the data analysis? Once we understand the data, we collect, prepare, and process the data. This is similar to the extraction, transformation/cleansing, and loading step in our IEBI loop. Once we have completed the ETL of the data to be mined, we begin the mining process. This process entails the selection of an algorithm, the construction of a model, and the training of the model. We can then use this model for prediction, which leads to some action. In the following sections, we look at each step in a bit more detail.

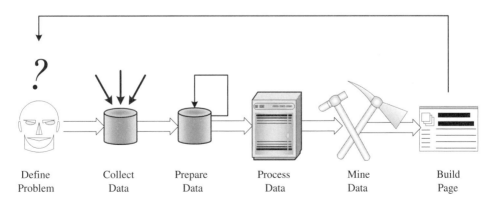

| Define Problem | Collect Data | Prepare Data | Process Data | Mine Data | Build Page |

**FIGURE 14.6**   The data mining process.

### 14.3.1 PROBLEM DEFINITION

It wasn't that long ago that many defined data mining as "the process that provided an answer to a question that you didn't even know you had." The image was that of an application that was let loose on a volume of data and out would flow gems of wisdom. As we can no doubt tell by now, this is far from the case. As we approach a data mining problem, we need to define the problem that we are attempting to solve. Part of that definition includes the anticipated results of the mining process. What is it we expect to get from the model: a description? a prediction? some combination of both? We also need to define the inputs from which we will derive these results. Are we trying to predict customer behavior based on some clickstream analysis? Are we trying to predict employee turnover based on human resources data?

Data mining can be applied to many areas within an organization. We can see it employed in manufacturing for quality assurance and in human resources for employee separation. In this chapter, we have focused on one specific use of data mining: the prediction of customer behavior. CRM is concerned with understanding our customers. Consider some of the questions we might attempt to answer as a result of our data mining process. Table 14.1 provides some examples.

**TABLE 14.1**  Questions that Data Mining Can Help Answer

| | |
|---|---|
| Profile Customer Behavior | • What are the characteristics of customers who return most frequently to our site?<br>• What are the characteristics of customers who return least frequently to our site?<br>• Which products are purchased most frequently by my most profitable customers? |
| Profile Customer Demographics | • What are gender and location of my most profitable customers?<br>• What is the gender and location of my least profitable customers? |
| Time Dependencies | • Is there a season in which my most profitable customers purchase less?<br>• How frequently do my most profitable customers return?<br>• How frequently do my least profitable customers return? |
| Customer Retention | • What is the average life of our relationships with our most profitable customers? |

### 14.3.2 COLLECTION

The second step of the process is to collect the data to be mined. If we are mining the customer activities on our Web site, we will obviously want to collect the clickstream data. As we collect this data, there are important decisions to make. For example, we must determine how far back in time our analysis should reach. If the market has relatively long-term trends, we will want to go back further than we would in a market that is very volatile. If we have a Web site dedicated to selling cars, the same trends that may have occurred in the past year or two may be relevant to the solution of our problem. In cases where these trends are short term, such as clothing or cosmetics, we would look at much shorter time spans.

In addition to the clickstream data, we want to include demographic data and buying patterns. In cases of financial institutions, we may wish to *household* the data, a process by which we relate the information of all the members of one household. In some cases, we may have brick-and-mortar outlets in addition to our Web site. Will it be relevant to our analysis to include this customer activity as well?

### 14.3.3 DATA PREPARATION

The data preparation stage of the data mining process is similar to the data transformation and cleansing stage of the IEBI loop. In this stage, we prepare the data for inclusion into the data set that we will use in our analysis. The same types of issues we face with the data warehousing ETL process are present when extracting data for data mining. Of course, we would hope that much of the data we extract from the data warehouse is clean, but this is only a hope. As we build our analysis, we must take measures to insure that we eliminate redundant data that may skew the results, typographical errors that may generate erroneous results, and stale data that may generate results that are no longer valid.

In addition to these quality issues, we must be concerned with issues such as qualification, binning, and derivation. Data qualification entails selecting data elements that are pertinent to the results we wish to achieve. For example, we may wish to understand the location of our most profitable customers and attempt to use postal codes as a means to classify them. While this may sound reasonable at face value, there are instances where the data may be inappropriate. For example, we may be an organization whose business is limited to a specific state. In such a case, a postal code would be perfectly reasonable. If, on the other hand, we were an international organization, segmenting our customer base by postal code may not be very helpful. Perhaps we have a handful of postal codes in New York, California, Norway, Latvia, and Fiji in our top 30 geographic areas. Does this really help us? It might be more beneficial to examine data that is coarser, perhaps at the country or state/province level.

Data preparation might also include the binning of data. The data warehouse may simply store the customer's age. Again, this may not meet the data qualification needs of our data mining process. To solve this problem, we may create age categories, or bins, to store customers' ages. Customers between the ages 18 and 25 are in one bin, while customers 26 to 33 are in another. In some cases, the data warehouse may store the year the customer was born and not their specific age. In this case, we have to derive the age. Data derivation calculates a data element to be included in the analysis from other data elements in the source data.

### 14.3.4  DATA MINING

We discussed the specifics of creating a data mining model in Chapter 8 when we discussed the Java Data Mining API. Remember that no single method drives personalization on our Web site. Instead, we employ a variety of algorithms on our Web site, deciding which model will be employed at which point in time depending on the objective to be accomplished.

For example, we may wish to segment our customer base in order to define the different market segments. Who is visiting our Web site? We can divide visitors by certain demographic characteristics or combinations thereof, such as gender, age, or income levels. Once we have established the different segments, we may wish to predict the propensity of these different groups to purchase a particular product or group of products. We could employ a neural network, tuning the model with a genetic algorithm. The taxonomy of a Web site refers to the structure of the page, how a page leads to other pages. Genetic algorithms are useful in optimizing this taxonomy.

## 14.4  Summary

In this chapter, we contrasted personalization with customization. Customization is something done by the consumer. Personalization is something done by the company. While customization is certainly of benefit to the consumer, it does little if anything to strengthen the one-to-one relationship. Through personalization, however, we develop an understanding of the consumer and use that understanding to strengthen the mutually beneficial relationship.

In our data warehouses, we capture huge volumes of information. Our Web sites can capture every click made by the customer. We can collect volume upon volume of information concerning our customers and their behavior. The only real solution to deriving quality information from this torrent of data is data mining. While we have reviewed just a small sample of the various data mining methodologies, we have seen them not as mutually exclusive, but as complementary. We have explored how these different methodologies can be used together to provide a more complete picture of our customer.

We concluded the chapter with an examination of the Oracle Personalization application. The application demonstrates how we can use data mining to provide a more personalized experience for visitors to our Web site. We have seen how we can use data mining to recommend products and compose Web pages that are of greater interest to individual consumers.

Just as we noted that the personalization of our Web site is not driven by one data mining methodology, the same is true of the topics discussed in this chapter. We should not look to replace customization with personalization, or even collaborative filtering with data mining. We use each of these in conjunction with one another to enhance the effectiveness of our site. We provide both customization and personalization. We can use data mining to cluster customers and visitors. We then can use collaborative filtering in conjunction with neural networks and decision trees to make recommendations.

We have come full circle. In this section, we discussed how our organization needs to become a customer-driven organization and how the Internet enables us to develop that relationship more completely. We have also seen how we can use clickstream data to capture customer activity. Finally, we discussed how to use that data to provide a more personalized environment. This concludes just part of our examination of IEBI. In Chapter 15, we put all the concepts we have discussed in this book into one complete and concise picture.

# THE ROAD GOES EVER ONWARD

*Thou ill-formed offspring of my feeble brain,*
*Who after birth did'st by my side remain,*
*Till snatcht from thence by friends, less wise than true,*
*Who thee abroad exposed to public view;*
*Made thee in rags, halting, to th' press to trudge,*
*Where errors were not lessened, all may judge.*

—*Anne Bradstreet*
The Author to Her Book

There is an old Abbott and Costello routine that, on occasion, I go through with my children. In the routine, the owner of a local Italian restaurant, Mr. Bacciagalupe, offers Costello a meatball. When Costello tells Mr. Bacciagalupe that he doesn't like meatballs, the restaurateur reviews each individual ingredient of a meatball. With each ingredient, Mr. Bacciagalupe asks Costello if he likes that particular ingredient. Costello responds by saying that he likes the ingredient. The routine proceeds in a similar fashion through each ingredient. After Mr. Bacciagalupe reviews each of the ingredients, he concludes that when Costello must like meatballs because he likes all the ingredients, a piece of seemingly sound logic. Costello would of course reply that he doesn't like meatballs. Mr. Bacciagalupe would go ballistic, scatter the ingredients, and grab Costello by the throat. Lou Costello would utter his catch phrase in which he calls for help from Abbott. While my retelling of the act is not as funny as the act itself, it does show that the whole is very different from the sum of the parts.

Throughout this book, we have presented IEBI as a solution, examining each ingredient. In Chapter 2, we discussed the Internet and its evolution; in Chapter 3 we discussed business intelligence in the Internet age. In later chapters, we discussed the enabling technologies: servers, networking, Java, XML, and CWMI. Finally, we discussed how we can use this technology to build mutually beneficial relationships with our customers. Like Mr. Bacciagalupe and Lou Costello, we have tasted each ingredient. It is now time to look at what we have created to see if the solution created by this recipe is palatable.

## 15.1  One Last Visit with Billy Boy

In Chapter 2, we painted a grandiose picture of a completely integrated value chain. In this picture, the Internet acted as the medium through which we were able to tie the information systems of these different organizations together, forming a single virtual organization. Spanning this virtual organization is the IEBI system. Just as traditional BI permeates the entire organization, IEBI permeates the virtual organization created by the Internet. While we have discussed this idea in brief throughout this text, let us now take a moment to examine it in detail.

Figure 15.1 presents the value chain for Billy Boy Bowling Balls. This is a rather simplified chain. We can see how raw materials flow from the suppliers, are transformed into products by the internal processes of the organization, and in turn are sold to customers. This diagram, however, presents another flow, a flow of information. In a customer-driven organization, the information flows in the opposite direction of the material. The source of the information is the customer, and it flows back through the organization to the supplier. To understand how IEBI acts as the nervous system of the virtual organization formed by the Internet, we need to understand the flow of this information.

Billy Boy interacts with his market through three primary channels. The first is composed of distributors. These organizations are the infamous middlemen that folks are always trying to cut out when buying wholesale or direct from the factory. We discussed Billy Boy's visit with one of these middlemen in Chapter 9, demonstrating the use of IEBI in the negotiating process. The second channel consists of the customers themselves. These folks buy from Billy Boy Bowling Balls directly over the Web. Finally, Billy Boy distributes slow-moving items and out-of-date products to a secondary market using a B2B exchange. Distributors who do not necessarily have distribution agreements with Billy Boy can purchase these products at reduced prices through the exchange. Since they are slow-moving items or last season's products, there is little if any channel conflict with Billy's other distribution channels.

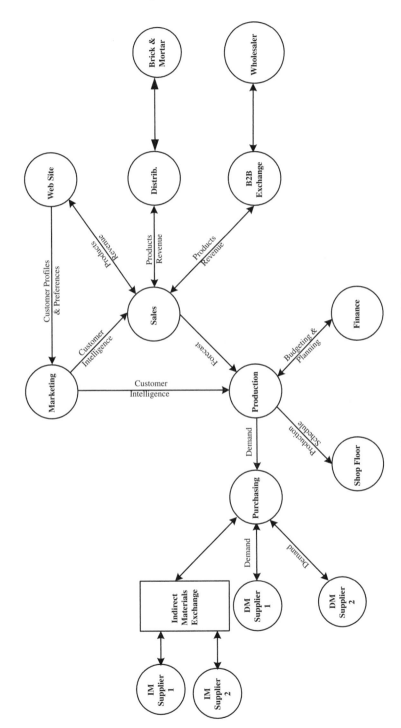

**FIGURE 15.1** Simplified value chain.

As products flow from Bill Boy Bowling Balls to customers through these channels, information flows from the customers to Billy Boy. The information the sales department receives from the first channel, the distributors, are sales forecasts. The distributors realize that providing this information to Billy Boy helps him plan production and meet their needs more efficiently. The forecast data from the different distributors is aggregated along with data from the Web site and secondary markets such as B2B exchanges. Once consolidated, it provides critical information to production and finance.

Production uses the information to plan the product mix. How much of which products should they produce to meet demand? They also use this information for budgeting. Once they understand production demand, they are better able to anticipate their resource needs. Production gives this information to the purchasing department so that they can plan the purchasing of both direct and indirect materials.

In addition to the forecasts, the finance department receives the resource requirements from the different departments. Finance uses the forecasts to predict revenue. They are able to predict spending from the resource requirements. With these two sources of information, they are able to compile a budget. This is all pretty much prima facie. Businesses have been running this way for hundreds of years. How does IEBI change this process?

In fact, IEBI doesn't change this process; IEBI strengthens it. Tighter integration with our distributors provides more timely information. Organizations can also apply data mining techniques to improve the accuracy of the forecast. Perhaps a distributor under- or over-forecasts demand at irregular intervals. Data mining can determine the conditions that cause these errors and adjust the projected demand accordingly.

Another important piece of information is data concerning the customers themselves. The sales department receives this information from their Web site, where they have direct access to their customers. This data is analyzed by marketing along with the all-important demographic data. The results of this analysis, customer intelligence, are sent to production for input into product design. Customer intelligence is also provided to the sales department to assist them in being more effective in reaching their customers.

The ultimate destination of the information, although they may never see it as such, is the suppliers. These are the companies that provide Billy Boy with both direct and indirect materials for production. We can see that Billy Boy is to these suppliers what the distributors and customers are to Billy. As Billy Boy is more able to see into the future, to forecast, to understand customer needs and wants, the better he is able to plan the strategy of his organization. By the same token, Billy Boy's suppliers will also benefit from understanding Billy Boy's needs and wants. The further out and the greater the reliability of this understanding, the greater the benefit of the insight. As the quality and timeliness of the data to Billy improves, we continue the process by improving the quality and timeliness of the data to Billy's suppliers.

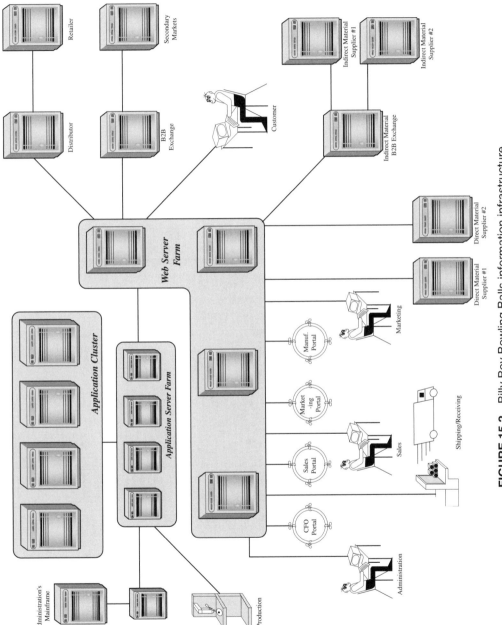

**FIGURE 15.2** Billy Boy Bowling Balls information infrastructure.

Our description of Billy Boy's virtual organization has been limited to the data flow. Figure 15.2 presents an information infrastructure that enables this data flow. If we compare this structure with what we had when we first met Billy Boy way back in Chapter 4, we will see a much cleaner structure. It is an environment providing complete integration both within the organization itself as well as with suppliers and distributors.

The first thing we notice is that all of the systems have been consolidated. Rather than maintaining a separate environment for each application, we have moved everything to an application cluster. In moving the operation to this one centralized environment, we have moved the data and metadata, including the business rules, to one place within the organization. We have quite literally created one instance of the truth.

We have continually described the information infrastructure as the organization's nervous system, with the IEBI system being the cerebral cortex in which the intelligence resides. The purpose of the organism's intelligence is to coordinate the activities of its various parts. This of course mandates that the intelligence of the organism be centralized. Proof of this is that there are no organisms with two brains. The same is true of the organization. To effectively coordinate the activities of the different parts of the organization, there must be a central system.

Examining this figure, many may be concerned with performance. Is it truly possible to support the processing demands of anything but a moderately sized organization? To solve this problem, we distribute the processing vertically and horizontally. We distribute the application vertically across tiers of our Internet-enabled information infrastructure. Within each tier, we distribute the application horizontally across application clusters and server farms.

In an application cluster, we create a single virtual server from multiple systems. There are several benefits to this strategy. First, this reduces cost. Rather than purchasing one large, expensive system, we can deliver the same processing power with several lower cost systems. A second important benefit is redundancy. In a single system environment, when that one server goes down, the entire business is brought to a screeching halt. In a clustered environment, when an individual system in the cluster fails, the other systems take on the additional load. While this *may* result in reduced performance, the business can still operate.

We should be careful not to underestimate the value of high availability in an Internet-enabled world. When we attempt to reach our customers over the Internet, we are establishing a 24/7 environment. When our system is down, so too is our communication with our customers and suppliers. Clustering provides a means to meet these demands. Consider situations in which we need to upgrade software or perform preventive maintenance on the system. In a clustered environment, we remove that system from the cluster, perform the maintenance, then reintegrate that system into the cluster. There is never an interruption of service.

Another concern with moving to a single instance is supporting both our data warehouse and our Enterprise Resource Planning (ERP) applications in a single operational environment. Traditionally, data warehouses have been kept separate from the ERP systems so as to not impact the operation of the business. To quote Emerson, "a foolish consistency is the hobgoblin of little minds, adored by little statesmen, and philosophers and divines." In considering whether we can practically run our ERP system and our data warehouse on one system, we should consider the ability to partition the cluster. It is possible to partition our systems in such a way that one set of servers in the application cluster give priority to the ERP system and another set give priority to the IEBI system. While at first this may not seem significantly different than running the systems in two different clusters, there is a significant difference, as shown in Figure 15.3.

**(a) Application Cluster under Normal Daytime Operation**

**(b) Application Cluster under Normal Nighttime Operation**

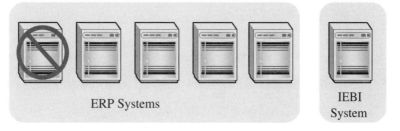

**(c) Application Cluster with a Failed Node**

**FIGURE 15.3** Application cluster partitioning.

Under normal operations, we can balance the load of the system based on our processing requirements. As shown in Figure 15.3 (a), during the day, when there is a heavy demand on the ERP systems, we give a higher priority to the ERP applications. In the evenings and off-peak hours, we shift the priority to the IEBI applications. This shift in priority is shown in Figure 15.3 (b). If an ERP system should fail during peak hours, as we see in Figure 15.3 (c), we shift the responsibility of an IEBI server to the ERP system until the failed system can be replaced.

Similar to application clusters, Billy Boy has clustered his Web servers into Web server farms. As you will recall from Chapter 6, resources are located on the Web by way of a domain name. The DNS server links that name with an IP address of a server that in turn is used to identify the machine address burnt into the server's network card. In a server farm, a single DNS name and IP address is used to identify the routing server. This server can take the form of a specialized device designed for this purpose. When a request is sent to server farm's IP address, the routing server redirects the request to another server within the farm. Each server within the farm has a unique IP address.

Another important change in the information infrastructure that makes the centralization of applications possible is the horizontal partitioning of the applications. While the architecture shown in Figure 15.2 may be reminiscent of a mainframe environment, there is an important distinction: the application server. In Chapter 5, we discussed in detail the evolution of the Internet. We saw the movement of the application from mainframe (or the client in two-tiered architectures) to the middle tier. In this way, we further distribute the processing, reducing the overall load on the central application cluster. From our previous discussions, we should have an appreciation for how the application server farm can improve overall performance.

It is important to note that by *front-ending* the central system, the application cluster, with an application server farm, we provide global access to the single source of information. As we can see in Figure 15.2, all decision makers and all line-of-business managers are given access to the one authoritative source of the truth through their information portals. This by itself is significant. More importantly, however, we can tightly integrate our information systems through this multitier architecture with those of our distributors and suppliers. We can do this through *Web services*.

## 15.2   Web Services

Simply having two systems on the network does not mean that they communicate. We need more than TCP/IP, ASCII, and XML. If we think back to the ISO/OSI reference model, we need to establish communication between systems at the application layer. This is the task of Web services. Web services are similar to objects in an object-oriented programming environment. Just as an object in Java is a self-contained unit or module, a Web service is a self-contained application unit. We can take this unit and publish it over the Internet where others can locate the module and invoke its functionality. Via these Web services, supplier and distributor applications can communicate directly with our own applications.

In the case of Billy Boy, suppliers may be given access to inventory data. When stock levels drop below a certain level, the supplier's application can immediately issue an order. The IEBI system can use past history to predict the appropriate level at which to issue the order. Billy Boy can of course replicate this scheme with his distributors, detecting when their stock levels drop. Distributors in turn can be given access to Billy Boy's finished goods inventory. In essence, Billy Boy's inventory becomes an extension of their own, allowing them to reduce their own stock levels.

Another application of Web services comes into play with third-party information sources. We have discussed the use of demographic information, but where do we get that information? More importantly, how do we integrate that data into our IEBI systems? As one might guess, Web services. Our IEBI system can communicate with the third-party suppliers of demographic information, integrating this information directly into our data warehouse. This holds promise for more than just demographic data. We can use this same strategy to incorporate data from our partner and supplier systems into our data warehouse. As we discussed throughout this text, we want to extend our IEBI system beyond the four walls of our organization; we want to understand the entire value chain. Web services provide us with a means of establishing this level of integration.

Billy Boy also uses a B2B exchange for acquiring indirect materials. We can use Web services to distribute a Request for Proposal (RFP) to different suppliers. They can in turn respond automatically. Billy Boy's system receives these responses and automatically sorts through them, selecting the best response.

Web services employs three XML-based protocols: Web Services Definition Language (WSDL), Universal Description, Discovery, and Integration (UDDI), and Simple Object Access Protocol (SOAP). Basing these protocols on XML, an accepted and popular standard, makes this technology readily accessible. Figure 15.4 presents how these protocols work together to expose services to suppliers, customers, and partners.

The process begins when the Web service provider publishes the availability of the Web service in a directory, using WSDL. The Web services directory is a UDDI repository of available Web services. Publishing a Web service over the Web entails creating an entry in this repository that describes the service as well as the protocols necessary to acquire the service. A Web service client that requires a service queries the directory and receives in return the WSDL descriptor.

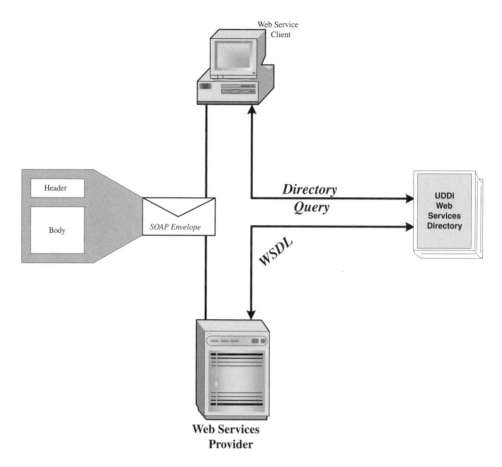

**FIGURE 15.4**   Web services data flow.

The Web service client uses the information provided in the Web service descriptor to construct a SOAP message. The SOAP message is contained within a SOAP envelope composed of a header, a body, and name space definitions. The header is an optional data structure that describes the data contained within the body. Header data might include user profiles used to grant or limit access to data. The body itself is an XML document that contains the actual request. The name spaces used in the header and body are defined within the SOAP envelope. Once the Web service provider has processed the request, the response is packaged in another SOAP envelope. The response itself is placed in the SOAP body.

Figure 15.5 demonstrates how we can use Web services in an IEBI environment. The process begins, as it does with any good company, with the customer. New visitors to our Web site select and purchase products. As part of this purchasing process, we receive from them registration information. On a periodic basis, the data warehouse extracts customer and clickstream data from the Web store.

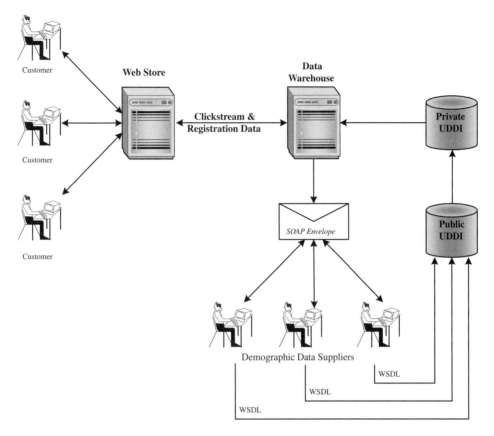

**FIGURE 15.5**   Web services in an IEBI environment.

Upon receiving new customers, the data warehouse data integration process seeks those customers' demographic data. It begins by querying its own private UDDI-based Web services directory for providers of demographic information. This private directory is an extraction of a public directory on the Web. Once the data warehouse has received the WSDL descriptors for the respective suppliers, it sends a SOAP envelope to each, containing a RFQ (Request for Quote) for the demographic data.

The quotation system of the demographic data suppliers responds to this request with its own SOAP envelope containing the quote. The data warehouse system evaluates the quotes based on price and completeness of the data. The system also takes into consideration the quality of the data the system received in the past from each supplier. A vendor is selected and a purchase order is issued. When received by the supplier, the data is sent directly to the data warehouse, where it is integrated into the system.

As we look at this example, we should notice one thing. Other than the consumer of the information in the data warehouse, this isn't necessarily an IEBI example. After all, couldn't these requests have been for powdered creamer for the office kitchen or urinal cakes for the men's room? Exactly! The fact that we are generating requests for demographic data simply shows another application of Web services. What makes this interesting from the IEBI perspective is not the data that is being transmitted between systems, but how that data is being transmitted.

The link between IEBI and Web services is that we now have captured our interactions between our suppliers, distributors, and partners. The Web store gave us insight into our customers' behavior that the brick-and-mortar environment couldn't. It did this by capturing the movements through our store in some electronic structure, the clickstream. We now had a tracking of each and every individual transaction that we could later analyze. This is what Web services do for IEBI. In addition to providing tighter integration between our systems and automating much of the process, it provides us a structure that captures the interactions with the other members of the value chain.

Web services have the potential of being the next big thing in software. So did XML. However, we should be wary of the hype. Web services are a structure by which applications can communicate. In this sense, they are very similar to XML and CWMI. Ultimately, data needs to be placed in this structure. If we place the wrong data in the structure or place the correct data in the wrong places, we still end up with garbage. There is still going to be some up-front investment in making these systems work together. It is not going to happen *auto-magically*.

At Oracle's 2002 Apps World in San Diego, Larry Ellison described the situation quite clearly. Allow me to paraphrase what he said. Let us say that I call someone, say Francois, in France from the *landline* in my home, and he picks up on his cell phone. After a brief attempt at conversing, it is clear that Francois speaks only French. Despite 3 years of French in high school with Mr. Lano, I don't understand a word he says. At that point, I hang up and call the same number, but this time from my cell phone. Can we now communicate any better?

The point is clear: It is not the technology that we use to facilitate communication as much as it is what we say to one another. We still need to understand how to speak the same language.

## 15.3  Go Gently Into that Dark Night

As our IEBI symphony draws to a close, there is one note of caution. Throughout this book, we have tried to sort the hype from the fact. In Chapter 1, we asked if the praise of the Internet is factual or flights of fancy. We examined the rhetoric surrounding XML, whether it was the panacea for communication some claimed. Our discussions of Java and CWMI were focused on the reality of what we can deliver, not on the far-flung hyperbole of a marketing department with an overactive imagination. So, what about IEBI? Is it really the solution to remaining competitive in an Internet Enabled age?

Well, yes.

And no.

Yes, in the sense that we are providing information to the decision maker, the crafter of our corporate strategy. Keep in mind, information is the meat upon which strategy feeds. If our strategy is based on solid, substantive information, we are in a much better position to develop a solid, winning strategy than if we didn't have this information. However, we are not guaranteed a successful and winning strategy. This is where the "no" comes in.

The most critical element of the BI loop is the decision maker. In his book *Investment Madness,* John Nofsinger notes that "Psychologists have found that people become overconfident when they experience early success in a new activity. Also, having more information available and a higher degree of control leads to higher overconfidence. These factors are referred to as the *illusion of knowledge* and the *illusion of control.*" We must be aware that simply providing quality information will *not* necessarily make an organization more strategic. As system architects, we can provide all the information in a timely manner, but ultimately it is the decision maker who is responsible for making better decisions. Nofsinger goes on to say, "Because most individual investors lack the training and experience of professional investors, they are less equipped to know how to interpret information. They may think they have access to all this incredible inside information and that may well be true, but without the proper training, they cannot begin to guess how that information might shape the future—any more than they can guess future rolls of the die from what was rolled in the past."

Analysis is so much more than providing multidimensional access to data; it is more than just determining the value of a particular KPI or the cost-object unit cost. Analysis is the ability to determine the nature of a thing. IEBI cannot do this. One might argue that data mining can perform this analysis, but this would be incorrect. Even in the case of data mining, there is always a human decision maker who evaluates the decisions being made by the automated process. A recommendation engine recommends products to a consumer who in turn makes the buy decision.

We need to understand this concept. We need to understand that as IEBI system architects, our product is information, not better decisions. The consumer of that information, our customer, is the decision maker. If our organization is to be customer-driven, we must be as well. We must always keep our customer's needs and wants in mind in order to establish our own *mutually beneficial relationship* with our own customers.

## 15.4   Summary

When I was 9 years old, there was a movie theater at the end of my street, the Rialto. My friends and I would spend many Saturday afternoons watching various B movies. One such black-and-white classic dealt with the end of the world and some sort of fog that enveloped the earth. For the life of me, the only thing I could remember about the film was the very last scene. After vanquishing the plague that had destroyed mankind, the hero, along with a lovely and voluptuous female costar, walked down a wooded path hand in hand. The words "THE BEGIN-NING" were emblazoned across the screen. The implication of course was that once out of the prying eye of the camera, they would, like Adam and Eve, set to repopulating the Earth. In a sense, we are in the same place.

I began this chapter with a quote from Anne Bradstreet's poem, "The Author to Her Book." Every author I have ever met feels that there is never enough time to complete his or her work. It always feels as if it has been ripped from your loving hands, prematurely thrust into the world. Be that as it may, while this text may draw to a close, it is more of a beginning than an ending. We have introduced many concepts and explored many technologies. It is now up to you to advance IEBI and to make your own organization more intelligent, more competitive, and ultimately more profitable.

# RECOMMENDED READING

Typically, when I complete a lecture I have audience members who are interested in continuing their study on that subject. Many ask for information sources so that they may do further reading. I have compiled a list of some of my personal favorites. Each book on this list is well worth reading.

There are three books that deserve "honorable mention." The first is *Building the Data Warehouse* by William H. Inmon. This is the first book I have read on the subject. It is well written and is required reading for anyone who is attempting to understand business intelligence. The second and third must-read books are *The Data Warehouse Toolkit* and *The Data Webhouse Toolkit* by Ralph Kimball. Both of Kimball's books provide a good understanding of the details of building a data warehouse. No library is complete without them.

*B2B Exchanges,* Arthur B. Sculley & W. William A. Woods, ISI Publications, 1999.

*Building the Data Warehouse,* William H. Inmon, John Wiley & Sons, 1992.

*Building, Using and Managing the Data Warehouse,* Ramon Barquin & Herb Edelstein (Eds.), Prentice Hall, 1997.

*Data Mining Your Website,* Jesus Mena, Digital Press, 1999.

*The Data Warehouse Toolkit,* Ralph Kimball, John Wiley & Sons, 1996.

*The Data Webhouse Toolkit,* Ralph Kimball, John Wiley & Sons, 2000.

*The Digital Economy,* Don Tapscott, McGraw-Hill, 1996.

*e-Enterprise,* Faisal Hogue, Cambridge University Press, 2000.

*Enterprise JavaBeans,* Richard Monson-Haefel, O'Reilly, 2000.

*e-Procurement,* Dale Neef, Prentice Hall, 2001.

*How Brains Think,* William H. Calvin, Basic Books, 1996.

*Investment Madness,* John Nofsinger, Prentice Hall, 2001.

*The Java Tutorial,* Mary Campione & Kathy Walrath, Addison Wesley, 1998.

*Making the Information Society,* James W. Cortada, Prentice Hall, 2002.

*Obect Oriented Data Warehouse Design: Building a Star Schema,* William Giovinazzo, Prentice Hall, 2000.

*Planning and Designing the Data Warehouse,* Ramon Barquin & Herb Edelstein (Eds.), Prentice Hall, 1997.

*Parallel Systems in the Data Warehouse,* Stephen Morse & David Isaac, Prentice Hall, 1998.

*Solving Data Mining Problems through Pattern Recognition,* Ruby L. Kennedy (Ed.), Prentice Hall, 1997.

# GLOSSARY

| | |
|---|---|
| **ABB** | See Activity Based Budgeting |
| **ABC** | See Activity Based Costing |
| **ABM** | See Activity Based Management |
| **Activity** | The actions performed as part of the production process to deliver a product or service. |
| **Activity Based Budgeting** | The process of creating a budget based on activity cost. The process begins with forecasting demand. It then projects the activities required to meet that demand and finally calculates the cost of those activities. The budget uses these projected costs to compile a budget. |
| **Activity Based Costing** | The calculation of costs based on the cost of the activities to deliver a product or service. |
| **Activity Based Management** | The use of activity-based costing in management of an organization. |
| **Aggregate Exchanges** | An exchange where products from multiple suppliers are collected together in one place. |
| **American Standard Code for Information Interchange** | A standardized binary code for the representation of letters, numbers, and specialized characters. |
| **Application Service Provider** | A business that hosts and manages computing services, such as email and web servers, for other companies. |

| | |
|---|---|
| **ASCII** | See American Standard Code for Information Interchange |
| **ASP** | See Application Service Provider |
| **Auction Exchange** | An exchange in which bids are made by consumers for products and services. |
| **B2B** | See Business to Business |
| **B2C** | See Business to Consumer |
| **Balanced Scorecard** | A tool to define an organization's strategy, communicate that strategy, measure the organization's performance in fulfilling that strategy, and communicate that performance. |
| **BI** | See Business Intelligence |
| **Brick & Mortar** | Traditional organizations that conduct business in actual physical structures. |
| **Brochure-ware** | An Internet version of corporate brochures. |
| **BSC** | See Balanced ScoreCard |
| **BSC Perspective** | The various strategic themes into which the organization's Key Performance Indicators are mapped and viewed. |
| **Business Intelligence** | Thinking abstractly about an organization, reasoning about the business, organizing large quantities of information about the business in order to define and execute a strategy. |
| **Business Rules** | The rules that uniquely define a business or industry. Often these rules are encoded in software to meet the requirements of a particular business. |
| **Business to Business** | An exchange in which the both the buyer and seller are businesses. Businesses selling to businesses. |
| **Business to Consumer** | An exchange in which Businesses sell directly to consumers. |
| **C2B** | See Customer to Business |
| **C2C** | See Customer to Customer |
| **CART** | See Classification and Regression Trees |

| | |
|---|---|
| **Centaur** | Consumers that are a combination of traditional and cyber shoppers. Consumers that act both rationally and emotionally, whose attributes are complex and often times conflicting. |
| **Central Nervous System** | The part of the nervous system that aggregates the input from the rest of the nervous system. It consists of the spinal column and the brain. |
| **Central Repository** | The portion of the business intelligence loop that stores the information driving business intelligence. It is the storage part of the data warehouse. |
| **Cerebral Cortex** | The part of the brain responsible for the higher level functions such as reasoning, voluntary action, memory, and thought. |
| **CGI** | See Common Gateway Interface |
| **CHAID** | See Chi-Square Automatic Interaction Detection |
| **Chi-Square Automatic Interaction Detection** | A method of constructing nonbinary, decision trees, useful in the categorization of data. |
| **Classification and Regression Trees** | A method of creating binary decision trees. The algorithm determines a *split value* which is used to determine paths through the decision tree. |
| **Cleansing** | The portion of the data integration process that removes errors from the data being loaded into the data warehouse. |
| **Click & Mortar** | Existing *brick & mortar* organizations that have integrated e-commerce into their operations. |
| **Clickstream** | The record of hits taken by a Web site. |
| **Collaborative Filtering** | A predictive algorithm based on comparing the attributes of candidates against known groups. |
| **Common Gateway Interface** | Protocol used by a Web server for communicating with an application. |
| **Common Warehouse Metadata Interchange** | An XML-based standard for the exchange of metadata. |
| **Consumption Quantity** | The number of times an individual activity is performed to create a cost object. |
| **Cookies** | A small piece of data stored on the client system and passed to the Web server with each request. |

| | |
|---|---|
| **Cost Object** | A product or service produced by a business. It is something that the organization produces or does to generate profit. |
| **Cost Object Unit Cost** | The sum of the cost of all activities necessary to produce one unit of a cost object. |
| **CRM** | See Customer Relationship Management |
| **Crossover** | The process of exchanging genetic information between the solutions in genetic models. |
| **CSN** | See Central Nervous System |
| **Customer Lifetime Value** | The sum of all profit generated by an individual customer over the entire life of the relationship with that customer. |
| **Customer Relationship Management** | A strategy whose main objective is to create a mutually beneficial relationship with each of its customers. |
| **Customer to Business** | Exchanges where the consumer determines the conditions of the transaction. Businesses compete with one another on these exchanges for the customer's business. |
| **Customer to Customer** | Exchanges where customers sell directly to one another. |
| **Customization** | The ability to tailor an environment to meet individual preferences. |
| **CWMI** | See Common Warehouse Metadata Interchange |
| **Data Administrator** | Team member responsible for the quality of the data in the data warehouse. The data administrator reviews the extraction log for metadata changes, inaccurate data, or data errors. |
| **Data Mart** | A data warehouse, or repository, whose scope is limited to a single subject area. |
| **Data Mining** | The discovery of information hidden within data. |
| **Data Transformation** | The process of converting data from many disparate systems into one standard format. |
| **Data Warehouse** | "A subject oriented, integrated, nonvolatile, time variant collection of data in support of management's decisions."[1] |

---

[1] W.H. Inmon, *Building the Data Warehouse.*

| | |
|---|---|
| **Decision Support System** | The presentation of data to support management in making decisions. |
| **Dependent Data Mart** | A data mart whose sole source of information is the data warehouse. |
| **DHCP** | See Dynamic Host Configuration Protocol |
| **Document Type Definition** | Defines the structure of a particular type of XML document. |
| **Drill-down** | Presentation of the data at a deeper level of detail. |
| **DSS** | See Decision Support System |
| **DTD** | See Document Type Definition |
| **Dynamic Host Configuration Protocol** | A protocol that dynamically leases IP addresses to workstations from a pool of IP addresses. |
| **Dynamic Metadata** | Metadata that primarily reflects the overall state of the system. Dynamic metadata is in a constant state of change. Dynamic metadata describes the quality, usage, and status of the system. |
| **e-business** | An organization whose internal processes are Internet based. |
| **e-commerce** | The process of conducting business over the Internet. |
| **EDI** | See Electronic Data Interchange |
| **EDM** | See Enterprise Data Model |
| **e-enterprise** | An organization whose entire value chain has been integrated over the Internet. |
| **Electronic Data Interchange** | Integration of the supply chain through the electronic exchange of information. This exchange is not necessarily Internet based. |
| **Engineering Driven** | An organization whose focus is selling what they are good at building. |
| **Enterprise Data Model** | A data model whose scope encompasses the entire organization. The Enterprise Data Model receives metadata from all systems within all departments in the organization, combining it into one cohesive model. |
| **e-procurement** | The electronic automation of the procurement process. |

| | |
|---|---|
| **eXtensible Markup Language** | A derivative of Standard Generalized Markup Language designed to be extensible, easy to use, structured, and self-validating. |
| **Extraction Log** | A record of the status of the extraction process. The extraction log records any exceptions to the extraction process. This log serves as input to the data administrator to verify the quality of the data loaded into the data warehouse. |
| **File Transfer Protocol** | RCF 959 – provides for the transfer of files between a client and a remote host. The protocol allows the client to access directories and files on the remote host and perform such operations as listing and renaming directories and files. The protocol is a process/application layer protocol of the TCP/IP stack. |
| **FTP** | See File Transfer Protocol |
| **GAAP** | See Generally Accepted Accounting Procedures |
| **Generally Accepted Accounting Procedures** | The accounting community's prescribed method of financial accounting. |
| **Genetic Algorithms** | A method of finding an optimal solution to a problem by using techniques found in natural selection, such as mutation and survival of the fittest. |
| **GIF** | See Graphics Interchange Format |
| **Graphics Interchange Format** | A standard image file format. |
| **Hits** | The number of files accessed on a Web site. A single Web page can generate multiple hits. |
| **HOLAP** | See Hybrid On-Line Analytical Processing |
| **HTML** | See Hypertext Markup Language |
| **HTTP** | See Hypertext Transfer Protocol |
| **Hybrid On-Line Analytical Processing** | On-Line Analytical Processing, whose underlying data structure is based on both relational and multidimensional data structures. |
| **Hypertext Markup Language** | A derivative of Standard Generalized Markup Language designed to describe the display of Web pages. It uses tags to define the display of text, embed graphics, and include links to other Web pages. |

| | |
|---|---|
| **Hypertext Transfer Protocol** | The protocol used to transfer HTML pages over the Internet. |
| **Independent Data Mart** | A data mart whose source of information includes the operational environment and external data sources. It is independent of the data warehouse. |
| **Information Superhighway** | A euphemism for the Internet. |
| **Intelligence** | The ability to think abstractly, to organize large volumes of information and then reason. |
| **International Organization for Standards** | A non-governmental organization founded in 1947, dedicated to establishing international standards. |
| **ISO** | From the Greek *isos*, meaning equal. It is the name used to identify the International Organization for Standards. |
| **Java Database Connectivity** | A standard Java API for communicating with relational databases. |
| **JDBC** | See Java Database Connectivity |
| **Key Performance Indicator** | A performance measure that is indicative of the organization's performance within a specific area. |
| **KPI** | See Key Performance Indicator |
| **Life Time Value** | The total value of an asset over its useful life. |
| **Limbic System** | The structures of the brain that control emotion, motivation, and autonomic functions. |
| **LTV** | See Life Time Value |
| **Market-Basket Analysis** | The analysis of customer behavior based on groups of purchases made by that individual. |
| **Mean Time Between Failure** | The mean of the time interval between system failures. |
| **Mean Time to Repair** | The mean of the time required to repair a failed system. |
| **Meta Object Facility** | Specifies the meta-metamodel, the semantics to describe the metamodels in a variety of domains. |
| **Metadata** | Generally described as data about data. It is the data, beyond the data, describing the context in which the data resides. |

| | |
|---|---|
| **Mixture** | A combination of ingredients or components in which each of the ingredients is unchanged by the other elements of the mixture. |
| **MOF** | See Meta Object Facility |
| **MOLAP** | See Multidimensional On-Line Analytical Processing |
| **MOSAIC** | First browser created by students of the NCSA in Champaign-Urbana based on Berners-Lee's proposal. |
| **MTBF** | See Mean Time Between Failure |
| **MTTR** | See Mean Time to Repair |
| **Multidimensional On-Line Analytical Processing** | On-Line Analytical Processing whose underlying data structure is based on a multidimensional database. |
| **Mutation** | A source of variations and diversity within a population. In data mining, mutation occurs when new values are created for attributes. |
| **Neural Networks** | A type of data mining that simulates the structures in the brain. It is a network of processes where each process has a specific set of inputs and outputs. The neural network algorithm provides a means by which these processes *learn*. |
| **Nervous System** | A system of cells and tissues in an organism that receives input and reacts to that input. |
| **Nonvolatile Data** | Data that remains unchanged once it is written to the data warehouse. |
| **Normalize** | A method of structuring relational databases to reduce the redundancy of data and improve transaction processing performance. |
| **Object Analysis & Design Facility** | Defined by the OMG, it specifies the *Unified Modeling Language* (UML) as a common meta-model. |
| **Object Management Architecture** | A standardized object-oriented architectural framework within which developers can create software. It addresses portability issues as well as the specification to address object interoperability. |

| | |
|---|---|
| **Object Management Architecture Guide** | Describes the Object Management Architecture. |
| **Object Management Group** | A software consortium established in 1989. It is the world's largest consortium, composed of more than 700 vendors, developers, and end-users. The mission of the Object Management Group is to promote the theory and practice of Object Technology for the development of distributed computing systems. |
| **ODBC** | See Open Database Connectivity |
| **ODS** | See Operational Data Store |
| **OLAP** | See On-line Analytical Processing |
| **OMA** | See Object Management Architecture |
| **OMAG** | See Object Management Architecture Guide |
| **OMG** | See Object Management Group |
| **OMG Object Model** | The OMG Object Model specifies an implementation-independent way of defining the attributes of objects that are visible to the outside world. |
| **On-line Analytical Processing** | The interactive accesses and display of data in multiple dimensions. |
| **Open Database Connectivity** | A standard established for communicating with relational databases. |
| **Open Systems Interconnection** | A protocol reference model established by ISO to define the layers of electronic communication. |
| **Operational Data Store** | A system independent of the operational environment used to capture snapshots of that environment. Where the data warehouse is a long-term strategic view of the organization, the Operational Data Store is more of a short-term tactical view. |
| **OSI** | See Open Systems Interconnection |
| **Personalization** | Tailoring the customer interactions to meet the needs and wants of the individual customer. |
| **Portlet** | A window within a portal. |
| **Present Value Interest Factor** | A value used to adjust a future value into present day terms. |

| | |
|---|---|
| **Proxy Server** | An intermediary server between the client and the rest of the Internet. Its purpose is to hide the client computer from the Internet by making requests on its behalf. |
| **PVIF** | See Present Value Interest Factor |
| **RDBMS** | A Relational Database Management System. |
| **Relational On-Line Analytical Processing** | On-Line Analytical Processing based on a relational database architecture. |
| **ROLAP** | See Relational On-Line Analytical Processing |
| **Roll-up** | The presentation of data at a coarser level of detail. |
| **Sales Driven** | An organization whose strategy is to make what they know how to sell. |
| **Solution** | A combination of ingredients or components in which each of the ingredients is transformed by the others. |
| **Static Metadata** | Data that describes data elements. Static data changes less frequently than dynamic metadata and is relatively stable. In addition to describing the format and domain of the data, static metadata also describes the business rules that govern the data elements. |
| **Strategy Map** | A graphical representation of the cause and effect relationships of the Balanced Scorecard's KPIs. |
| **Subject Orientation** | The structure of the data that groups the information pertaining to a specific subject. Subjects include such things as products, customers, competitors, or employees. |
| **TCP** | See Transmission Control Protocol |
| **TELNET** | Resides in the Application Layer of the TCP/IP stack. The application emulates a terminal connected to a remote host, allowing the user to work as if directly connected to the remote host. |
| **Time Variant** | Allows the time variable to be manipulated by the business strategist. |

| | |
|---|---|
| **Trading Hubs** | A trading hub is a virtual marketplace in which vendors can advertise and sell their products. Trading hubs have a distinct benefit to the buyer in that they typically set up communities comprising both buyers and sellers. These communities provide the buyer with information concerning their businesses. |
| **Transfer Log** | Records the hits taken by a Web site. |
| **Transformation** | The process of changing a value format or structure to be more consistent with the data warehouse data. |
| **Transmission Control Protocol** | A protocol that resides in the Host-to-Host Layer of the TCP/IP stack. The protocol establishes a virtual circuit between the two systems. The protocol ensures the reliable exchange of data by sequencing and acknowledging packets. |
| **UML** | See Unified Modeling Language |
| **Unified Modeling Language** | A common metamodel that provides a set of interfaces for the support of dynamic construction and traversal of user models. |
| **Value Added Networks** | The "middleman" in an electronic business relationship. Generally used in conjunction with EDI to accept and forward electronic business documents. |
| **VANs** | See Value Added Networks |
| **Video Dating exchange** | These exchanges provide introductions between potential buyers and sellers. The exchange is only involved in the initial introduction of the two parties. Subsequent activities occur outside of the exchange. |
| **XMI** | See XML Metadata Interchange |
| **XML** | See eXtensible Markup Language |
| **XML Metadata Interchange** | The method by which data warehouse metadata that conforms to the CWMI metamodel is communicated. |

# INDEX